STREET FOOD
CHICAGO

Chef Michael J. Baruch

Jacket: Chicago Skyline Facing Southwest

Text © Michael J. Baruch 2007
Photography © LBCM Publishing, Inc. 2007
Design and Layout © Odez Dezigns

First Published 2007 by La Baruch Cuisine Moderne

The rights of the author have been asserted

LBCM Publishing Inc.
P.O. Box 55
Del Mar, CA 92014-0055
Chefmb@earthlink.net

Library of Congress Cataloging -in- Publication Data is on file with the publisher
ISBN: 0-9715313-1-5

First U.S. edition, 2007
Manufactured in China

1 2 3 4 5 6 7 8 9 10

DEDICATION

I dedicate this book to all the hard working mom and pop joints throughout the city who have fueled our appetites and satisfied our cravings with the finest street food known to man! I love and want to eat you all!

Peace - Mike the Chef, 2007

ACKNOWLEDGEMENTS

To my beautiful Sicilian wife Pam, who diligently typed the book's text and fondly refers to me as her fourth son.

Love and Kisses!

To my beautiful neighbor Eve who we like to call Mom. A truly heartfelt thank you for professionally revising and editing all the book's intros. The book now truly shines because of your diligent and loving effort.

Love and Kisses!

To my beautiful friend Olivia. 7,000 restaurants, 90 different ethnic groups, where does a book designer start? Olivia's keen attention to detail, artistic finesse and style captures the heart and soul of the city.
You are now officially a Chicagoan.

Love and Kisses!

TABLE OF CONTENTS

Street Food
CHICAGO

The Man Hello from Mike the chef! Wow, what a few interesting years I've had since the release of my first book The New Polish Cuisine. Some critics panned it, chef's loved it and a lot of really appreciative fans wrote me some heartfelt letters asking for more great recipes and stories about growing up in Chicago. Man, I'm flattered!

For those of you who don't know me, let me tell you a little bit about myself. I'm a sixth generation Polish kid who grew up on the Northwest side of Chicago. Through some god given fate, I managed to work my way through many of the city's top four-star restaurants over the last 25 years. I made my bones the hard way, knocking on a lot of back doors, and I'm proud of that fact. I've never considered myself to be a tyrannical chef who wears a big tall hat, but more of a personable kind of guy who just really likes to cook and experience life's adventures!

Chi-town Cuisine Check this out! The latest 2005 census poll denotes there are about 3 million people living in the Chicago land area with an estimated 80 to 90 different ethnic groups comprising that number. That's a big group to contend with on a culinary scale, so local food writers group together certain ethnic cultures and cooking styles, such as, eastern Europeans, Hispanics, Pan-Asians, Middle Easterners and South Americans to make up a more reasonable list of actual cuisines in the city, about 40 to be exact. That list also includes such things as bakeries/delis, burger and hot dog joints, coffee shops and diners, pizza and steak houses, to name a few.

There is no question that the largest and oldest ethnic groups in the city are the Germans, Irish, Polish, African-Americans, Italians, Hispanics and Swedes who have all contributed to the spice blend that makes Chicago a true "culinary melting pot." Not to be excluded are the French, Greeks, east Indians, Japanese, Koreans, Scottish and Spanish, who have also made a considerable mark on our culinary history. I tend to view it like this: the Europeans add the backbone and heartiness to the broth, whereas the emerging Asians, Middle Easterners and Africans tantalize and excite our taste buds with new and interesting sweet spices, fiery chilies, vibrant micro greens and a big splash of the exotic. Trust me, it all comes together; you've just got to find it!

In my younger days I hung out with guys whose folks owned mom and pop joints along Belmont, Milwaukee and Harlem Ave., three gateways to the city that showcase its ethnic diversity in less than a five-mile radius. (Think of it as kind of a Midwestern Bermuda Triangle of food). These bakeries, taverns, sausage shops, grocery stores and restaurants were family-run operations that tied these people to their communities and in turn flavored the neighborhoods with a patchwork of ethnic backgrounds. For any one of you that has ever had to endure a long tedious ride on our local CTA bus lines from the suburbs to the inner city, you will have most assuredly internalized a myriad of ethnic food neons proclaiming "Old Style beer," "Vienna hot dogs," "Homemade Polish & Rye," etc. There was a lot of hard work, love and joy that went into keeping those businesses alive and thriving through the years. When I was a kid, I used to joke around about whose house was the most aromatic. I could tell the nationality of the friend I was hanging out with (Italian or

Greek) by the smell of garlic and basil or olive oil and oregano. In high school, I worked my way through a number of bakeries and sausage shops, and undoubtedly, all of these experiences have molded my cooking style and culinary career. Even though I am usually associated with some kind of four-star operation, my heart has always been with the working man's fare which I like to call "Street Food."

I've been slinging skillets around the city for a long time and I classify Chicago cuisine into 4 different types:

❶ Everyday working man's "street food."

❷ Ethnically oriented joints.

❸ Local chains.

❹ Four-star gourmet dining.

You can discount #4 because this ain't no fancy Dan type of cookbook! You can also discount #3 for the pure fact that Chicago has its own unique style of fast food that doesn't fall under the guise of the "golden arches." The true heart and soul of the city revolve around #1 and #2.

The great chef, Jean Banchet of Le Francais fame, told me a long time ago that "to define a cuisine is to live it, love it, and be intimately familiar with it for a good part of your life." Chicago's diverse ethnic community has most definitely transformed and evolved into a beautiful kaleidoscope of ever-changing culinary nirvana that is second to none.

The Quest Over the last two years I've spent more down time at airports in cities such as Warsaw, New York, Boston, Cleveland, Detroit and Dallas in my quest to become a Midwestern food writer. People who know me can attest to the fact that I possess the gift of gab, so conversations come easily with fellow flyers and they usually center around Chicago food. When I was a young apprentice cook, I was strongly advised to carry around a pocket notebook to sketch dishes and scribble recipes for later use, a practice I still use today. Early in my career I was befriended by the great writer, Mike Royko, a daily columnist for the Chicago Tribune. Mike's ability to transfer everyday stories or life experiences into enjoyable print is unsurpassed in the publishing world and I took a lot of his advice to heart.

"Give em what they want, kid, not what you think they need." "The everyday plight of the working man in Chicago is where the story's at." Sadly, Mike passed, but his spirit, wisdom and humor ignited my passion for food writing and preserving our city's culinary culture. Taking his advice, my down time at airports became my creative playtime and I quickly filled reams of notebooks with shared stories, humorous anecdotes and other's life experiences centered around Chicago's street food.

The Book & Recipes *Street Food Chicago* just didn't happen overnight; I've been livin', cookin' and eatin' it for years! Lately my dining room table has become my publishing office, stacked with reference books, legal pads, notebooks and tons of pens. People say that chefs and writers, like most artists, make quirky bedfellows and my kids find it amusing that I find solace in working in my underwear sans pants or shirt to keep cool and help concentrate on the chapter at hand. Before I started this project I was advised by a few luminary food writers to tread carefully in dealing with a subject of this magnitude. With Chicago's 3 million plus people, 7000 restaurants and 90 different ethnic groups, it was quite a task to pick and choose what to include and what would appropriately fall under the guise of street food, since Chicago is not a push cart kind of town.

Let me digress. There was a time in the city's history that street vendors and push carts ruled. However, there are many factors which led to their demise way back when: a polluted river called "The Loop;" fore-founding politicians who didn't accept or want the immigrant population clogging up their downtown city streets; the stock yards and a devastating fire that demolished every wooden structure that stood. I recently had a conversation with a health inspector about our lack of street vendors and it was her observation that the Chicago stockyards really changed the way the city did business with regard to permits, regulations and food sanitation. It was also her opinion that certain practices like cooking are better left indoors so that they can be regulated and controlled. Many of the earliest German, Jewish and Italian immigrants would sell their wares outside and it's worthy to note that Chicago is still home to one of the last bastions of open-air merchants, called "Maxwell Street Market."

Chicago's street cuisine, like that of other big cities, gets its identity from, and flourished under, the vast influx of immigrant populations that flocked to its gates. Bringing with them their unique ethnic foodstuffs and spices, these Europeans, Asians, Latinos etc. integrated their diverse cultures by sharing and changing their recipes slightly to fit into an American lifestyle. Food writers around the world proclaim Chicago as an essential visiting destination for a culinary experience. Yeah, we got hot dogs, pizza and beefs, but we also have a treasure trove of outstanding ethnic delights and it would be virtually impossible to do them all justice in this book. I'm often asked what makes our cuisine so good, and with humility I respond that "we cook, we eat, we care!" San Francisco touts the virtues of "Chinatown," whereas New Yorkers boast of their larger than life delis, dirty dogs and foldable pizza. I'm just a Polish kid from the northwest side of Chicago, and like my city, I have a down-to-earth, blue collar, working man's view of our local food. Even though I've worked for some of the best chefs in the world, my favorite four-star restaurant is a corner hot dog stand, tavern, bakery or ethnic joint. I take comfort in having to stand while I eat my beef sandwich and being able to watch the guys work the fries. I take comfort in going to my local Polish restaurant and peeking through the velvet curtain to see some old Busias making their pierogi by hand. I feel at home with that red-checkered tablecloth in the local pizza parlor and that old string of colored lights lining the bar. And last but not least, I like the fact that I could go to any local tavern around the city, put a fiver on the bar and not get gouged for the price of a ham sandwich, cup of soup and a beer!

I spent a lot of sleepless nights determining what recipes I should include in this book, since as of late, Chicago is churning out more four-star chefs than it has in its past, but fame is fleeting! It's unavoidable to try to hop, skip and jump over our beloved hot dog, beef and pizza, even though Chicago street food is so much more than that. **I'm a big proponent of the slow foods movement, and it's my opinion that local ethnic cooks in the city are leading the pack and preserving that tradition.** So this is what I did. Over the last year while on the road, I interviewed as many as one thousand weary travelers, military personnel, businessmen and stewardesses at different airports around the country seeking to find out about Chicago's street foods. The obvious was obvious, there were a few surprises, but the winning consensus was "most definitely give me good Chicago style food!" Nothing frou-frou or cutesy. **Pizza, steaks, Asian, Greek, Soul, and Polish cuisines still rule the roost.** The chapters and recipes in this book are my interpretations of what Chicago eats and has loved through the generations. You will find that the most popular foods have been included. As a chef, I find balance by juggling the old with the new, and if your favorite street food is not in the book, send me a note and I will try to include it in a revised copy. Lastly, good restaurants come and go, and those that I've mentioned are worth checking out, but please keep in mind that this is a cookbook I want you to use, not a guidebook to Chicago restaurants.

BEER WARS, OLD POLISH GEEZERS, POLITICS AND STREET BOOZE

STUFF IN JARS

You know, I have to admit that I might not be the smartest guy when it comes to book learning, but I've truly learned a lot of weird and interesting facts from old Polish geezers while sitting in local taverns. Chicago's love of neighborhood beer joints and their history should and could easily be put into some kind of downtown museum or shrine, for its depth of historical fact, but also for the political plight of being able to enjoy a bucket of suds on a Sunday afternoon. Most people equate Chicago's illustrious fascination with street booze with old glorified movies depicting Al Capone as some crazed hooch lord. The truth of the matter is that Chicago's love of suds makes Big Al look like a puny, dead smelt compared to the city's past brewing history.

Check this out; a week back, I was in the mood for some homestyle cooking and libation, so I cruised down to my favorite joint on Wabansia. This Polish bar/restaurant is family owned and I've known the proprietors for years. As stools are at a premium at lunchtime, I nabbed a four top and was immediately, forcibly nudged up against the wall by three Streets and Sans guys who also needed seating quickly. I politely obliged. For you out-of-towners, Streets and Sanitation workers are the guys who drive around the city in the powder-blue trucks filling in massive pot holes, rescuing kids who climb down sewer drains and spreading salt during the winter; basically, they are the street troops who keep the city clean and working. These city workers are a breed among themselves. My observation is that they are usually of Italian or Irish decent with big shoulders, thick necks, Moose Cholak weathered hands, real "Chicago street accents" and Aqua Velva undertones. One other observation I have about these guys is that they take their lunch very seriously and are always looking for the best deal. (If you ever see the big blue trucks parked in front of a restaurant, be sure to eat there because the food is probably really good and a great value.)

Since it was the holidays, I bought a round of long necks and the conversational shtick started a flowin'. When I was getting ready to order, one of the Sans guys by the name of "Big Reilly" grabbed my menu and said, "We'll order for you ." So who am I to argue with my new best Irish friend? Hot corned beef sandwiches with kraut and dilled potatoes was the daily special and my new pals requested to be served "family style." I was really in the mix now with no escape! The conversation gets deep and heavy with these guys and once I told them I had written a Polish cookbook and was working on another the wise cracks were coming on fast and furious. "Polack food," one guy says. "Man, I haven't had good Polish food in quite a while." My buddy, Reilly, chimes in with his thick Irish street accent, "The reason we haven't had that food in a while is because last time we had it at Sofia's, you were fartin' in the truck all afternoon and we couldn't even drive straight!" Now the other guy chimes in with his Sicilian street accent and says, "Dat's right, your ass was smellier den dat sewer job we jus finished up over der on eighteent street." It was obvious to me that my Polishness was now the brunt of the lunch hour tomfoolery and I was going to have to endure this banter throughout the entire meal. By this time, Stash, the young bartender who's known me for years, brings this huge platter of sandwiches with a cynical smile on his face and "Reilly" requested more pickles for the Polish guy at the table, meaning me.

After about a half hour of lively loud conversation, ethnic jokes and street banter, the talk turned to the history of the tavern and how many lunch tavern/bars there are in the city. "Italian Tony" says, "ders got to be thousans' of dem wit jus as many pizza and hot dawg places" and then Stash, behind the bar, chimes in and says, "Yea, dat doesn't include the shot and beer bars up in Berwyn or the cash and carry joints on the Southside." By this time, the topic of our conversation had peaked the interest of a few lone Polish geezers that were earring in on the discussion. "Reilly," who fancies himself now as a historian, comments that if it wasn't for the Czechs and Slovaks, we probably wouldn't have beer in the city. One of the old Polish geezers, clad in his Archie Bunker attire, turned around on his stool and says, "No, dat's wrong, everyone knows it was the Micks and the Jerrys." Stan, the third Sans guy, of unknown origin, contributed with his pearl of wisdom saying, "Dat's right, the potato and kraut eaters are the real ones." So now, it's me, the two old Polish geezers, the three Sans guys, junior Stash and old Stash intertwined in this historic fact-finding mission.

At this time, one of the old Polish geezers steps up to the plate and lays on us all such a beautiful and interesting story that I have to retell it here in some logical sequence.

The Beginnings 1800

Chicago's brewing history just didn't appear on the horizon one day. It was well noted in books that fur traders and Indians boasted about the rich untouched fields of grains and hops, God Given fuel for making quality beer, that line the borders and outskirts of areas we now call the suburbs. There was one problem, though; unless you lived near the Mississippi River, these quality grains were hard to get to market to be processed and dried. In 1848, the Illinois and Michigan canal project opened, allowing ships to unload quality goods along the Chicago River and providing a huge boost for the city's economy and building structure. By 1850, displaced canal workers turned their attention to building Chicago's great train lines that ventured out West to mostly accommodate farm and cattle trade. These trains enabled Chicago's business and trade section to flourish and become a major hub of commerce between the east and west coasts.

The vast influx of Irish and German immigrants took the lead in opening up breweries.

Breweries in the City

1827 - First liquor store, called "The Miller House," opened by Samuel Miller and Archibald Clybourne

1833 - German-owned brewery named "Lill and Diversey," making English- style ales and porters.

1847 - John Huck opens a plant and beer garden on the northwest side that specializes in German-style lager beers.

1854 - German-owned Conrad Seipp Brewing Company opens, manufacturing about 100,000 barrels of beer a year. Noted for being the first company to deliver beer to your home.

1861 - Prussian immigrant Peter Schoenhofen opens a brewery that specializes in edelweiss-style beer.

1891 - Peter Hand, another Prussian, opens his own brewing company, and invents the beloved "Meister Brau". Probably the most influential and longest running company, it closed in 1978.

By the early 1900s Chicago was the proud home of over 60 large breweries, mostly German owned, that knocked out 100 million gallons a year.

The Instigators

If you ever want to see some cool old pictures, visit the Chicago Historical Society on the web and look up early Chicago. It was really a city built on swamplands with dilapidated accommodations, muddy streets, a polluted river called "The Loop" and a lot of unsavory types who gravitated towards drinking beer instead of lake water. Since beer was a pasteurized science, it made more sense to drink it than gamble on bacteria ridden lake water that killed thousands a year. Old geezers I know tell me stories about when they were kids and their uncles would give them a nickel to run down to the local corner tavern to get a wash bucket full of suds and a block of ice to keep it cold. Even older geezers whose relatives worked at the stockyards recall that when barrels of beer would go flat, the suds were taken to the stockyards and given to the hogs to fatten them up and also be used to clean the floors!

As usual, not everyone agreed with this practice of drinking beer. Around 1833, a few Chicagoans started organizations such as "The Chicago Temperance Society" and "The Chicago Benevolence Society" to combat drunkenness and to fight tavern owners from purchasing liquor licenses. By the 1900s, this semi-frontier town was on the fast track and city politicians were forced into reform to clamp down on all city evils.

Chicago Beer Riots

For you out-of-towners, Chicago streets and neighborhoods (we call 'em wards) are built upon a grid system that kind of looks like a piece of graph paper. Each line is a street or block, the middle containing the housing or buildings. Early settlers had to buy their land from the city, which in turn would designate an area that would accommodate their specific ethnic group. Basically, it was Germans in up town, Irish and Poles on the northwest side, African Americans south and the rest on the near west side. These early settlers actually got along pretty well. They worked 6 days a weeks and really enjoyed their suds, especially the Germans and the Irish, who history notes had great alliances through the 1800s and hated anything British.

This philosophy didn't exactly sit well with the city's founding fathers, who took a jaded view of Europeans as filth mongers, breeders and non-Americans. It just so happens at this time that an ultra-conservative group called "The Know Nothings" aligned with the city's mayor, Dr. Levi Boone, to teach these beer-drinking filth mongers a lesson by attacking their beer consumption and licensing policies. Not only did Boone propose to raise license fees by 600%, he also wanted to shut down taverns on Sundays so no one could have a Sunday afternoon beer (package stores didn't exist at that time).

Rumor has it that the first Sunday of the city's enactment of this law, 200 Germans were arrested and a hearing was set for April 21, 1855. On the 21st, a group of 400 bar owners converged on the courthouse to hang the judge but were forced back by police to the near north side. Later that day around 3:00 p.m., the crowd again returned with their Irish friends, who were well armed. A gunfight broke out. Casualties were excessively heavy and that was the last time anyone heard from "The Know Nothings," who ran away to pick on other less fortunate and less powerful ethnic groups.

Demise

The word demise might seem a little rough for this chapter as it was really technology, automation and politics that brought down all of Chicago's great breweries. From 1860 to 1900, Chicago brew meisters were introduced to newfangled technologies that centered around yeast production, malting and cooling applications. Gone were laborious days of experimentation and rampant spoilage. It's at this same time that The Siebel Institute of Technology opened its doors in the city to emerging scientists, who replaced most of the old-world brew meisters and their antiquated ways. Deeper investigation also points to three other significant historical events, the city's 1907 Act, World War I and Prohibition. The 1907 Act gave individual wards in the city the power to enforce their own prohibition laws, thus leading to about a two-third reduction of saloons! World War I put a kabash on Midwestern grain production by the enactment of strict conservation. Also, the animosity toward the Germans affected their beer hall popularity. Last, but not least, with the thirteen-year reign of Prohibition and a long Midwestern drought, brewers found it more economical to produce hard booze, which was easier to carry and easier to hide than laborious beer.

On a sad note, by 1984, 94% of all American beer was being produced by 6 large national companies, not one originating in Chicago. Beer Ho Bastards!!!!!

New Horizon

Wow! That's an amazing story about Chicago's beer-making history, but don't feel too bad as the city now boasts at least a good dozen micro breweries that are getting back to the old way of creating suds. In researching this chapter, I was consumed with a couple of culinary questions: What exactly did Chicago-style beer taste like back then and is there anything equivalent to it on the market today? Did it taste like the ever popular Hamm's, Meister Brau, Schlitz or Pabst Blue Ribbon that we all used to steal from our old man's stash during our high school 70's? Hmmm! Very interesting question, Colonel Klink. Hogannnnn! We must find the answer!

So this is what I did. I contacted a few local brew meisters to get a quick education about brewing technique and history. Pre-prohibition beer production was dominated in the city by the Germans who were really obsessed with using primo barley grain that mimicked the strain they had back home. The two most popular types of brews back then were called lagers and ales. For your info, lager beer is bottom fermented for up to three months and produces suds with a light clean body and taste. On the other hand, ales are fermented from the top for a few days and produce a beer that is heavy bodied, alcohol laden and darker in color. Local beer enthusiasts informed me that there is one beer on the market today that traces its roots back to these pre-prohibition strains. The year was 1842, the town was Pilsen, which today is part of the Czech Republic, and the name of the beer is Pilsner Urquell, often referred to as the original Pilsen. It seems that beers up until that time varied from amber pale colors to deep murky browns or blacks. An interesting fact that I uncovered was that even though it was well noted that the German immigrants were responsible for starting the beer-making process, it was the Irish-American influence in Chicago around the turn of the century that demanded a lighter and more palatable beer style that we now know as pale lager, ie. Miller, Milwaukee's Best or Bud. From what I understand, brewing a true Pilsner can be a real pain in the ass due to the fact that it uses all grain and soft water in its production.

Another fact well noted is that the Great Depression put a stranglehold on beer makers who were forced into stretching recipes and lightening the taste of beer in general. In the 1930s, America's heartland known as the Grain Belt was suffering though one of history's worst droughts. Barley supplies shrank and prices skyrocketed, causing beer makers to turn to other cereal grains called "adjuncts" to continue production. This separated the old world style brewing process into what we know now as a cheap six pack. Chicago, like many other blue collar cities, has an abundance of geezer beer halls, taverns and bars to satisfy its working man's thirst. Who could forget the late, great Harry Carey on WGN radio sipping a few cold ones up in the press box at Wrigley Field or the 60s Hamm's beer commercial with the dancing bear? There also was a time in our history when Mayor Daley Sr. held a press conference proclaiming that office workers in the loop should grab a fishing rod and a beer and head down to the Chicago River for a relaxing lunch! **I love that guy!**

All right, enough said; I hope you get the drift. Not that I want to leave you hanging, but want to know what Chicago style beer tasted like way back when? I uncovered a very secret recipe I know you will like. This is it. Oh yeah, you'll have to talk to your local beer meister to figure it out. Recipe courtesy of master brewer Jeff Renner.

Chicago Style Lager

MALTS	Gravity Contribution
7 lbs. of 6 Row Base Malt	37
1.75 lbs. of Flaked Maize	10
BG for 6 Gallons	1.047
OG for 5 Gallons	1.056

HOPS	IBU Contribution
1 oz of Cluster (7.5%) at 60 minutes	28
1/4 oz of Styrian Goldings (5%) at	2
10 min.1/4 oz of Styrian Goldings	0
(5%) at 0 min.	
Total IBUs	30

YEAST	Fermentation Schedule
Bavarian Lager	Primary at 50°F for 2 weeks, Lager at 34°F for 7 weeks.

MASH SCHEDULE - MULTI REST MASH

Rest	Temperature	Time
Protein Rest	122° F	30
Beta	140° F	15
Conversion	158°F	40
Alpha Conversion Mashout	170°F	10

I know you like the beer wars story so I thought I throw in a few oldies but goodies that need no introduction.

Fried Pork Rinds

MAKES 3 TO 5 POUNDS

"Chicharrones" are most definitely a Mexican delicacy or snack that are prepared all over the city, best when made fresh. Try to get the whole skin from a small butchered pig.

INGREDIENTS

5-10 pounds fresh pork skins, no fur
1 cup sea salt
5 pounds lard for frying
1/3 cup Creole spice or hot Mexican
   spice blend

BRINE

1 gallon warm water
1/4 cup white vinegar
1/4 cup sea salt
1 whole lemon, halved

Place all the ingredients for the brine in a large bucket, stir to mix and then layer in the fresh pork skins. Cover the skins with a heavy weight or plate to keep them under the water After two hours remove the skins, rinse under cold water, dry and lay on top of a sturdy picnic table. Sprinkle on top of the skins one half cup sea salt and using a small bristle scrub brush, scrub the skins on both sides to remove any small hair or excess fat. Repeat with all the skins and then rinse under cold water to remove any excess salt. Bring another gallon of water plus 1/4 cup sea salt to a boil and then take off the fire. Dump all the skins into the hot water and let rest 20 minutes to remove any excess fat. Pour into a large strainer to drain then dry and cut into 2 X 6-inch strips. Pre-heat the oven to 250°, line a few large baking pans with parchment paper, place the strips on the pan and let dry in the oven for three hours After three hours, heat the lard in a large turkey fryer to 350°. Place the dried rinds into a frying basket and deep fry to 3 to 4 minutes until crisp and golden brown. Drain on newspapers, sprinkle with the Creole spice and serve with lime wedges, pickles jalapenos or tio peppers.

Polish Red Pickled Eggs

There was a time in the city's history when tavern owners would offer up for free these delicacies to their patrons to go along with a schooner of beer. The trick is to let them sit in the brine a good two weeks before eating.

INGREDIENTS

12 large hard-boiled eggs, peeled

BRINE

3 cups white vinegar
1 cup canned beet juice
1/4 cup brown sugar
1 tablespoon sea salt
8 whole black peppercorns
1 teaspoon dry mustard
1 teaspoon celery seed
1/2 teaspoon whole cloves
1/2 small cinnamon stick

Gently place the peeled hard-boiled eggs into the bottom of a large mason jar. Place all the brine ingredients into a saucepan, bring to a boil, simmer for 5 minutes and cool. When the brine is cool, strain over the eggs, seal tightly and refrigerate for two weeks before eating. Be sure to shake the jar every once in a while.

Mexicali Style Bar Eggs

I've seen these cropping up around local taverns over the past few years and they are actually pretty good when you're juiced up.

INGREDIENTS

12 large hard-boiled eggs, peeled

BRINE

2 cups white vinegar
1 heaping cup jarred sliced jalapenos with juice
1 heaping cup jarred hot chili picante peppers, quartered with juice
1/4 to 1/2 cup Tabasco sauce
1 tablespoon Lawry's garlic salt
Dash of red pepper flakes
1 small onion, sliced
4 large garlic cloves, sliced
1 large carrot, peeled and sliced

Gently place the peeled hard-boiled egg into the bottom of a large mason jar. Combine the remaining ingredients in a mixing bowl, stir to combine, pour over the eggs, seal tightly and then refrigerate for 2 weeks before eating. Be sure to shake the jar every once in a while.

Pickled Polish Sausage

I know a Polish tavern owner who makes this every year and gives it away as Christmas presents. Any kind of smoked sausage can be used.

INGREDIENTS

2-3 pounds kielbasa or hot links

BRINE

2 cups cider vinegar
1 1/2 cups water
1 small red onion, sliced
4 large garlic cloves, sliced
1 tablespoon sugar
1 teaspoon sea salt
8 whole black peppercorns
Pinch of red pepper flakes
1 tablespoon pickling spice

Cut the kielbasa into 1 1/2-inch pieces and place in the bottom of a mason jar. Combine the remaining ingredients in a saucepan, bring to a boil, simmer 5 minutes and then pour directly over the sausage pieces. Cover tightly and when cool, place in the refrigerator for a week before eating.

THE CORNER BAKERY

BREAD
RECIPES

When I released my first cookbook, I included a generous chapter on bread baking and also a squib in the book asking readers to feel free to e-mail me and exchange recipes. To my surprise, I received about a thousand requests for obscure and obsolete recipes that mostly centered on pastry and bread baking. Now mind you, I'm a pretty competent chef, but a baker's hat I'm not ready to don since most bakers I know are a little bit too sugar crazy for my new diet lifestyle. Don't get me wrong, I love bakers, but the art of baking bread and pastry is truly a gift from God to their hands, which is almost a literal statement as bread and beer have been around since 10,000 B.C. However, it wasn't until the middle of the great 19th century when the art of cake and torte making steadily evolved into what we know as pastry today. Chicago has a deep-rooted history of great baking and bakers, some dating back to the 1800s and still going strong. Now you might be saying to yourself, "Hey Mikey, what does bread have to do with street food?" The answer is simple. Just as hot dog stands and taverns line corners of the city, Mom and Pop bakeries are nestled somewhere in between the two and deserve the same attention.

The city's influx of Irish, German, Swedish, Poles, Slovaks, Jews, Hungarians, Ukrainians and Greeks around the 1850s brought not only a wave of immigrants, but a generation of young and adventurous bakers who were anxious to feed their fellow countrymen. However it came at a very steep price! Unsanitary conditions, rat infestations and distribution issues ran most newfound bakeries into the ground. Some survived and prospered, but most found themselves in the middle of a consolidation war that put a premium on wheat flour and those who supplied it. In the 1890s, the National Biscuit Company, now known as Nabisco, decided to expand the baking industry and consolidate local companies into the union fold on a national basis, ultimately undercutting local bakers and depriving them of earning a fair profit. Chicago's American Biscuit Manufacturing Company was formed from 40 Midwestern bakeries in the 1830s and gave into the pressure. Most people are surprised to learn that one of the hottest selling biscuits of that era were Animal Crackers, the kind in the cutesy little box with the string on it. For your information, animal crackers in the box were typically hung on the Christmas tree as an ornament for the kids. (Eighteen animals to a box and the latest addition to the zoo is the koala bear.) Another surprising fact is that bread took the form of Viennese-type soft buns and rolls rather than the crispier types we are familiar with now. Nabisco gained inspiration from their partnering companies located in England in the form of cracker-like products that could readily be stored in fanciful tins, barrels and sealable packages to insure freshness for overseas travel. Another setback for local bakers was the Columbia Exposition that showcased newfangled mechanical mixers, ovens and utensils, all too steep in price for small bakers. Many went under but some stayed afloat by improvising and avoiding the mass-marketed goods in favor of local or ethnic delicacies.

There is no question that the eastern Europeans led the forefront of modern baking in the city. Most people consider loaf bread to be Chicago's claim to fame, but in reality our past was filled with crackers, biscuits, quick breads and sweet doughs that still seem to fill doily-clad shelves of local ethnic markets and bakeries. In my younger years, I worked summer jobs at a few local bakeries, usually Swedish, Polish or German owned, and although different cultures, their breads and pastry were similar in texture, taste and feel. Handed-down recipes from old Europe were filled with exceedingly fresh eggs, butter and cream, while breads were steeped with the sourness of kvas, caraway and fennel. A far cry from what you can get at your local grocery store!

I've always loved Mom and Pop joints not only for their simplicity, but also for their attention to detail in the product. I come from an ethnically diverse and religious neighborhood and some of my best friends' parents owned small grocery stores, taverns, sausage shops and bakeries. When you're in Chicago, bakery doesn't just mean bread. Chicagoans are fond of savory sweet treats such as almond coffee cakes, houska, lemon babka, raisin stollen, mazurkas, kringle and Danish, with cravings that are satisfied daily by visiting small joints that knock out these fresh delicacies typically sold by the pound. Most are heavy sweet doughs that contain yeast and are usually filled with farmers' cheese, quality preserves or a dose of sugared walnuts or pecans. Flavorings such as lemon, vanilla, cardamom, mace, cinnamon and rum intensify the taste sensation of these breads, usually best accompanied by a steaming cup of joe. I guess you get my drift!

Not to be left out in the cold, my oldest and dearest friends, the rye bread and its distant cousins, have always held a special spot in the hearts of all Chicagoans. If you're a city kid like me, nothing brings more joy to your heart than memories of leaving church on Sunday and heading to your local bakery to get freshly cut rye bread and coffee cake to eat throughout the week.

Chicago's bread history is pretty cool in the fact that French Canadian explorers in the 1600s, while mapping the Mississippi, lingered long enough to take notes and sketch the beautiful flowing fields of wild wheat. The first true bread bakers in the city were the Germans and the Swedes. Matthias Meyer of Frankfurt, Germany opened the first full-service bakery in the city in 1831. Food historians note that at about the same time, Germans started brewing local beer and the leftover yeasty foam was used as a starter to make heavy Bavarian-style rye breads that were typical of their homeland. Historians also relate that it wasn't until the Columbian Exposition that new thrashing machines and farming equipment provided the local markets lighter and softer flours to work with, thus fueling the fine baking trend.

Chicago's oldest and most recognized baking company is Gonnella, started by Alessandro Gonnella in 1886. This paesan introduced Chicago to the infamous 3-foot-long, hearth-baked French-Italian baguette frequently squeezed today by frugal shoppers around the city. Two years later in 1888, Edward Katzinger started the Ekco Housewares Company that still produces some of the best commercial baking pans known to man. With the insurgence of eastern European immigrants invading our shore, the hits kept coming. Some of the oldest bakeries in the city that still survive are Roeser's (1905), Ferrara (1908), Swedish Bakery (1920), Dinkle's (1922), Weber's (1930) and Sara Lee (1935). That's some heavy-duty baking and the tradition continues. Chicago's bread history has been a steady climb through the years and it would seem to be a simple operation to run, but the 1980s brought reform and change into the way the system works. According to Mike Marcucci, Chairman and CEO of Alpha Baking Company (MaryAnn and S. Rosen Brand), "The over population of suburbs in the Midwest led to an upheaval in supply and demand issues that led to a pac man effect of larger companies acquiring smaller just to get a decent loaf of bread to market." Trucking issues, mergers, acquisitions, prime rates of 21% plus the bosses' shoe size kicked a lot of companies into high gear to expand their product line. Mike's company and family baking background earned them the prestigious Wholesale Baker of the Year Award in 2003, with over 150 million is sales. Kudos to Mike!

To say who produces the best bread in the city is a tricky question because there are so many great pastry shops and bakeries. You have to choose one that you enjoy for its consistency and patronize it. It's my observation that your ethnic heritage dictates your preference, but I truly believe that Chicago is a rye bread kind of town. Rye bread in the city is classified as being a tight crumbed, slightly sour tasting, chewy crusted loaf with a hint of caraway. Oh, they love other breads too, but light rye bread is the working man's daily choice. The lightness of the loaf lifts the working man to aristocratic ranks, whereas the sourness of the bread keeps him well rooted in the peasant tradition. Chicago bakeries have a special lingo that one must know to order breads. First, the shape and size, meaning does one want it long or short, bucket rolled or braided? Second, light or dark, meaning light rye or dark rye or pumpernickel. Next is seeded or unseeded, meaning with or without caraway seeds, poppy seeds or sesame seeds. Finally, should it be sliced or left whole? My advice to you is to get to the bakery early, grab a number and pay close attention to the action because by mid-morning all the good stuff is gone.

Bread baking is a very easy, but sometimes very exacting science. I've seen many a great chef break down and cry with frustration over the fact that his bread didn't turn out like the corner bakery's. But don't despair, commercial bakeries have all kinds of specialized equipment and ingredients that make their bread look perfect. Bread dough has a mind of its own. If it's too cold when mixed, it gets lethargic and moves really slowly. If it gets too hot, it just gets plain ornery, rising too quickly and taking on a yeasty taste. With that said, I've included in this book 8 breads (3 breakfast sweet breads and 5 street loafs) that have been very loyal to me over the last 25 years. I wanted to give you a wide spectrum of taste, flavors and textures.

For first-time bread bakers, I would be more concerned about the taste than the appearance, so don't get aggravated; it takes time to master. I've included a whimsical story about my early bread baking experiences and also a Bread Bakers Workbench that will give you more insight into the proper ingredients used. Lastly, for all you paesans, I have a few more bread recipes in the Italian Sub Grinders section of this book. So get up, stop loafing and make some bread!

Mike, The Apprentice Polish Baker

I've got to be honest; I have a love-hate relationship with bread and pastry. I think it all stems from my earlier days as an apprentice cook working at a local bakery on the Northwest side of Chicago. When I was hired for the job over the phone, I was told by the owner in his broken English, "Yeah! You'll be working in the back with the bakers, so be here tomorrow at 6:00 a.m. sharp." "And wear comfortable shoes." So with that said and a promise to make minimum wage, I went to bed early that night so that I could be awake by 5:00 a.m. As I trudged 2 miles through the early morning snow, my thoughts of sweet anticipation could barely hold back my enthusiasm. Swirling hot babkas, almond coffee cakes, rye breads, and tortes whipped through my head, and maybe a cup of hot cinnamon krupnik to welcome the new kid on the job. As I turned up the alley, I could see the back of the bakery, and low and behold there were four bakers, two Poles and two Germans to be exact, sitting on old dairy crates waiting for me. As I approached them, I was greeted with an enthusiastic "Hello," and at the same time I thought it was strange that they were all red-cheeked, sitting there in 5-below weather, wearing nothing but white, short-sleeved T-shirts, stained aprons and those crazy Chicago Tribune formed baker hats. One baker by the name of Stanley said, "Hey, you're early so have a cup of coffee," and then he offered me an unfiltered cigarette that he pulled from behind his ear. I declined the smoke but accepted the coffee that was in a mug, which resembled my grandfather's old shaving cup, and the coffee didn't taste much better. For an uneasy five minutes of small talk, all I could do was stare at their thick necks and massive arms, which obviously were built by years of mixing dough and hoisting pans into the hot ovens. Alas, one of the bakers let me into paradise. I can still remember it today; it was like walking into heaven, the warmth of the kitchen and the sweet smell of fresh baked pastries and breads. As my eyes gleamed at the massive sized bakery, a long building with a center aisle of wood worktables down the middle and baking equipment on each side, I was in awe. And while my coat and scarf were lifted off of me, I was donned with one of the bakers used aprons, and another's sweat-filled hat was placed on top of my head. I was ready to bake! I asked with anticipation, "Where do I start?" And now my new friend, Stanley, put his arm around me and said, "You're going to work with the sugar."

"Oh," I said, "I always wanted to work with sugar." With that said, he handed me two wood- handled metal pastry scrapers, and said, "Now get on your hands and knees, and start scraping the trampled sugar off the oak floors, all the way up and all the way down." No joke! Two bowling- alley sized lanes were laid out before me. As Stanley walked out the back door, he reminded me that the shop opened in one hour. So on my hands and knees, I began my apprenticeship. Every foot of the way was an adventure, huge tables to the left of me, huge containers full of sugar and flour to the right, and let's not forget, gargantuan bakers' ovens, bowls, mixers and a million stack trays. As I eagerly scraped, I noticed that I was, eerily, the only one in the dimly-lit bakery, except for the voices speaking in Polish behind the red velvet curtain at the front of the store. Scrape, scrape, scrape, crawl, crawl, crawl "Hey," I said to myself, "This must be some kind of Polish joke, right. Maybe if I get up to the curtain, I'll be saved." Dare I not get up, but to stretch my aching back and swollen hands? So alas, in pain, I popped up and to my amazement, I saw that on the wood work tables were hundreds of freshly baked breads of all shapes and sizes, beautiful pastries, tortes, coffee cakes, chocolate pachki, cookies galore, and because it was around Christmas, Chrusticki and almond crescents gloriously coated with powdered sugar. My stomach reeled in pain from the cheap coffee, so I grabbed the closest item off the table to ease the pain, and now while I'm scraping again and choking on the powdered sugar crescents, I hear the distinct sound of Christmas bells emulating from the front of the shop. The store is open. I quietly crawl up to the velvet curtain, and peek my head through to see a beautiful wood-paneled European storefront, with glass-lined shelves adorned with dainty Polish lace, and two bread cutting machines running full tilt at 7:00 a.m. The steady clientele of Busias, dressed in car coats, scarves, and galoshes, were streaming through the front door, fighting over the number machine. As I sat there in amazement watching this fevered excitement, my eyes were affixed to one of the countertops which had a spool of kitchen twine that was rapidly being wound around every box and package that left the store. At the same time, the velvet curtain was drawn, and I was knocked on my butt by one of the Polish girls hurriedly racing to get more rye breads and Babkas. Not a word was said, or an apology given, so dejectedly I went back to my scraping and table foraging, and just about the time I got down to where I had begun, I was tapped on the shoulder by one of the shop girls named Sophie. A big girl with a huge chest and a lot of makeup, and a hairnet to boot, she said in her sweet Polish accent, "Welcome to the bakery, and here's a cup of coffee and a chocolate pachki for you." She also added two other phrases that I will always remember; "All employees get 50% off on all unsold bakery, and when you're done with the floor, don't forget to clean the baking pans."

Bread Baker's Work Bench

There is nothing more satisfying in life than the smell of freshly baked bread coming from your kitchen, and with a little trial and error, anyone can knock out a beautiful loaf. Before you begin, please follow my guidelines and read about the ingredients that I use at home.

Proper Measuring

Every recipe in this book, whether it is bread or pastry, uses the spoon and sweep method. That means you pour a bag of flour into a plastic container, then using a large kitchen spoon, spoon the flour directly into a metal measuring cup, then using a flat icing spatula, remove any excess flour by running the flat edge across the top of the cup. (Do not dip your measuring cup into a bag of flour because it compacts the flour too much and the recipes won't work.)

Proper Mixing

Breads in this book are best kneaded in a heavy-duty tabletop mixer to build gluten. All of the breads can be mixed in a large capacity food processor, but I prefer the other. One good word of advice is to never walk away from the machine while it is on, because certain dough will torque the machine and may cause it to hop around the counter and land on the floor.

Oven Temperature

Always make sure that your oven is cleaned and properly calibrated. A few degrees off here and there can ruin your precious dough. It is wise to invest in a good oven thermometer.

Ingredients

Never short yourself by buying inferior products. Good ingredients make all the difference in baking.

Active Dry Yeast - I only use Red Star (granular) in the jar, stored in the freezer to keep fresh. Rapid rise is a no-no, and fresh yeast is too hard to work with. Old recipes call for too much yeast, so please follow my guidelines for measuring yeast. Use 1/2 teaspoon yeast per cup for regular flour dough, and use 3/4 teaspoon yeast per cup for heavy and sweet dough.

Butter - I like good old Land O' Lakes Unsalted Butter for its never-ending consistency and exceptional taste.

Shortening - Crisco all-vegetable shortening in the blue can is my favorite for its frying and baking consistency.

Vegetable Oil - Wesson Canola Oil is great because of its pure clean taste and versatility.

Eggs - Grade A large eggs are perfect for all of my recipes.

Milk - I only use Grade A pasteurized whole milk.

Powdered Milk - Powdered milk is sometimes used instead of whole milk to keep a bread or dough light and fluffy without adding extra fat or weight.

Sea Salt - I only use sea salt in all of my cooking for its clean and pure taste. Regular iodized table salt will give your food an unpleasant after taste.

Malt Syrup - A honey-like syrup made of roasted grains that has a more concentrated taste than regular sugar. Dark honey can also be substituted if needed.

Molasses - Brer Rabbit green label molasses is excellent for providing flavor, color, and moisture to baked products.

Chef's Tip About Flour While the home cook depends almost exclusively on a product called all-purpose flour, the professional baker has available a wide variety of flours with different qualities and characteristics. It is vitally important that you seek out the best flour you can get your hands on to replicate the quality of bakery shop results.

Powdered Sour - An integral ingredient that gives rye bread its distinctive mellow, tangy, sour flavor. Powdered sour is available at any quality baking supply house or through mail order.

Vital Wheat Gluten - Not all flours are created equal, so a tablespoon or two added to any bread dough will give your loaves more strength and boost while lightening the texture and promoting a good rise. I recommend using 1 teaspoon per cup of regular flour, and 1 1/2 teaspoons per cup of whole grain or rye flours.

All-Purpose Flour - Store bought flours are adequate; however, I like to search out and find quality flour milled from hard red winter wheat that has a significant amount of gluten-producing protein in it. Most whole food markets carry a variety of great brands, but read the label for brands that carry a minimum of 11.7% protein.

Bread Flour - I prefer to use bread flour that is unbleached, unbromated and made from hard red spring wheat. Bread flours naturally have higher protein content than other flours and this will give your loaves more structure. Try to find a brand that contains at least 12.7% to 14.2% protein content.

Rye Flour - Rye flours come in so many different varieties that it is often difficult to know what to buy. I prefer using light rye flour, but sometimes I combine it with darker rye flours or whole rye meal (pumpernickel flour) to give my breads a richer taste or texture. Rye flours are naturally low in protein so most bakers use a rye bread improver or high protein wheat flour that gives the bread its chewy texture. My recipes use a combination of high protein bread flour and vital wheat gluten to give the loaves that extra lift.

Rye Blend - Whole food markets sometimes sell this mixture which is a combination of light rye and a strong wheat flour that is an excellent mix for the beginning rye bread maker. Feel free to substitute this blend for all the flour in any rye bread recipe.

As I stated in the introduction, Chicago is loaded with mom and pop bakeries that knock out beautiful breads and breakfast cakes on a daily basis. This small collection of recipes has been very loyal to me over the years and with a little practice you also can produce a taste of Chicago in your own home.

Almond Coffee Cake

MAKES 1 CAKE

Bakeries on the northwest side easily make the most delicious coffee cakes I've ever had. Their beautiful cakes are sold in a large flat shape, lightly braided and stuffed with a sweet almond or walnut filling then topped with a fresh sugary streusel, baked and drizzled with a warm butter cream icing.

INGREDIENTS

6 tablespoons sugar
1 teaspoon sea salt
1 stick unsalted butter, softened
1 teaspoon vanilla extract
1/2 teaspoon ground cardamon
2 whole large eggs
1 cup half and half (about 110F)
3 1/2 cups all-purpose flour
1 cup cake flour
4 teaspoons active dry yeast

1 Recipe Walnut Filling, see Pantry
1 Recipe Clear Glaze, see Pantry
1 Recipe Butter Cream Icing, see Pantry

EGG WASH

1 egg well beaten with a little milk

Thoroughly combine the flours and yeast in a mixing bowl and set aside. To mix the dough in a kitchen aid machine, place the sugar, salt, butter, vanilla and cardamon in the mixer bowl, attach the paddle and mix on low speed for 1 minute to blend. Add the eggs one by one then add the half and half and mix briefly until well combined. Now slowly add all the flour until the dough forms a mass around the paddle. Turn the machine off and re-place the paddle with the dough hook. Knead the dough on medium low speed for about 5 minutes until it is smooth and elastic. If the dough is excessively soft and sticky, add a little more flour. Place the dough in a large lightly oiled bowl, turn to coat on all sides, cover with plastic wrap and allow to rise for 6 to 8 hours in the refrigerator or overnight until doubled in bulk. The next day deflate the dough, divide into 2 equal pieces and freeze one for later use. When the piece comes to room temperature, using a rolling pin, roll out the dough into a 8 by 15-inch oblong and place onto a parchment lined sheet pan. Place the long end of the sheet pan in front of you, and using a 12-inch ruler, lightly mark but don't cut the dough into 3 equal sections working your way from the bottom to the top. You should now have 3 sections that are 3-inches each, a left side, middle and right side. Using a rolling cutter, cut through the 2 outer most sections of the dough diagonally downward at 3/4 -inch intervals. Evenly spread half of the almond filling down the center then fold the slashes one at a time over the center filled section alternating the strips of dough. Brush the loaf with the egg wash, sprinkle on the remaining almond filling then cover the coffee cake loosely with plastic wrap and let rest for 1 hour until almost doubled. Pre-heat the oven to 350° and when hot, bake on the middle rack for 25 to 30 minutes until the cake is a deep golden color. When thoroughly baked, slide the coffee cake still on the parchment paper onto a rack to cool. After 5 minutes, brush the entire loaf with the clear glaze then after 1/2 hour, sprinkle on the butter cream icing.

Lemon Babka

Chicago bakeries specialize in all different kinds of babka-like products but I prefer mine just on the basic lemony side along with some fresh fruit.

INGREDIENTS

10 tablespoons sugar
1 teaspoon sea salt
1/2 pound unsalted butter, softened
1 teaspoon lemon extract
1/2 teaspoon vanilla extract
2 teaspoons grated lemon zest
3 whole large eggs
1 cup half and half (about 110F)
2 1/4 cups bread flour
2 1/4 cups all-purpose flour
4 teaspoons yeast

Powdered sugar for dusting
1 non-stick fluted bundt pan, unbuttered

Thoroughly combine the flours and yeast in a mixing bowl then set aside. To mix the dough in a kitchen aid machine, place the sugar, salt, butter, extracts and zest in the mixer bowl, attach the paddle and mix on low speed. Now slowly add the eggs until they are absorbed then add the half and half and mix briefly. Add all the flour until the dough forms a mass around the paddle, re-place with the dough hook and knead on low speed for about 5 minutes until the dough is smooth and elastic. If the dough is excessively soft and sticky, add a little more flour. Place the dough into a large bowl, cover with plastic wrap and refrigerate for at least 4 hours. After a couple hours, turn the risen dough out onto a lightly floured work surface and punch it down. Using your hands, roll the dough into a flat cigar shape about 12-inches long, form into a small tire and pinch together the open ends. Place the dough into the unbuttered pan, cover with plastic wrap and let rise slowly until doubled in bulk. Pre-heat the oven to 350°, and when the babka is risen, place into the hot oven and cook for 35 to 45 minutes until the top is golden brown. Remove the babka from the pan to a cooling rack and when the cake is cool, dust with powdered sugar.

Chocolate Glazed Paczki

MAKES ABOUT 14 TO 16 DOUGHNUTS

Paczki "pronounced Poonch key" fever has gone wild all over the country but unfortunately most are made from a commercial mix. This is a true to heart recipe that takes a little practice but it's well worth the effort once you get the hang of it.

INGREDIENTS

5 tablespoons sugar
3/4 teaspoon sea salt
3 tablespoons shortening
1/2 teaspoon vanilla extract
1 heaping teaspoon orange zest
2 large egg yolks
1 scant cup water (about 110F)
2 tablespoons dry milk powder
1 3/4 cups all-purpose flour
1 3/4 cups cake flour
4 1/2 teaspoons yeast
1 tablespoon baking powder
2 tablespoons Spiritus or rum (optional)

1 Recipe Chocolate Glaze, see Pantry
Crisco shortening for frying

Thoroughly combine the flours, milk powder, yeast and baking powder in a mixing bowl then set aside. To mix the dough in a kitchen aid machine, place the sugar, salt, shortening, vanilla and zest in the mixer bowl, attach the paddle and mix for 1 minute to blend. Add the yolks until they are absorbed, then add the water and liquor and mix briefly. Add the flour until the dough forms a mass around the paddle then replace with the dough hook, and knead the dough on medium speed for about 5 minutes until the dough is smooth and elastic. If the dough is excessively soft and sticky, add a little more flour. Place the dough in a large oiled bowl, cover tightly with plastic wrap and allow the dough to rise In a warm place for about 20 minutes. After 20 minutes turn the dough out onto a lightly floured work surface, and using your hands, pat down the dough until it is exactly 1/2 -inch thick. Cover the dough with a kitchen towel and let it rest for 15 minutes more. After 15 minutes, cut the dough using a 2 1/2-inch round pastry cutter. Carefully remove any excess dough around the cut circles, re-cover the circles and let rest 20 minutes more until they are 3/4 risen. (Re-use the excess dough to make more pachki.) Heat a good amount of shortening in a medium sized heavy duty pot until it reaches 375°. After the doughnuts have rested, fry one or two at a time in the hot fat until golden brown on each side. Drain the pachki on brown paper bags then transfer to a cooling rack. Dip the slightly cooled pachki into the warm chocolate glaze and serve.

Milwaukee Avenue Caraway Rye

MAKES ONE PLUMP LOAF

This is the real deal that I learned how to make some 25 years ago while working at Forest View Bakery on the northwest side. The recipe produces a medium sized loaf, tight grained with slightly sour caraway undertones complimented by a shiny, chewy crust. The bread is great with smoked Polish sausage, kraut or kiszka and eggs.

INGREDIENTS

Starter
1 cup light rye flour
1 cup whole wheat flour
1 1/4 teaspoons yeast
Pinch of sugar
1 1/4 cups warm water (about 110F)

Dough
2 cups bread flour
2 teaspoons sea salt
1 1/4 teaspoons yeast
1 1/2 teaspoons powdered sour
1 tablespoon caraway seeds
2 tablespoons shortening, softened
1/4 cup warm water (about 110F)

INGREDIENTS

Starch Wash
1/4 cup water
1/2 teaspoon cornstarch

To make the starter, place all of its ingredients into the bowl of a kitchen aid mixer and stir with a spoon until well combined. Cover tightly with plastic wrap and leave in a warm place to let the starter rise, bubble and ferment for about 2 hours. (This is accentuating the flavor of the rye.) When the starter is doubled, place the bowl onto the machine and attach the paddle. Add the remaining ingredients for the dough, turn the machine on and let the dough mix until it forms a shaggy mass around the paddle about 1 minute. Now replace the flat beater with the dough hook and knead at medium speed until the dough is smooth and elastic around 3 to 4 minutes. Remove the ball to a lightly floured work surface, hand knead for 1 minute then place into an oiled bowl, cover with plastic wrap and let rise until doubled about 1 1/2 to 2 hours. When the dough is risen flatten the ball, return to the bowl, cover and let rise until doubled again. When the dough is risen again, pour onto a lightly floured work surface without deflating it. Carefully using your hands, flatten the piece into a 10 by 8-inch rectangle. With the dough sitting in front of you on the counter, fold the top edge over onto itself about 1/4 of the way down and tightly seal the seam with your fingertips. Fold it over again then seal again with your fingertips. Fold the dough over one more time, re-seal and form the dough into a plump salami with the seam on the bottom. Pinch both ends, fold the pinch underneath the dough then place onto a lightly cornmeal dusted piece of parchment paper set on a baking sheet. Cover the dough with a piece of plastic wrap and let it re-rise. After 30 minutes of rising, pre-heat the oven to 450° and adjust the oven rack to the middle setting. When the oven is hot, fill a spray bottle with cool water and sprits the oven to create steam then immediately close the door. When the dough is doubled, lightly score the top with a few slashes from a razor blade and bake in the hot oven for 10 minutes. Re-sprits the oven, reduce the heat to 400° and let the bread bake for another 20 minutes until golden brown then remove it to a wire rack. Place the starch wash ingredients into a small saucepan, bring to a boil to mix then brush over the hot bread to glaze.

Light and Sweet Pumpernickel

Most pumpernickel bread are too heavy for my liking so I devised this recipe for those of you who enjoy it on the lighter side. The recipe produces 2 huge round loaves that are medium crumbed and lusciously sweet from the molasses. I recommend serving this bread with any smoked fish, pickled herring or creamy cheese.

INGREDIENTS

Starter
1/2 cup warm water (about 110F)
1 teaspoon yeast
2/3 cup bread flour

Dough
5 1/4 cups bread flour
1 3/4 cups pumpernickel or rye flour
2 1/4 teaspoons yeast
2 tablespoon unsalted butter, softened
1 tablespoon plus 1/4 teaspoon sea salt
1 3/4 cups warm water (about 120 to 130F)
1/4 cup dark molasses
1/4 cup sugar

To make the starter, place all of its ingredients into the bowl of a kitchen aid machine and stir with a spoon until well combined. Cover tightly with plastic wrap and leave in a warm place to rise, bubble and ferment about 1 hour.

When the starter is doubled, place the bowl onto the machine and attach the paddle. Add the remaining ingredients for the dough, turn the machine on and mix the dough until it forms a shaggy mass around the paddle about 1 minute. Now replace the flat beater with the dough hook and knead at medium speed until the dough is smooth and elastic about 3 to 4 minutes. Remove the ball to a lightly floured work surface, hand knead for a minute then place into an oiled bowl, cover with plastic wrap and let rise until doubled in bulk about 1 1/2 hours. Turn the risen dough out onto a work surface, deflate and divide into 2 equal pieces. Cover the pieces with a kitchen towel and let rest for 10 minutes. To form a loaf using your hands, grasp the dough and form it into a rough shaped ball. Now gently using both hands, tuck the dough underneath itself to form a tight ball. Repeat with the remaining dough then place them onto a parchment lined sheet pan dusted with cornmeal. Cover the dough balls with slightly oiled plastic wrap and allow to rise in a warm place until doubled. When the loaves are almost doubled, pre-heat the oven to 475° and set the rack to the middle position. Using a spray bottle filled with water, sprits the inside of the oven to create steam then close the door. Bake the bread in the hot oven for 10 minutes, re-sprits then lower the heat to 425° and bake for another 20 minutes until the crust is well browned. Now turn the oven off and let the bread sit in the oven for 5 minutes more then remove to a wire rack and cool before slicing.

Harlem Avenue Crispy Italian

MAKES 2 PLUMP LOAVES

Everyone loves a good loaf of Italian bread and in Chicago you are easily looking at a good 20 or 30 different bakeries vying for your business. This recipe produces a light, airy and crisp loaf that stands up well to any Italian sandwich or generous dunk in homemade spaghetti sauce!

INGREDIENTS

1 3/4 cups water
1 teaspoon sugar
1 teaspoon sea salt
5 cups bread flour
4 1/2 teaspoons yeast
2 tablespoons canola oil

In a small saucepan, combine the water, sugar and salt, bring to a boil, stir then remove from the fire and cool until 105 to 115F. In the bowl of a kitchen aid mixer , add the remaining ingredients. Attach the flat beater, put the machine on low speed and mix for 1 minute. While the machine is running, slowly add the water until it forms a shaggy mass around the paddle about 1 minute. Now replace the flat beater with the dough hook, and knead at medium speed until the dough is smooth and elastic and forms a round ball, around 3 to 4 minutes. If the dough seems a little sticky and won't form a ball, add a little bit more flour until it does. Remove the ball to a lightly floured work surface, hand knead for 1 minute, then place into an oiled bowl and cover until risen and doubled in size about 1 1/2 to 2 hours. Turn the risen dough out onto a lightly floured work surface. Deflate the dough and divide into 2 equal pieces. Cover the loaves with a kitchen towel and let rest for 10 minutes. To form, use your hands to punch the dough back and flatten it out into a 12 by 6-inch rectangle. With the dough sitting in front of you on the counter, fold the top edge over onto itself about 1/4 of the way down and tightly seal the seam with your fingertips. Fold it over again then seal again with your fingertips. Fold the dough over one more time, re-seal and form the dough into a slender salami with the seam on the bottom. Pinch both ends, fold the pinch underneath the dough then place onto a parchment lined sheet pan that is dusted with cornmeal. Repeat with the remaining loaf then cover with a kitchen towel and let rise until doubled. Pre-heat the oven to 425° and adjust the oven rack to the middle. (You have to inject a little steam into the oven while the bread is baking so the loaves will crisp up, so fill a spray bottle with some cool water.) When the oven is hot, open the door and mist the walls of the oven with a good 10 sprits from the spray bottle and then close the door. Lightly spray the loaves then place directly into the hot oven and bake for 5 minutes. Quickly open the door, sprits 10 more times then close the oven door. Repeat after another 5 minutes. The loaves take around 30 minutes to bake.

Daily White Filone

Please refer to the ITALIAN SUB GRINDER CHAPTER for this recipe.

Sesame Seeded Pane Siciliano

Please refer to the ITALIAN SUB GRINDER CHAPTER for this recipe.

Balice Bread

Please refer to the ITALIAN SUB GRINDER CHAPTER for this recipe.

Farm House Potato

MAKES 2 LOAVES

This is an excellent and easy bread to make if you are a beginner. The loaves have a nice, supple, light and airy crumb with a slightly sweet chewy crust. Best served with a slather of unsalted butter and homemade strawberry jam.

INGREDIENTS

1 medium sized baking potato
2 1/2 cups water

Dough
6 cups bread flour
4 teaspoons yeast
1/4 cup unsalted butter, softened
2 1/2 teaspoons sea salt
2 cups cooking potato water (about 120 to 130F)
5 tablespoons powdered milk
3 tablespoons sugar

Two 8 1/2 by 4 1/2 by 2 3/4 -inch loaf pan, lightly oiled

Peel the potato, place into the water, bring to a boil and simmer for 20 minutes until the potato is able to be mashed. Drain the potato being sure to save 2 cups of the cooking liquid. Mash the potato until completely smooth then set aside. To make the dough in a kitchen aid mixer, place the flour, yeast and butter in the mixing bowl and attach the paddle. Dissolve the salt, powdered milk and sugar into the reserved potato water. With the machine running, slowly add the liquid to the flour until the dough forms a rough mass around the paddle. Now add the reserved mashed potato and let the machine run another minute. Turn the machine off, remove the paddle, replace it with the dough hook, and knead the dough on medium low speed for 4 to 5 minutes until the dough is smooth and elastic. Place the dough into a large oiled bowl, cover with plastic wrap and allow to rise in a warm place until doubled in bulk about 1 1/2 hours. Turn the risen dough out onto a lightly floured work surface, deflate and divide into 2 equal pieces. Cover the pieces with a kitchen towel and let rest 10 minutes. To form into loaves, use your hands to punch the dough back and flatten it out. To form a loaf, stretch the dough into a rough rectangle. Fold in the short ends of the dough until it is approximately the length of the pan, then fold the far long edge over to the middle. Fold over the other long side and compress to form a tight loaf. Place the loaf in the oiled pan seam side down. Repeat with the other piece, place in the pan, cover with a kitchen towel and let rise until doubled in bulk about 1 hour. Pre-heat the oven to 400°, set a rack in the middle and bake the loaves until golden brown and firm about 30 minutes. Cool on a wire rack before slicing.

Poppy Seed Challah

My all time favorite a.k.a. Egg twist. Who can resist a beautifully braided loaf, speckled with poppy seeds or white sesame seeds? I've reduced the traditional quantity of eggs in the recipe and increased the sugar to produce a truly magnificent loaf. Medium grained, slightly sweet and egg enriched accentuates a soft but sliceable crust. Bakers sometimes add saffron water to the dough to give it a deeper color. Any leftovers make an excellent French toast!

INGREDIENTS

6 1/2 cups bread flour
4 teaspoons yeast
2 large whole eggs
2 1/2 teaspoons sea salt
1 1/2 cups warm water (about 120 to 130F)
1/2 cup sugar
6 tablespoons canola oil

EGG WASH

1 egg yolk well beaten with a little water
Poppy seeds or sesame seeds

In the bowl of a kitchen aid mixer, place the flour, yeast, eggs and salt, attach the paddle and mix on low speed for a minute to blend. Dissolve the sugar into the warm water and while the machine is still running, slowly add the liquid and oil to the flour until the dough forms a shaggy mass around the paddle. Turn the machine off, replace the paddle with the dough hook and knead on medium speed for 5 minutes until the dough is smooth and elastic. If the dough is excessively soft and sticky, add 1 to 2 more tablespoons of flour. Place the dough in a large oiled bowl, cover with plastic wrap and allow to rise in a warm place until doubled in bulk about 1 1/2 hours. Turn the dough out onto a lightly floured work surface, deflate and divide into 4 equal pieces. Cover with a kitchen towel and let rest for 10 minutes. To form a loaf using your hands, roll each piece into a cylinder 12 to 15 inches long. Arrange two strands side by side. Begin to braid in the middle of the strands and braid to one end then turn the dough around and braid from the middle to the other end. Repeat with the other two strands. Pinch each end to seal and turn the pinched parts under the loaves. Place the loaves on a parchment lined sheet pan dusted with cornmeal. Cover the loaves with oiled plastic wrap and allow to rise until doubled, about 1 hour. Pre-heat the oven to 375° and set a rack to the middle level. Brush the top and sides of the loaves with the egg wash, liberally sprinkle on the poppy seeds and bake for 20 to 25 minutes until the tops are golden brown.

JUST GOOD FRIGGIN SOUP!

SOUP

RECIPES

Since I've become a chef/writer, a lot of things have changed in my life and probably the biggest is that I've become a nocturnal insomniac. It's not easy working out of your home when your wife is vacuuming or running the washing machine, or listening to the kids argue about who's going to get on Sony Play Station first. As a writer you have to learn how to zone out, and I find a lot of solace late at night sitting at my dining room table in my underwear, sipping a cocktail and filling reams of paper with thoughts and memories of past cooking experiences. I've been lucky in my career to have learned the art of soup making from some really great chefs who were generous enough to share their secrets. In a French kitchen, I was known as the saucier, or the cook who makes soups, stocks and sauces. This position, although respected, is often neglected because of the complexity of the art. As a young cook, you quickly learn that anyone can grill a steak, but the guy who can make a sauce or soup is the king!

My earliest memories with soup, I guess, are like everyone else's. When you were sick, your mom would bring you a folding T.V. tray with the mandatory Campbell's tomato soup, flat ginger ale and oyster crackers. As I got older and was forced into becoming a boy scout, the only salvation when stuck in Rockford camping was most definitely clean socks, underwear, toilet paper, a pocket knife and a can of Hormel chili. Maybe not gourmet fare, but I think you get my drift. My progression into appreciating and learning how to make soup was actually through experiences I had while spending time on my aunt's farm in Wausau, Wisconsin. My Aunt Minnie, who was a dairy farmer, used to make the best chicken noodle soup with fresh ingredients that she pulled from her garden, and by a quick head wackin' of a really plump chicken that she had raised. I remember that my aunt used to say, "From God to the ground to the pot to your heart." It's funny that I remember that after all these years, but all in all, soup making is about comfort and security.

Before I actually became a chef, I used to clerk for a couple of law firms located in the loop. Part of my studious duties were not only to schlep around brief cases full of files and get documents stamped before judges, but I was also the designated "lunch boy!" Lunch boy is a very prestigious position at a law firm because, let's face it, when it's mid December, 5 degrees above, 4 inches of slush and the wind is blowing, no self respecting judge or attorney wants to pull on his Florsheim galoshes and overcoat for a sandwich and a bowl of soup. Pulling files gets boring for a young guy after a while, so I loved being lunch boy. It was actually my first experience with downtown restaurants and delis. The process is simple. At 11:30 A.M. you get a pen and a pad of paper, visit each attorney for his order, get some petty cash and try to narrow your expedition down to one place that will satisfy everyone's cravings for that day. During the late 70s, my places of choice were usually Stop N Shop, Berghoff's, Cordoza's, Manny's, Woolworth's lunch counter, Marshall Field's or Abe's Deli. The trick was how to get there and back in about a half hour and not get sleeted on, wind blown or killed by some crazy driver. So everything I did was underground.

At this time in Chicago's culinary history, burger joints were a rare find in the Loop so more substantial fare was the way to go. Back then restaurants used to fill up really fast so you had to get your order in quickly, and as usual it takes time when handing a written order in for ten different items at a time. Since I visited these places frequently, the waitresses knew me and also knew that lunch boy needed some sustenance for himself. I would have just enough time to scarf down a cup of cream of chicken and rice soup and a Kaiser roll before the order was filled. Maybe it's just me, maybe I was just young, or maybe it was the climactic conditions outside, but it seemed at the time that sitting on that barstool at that lunch counter with all the frenzied activity around me, nothing mattered more than the goodness and heartiness of that soup.

I know it might seem strange to you that I would include this chapter in the book, but I have spent so much time in my life sitting at greasy spoon joints, taverns or quality restaurants sipping a cold one, enjoying friendly conversation and diving into a good cup of soup, usually the house specialty that it seems strange to me to leave it out! Soup is comfort and security on a cold winter's day; it's childhood memories revisited, a quick nourishing lunch remembered, and nothing defines street food more than a hot bowl of soup.

This is a good collection of local favorites that I've been making throughout the years. I've scaled down the recipes for the home cook but they can easily be doubled to accommodate more guests.

Breakfast Menudo 2007

SERVES 6 TO 8

This is my updated version of the beloved Mexican breakfast soup. Pre-blanching the tripe 2 to 3 times removes a lot of the gamey smell that people find offensive.

INGREDIENTS

2 to 3 pounds tripe, pre-blanched
1/2 small calves foot, cleaned
1 1/2 pounds beef short ribs
1/4 cup all-purpose flour
4 tablespoons canola oil
4 large garlic cloves, minced
1 medium onion, diced
2 medium carrots, sliced
1 large celery stalk, sliced
1 small leek, sliced
1/2 medium red and green pepper, diced
1 cup diced tomatoes
2 tablespoons tomato paste
10 cups chicken stock
One 14 oz. can hominy, rinsed and
   drained

SPICE

1/2 teaspoon sea salt
1/4 teaspoon black pepper
2 small bay leaves
1 large pinch red pepper flakes
1 teaspoon comino seeds, crushed
1 1/2 teaspoons dried Mexican oregano
2 tablespoons hot New Mexican red chili powder
Dash of Tabasco and Worcestershire

Pre-blanch the tripe and cut into half inch strips. Heat 2 tablespoons of oil in a medium sized pot, flour and brown the short ribs then remove to a platter. Return the pot to the fire, add the remaining oil then saute the garlic, onion, carrots, celery, leek and peppers for 3 to 4 minutes. Add the tomatoes and tomato paste, stir, then add the spice blends to the pot and cook for 1 minute to infuse. Add the remaining ingredients to the pot except the hominy, bring to a boil, reduce the heat and simmer slowly for about 2 hours. Add the hominy and cook the soup for another half hour. Ladle the soup into bowls and garnish with diced pequin chilies, lime wedges and fresh tortillas.

Chi-town Chili

Everyone loves chili! This is a basic Midwestern recipe that's not too spicy but will most definitely warm your belly up.

INGREDIENTS

2 tablespoons canola oil
1 1/2 pounds ground beef, 85% lean
1/4 teaspoon garlic powder
1/4 teaspoon onion powder
1/4 teaspoon oregano
1/2 teaspoon cumin
2 teaspoons paprika
1 heaping tablespoon chili powder
1/2 teaspoon black pepper
Dash of sea salt and red pepper flakes
4 cups beef stock
1 cup tomato puree

THICKENER

2 tablespoons all-purpose flour
2 tablespoons cornmeal
1/3 cup warm water
One 15 ounce can light or dark red kidney beans, rinsed and drained

In a non-stick saucepot, heat the oil and brown the ground beef until it renders its fat. Drain the meat in a colander then return to the pot, add all of the remaining ingredients except the thickener, bring to a boil then reduce to a slow simmer to cook for about 45 minutes. Mix the flour and cornmeal with the warm water until it forms a smooth paste, add to the pot and stir with a spoon to combine. Also add the drained kidney beans to the pot and let the chili cook for another 15 minutes. Serve with a splash of hot sauce and some oyster crackers.

"Baked" Stuffed Pepper Soup

SERVES 6 TO 8

This is a south side favorite that I have enjoyed at several taverns around town. I like a little bit of a fancier presentation but feel free to chop up everything, throw all the crap in a crock pot and let it stew all day. Just be sure to brown the ground beef first and omit the egg!

INGREDIENTS

4 medium green peppers

FILLING

2 tablespoons canola oil
3 large garlic cloves, minced
1 small onion, diced
1/2 pound ground beef, 85% lean
1/2 pound lean ground pork
1/2 cup long grain rice, pre-cooked and cooled
2 tablespoons parsley, minced
1/2 cup tomato sauce
1 large whole egg
1 teaspoon sea salt
1/8 teaspoon black pepper
Dash of Tabasco and Worcestershire sauce

SPICY TOMATO SAUCE

2 tablespoons canola oil
2 large garlic cloves, minced
1 medium onion, diced
1 medium red pepper, diced
3/4 teaspoon dried thyme
1 bay leaf
3 tablespoons tomato paste
2 cups tomato sauce
4 cups beef stock
1/4 cup dry white wine
Dash of cayenne pepper, Tabasco, Worcestershire
1/4 cup brown sugar, optional

To prepare the sauce, heat the oil in a saucepan and sauté the garlic, onion and pepper for 3 to 4 minutes. Add the remaining ingredients, bring to a quick boil then reduce the heat and simmer for 10 minutes. To make the filling, heat the oil in a small skillet, sauté the garlic and onion for 3 to 4 minutes, remove from the fire and chill. Place the remaining filling ingredients into a mixing bowl, add the garlic-onion mixture and combine with a wooden spoon. Pre-heat the oven to 350°. Cut the peppers in half horizontally, scoop out the insides and equally divide the filling among all 8 pieces. Place the stuffed peppers into an oval high-sided casserole, pour on the sauce, cover and bake in the oven for 2 hours until the soup takes on a good taste. To serve, carefully place a stuffed pepper in the middle of a soup bowl and ladle over a generous amount of the sauce.

Spicy Chorizo and Red Bean Soup

SERVES 6 TO 8

"Que pasa, amigo?" You like your chili mucho caliente, then this is the recipe for you my friend. Somewhat like a chili but more Southwestern in feel. Do not use pre-packaged chorizo!

INGREDIENTS

2 tablespoons canola oil
I pound freshly ground bulk chorizo sausage
I pound ground beef, 85% lean
3 large garlic cloves, minced
I medium onion, minced
I large red pepper, minced
2 medium celery stalks, minced
I small jalapeno, minced
I bay leaf
2 tablespoons Creole spice
I heaping cup diced tomatoes
6 cups beef stock
3 to 4 cups canned small red chili beans, rinsed
   and drained

THICKENER

I tablespoon cornstarch
I/4 cup cool water

Heat the oil in a non-stick saucepot and when hot, brown the chorizo and ground beef until they render their fat. Drain in a colander and set aside. Add a little more oil back to the pot and saute the garlic, onion, pepper, celery and jalapeno for 3 to 4 minutes. Add the remaining ingredients back to the pot except the beans and thickener, bring to the boil, reduce the heat to a simmer and cook for 30 minutes. Add the beans to the pot and cook for another 30 minutes. Combine the cornstarch and water, add to the pot and let the soup cook for 15 minutes more until its slightly thickened and has good taste.

Mexican Posole Por Favor!

This is a real home style Mexican soup that will definitely warm your heart on a cold winter's day. The smoked hock adds a lot of extra flavor to the broth.

INGREDIENTS

2 tablespoons canola oil
2 to 3 pounds country style pork ribs
2 tablespoons Creole spice
1 small smoked pork hock
4 large garlic cloves, minced
1 medium onion, diced
2 medium carrots, sliced
2 medium celery stalks, sliced
2 cups diced tomatoes
2 tablespoons tomato paste
9 cups chicken stock
One 28 oz. can white hominy, rinsed and drained

POSOLE SPICE

1 tablespoon pure ground red chili powder
2 teaspoons ground cumin
1 1/2 teaspoons dried Mexican oregano
1 1/2 teaspoon dried basil
2 bay leaves
8 whole black peppercorns
1/4 teaspoon sea salt
Pinch red pepper flakes, Tabasco and garlic powder

GARNISH

chopped lettuce
radish
onion
cilantro
avocado
monterey jack cheese
quartered limes

Season the pork ribs with the Creole spice and sauté until brown in the oil then remove from the pot. In the remaining oil add the garlic, onion, carrots, celery and sauté for 3 to 4 minutes. Add the tomatoes, paste and spice and cook for another 2 minutes. Now add the chicken stock, hock and meat, bring to a boil, reduce the heat and simmer slowly for about 1 hour and forty-five minutes. Using a kitchen fork, break apart the pork ribs that are in the pot then add about 3/4 can of the hominy and simmer for another 45 minutes. Ladle the soup into soup cups and garnish.

Chicago-Style Green Split Pea

SERVES 6 TO 8

Often imitated but never duplicated, this is the real deal. I've made this soup for great chefs all over the world with rave reviews so don't throw out your ham bone!

INGREDIENTS

2 tablespoons canola oil
3 medium garlic cloves, chopped
1 small onion, chopped
2 medium carrots, chopped
2 medium celery stalks, chopped
1 bay leaf
1 1/2 teaspoons dried thyme
6 whole black peppercorns
1 cup green split peas, rinsed
6 cups chicken stock
Dash of Tabasco, garlic powder and sea salt
1 small smoked hock or ham bone

Heat the oil in a non-stick saucepot and sauté the garlic, onion, carrots and celery for 3 to 4 minutes. Add the remaining ingredients, bring to a quick boil, lower the heat and simmer for 1 1/2 hours until the vegetables are tender. Turn the heat off, remove the bay leaf and ham bone, and puree the soup in batches in a food blender until completely smooth. Using a fine mesh conical sieve, strain the pureed soup into a clean pot and bring back to a quick boil. Simmer 2 minutes more and serve.

Bavarian Brown Lentil

SERVES 6 TO 8

A Bavarian classic revisited without the hotdogs! Most joints overcook the soup so let me give you a good piece of advice. Cook it very slowly in a non-stick pot and don't stir the soup just swirl the pot once in a while and the lentils will stay whole.

INGREDIENTS

1 small smoked hock, rinsed
2 tablespoons canola oil
3 medium garlic cloves, minced
1 small onion, diced
2 medium carrots, diced
2 medium celery stalks, diced
1 bay leaf
1 teaspoon dried thyme
1/4 teaspoon dried oregano

1/4 teaspoon caraway seeds, crushed
1 1/2 tablespoons tomato paste
1/2 cup brown lentils, rinsed
6 cups chicken stock
1 tablespoon red wine vinegar
1/4 teaspoon sea salt
1/8 teaspoon black pepper
Dash of Tabasco and Worcestershire sauce
1/4 cup small soup pasta

Heat the oil in a non-stick saucepot and saute the garlic, onion, carrots and celery for 3 to 4 minutes. Add the remaining ingredients except the pasta, bring to a boil, lower the heat and simmer for 1 1/2 hours until the lentils and vegetables are tender. Remove the pot from the heat and stir in the pasta which will cook in about 20 minutes.

Midwest Ham Bone and Bean

This is one of those "warm your guts" kind of soups that will clean out your pipes (if you know what I mean) so drive with the windows wide open!

INGREDIENTS

3 cups high quality canned Great Northern white
   beans, rinsed
1 small meaty ham bone or shank
2 tablespoons canola oil
3 medium garlic cloves, minced
1 small onion, diced
2 medium carrots, diced
3 medium celery stalks, diced
1 bay leaf

1 teaspoon dried thyme
1 1/2 teaspoons dried basil
1/4 teaspoon sea salt
1/8 teaspoon black pepper
1 cup crushed tomatoes
6 cups chicken stock
1 large baking potato, diced
Dash of Tabasco

Heat the oil in a non-stick saucepot and sauté the garlic, onion, carrots and celery for 3 to 4 minutes. Add the remaining ingredients except the potato, bring to a boil, lower the heat and simmer slowly for 1 hour. Now add the potatoes and simmer the soup for another 20 minutes. When the potatoes are almost cooked carefully using a ladle, remove about 2 to 3 cups of the soup to a blender and puree until smooth. Return the puree back to the pot and simmer the soup for another 20 to 30 minutes until the beans are tender and the soup has good taste.

Dill Pickle Soup

A tart and refreshing soup that you should try.

INGREDIENTS

4 tablespoons unsalted butter, melted
3 medium garlic cloves, minced
1 medium onion, minced
1 medium carrot, diced
1 medium celery stalk, diced
1 bay leaf
Pinch of thyme
6 tablespoons all-purpose flour
5 cups low sodium chicken stock

1 cup dill pickle juice
1/4 cup dry white wine
1/8 teaspoon sea salt
1/8 teaspoon black pepper
Dash of Tabasco and Maggi
1 cup dill pickles, chopped
1 large baking potato, peeled and cubed
1/2 to 1 cup heavy cream
2 tablespoons fresh dill, minced

Heat the butter in a non-stick saucepot and sauté the garlic, onion, carrots and celery for 3 to 4 minutes. Add the bay leaf, thyme and flour to the pot and stir cook for 2 minutes. Add the remaining ingredients except the heavy cream, pickles ,potato and dill, bring to a boil then lower the heat and simmer for 30 minutes. Now add the pickles and potatoes and simmer for another 20 minutes. Stir in the heavy cream and dill and cook for 20 more minutes until the soup has good taste. You can enliven the soup with a splash of vinegar, sugar and Worcestershire sauce.

French Onion Soup

This is a great and easy recipe that I know everyone will love.

INGREDIENTS

4 tablespoons unsalted butter, melted
2 large garlic cloves, minced
1 1/2 pounds onions, thinly sliced
Pinch of sugar
1/4 teaspoon sea salt
1/8 teaspoon black pepper
8 cups beef stock
1/4 cup dry white wine
2 teaspoons cornstarch
1 small bay leaf
Dash of Maggi
Pinch of dried thyme

TOPPING

12 thin slices French bread, toasted
1/2 pound thinly sliced Gruyere or Swiss cheese
1/4 cup grated Parmesan cheese

Heat the butter in a non-stick saucepot and sauté the garlic and onions until lightly browned about 10 minutes. Add the sugar, salt and pepper, and continue cooking for another 5 minutes until the onions take on a deep golden color. Add the remaining ingredients except the topping and simmer the soup for 1 hour. Pre-heat the oven to 375°. Place earthenware soup cups into a medium sized roasting pan filled with about 1/4-inch of water. Ladle the hot soup into the cups leaving about 3/4-inch head room between the soup and the rim of the cup. Place 3 of the bread slices into each cup, layer on 2 slices of cheese and sprinkle on the parmesan. Place the pan in the hot oven and bake for 20 to 25 minutes until the tops are bubbly and golden brown.

Baked Potato Soup

This soup was actually developed by corporate chefs at Houlihan's, Bennigan's and TGIF's, local food chains who knock out some pretty decent soups.

INGREDIENTS

1 1/2 pounds baking potatoes, cleaned
6 tablespoons unsalted butter, melted
1/3 cup hickory smoked bacon, finely diced
4 medium garlic cloves, minced
1 small onion, minced
1 medium carrot, diced
1 large stalk celery, diced
8 tablespoons all-purpose flour
7 cups low sodium chicken stock
1/2 teaspoon dried basil
Pinch of dried thyme
1 bay leaf
1/4 teaspoon sea salt
1/4 teaspoon black pepper
Dash of Tabasco, Maggi, garlic powder
   and nutmeg
3/4 cup heavy cream

GARNISH

6 strips bacon, cooked and crumbled
1 cup Colby cheese, shredded
2 tablespoons chopped scallions or chives

Pre-heat the oven to 400°. Pierce the potatoes and bake for about an hour until tender. Remove from the oven and cool. When you can handle the potatoes, cut them in half and gently remove the soft interior, cut into large cubes and set aside. (You should have about 4 cups diced) Heat the butter in a non-stick saucepot and saute the bacon until its lightly brown then add the garlic, onion, carrot and celery and saute for 5 minutes. Add the flour to the pot and stir cook for 2 minutes more. Add the stock and seasonings, bring to a boil then reduce the heat and simmer for 40 minutes. Now add the heavy cream, let the soup cook for 10 minutes then add the cubed potatoes and cook for 10 minutes more. Ladle the soup into decorative crocks then crumble on top the cooked bacon, cheese and scallions.

Jewish Penicillin "Loaded"

Just what the doctor ordered!

INGREDIENTS

One 5 to 6 pound kosher chicken, excess fat
   removed
1 pound assorted chicken neck, wings and feet
12 cups cold water
2 tablespoons chicken base
4 large garlic cloves, sliced
1 medium onion, chopped
2 large carrots, peeled and halved
2 large celery stalks, halved
1 small leek, chopped
1 small parsnip, peeled and quartered
1 small celery root, peeled and quartered
1/2 teaspoon sea salt
10 whole black peppercorns

GARNISH

2 tablespoons fresh dill, minced
2 tablespoons parsley, minced
1 cup long grain rice, pre-cooked and chilled
1 cup fine vermicelli, pre-cooked al dente

1 Recipe Matzo Balls
1 Recipe Kreplach

Rinse the chicken and assorted parts under cold water and place in a large stock pot. Add the water and base, bring to a boil then reduce the heat and simmer for 20 minutes skimming the surface with a kitchen spoon to remove any impurities. Add the remaining ingredients except the garnish and simmer slowly for 2 hours. Remove the chicken from the pot and let it cool for 20 minutes. While the chicken is cooling, skim any grease with a large kitchen spoon that has risen to the top of the soup then carefully strain into a clean pot. Reserve the carrot, celery, parsnip and celery root to garnish the soup. While everything is cooling, proceed with the rest of the recipe.

Matzo Balls

INGREDIENTS

6 large whole eggs
1 1/2 teaspoons sea salt
1/3 cup melted butter or smaltz
1 1/2 cups matzo meal
1/4 teaspoon baking powder
3/4 cup cold water

In a mixing bowl beat the eggs with the salt and butter until foamy. Stir in the rest until it comes together, cover and refrigerate for 2 hours.

Kreplach

INGREDIENTS

1 pack fresh wonton skins
2 tablespoons canola oil
2 large garlic cloves, minced
1 small onion, minced
1/2 pound lean ground beef
1/2 teaspoon sea salt
1/4 teaspoon black pepper
2 tablespoons matzo meal
1 egg white

In a small skillet heat the oil and saute the garlic and onion for 2 to 3 minutes. Add the ground beef and cook for 3 to 4 minutes until it releases its grease and turns gray. Remove from the fire and pour into a strainer to be rid of any excess liquid. Place the meat in a bowl and when cool, using a wooden spoon, mix in the salt, pepper, matzo meal and egg white until it comes together in a ball. Refrigerate for 1 hour.

Now to prepare the soup, bring a large pot of lightly salted water to the boil and reduce to a simmer. Using a 1/2 cup measuring spoon, scoop the chilled matzo balls, roll into a ball then gently place into the boiling water. Slightly cover the pot and simmer slowly for 20 to 25 minutes. While the matzo balls are cooking, prepare the kreplach by placing the wonton shells onto a clean work surface. Place a teaspoon of the beef filling into the center of each wonton square, lightly brush the edge with a little water, fold over the wrapper and form into a wonton shape. After 25 minutes remove the matzo balls to a large bowl and cover with a piece of plastic wrap. Now using the matzo water, cook the kreplach for 2 to 3 minutes until they float to the top, remove with a slotted spoon then place into a bowl and cover with plastic wrap.

To serve the soup, remove the chicken meat from the carcass and cut into bite-size pieces. Also cut the reserved vegetables into bite-size pieces and set aside. Bring the strained chicken stock to a simmer and then add the reserved garnish of dill parsley, rice and noodles and cook for 2 minutes. Now add the reserved chicken and vegetables and cook for 2 minutes more. Lastly, add to the pot the matzo balls and kreplach to warm through. Gently ladle into an old fashioned tureen to serve.

Chicken Kluski Noodle

SERVES 6 TO 8

Everyone's grandmother makes a really good Jewish penicillin. The secret is to use exceedingly fresh ingredients and to let the soup cook slowly. For more body, add a couple of chicken feet to the pot and don't cook the noodles in the soup, do it separately.

INGREDIENTS

One 5 to 6 pound fresh chicken, excess fat
   removed
10 cups cold water
3 large garlic cloves, sliced
1 large onion, chopped
2 large carrots, chopped
2 large celery stalks, chopped
1 small leek, chopped
1 1/2 teaspoons dried thyme
2 whole cloves
2 bay leaves
1/4 teaspoon sea salt
8 whole black peppercorns
1/4 cup parsley, chopped
1/4 cup dill, chopped
2 cups kluski noodles, pre-cooked

Rinse the chicken under cold water and place into a large stockpot. Add the water, bring to a boil, then reduce the heat and simmer for 20 minutes, skimming the surface with a kitchen spoon to remove any impurities. Add the remaining ingredients except the parsley, dill and noodles and simmer slowly for 2 hours. Remove the chicken from the pot and let cool for 20 minutes. While the chicken is cooling, skim any grease with a large kitchen spoon that has risen to the top of the soup. Remove the chicken from the bone, add back to the pot with the parsley and dill and serve over the cooked kluski noodles.

Creamed Chicken and Rice

This is one of the first soups I learned how to make at chef's school and it comes together in a snap. It's always best to pre-poach the succulent chicken breast in chicken stock before adding it to this soup.

INGREDIENTS

- 4 tablespoons unsalted butter
- 4 large garlic cloves, minced
- 1 small onion, diced
- 1 medium carrot, diced
- 2 medium celery stalks, diced
- 1/2 small red pepper, diced
- 1/2 small green pepper, diced
- 1 teaspoon dried thyme
- 1 bay leaf
- 1/4 teaspoon sea salt
- 1/8 teaspoon black pepper
- 2 whole cloves
- 4 tablespoons all-purpose flour
- 7 cups chicken stock
- Dash of Tabasco, Maggi and garlic powder
- 1 1/2 pounds chicken breast, pre-cooked and cubed
- 1/2 cup long grain rice
- 1/4 cup heavy cream
- 1/4 cup parsley, chopped

Heat the butter in a non-stick saucepot and sauté the garlic, onion, carrot, celery and peppers for 3 to 4 minutes. Add the thyme, bay leaf, salt, pepper, cloves and flour and stir cook for 2 minutes more. Add the chicken stock and seasonings, bring to a boil, reduce the heat and simmer for 40 minutes. Now add the chicken and rice, and cook for another 20 minutes. Stir in the heavy cream and parsley and cook for another 10 minutes until the soup has good taste.

Cream of Whatever with Rice

SERVES 6 TO 8

Canned soups are good for an emergency meal, but the sodium content is just ridiculous. This is a great recipe because you can use any kind of vegetable you want, so feel free to reinvent yourself.

INGREDIENTS

1 1/2 pounds of your choice; broccoli, cauliflower, celery, artichoke or potato
4 tablespoons unsalted butter
4 large garlic cloves, chopped
1 small onion, chopped
1 medium carrot, chopped
2 medium celery stalks, chopped
1 small leek, chopped
1 bay leaf
1 1/2 teaspoons dried thyme
10 whole black peppercorns
2 whole cloves
4 tablespoons all-purpose flour
8 cups chicken stock
Dash of Tabasco, Maggi and garlic powder
1/4 teaspoon sea salt
1/2 cup long grain rice
1/2 cup heavy cream

Prepare the vegetable of your choice by chopping it into medium sized pieces. Heat the butter in a non-stick sauce pot and sauté the garlic, onion, carrot, celery and leeks for 3 to 4 minutes. Add the bay leaf, thyme, peppercorns, cloves and flour and stir cook for 2 minutes more. Now add the vegetables, chicken stock and seasonings, bring to a boil, reduce the heat and simmer for 40 minutes. At this point, turn the heat off and remove the bay leaf and cloves from the pot. Puree the soup in batches in a food blender until completely smooth. Using a fine mesh conical sieve, strain the pureed soup into a clean pot and bring back to a boil. Reduce the heat to a simmer then add the rice and cream, and cook stirring for another 10 minutes until the rice is tender.

Polish Creamed Mushroom and Dill

Great Polish cooks have handed down this recipe for generations and it can be found on the menu of most Eastern European restaurants in the city.

INGREDIENTS

4 tablespoons unsalted butter, melted
3 medium garlic cloves, minced
1 small onion, diced
1 large celery stalk, diced
1 small leek, diced
1 pound sliced domestic mushrooms and stems, cleaned
1/2 teaspoon dried thyme
1 bay leaf
4 tablespoons all-purpose flour
6 cups chicken stock
1/4 teaspoon sea salt
1/8 teaspoon black pepper
Dash of Tabasco and Maggi
1/2 to 1 cup heavy cream
2 tablespoons fresh dill, minced

Heat the butter in a non-stick saucepot and sauté the garlic, onion, celery and leeks for 2 minutes. Now raise the heat to medium high, add the thyme, bay leaf and mushrooms, and cook stir until the mushrooms start to release their liquid about 3 to 4 minutes. At this point, it is imperative to reduce the liquid in the pot to a syrup-like consistency. Add the flour and cook exactly 1 minute more. Add the rest of the ingredients except the heavy cream and dill, bring to a boil, reduce the heat and simmer for 40 minutes. Remove the pot from the fire, remove the bay leaf then puree in a food blender, pass through a fine mesh strainer and pour the soup into a clean pot. Return the pot to the fire, stir in the heavy cream and dill and cook for another 10 minutes.

Wild Mushroom, Barley and Dill

Easily the king of all Polish soups! I have a beautiful picture of this on the cover of my cookbook, "The New Polish Cuisine".

INGREDIENTS

4 tablespoons unsalted butter, melted
3 medium garlic cloves, minced
1 small onion, diced
1 large carrot, diced
1 large celery stalk, diced
1 pound sliced assorted wild mushrooms, caps and stems cleaned
1/2 teaspoon dried thyme
1 bay leaf
2 tablespoons all-purpose flour
7 cups chicken stock
1/4 teaspoon sea salt
1/8 teaspoon black pepper
Dash of Tabasco, Maggi and mushroom powder
1/2 cup pearl barley, pre-cooked al dente
1/2 cup heavy cream
3 tablespoons fresh dill, minced

Rinse the pre-cooked pearl barely until the liquid runs clear then set aside. Heat the butter in a non-stick saucepot and saute the garlic, onion, carrot and celery for 2 minutes. Now raise the heat to medium high, add the thyme, bay leaf and mushrooms, and stir cook until the mushrooms start to release their liquid about 3 to 4 minutes. At this point it is imperative to reduce the liquid in the pot until it is a syrup-like consistency. Add the flour and cook exactly 1 minute more. Now add the rest of the ingredients except the heavy cream and dill, bring to a boil, reduce the heat and simmer for 45 minutes. Stir in the heavy cream and dill and cook for another 10 minutes.

Mother-in-law's Minestrone

Everyone loves a good minestrone and I learned how to make this from my mother-in-law, Geri. The trick is to let the soup actually cook for about a good 3 hours so don't skip any steps especially towards the end of the recipe.

INGREDIENTS

2 tablespoons olive oil
4 ounces salt pork, minced
4 medium garlic cloves, minced
1 medium onion, chopped
2 large carrots, chopped
2 large celery stalks, chopped
1/4 head medium cabbage, chopped
1 1/2 teaspoons dried basil
1/2 teaspoon dried thyme
2 medium bay leaves
1/4 teaspoon sea salt
1/4 teaspoon black pepper
Pinch of red pepper flakes and Tabasco
2 cups crushed tomatoes
12 cups low sodium beef stock
1 cup dry Northern beans, rinsed

INGREDIENTS

Uno
1 large baking potato, peeled and cubed
1 medium zucchini, sliced

Due
1/2 cup small elbow macaroni, raw
1 heaping cup fresh green beans, large diced

Trece
1/3 cups Parmesan cheese, grated
1/4 cup parsley, minced

In a large soup pot, heat the oil and sauté the salt pork until it melts and turns slightly golden brown. Add the garlic, onion, carrots, celery and cabbage and stir cook for 3 to 4 minutes. Add all the seasoning, tomatoes, beef stock and Northern beans, bring to a boil, reduce the heat and simmer for 2 hours. After 2 hours add Uno to the pot and let it cook for 20 minutes. After 20 minutes more add Due and let it cook for 20 minutes. Now remove the pot from the fire, add Trece and stir to combine.

Fran's "Pasta e Fagioli"

Auntie Fran from the South side loved to make soup for her 3 growing Italian boys, Doug, Donny and Dennis. She passed this recipe on to my wife who now makes it for our 3 boys, Anthony, Frank and Nick.

INGREDIENTS

2 tablespoons olive oil
1/3 cup pancetta, diced
4 medium garlic cloves, minced
1 medium onion, diced
2 medium carrots, diced
2 medium celery stalks, diced
1 teaspoon dried basil
Pinch of dried thyme
Pinch of dried rosemary
1/4 teaspoon sea salt
1/8 teaspoon red pepper flakes
One 28 oz. Can plum tomatoes, drained and chopped
6 cups chicken stock
Two 15 ounce cans cannelloni beans, rinsed and drained
1 heaping cup dry D'itali pasta
1/3 cup Romano cheese, grated
1/4 cup parsley, minced
Olive oil to drizzle

Heat the oil in a medium sized soup pot and sauté the pancetta for 2 minutes. Add the garlic, onion, carrots and celery and cook for another 5 minutes. Add the tomatoes and seasonings then cook another 2 minutes. Add the remaining ingredients except the pasta, bring to a boil, reduce the heat and simmer slowly for about 45 minutes. Now add the pasta and simmer for another 10 minutes until the pasta is al dente and the soup is thick. Ladle into soup bowls and garnish with the cheese, parsley and olive oil.

Pam's Italian Wedding Soup

SERVES 6 TO 8

This is a really nice version of the Italian classic soup that my wife has enjoyed at many Italian weddings. Make sure the meatballs are marble sized and serve in fancy cup like soup bowls with plenty of parmesan and pepper flakes.

INGREDIENTS

1/2 Recipe Mama D's Meatballs, see page 220

2 tablespoons olive oil
3 large garlic cloves, minced
1 medium onion, diced
2 medium carrots, diced
2 medium celery stalks, diced
1 teaspoon dried basil
1/2 teaspoon dried oregano
1 bay leaf
1/4 teaspoon sea salt
1/8 teaspoon black pepper
Pinch of red pepper flakes
1 1/2 cups diced tomatoes
2 tablespoons tomato paste
2 tablespoons parmesan cheese
8 cups beef stock
1 bunch escarole, cleaned and chopped

Prepare the meatball recipe and roll the batch into marble sized balls. In a large non-stick skillet, saute the balls in a little olive oil until lightly browned on all sides, about 5 to 6 minutes. Place on a paper towel lined plate and refrigerate until needed. Heat the oil in a medium sized soup pot and saute the vegetables for 3 to 4 minutes. Add the seasoning and saute for 2 minutes more then add the rest of the ingredients except the meatballs and escarole. Bring to a boil, reduce the heat and simmer slowly for about an hour and a half. Stir the escarole into the pot and cook for 10 minutes then add the chilled meatballs and cook for 10 minutes more.

Mom's Autumn Vegetable Beef

If there was ever a time of the year in Chicago that I truly love, it would be late September early October. The changing colors of the leaves and the ever present light mist in the air always made this warm inviting soup a staple on our kitchen table.

INGREDIENTS

2 pounds meaty beef shanks or neck bones
2 tablespoons canola oil
3 large garlic cloves, minced
1 small onion, diced
2 medium carrots, diced
2 medium celery stalks, diced
1/4 head small green cabbage, chopped
1 bay leaf
1 teaspoon dried thyme
1 1/2 teaspoons dried basil
1/4 teaspoon sea salt
1/8 teaspoon black pepper
1 1/2 cup diced tomatoes
3 tablespoons tomato paste
Dash of Tabasco, Maggi and red pepper flakes
2 tablespoons parmesan cheese, grated
9 cups beef stock
1 cup green bean, diced
1 large potato, cubed
1/2 cup soup pasta shells

Heat the oil in a medium sized soup pot and saute the beef shanks until golden brown on both sides about 5 minutes. Remove the shanks to a platter. Return the pot to the fire and saute the garlic, onion, carrots, celery and cabbage for 3 to 4 minutes. Add the remaining ingredients to the pot except the beans, potato and pasta, bring to a boil, reduce the heat and simmer slowly for about 1 1/2 hours. Add the potatoes and green beans and cook for another 1/2 hour. Now add the pasta and cook for 1/2 hour more.

Scotch Broth

A lot of the old time restaurants around the city used to serve this savory lamb and barley soup on a regular basis. It's an oldie but a goodie that I know you'll enjoy.

INGREDIENTS

1/4 cup canola oil
2 1/2 pounds lamb shoulder, 1-inch cubed
3 medium garlic cloves, minced
1 medium onion, diced
2 medium carrots, diced
2 medium celery stalks, diced
1 small leek, diced
1 tablespoon fresh rosemary, minced
1 teaspoon fresh thyme, minced
1 bay leaf
1/2 teaspoon sea salt
1/4 teaspoon black pepper
3/4 cup pearl barley, rinsed
1/3 cup dry white wine
10 cups beef stock
Dash of Tabasco, red pepper flakes and
  mushroom powder

GARNISH

1 medium turnip, peeled and cubed
1 medium potato, peeled and cubed

Heat the oil in a medium sized soup pot and brown the lamb cubes on all sides for 4 to 5 minutes then remove to a platter. In the same oil, saute the garlic, onion, carrots, celery and leek for 2 to 3 minutes then add the remaining ingredients except the garnish. Bring to a boil, reduce the heat and simmer for 1 1/2 hours. After that time, add the turnip and potatoes and let the soup cook for another 20 to 30 minutes.

"Das Der Goulash Zupen"

Achtung, Colonel Klink!

INGREDIENTS

4 tablespoons canola oil
2 1/2 to 3 pounds beef stew meat, 1-inch cubed
4 medium garlic cloves, minced
1 medium onion, chopped
2 medium carrots, chopped
2 celery stalks, chopped
1 small red pepper, chopped
1 cup wild mushrooms, chopped
2 tablespoons Hungarian sweet paprika
1/4 cup all-purpose flour
2 teaspoons dried marjoram
1 1/2 teaspoons dried thyme
1 bay leaf
2 teaspoons caraway seeds, crushed
1/4 teaspoon sea salt
1/8 teaspoon black pepper
1 teaspoon Worcestershire sauce
Dash of Tabasco and cayenne pepper
1/2 cup dry red wine
8 cups beef stock
1/4 cup tomato paste
1/4 cup cider vinegar

GARNISH

1 cup small new potatoes, quartered
One 14 ounce can sauerkraut,
    well drained (optional)

Heat the oil in a medium sized soup pot and brown the beef cubes on all sides then remove to a platter. In the same oil, saute the garlic, onion, carrots, celery, pepper and mushrooms for 3 to 4 minutes. Now add to the pot the flour, paprika, marjoram, thyme, bay leaf, caraway seeds, salt and pepper and stir cook for 2 minutes. Add the red wine, reduce for 1 minute and then add the rest of the ingredients except the garnish, bring to a boil, reduce the heat and simmer for 2 hours. After 2 hours, add the potatoes and sauerkraut and simmer for another 20 minutes.

Chicken and Kielbasa Gumbo

SERVES 6 TO 8

Creole gumbo has always been one of my favorite dishes because of the variety of the ingredients used, and for the way the spices meld together to create a pure taste sensation.

INGREDIENTS

3 to 4 pounds skinless chicken thighs, trimmed of all fat
2 tablespoons Creole spice
1/2 cup canola oil
1 pound smoked kielbasa, pre-blanched and sliced 1/2-inch thick

GUMBO SOUP

1/3 cup canola oil
3/4 cup all-purpose flour
4 large garlic cloves, minced
1 medium onion, diced
2 large celery stalks, diced
1 medium red pepper, diced
1 medium green pepper, diced
1/4 cup parsley, chopped
1/2 teaspoon dried oregano
1/2 teaspoon dried basil
2 small bay leaves
1/4 teaspoon black pepper
2 teaspoons Creole spice
8 cups chicken stock
Large dash of Tabasco, Maggi and cayenne pepper
1 cup diced tomatoes with juice
2 tablespoons tomato paste
1/2 pound sliced okra
1 teaspoon gumbo file powder

Liberally sprinkle the Creole spice onto the chicken thighs and let them rest for 1/2 hour. Heat the 1/2 cup of oil in a medium sized heavy duty gumbo pot and brown the chicken on both sides about 3 to 5 minutes then remove to a platter. Now add the kielbasa slices to the hot oil and sauté for 3 minutes until lightly browned then remove to a platter. **(At this point, you should have 6 tablespoons of oil in the pot, if you don't think you have it, measure and add some more in.)** To the hot 6 tablespoons of oil, add the flour and cook stir for 3 to 5 minutes until the flour has turned a dark golden and smells nutty. Now to the hot roux, add the garlic, onion, celery, peppers, parsley and dried spices and cook stir until slightly softened about 2 minutes. Add the rest of the gumbo soup ingredients except the okra and gumbo file powder, bring to a boil, reduce the heat then add the chicken and sausage and simmer slowly for 1 hour. After 1 hour, add the okra and continue cooking for 1/2 hour more. Sprinkle on the gumbo file, cook for another 10 minutes and serve with rice.

Real Polish Borscht

Pure Polish Elixir!

INGREDIENTS

2 tablespoons canola oil
2 - 3 pounds meaty beef bones or shanks
10 cups beef stock
5 medium garlic cloves, sliced
1 medium onion, chopped
4 medium celery stalks, chopped
1 small leek, chopped
1 small fennel bulb, chopped
2 large beets, peeled and chopped
1 small parsnip, peeled and chopped
1 medium tomato, chopped
1 bay leaf
4 tablespoons parsley, chopped
1 tablespoon fresh thyme
1 whole clove
8 whole black peppercorns
2 tablespoons fresh dill, chopped

Heat the oil in a large skillet and brown the bones for 5 minutes then remove to a paper towel lined platter to absorb any excess grease. When the meat is chilled, place into a large soup pot and add the beef stock. Over high heat, bring the stock to a boil then reduce and slowly simmer for 30 minutes. (Be sure to skim the surface with a kitchen spoon to remove any impurities that rise to the top.) Now add all the vegetables and seasonings except the chopped dill, and simmer the soup slowly for about 2 hours. Strain the soup through a fine mesh conical sieve into a clean saucepan and stir in the dill. Re-season and serve.

Duck Blood Soup (Czarnina)

SERVES 6 TO 8

I purposely left this recipe out of my first cookbook and I was severely beaten by old busias with walking canes. This rustic soup is one of those old dishes that you either love or hate depending on how juiced up you are. *Chef's word of advice, "Don't get goofy with the duck blood!"*

INGREDIENTS

One 5 pound duck or wild goose with giblets
2 pounds spare ribs, trimmed of fat
3 tablespoons canola oil
3 medium garlic cloves, chopped
1 medium onion, chopped
1 medium carrot, chopped
1 medium celery stalk, chopped
1 small leek, chopped
1 bay leaf
1 teaspoon dried thyme
2 whole cloves
5 all-spice berries
2 teaspoons chopped ginger
2 teaspoons sea salt
8 whole black peppercorns
2 heaping tablespoons sugar
1/3 cup red wine vinegar
1/2 cup brandy or burgundy wine
10 cups chicken stock

GARNISH

2 tablespoons unsalted butter
1 pound pitted prunes
3/4 cup golden raisins
2 small tart apples, peeled and chopped
Pinch of sugar and dash of lemon juice

THICKENER

4 tablespoons all-purpose flour
1/2 cup heavy cream
3/4 cup duck blood

Remove the giblets from the duck, clean and set aside. Using a sharp knife cut the duck into 4 equal pieces and remove any excess fat. Also trim the spare ribs of any excess fat. In a medium sized stock pot, heat the oil and saute the duck pieces on each side for 3 to 4 minutes until golden brown, then remove to a paper towel. Add the spare ribs to the pot and also brown on both sides then remove. Remove all but 2 tablespoons of oil from the pot and saute the garlic, onion, carrot, celery and leek for 3 to 4 minutes. Add the seasoning and let cook for 1 minute more. Now to the vegetables and seasoning, sprinkle on the sugar and stir cook until the sugar caramelizes with the vegetables to a light amber brown. Add the vinegar to the pot, reduce by half then add the brandy and reduce until almost dry. Stir in the stock and bring to a slow simmer then add the browned duck and spare ribs. Cook the stock for 2 hours or until the soup has good taste, then remove from the fire. Carefully pour the soup through a fine mesh strainer into a mixing bowl. **At this point, the soup must be cooled and placed in the refrigerator overnight to de-fat the stock.** When the duck and spare ribs are cold enough to handle, remove from the strainer and pick the meat off the bones. Chop into bite size pieces and refrigerate overnight. The next day scrape the fat layer off the top of the stock, return to a clean pot and bring to a brisk simmer. In a medium sized skillet heat the unsalted butter, saute the prunes, raisins and apples for 2 to 3 minutes. Sprinkle on the lemon juice and sugar then add the garnish to the simmering stock. Simmer the soup for 30 minutes then add the chopped meats. At this point, re-season the soup with some salt, pepper and a little lemon juice. In a mixing bowl combine the flour, heavy cream and duck blood and whisk until you have a smooth paste. Remove about 1/2 cup warm stock from the pot and slowly using one hand, whisk the duck blood mixture while pouring in the warm stock until it forms a loose slurry. Now slowly pour the blood mixture back into the pot stirring constantly with a wooden spoon until the soup comes to a boil and thickens. Immediately remove from the fire and serve over freshly made soup noodles.

CAFETERIA COUNTER CULTURE

COUNTER

CULTURE

I 've always been a curious cat when it comes to exploring Chicago's history and its formidable years of growth. The good people at The Chicago Historical Society turned me on to a chapter in our history called "The Jazz Age" (1893 to 1930) when commerce, architecture, a burgeoning night life and financial clout ruled the roost in the city, specifically at Michigan Avenue and "the Loop." For you out-of-towners, let me provide a quick lesson in Chicago history leading up to that point.

In 1779, the Potawatomi Indians called the swamp land around the city "Checavgou," meaning wild onion or swamp grass. Early French explorers doomed the area from the start by proclaiming that the stagnant water and muddy bogs left no place to build a shipping port. Alas, in 1825 the Erie Canal was built allowing waterway freedom for incoming immigrants to make the journey and settle in the Midwest. Chicago got a second chance. Now our beginnings were rough to say the least, as the entire new sprawling wood-built city was burned to the ground in 1871. Major speculators and investors from San Francisco and New York began gobbling up the city's devastated prime real estate and the newly built waterways and railways were the perfect route for bringing in supplies and more manpower for manual labor. The early Chicago Tribune demolished by the fire borrowed neighboring printing machines and rallied the troops by handing out free papers proclaiming that "Chicago will rise again" and the city took on an "I will" spirit. In less than five years, most of the city was rebuilt and the population soared to 1 million. At a parallel time in our history, major department stores such as Mandel Brothers (1857), the Fair (1875), Marshall Field's (1877) and Sears Roebuck (1893) started to open up locations along Michigan Avenue to accommodate the demands of supplies for the founding fathers and business tycoons who were becoming increasingly wealthy building the city.

That's a really cool story about Chicago's history and growth, but do you know that those rich guys left out the most important factor-- the poor working man and his needs. You see, these debonair numb skulls were so busy building our magnificent "mag mile" as the city of their future that they forgot to take into account whose shoulders it was being built on. For immigrant workers, the political clout unfortunately took on an attitude of "look but don't touch" and forced them to retreat to the outskirts of the city to fend for themselves and build their own less than luxurious communities.

The lord moves in mysterious ways and a blessing came to those less fortunate in the form of "five and dime" stores. The father of this invention was Frank Winfield Woolworth, a kid from upstate New York. Rumor has it Frank hated working on his dad's farm so he went to a local merchant and got a job as a sales clerk. Now check this out. Back then merchandise was kept behind the counter with no prices marked, as it was common practice to negotiate for the sales amount. Young Frank didn't like to negotiate with his fellow poor farmers so he brainstormed, gathered a bunch of items that weren't selling, and placed them on a long table in front of the counter with a sign proclaiming everything five cents. People went nuts, bought up all the goods and clamored for more. In 1879, young Frank and his family opened up their own store, selling everything for five or ten cents. People loved the idea of being able to handle merchandise, as well as not feeling humiliated by a middle man if they couldn't afford it. Young Frank also noticed that his customers liked to linger, as often they came from great distances in horse and buggy. His store was becoming not only a retail outlet, but also a meeting place where fellow shoppers felt comfortable with each other and their common plight, so Frank had lunch counters and soda fountains installed to capitalize on this new phenomenon.

The word spread quickly to other cities. Woolworth's expanded and the "five and dimes" were all the rage among the lower-earning working class set. By the turn of the century, the Northwest side of Chicago was overflowing with immigrants from Germany, Sweden, Ireland and Poland who were beginning to acquire a meager income and a little free time and found the city's "loop," the major retailing center, out of reach. So along came a second blessing by the name of W.A. Wieboldt Company. William Wieboldt, a German American, retailer loved his immigrant neighbors and opened up a department store on Milwaukee Avenue in 1884. His claim to fame was bargain basement prices, unpretentious merchandise and a multi-lingual sales staff, all in a fashionable store that mimicked those on Michigan Avenue. Wieboldt's later expanded to other ethnic working-class neighborhoods and literally undercut the entire downtown retailing competition. Other companies quickly followed suit, including Lindys, Walgreen's, Goldblatts, S. S. Kreskee's, Woolworth's and Steinways.

Along with fair prices and a welcoming attitude came the beginnings of our cafeteria counter culture. The "Jazz Age" most definitely brought fun and excitement to the Loop, which became the city's premier retail and entertainment district. Late night juke joints, the theaters and department stores were forced into adding lunch counters or cafeteria style eateries to satisfy the masses of people flocking into the city to be entertained. At the time, most tenement housing around the city didn't allow kitchenettes for renters to cook in, so it made sense for retailers to offer sustenance to the work force and their patrons at budget prices. Twenty-four hour luncheonettes and cafeterias started cropping up in basements of stores around the city to maintain the façade that the wealthy ate upstairs and the working class down. Late night musicians, artists and an emerging gay community loved to gather at the dinettes, using them as a social meeting place and in the summer as a way to avoid the sweltering heat of their tenement housing. Also women, who were the majority of the work force at the downtown retailers, found it safer to eat at the company cafeteria then to venture out into a city that still had its share of unsavory types.

If you're from the Midwest or any small town around the country, you undoubtedly have a fond childhood memory of eating at a lunch counter or soda stand. When I was a kid, my grandparents both worked for Sears in the Loop and at the end of each summer, we used to take the elevated train downtown to get a company discount on socks, underwear and clothes for Catholic grammar school. The highlight of the trip for me was eating at a local Woolworth five and dime that had a really cool, old-fashioned lunch counter. Actual waitresses wearing uniforms and pink hairnets served up the standard fare: patty melts, grilled cheese, ham, tuna, or egg salad sandwiches with potato chips. My Grandpa favored a lime-aid citrus drink that churned in a see-through plastic contraption, and was served in a paper cone that sat in a plastic holder. The coup de gras was most definitely the dessert menu that showcased fresh apple pie, tulip sundae and outstanding freshly made chocolate shakes that were poured into a tall fountain glass and served with a straw and spoon. The extra malted was left for you to polish off from an aluminum mixing container. After lunch, Grandma would stock up on toiletry items while my Grandpa and I would cruise the toy aisle for such things as the plastic parachute man, cap guns, silly putty and a rubber band windup airplane. When I got older and began working in the Loop, occasionally I would dodge into the same Woolworth's to feel the excitement I did as a kid by buying some socks, shoe strings and a lime aid just for the hell of it.

I hope you can all feel the love I'm trying to convey in my writing about these places, but history and economics dictate a nation. The 1930s brought depression, suburban mall sprawl, conglomerate takeovers and low, low, discounts. Chinese take-out, frozen dinners and fast food joints slowly sucked the wind out of the five and dimes and local cafeterias. Retailers and restaurants work off very slim margins and when the party's over, it's over! Bigger, faster, cleaner and fresher ideas swept through the Midwest like an autumn breeze and almost everything changed. Over the years I've heard a lot of scuttlebutt about the lack of good delis in Chicago, as well as the comparisons with New York that are bantered about by luminary food writers. With all graciousness and in defense of my city and fellow Chicagoans, as well as out of respect for the restaurateurs I'm about to name, I'm not about to get into a pissing match over who's got the best corned beef; it's all good! Don't kid yourself; Chicago has a good 150 year tradition of coffee shops, delis and cafeterias that rose from an emerging immigrant population. Some were able to pull it off and others bit the dust soon after they opened their doors, their sole demise due to the fact that they lacked street soul. In my first cookbook ,"The New Polish Cuisine," I quoted a great chef, friend and mentor who described ethnically oriented cooking as "a cuisine that is founded on sympathy. It is only done well with deep instinctive feelings and is done best if you have been familiar with it all your life."

Ninety-five percent of Chicago's mom and pop restaurants, taverns and bakeries are the backbone as well as the driving force that fuels the nation's appetite to return for that good old Chicago soul. You see, around the 1880s to the 1920s, central and eastern Europeans, mostly Jewish immigrants from Russia, Hungary, Bohemia, Poland and Germany descended upon the near west side of the city, which at that time comprised the Maxwell Street ghetto. In a nutshell, these vibrant and ambitious immigrants transformed Maxwell Street into one of the largest and most diversified open air flea markets or street fairs in the world. Along with their entrepreneurship and spirit came a sense of unity and community regardless of race, creed or color. Some say that poverty and indignity bring about the worst in human nature, but these blessed souls overcoming great obstacles showed those elite uptowners what the true ethnic feel, heart and soul the city's cuisine was all about.

Two restaurant owners that I've known through the years, Sophie Madej of Busy Bee fame and Ken Raskin of Manny's Coffee Shop and Deli have been serving up some of the best Polish/Jewish Eastern European delicacies since the 50s. I've known Sophie and Ken for most of my life and find that their genuine loving nature and style of cooking truly exemplify the heart and soul of the varied immigrants who needed a place to gather and eat. Sophie, now retired, owned a Polish restaurant up on North Damon that was fondly referred to as "the diamond ring" that united Damon, Milwaukee and North Avenue. Ken Raskin (Manny's son), current owner of Manny's Coffee Shop and Deli since 1942, was most definitely born with chicken soup in his blood. Both the Busy Bee and Manny's are famous in Chicago's culinary history for churning out some of the best eastern European foods known to man. In a quasi lunch counter/cafeteria/delicatessen/restaurant type setting, these two pioneers dished up such delicacies as pierogi, potato pancakes, stuffed cabbage, matzo ball soup, lamb shanks, breaded pork cutlet and corned beef sandwiches to adoring business people, college students, cops, politicians and wise guys.

My fondest memory of the Busy Bee was a horse shoe like lunch counter called "millionaire's row" that housed old geezers who were quick with a joke or old tale about the neighborhood. Sophie and her son were always warm and generous with their family-friendly style and oversized plate portions. On the other hand, Ken Raskin has always struck me as the consummate businessman/restaurateur, who should be given 4-star status and a tall chef's hat for his attention to detail in every part of his empire. I've worked at many opulent restaurants around the world, but I could tell you in fact that I've seen more business/political deals closed and hashed out over a corned beef sandwich and cup of matzo ball soup at Manny's than any where else in the world. Manny's Coffee Shop and Deli is unique because it stuck to the old world style cafeteria line where you grab a tray, work your way past steam tables loaded with daily delicacies to choose from, seat yourself and pay as you go. Other restaurants around the city might offer up one or two specials a day, but at Manny's the selection is mind blowing and endless. In honor of Sophie and Ken, I'm offering up this extensive chapter in tribute to their tenacity and graciousness as well as the comfort they've brought to those local Chicagoans seeking security in a busia and bubbie home cooked meal!

As noted in the introduction, I have an affinity for foods that are slow cooked and braised as do the good people of Chicago. When the digits fall, you could find any one of these great old comfort foods at lunch counters around the city. If you're a hot open-faced sandwich kind of guy or gal, most joints I know will serve it up to you with the mandatory mushroom gravy, garlic mashed, side of kraut and canned vegetables. I've included those recipes for your enjoyment.

Master Mushroom Gravy Sauce

MAKES ABOUT 3 CUPS

INGREDIENTS

5 tablespoons roasted pan drippings
   and grease
1 pound button mushrooms, sliced
4 tablespoons all-purpose flour
1/2 cup dry white wine
3 1/2 cups chicken stock
1/4 teaspoon sea salt
1/8 teaspoon black pepper
Large dash of garlic powder, Tabasco,
Magi, dried dill or sage

Heat the dripping in a non-stick saucepan and sauté the mushrooms until they turn lightly brown and all the liquid is evaporated. Add the flour and stir cook for 1 minute then add the white wine and reduce by half. Add the remaining ingredients, bring to a boil then simmer for 20 to 25 minutes until the sauce has good taste.

Garlic Mashed Potatoes

SERVES 4

INGREDIENTS

2 pounds Russet potatoes, cleaned,
   peeled and quartered
1 stick unsalted butter, softened
1 cup half and half
1 1/2 teaspoons sea salt
1/2 teaspoon black pepper
Large dash Tabasco and garlic powder
1 heaping tablespoon garlic puree

Boil the potatoes in lightly salted water for 20 to 25 minutes until tender then drain. Return to the pot and over low fire, beat in the remaining ingredients with a hand mixer until the potatoes are light and fluffy about 2 to 3 minutes.

New Potatoes and Dill

SERVES 4

INGREDIENTS

2 pounds new potatoes, cleaned
1/3 cup unsalted butter, melted
Large dash of sea salt and black pepper
1 to 2 tablespoons fresh dill, minced

Cook the potatoes in lightly salted water for 15 to 20 minutes and drain reserving 1/2 cup of the hot liquid. Return to the pot with the reserved liquid, toss with the remaining ingredients and cover until needed.

Excellent Polish Sauerkraut

MAKES ABOUT A QUART

INGREDIENTS

2 thick slices hickory smoked bacon, diced
2 large meaty pork bones
4 medium garlic cloves, minced
1 medium onion, diced
1 large carrot, shredded
1 large celery stalk, shredded
1/2 pound domestic mushrooms, sliced
1/2 pound green cabbage, shredded
2 pounds sauerkraut, well drained twice
2 tablespoons all-purpose flour
1 bay leaf
2 1/2 teaspoons Polish spice
Pinch of sugar
1 tablespoon tomato paste
2 dashes Maggi and Tabasco
4 cups chicken stock

Pre-heat the oven to 350°. Sauté the bacon and pork bones in a large non-stick saucepan and when they turn lightly brown and release their fat, add the garlic, onion, carrot, celery, mushrooms, green cabbage and sauerkraut and stir cook for about 3 to 4 minutes. Add the flour to the pot and cook for 1 minute more, and then add the remaining ingredients, bring to a boil, stir the pot, pour into a casserole and bake for 2 hours.

Corned Beef Hash

SERVES 4

INGREDIENTS

2 tablespoons unsalted butter
2 tablespoons bacon grease
2 small garlic cloves, minced
1/2 small onion, minced
1 small green bell pepper, diced
2 cups pre-boiled red potatoes, cubed
2 cups pre-cooked corned beef brisket, cubed
1/4 teaspoon sea salt
1/8 teaspoon black pepper
Dash of Tabasco, Worcestershire and nutmeg

4 whole large eggs

Pre-heat the broiler to high and place the oven rack in the top slot. On the stove, heat a 10-inch non-stick skillet and then add the butter, bacon grease, garlic, onion and green pepper and saute for 3 to 4 minutes. Now add to the skillet the diced potatoes and saute for another 3 to 4 minutes until lightly browned. Stir in the corned beef, saute for another 2 to 3 minutes, add all the seasoning except the eggs and give a good toss. Using a wooden spoon, divide the hash into four equal parts. Again using the spoon, dig an indent into the center of each of the four triangles that are now in the skillet. Carefully crack each one of the eggs into the well of each triangle and place under the broiler for 2 to 3 minutes until the eggs turn glossy and are slightly cooked over-easy style. Remove the pan from the broiler, divide into four equal parts on a breakfast plate, and serve with a good dollop of ketchup and Tabasco sauce.

"Open-Faced" Hot Roast Beef

SERVES 4

INGREDIENTS

1 top sirloin or chuck roast, 3 to 4
   pounds tied
2 tablespoons canola oil
1 tablespoon Lawry's garlic salt

1 recipe Mushroom Gravy
Garlic Mashed Potatoes
Canned vegetables

Pre-heat the oven to 350° Liberally season the piece of meat with the garlic salt then brown on all sides in a hot skillet with the canola oil. Roast in a baking pan until you reach an internal temperature of about 130° about 1 1/2 hours. Remove the pan from the oven and let the meat cool for about 20 minutes before slicing. Serve on a piece of bread with mushroom gravy, mashed potatoes and vegetables.

Fancy Beef Tongue with Horseradish Garnish

SERVES 4

INGREDIENTS

One 3 to 4 pound smoked beef tongue
1 quart chicken stock
1 teaspoon pickling spices

GARNISH

1 small red onion, peeled and thinly
   sliced into rings
2 tablespoons small capers
4 hard boiled eggs, peeled and sliced
1/2 cup sweet gherkins, julienne
1/2 cup radishes, julienne

HORSERADISH CREAM

1 cup heavy cream
1/4 teaspoon sea salt
2 tablespoons prepared horseradish
Dash of Tabasco

Place the tongue, chicken stock and pickling spice into a saucepan, bring to the boil then reduce the heat and simmer for 30 minutes to warm through. While the tongue is cooking, prepare the horseradish sauce by whipping the heavy cream, salt and Tabasco in a mixing bowl with a whisk until it forms stiff peaks. Gently fold in the horseradish then put it in a decorative sauce bowl to serve. After 30 minutes remove the tongue, completely chill, skin and then thinly slice. On a large serving platter, arrange the tongue slices in a circular fashion, top with a slices of egg and red onion rings, and then sprinkle on top the capers, gherkins and radishes. Serve with the horseradish cream sauce.

"Open-Faced" Turkey Breast Plate

SERVES 4

INGREDIENTS

One 3 to 4 pound free-range turkey
   breast with skin
1/3 cup unsalted butter, melted
1 tablespoon Lawry's seasoned salt

1 Recipe Mushroom gravy with sage
Garlic Mashed Potatoes
Canned Corn
1 can jellied cranberries

Pre-heat the oven to 450°. Rub the breast with the melted butter and seasoning, place skin side up in a baking dish and add 1 cup chicken stock to the pan. Roast the breast, basting frequently until the internal temperature reaches 160°. Let the breast stand 10 to 15 minutes before slicing into thin slices then serve on a piece of bread with a dollop of mushroom gravy, mashed potatoes, corn and cranberries.

"Open-Faced" Pork Tenderloin Cutlet

SERVES 4

INGREDIENTS

4 boneless pork cutlets, six ounces each
1/2 cup all-purpose flour
2 large whole eggs
1 cups fresh breadcrumbs
1 1/2 teaspoons dried oregano
1 1/2 teaspoons dried basil
1/4 teaspoon Hungarian sweet paprika
1/4 teaspoon sea salt
1/8 teaspoon black pepper

1 cup canola oil for frying

Pre-heat the oven to 400°. Lightly flatten the pork cutlets with a meat mallet and then dredge in the flour. Beat the eggs in a separate bowl and set aside. Combine the remaining ingredients in another bowl and mix. Heat the canola oil in a medium sized skillet and when hot, dip the flour coated cutlets into the egg, then into the seasoned breadcrumbs and gently sauté for 2 to 3 minutes on each side until golden brown and crisp. Place the skillet in the hot oven for 10 minutes then serve on a piece of bread with garlic mashed potatoes, mushroom gravy and Polish sauerkraut.

"Open-Faced" Meatloaf Plate

SERVES 4

INGREDIENTS

2 tablespoons canola oil
3 medium garlic cloves, minced
1 small onion, minced
2 pounds fancy meatloaf mix
1 teaspoon sea salt
1/2 teaspoon black pepper
Large dash Tabasco, Worcestershire,
Maggi, garlic and onion powder
2 whole large eggs
1/2 cup whole milk
1 heaping cup breadcrumbs
1/3 cup parsley, chopped

Pre-heat the oven to 350°. Heat the oil in a small skillet, sauté the garlic and onion and then cool. Place the meat into a large mixing bowl and using your hands, combine with all the remaining ingredients until you are able to form a loaf. Place the meat into a lightly oiled 9 X 5-inch glass Pyrex loaf pan and cook in the hot oven for 1 hour until the top is golden brown. Remove from the oven, drain the grease and slice into generous portions. Serve on a piece of bread with garlic mashed potatoes, mushroom gravy and Polish sauerkraut.

Greek Style Lamb Shanks

INGREDIENTS

4 medium lamb shanks, one pound each (average)

2 tablespoons olive oil
4 large garlic cloves, minced
I medium onion, diced
2 medium carrots, diced
2 medium celery, diced
2 tablespoons tomato paste
I cup diced tomatoes
1/2 teaspoon sea salt
1/4 teaspoon black pepper
I teaspoon dried thyme
I teaspoon dried rosemary sprigs
I cup dry white wine
5 cups chicken stock
Dash Tabasco, garlic, powder and Maggi

Pre-heat the oven to 350°. In a large non-stick skillet, heat the olive oil and brown the shanks on each side for 4 to 5 minutes and then place into a tight fitting earthenware casserole. In the remaining oil, saute the garlic, onion, celery and carrots for 3 to 4 minutes then add the tomato paste, diced tomatoes, salt, pepper, thyme, rosemary and bay leaf and saute for I minute more. Add the white wine to the skillet, reduce by half and then add the remaining ingredients. Bring to a boil, pour over the shanks, cover and cook in the oven for 2 1/2 to 3 hours until juicy, moist and tender. Serve with a side of rice orzo pilaf.

Salisbury Steak

INGREDIENTS

2 tablespoons canola oil
2 large garlic cloves, minced
1 small onion, minced
1 1/2 pounds ground round
1 whole large egg
1/4 cup whole milk
1/3 cup breadcrumbs
1/2 teaspoon sea salt
1/4 teaspoon black pepper
1/4 teaspoon dried marjoram
Large dash Tabasco, Worcestershire,
Maggi, garlic powder and onion powder

1 recipe Mushroom Gravy
1/2 cup sour cream

Heat the oil in a small skillet and sauté the garlic and onion until slightly brown then cool. Place the meat into a large mixing bowl then add the remaining ingredients and mix with your hands until well combined. Form the meat into 8 equal sized patties and lightly sauté in a medium sized non-stick skillet until brown on each side. De-grease the pan then add the full recipe for the above mushroom gravy. Cover and simmer slowly for 25 minutes. Remove the cover, flip the steaks over and stir into the sauce 1/2 cup sour cream then cook for another 10 minutes. Serve with a side of mashed potatoes and Polish sauerkraut.

Pepper Steak

See recipe called Cousin Gladys' Smothered Pepper Steaks

Goulash

INGREDIENTS

1/4 cup canola oil
2 1/2 to 3 pounds cubed veal stew meat
3 large garlic cloves, minced
2 medium onions, thinly sliced
1 small red pepper, thinly sliced
1 large carrot, diced
1 large celery stalk, diced
2 cups domestic mushrooms, sliced
1 bay leaf
1/2 teaspoon dried thyme
1/2 teaspoon dried marjoram

INGREDIENTS

1 1/2 teaspoon caraway seeds, crushed
2 tablespoon tomato paste
2 tablespoons Hungarian sweet paprika
2 tablespoons all-purpose flour
2 tablespoons red wine vinegar
1/2 cup dry white wine
3 cups beef stock
1/4 teaspoon sea salt
1/8 teaspoon black pepper
Dash of Tabasco and Worcestershire

In a large heavy pot, heat the oil and brown the veal cubes about 3 to 4 minutes and then remove to a serving platter. In the remaining oil, add the garlic, onion, red pepper, carrot, celery and mushrooms and stir cook for 2 to 3 minutes. Now add the remaining ingredients to the pot including the veal, bring to a boil, reduce the heat to a simmer, cover and cook for 2 hours until the meat is fork tender.

Hearty Beef Stew

INGREDIENTS

3 pounds cubed beef stew meat
1/2 cup all-purpose flour
4 tablespoons canola oil
4 large garlic cloves, sliced
1 medium onion, large diced
2 large carrots, large diced
2 large celery stalks, large diced
2 cups domestic mushrooms, sliced
1 bay leaf
1 teaspoon dried thyme
1 1/2 teaspoons dried marjoram or basil

INGREDIENTS

1 tablespoon all-purpose flour
1/4 teaspoon sea salt
1/8 teaspoon black pepper
Dash of Tabasco
1 cup tomato puree
1 heaping tablespoon tomato paste
3 cups beef stock
1/2 cup dry red wine

12 small new potatoes
1 can sweet peas, drained

Pre-heat the oven to 350°. Heat the oil in a medium sized pot and working quickly, dredge the beef cubes in the flour and saute for 3 to 5 minutes until golden brown. Remove the meat to a serving platter. In the remaining oil, saute the garlic, onion, carrots, celery and mushrooms for 2 to 3 minutes. Add the remaining ingredients to the pot except the potatoes and peas, bring to a boil then pour into an earthenware casserole. Bake in the hot oven covered for 2 hours. After 2 hours, add the potatoes and peas, re-cover and cook for a half hour more.

Hungarian Stuffed Cabbage

INGREDIENTS

1 large head green cabbage

2 tablespoons canola oil
3 large garlic cloves, minced
1 small onion, diced
1 pound ground beef, 85% lean
1/2 pound lean ground pork
3/4 cup long grain rice, pre-cooked
1/2 cup tomato sauce
1 large whole egg
1/2 teaspoon sea salt
1/4 teaspoon black pepper
Large dash of Tabasco and Worcestershire

1 recipe Spicy Tomato Sauce, see page 399
One 15 ounce can sauerkraut, well drained

Pre-heat the oven to 350°. Bring a large pot of lightly salted water to a boil, add the whole head of cabbage, cover and let simmer slowly for 5 to 10 minutes. Remove the cabbage, drain and cool and then using a small knife, cut around the core, remove all the cabbage leaves and dry. In a small skillet, heat the oil and sauté the garlic and onion for 2 to 3 minutes, remove from the fire and cool. Place all the remaining ingredients into a large mixing bowl except the spicy tomato sauce and kraut and using your hands, thoroughly combine. Lay the cabbage leaves out onto a counter, fill with 3 to 4 tablespoons of the beef mixture, fold the edges over, roll into a tight package and secure with a toothpick. Continue until all the cabbages are rolled. Pour a little of the sauce into the bottom of an oval earthenware casserole. Sprinkle on all of the kraut, arrange the stuffed cabbages on top, pour on the rest of the sauce, cover and bake in the hot oven for 2 hours. Serve with a side of garlic mashed topped off by a dollop of mushroom gravy.

Jewish Style Beef Brisket

SERVES 4

INGREDIENTS

2 tablespoons canola oil
3 pounds fresh beef brisket

SAUCE

2 tablespoons canola oil
3 large garlic cloves, sliced
3 medium onions, sliced
1/2 teaspoon sea salt
1/4 teaspoon black pepper
Dash of red pepper flakes
One 12 ounce jar chili sauce
14 ounces tomato puree
1 cup beef stock
1 to 2 tablespoons brown sugar
Large dash Tabasco, Worcestershire,
    garlic powder, onion powder
2 bay leaves

Pre-heat the oven to 350°. In a large non-stick skillet, heat the oil and sauté the beef brisket on both sides for 3 to 4 minutes until golden brown and then place into a tight fitted roasting pan. Add the remaining oil to the skillet, sauté the garlic and onion for another 4 to 5 minutes until the onion is lightly brown and golden, then add the remaining ingredients, bring to a boil and pour over the brisket. Cover the roasting pan with a piece of aluminum foil and bake in the hot oven for a 2 to 3 hours until the brisket is tender, juicy and easy to slice. Serve with a side of boiled potatoes or garlic mashed.

Spaghetti and Meatball Dinner

SERVES 4

INGREDIENTS

1 pound Barilla spaghetti
1 recipe Geri's Tomato Sauce, see page 219
1 recipe Mama D's Meatballs, see page 220

1 cup Pecorino Romano cheese, grated

Bring a large pot of lightly salted water to a boil and cook the pasta for 8 to 9 minutes until al dente. While the pasta is cooking, be sure to heat the meatballs in the tomato sauce. Thoroughly drain the pasta reserving 1/4 cup water in the pot, return the pasta to the pot, toss and cover. To serve, ladle a generous amount of tomato sauce into the bottom of a large pasta bowl, add half the pasta, some more sauce and cheese, the rest of the pasta and then mix with a large tong until the pasta is evenly coated. Serve with the meatballs, cheese and garlic bread.

Classic Corned Beef and Cabbage

SERVES 4

INGREDIENTS

One 3 1/2 pound corned beef brisket
   with season packet
3 quarts light chicken stock, cold

AROMATICS

One large head green cabbage
12 medium garlic cloves, peeled
2 small onions, peeled and quartered
4 medium carrots, peeled
4 medium celery stalks
12 new red potatoes, cleaned

Rye bread, horseradish mustard and dill pickles

Remove the corned beef from its package and rinse under cold water to remove all the slime. Place in a large pot with the chicken stock and seasoning pack, bring to a slow simmer and cook for 2 to 3 hours until the brisket is tender. (Be sure to skim the broth.) When the brisket is cooked, remove it to a shallow roasting pan and strain some of the cooking juice over the top of it until it is just barely covered. (This prevents it from drying out.) While the corned beef is resting, prepare the vegetables by cutting the cabbage into 6 quarters, onions into 4 quarters, carrots and celery into 4 quarters and the leave the potatoes whole. Arrange all the vegetable pieces into the bottom of a clean stockpot that is large enough to hold them. Strain the remaining cooking stock over the vegetables, bring to a slow simmer and cook for 45 minutes until they are tender. Slice the corned beef into thin slices and place on a serving platter surrounded by the cooked vegetables and pass around the compliments.

Savory Stuffed Pork Chops with Dressing

SERVES 4

INGREDIENTS

6 tablespoons unsalted butter, melted
4 bone-in rib loin pork chops 10 to 12
   ounces each, 1 1/2 -inches thick
One 6 ounce bag Mrs. Cubbison's
Seasoned Dressing Mix

1 recipe Mushroom Gravy with Sage
1 can Jellied cranberries

Pre-heat the oven to 400°. Prepare the dressing being sure to include the onion, celery and chicken bouillon and then cool. Lay the pork chops on top of a cutting board and using a sharp knife, make a horizontal cut exactly through the middle 3/4 of the way before hitting the bone. Stuff the chops with the prepared dressing and then secure the cut with 1 or 2 toothpicks making sure the stuffing doesn't fall out during the cooking process. Heat the butter in a non-stick skillet and when hot, carefully sauté the pork chops on each side for 2 to 3 minute until lightly golden brown, place into an earthenware casserole and bake in the hot oven for 10 minutes. After 10 minutes, flip the chop over, ladle on 2 to 3 cups mushroom gravy and continue baking for another 5 minutes. Serve with a side of canned vegetables and cranberry.

South Side Ham and Sweets

See recipe called Auntie Phyllis' Orange Marmalade Dinner Ham

See recipe called Glazed Sweet Potatoes Gratinee

"Nort Side" Chop Suey

SERVES 4

INGREDIENTS

4 tablespoons canola oil
2 1/2 pounds pork or beef stew meat, cubed
4 medium garlic cloves, minced
1 medium onion, diced
1/2 cup green onion, diced
2 1/2 cup carrots, sliced
2 1/2 cups celery, sliced
6 cups chicken stock
1/2 cup soy sauce
2 tablespoons black bead molasses
1 tablespoon hoisin sauce
1 tablespoon fresh ginger, minced
1 tablespoon cornstarch
Dash of Tabasco, garlic powder and onion powder

GARNISH

One 14 ounce can bean sprouts, rinsed and drained
One 8 ounce can sliced water chestnuts, rinsed and drained

Heat the oil in a large non-stick pot and brown the meat on all sides then remove to a serving platter. In the same hot oil, saute the garlic, onions, carrots and celery for 2 to 3 minutes. Add all the remaining ingredients to the pot except the garnish, bring to a boil, reduce the heat and slowly simmer for 1 hour until the meat is tender. Add the garnish, simmer for another 10 minutes and then serve over steamed white rice.

Chicken Cacciatore

SERVES 4

INGREDIENTS

1/3 cup olive oil
8 large bone-in chicken thighs, excess
   fat removed
1 cup all-purpose flour
Large dash sea salt and pepper

1 recipe Spicy Tomato Sauce, see page 399

Pre-heat the oven to 350°. Prepare the sauce as indicated and set aside. Put the olive oil in a large skillet and when hot, dredge the thighs in the flour and seasoning and sauté for 3 to 4 minutes on each side until golden brown. Remove to a large baking dish. Pour the sauce over the thighs, cover tightly with aluminum foil and bake for 2 hours until cooked. Serve with a side of fettuccine.

The Best Chicken and Dumplings

SERVES 4

INGREDIENTS

4 tablespoons canola oil
One 4 to 5 pound fresh chicken,
   quartered excess fat removed
1/2 cup all-purpose flour

SAUCE

4 tablespoons unsalted butter, melted
6 tablespoons all-purpose flour
3 garlic cloves, minced
1 small onion, cut julienne
2 medium carrots, cut julienne
2 medium celery stalks, cut julienne
1 small leek, cut julienne
1 cup domestic mushrooms, sliced
1 1/4 teaspoon Polish spice
1 bay leaf
1/4 cup dry white wine
5 1/2 cups chicken stock
Dash of Tabasco and Maggi

1 recipe Parsley Dumplings

Heat the oil in a medium sized non-stick saucepan, dredge the chicken pieces in the flour and sauté in the hot oil for 3 to 5 minutes until golden brown and then remove to a serving platter. Remove the excess grease from the pot, then add the butter and flour and cook stir for 1 to 2 minutes until the flour has turned a light golden and smells slightly nutty. Now add the garlic, onion, carrots, celery, leek, mushrooms, Polish spice and bay leaf and cook stir until slightly soft about 2 minutes. Now add the rest of the sauce ingredients to the pot, bring to a boil, reduce the heat and simmer the chicken slowly with the pot slightly covered for 1 hour. **After 45 minutes of simmering, remove exactly 3/4 cup of the cooking liquid, chill in the freezer and use to make the parsley dumplings.** After 1 hour, remove the lid from the pot and turn the fire down to low. Gently place the dumplings on top of the stewing chicken, cover the pot completely and let the dumplings cook for another 25 minutes.

Parsley Dumplings

INGREDIENTS

2 cups all-purpose flour
3 teaspoons baking powder
1 teaspoon sea salt
1/4 teaspoon white pepper
1/4 cup parsley, minced
3 tablespoons unsalted butter, softened
3/4 cup braising liquid from recipe

In a mixing bowl stir together the flour, baking powder, salt, pepper and parsley. Working quickly, cut the butter into the flour mixture with a pastry blender. Add the reserved braising liquid and stir with a wooden spoon until the dry ingredients are just moistened and the dough holds its shape. Turn out the dough onto a lightly floured work surface and carefully with floured hands, pat out the dough into a 6 X 6 - inch square about 1/2-inch thick. Using a chef's knife, cut the dough into 1-inch squares, roll into a round and follow the rest of the above recipe.

Chicken a la King

INGREDIENTS

2 tablespoons unsalted butter, melted
3 medium garlic cloves, minced
1 small onion, diced
1/2 small red pepper, diced
1/2 small green pepper, diced
1 cup domestic mushrooms, sliced
1 can Cream of Chicken soup
1 equal can of chicken stock
1/2 teaspoon sea salt
1/4 teaspoon black pepper
Dash of Tabasco, garlic powder, onion powder and nutmeg
2 cups pre-cooked chicken breast, cubed
1 cup canned baby peas, drained

8 pieces white bread, toasted

In a non-stick saucepan, heat the butter and sauté the garlic, onion, peppers and mushrooms for 3 to 4 minutes. Add the remaining ingredients except the chicken breast and peas, bring to a boil and simmer slowly for 5 minutes. Add the chicken and peas, simmer for another 10 minutes then ladle over the toasted bread and serve hot.

Easy Turkey Tetrazzini

SERVES 4

INGREDIENTS

2 tablespoons unsalted butter, melted
3 medium garlic cloves, minced
1/2 pound domestic mushrooms, sliced
2 tablespoons dry sherry (optional)
1 can Cream of Chicken soup
1 equal can of chicken stock
6 tablespoons parmesan cheese, grated
1/4 teaspoon sea salt
1/8 teaspoon black pepper
Large dash Tabasco, garlic powder, onion powder
   and red pepper flakes
2 cups pre-cooked turkey breast, cubed
1 cup canned baby peas, drained

3/4 pound Barilla spaghetti
Parmesan cheese for sprinkling

Heat the butter in a non-stick saucepot and sauté the garlic and mushrooms until the mushrooms release their liquid and dry. Splash on the sherry, reduce, add the remaining ingredients except the turkey and peas, bring to a boil and slowly simmer for 5 minutes. Add the turkey and peas to the pot and simmer for another 5 minutes. While the sauce is cooking, cook the pasta, divide among four soup bowls, ladle on the turkey sauce and sprinkle on the cheese.

Turkey Divine

SERVES 4

INGREDIENTS

4 tablespoons unsalted butter
12 large slices deli turkey breast, cooked
2 pounds fresh broccoli florets, pre-cooked al dente
1 Recipe Sauce of Turkey Tetrazzini, cooled
2 to 3 cups cheddar cheese, grated

Pre-heat the oven to 350°. Using the unsalted butter, grease a high sided earthenware casserole. Lay the turkey breast out onto a work surface and place the broccoli florets on to the center of each piece. Carefully roll each turkey breast up into a tight roll and place seam side down in the casserole. Ladle the sauce over each roll, sprinkle on the cheddar cheese and then bake in the hot oven for 40 minutes until the cheese is melted and slightly golden brown.

Classic Tuna Noodle Casserole

SERVES 4

INGREDIENTS

4 tablespoons unsalted butter
I can Cream of Mushroom soup
5 ounces whole milk
5 ounces chicken stock
I teaspoon sea salt
1/2 teaspoon black pepper

INGREDIENTS

Large dash Tabasco, garlic powder and
  onion powder
Two 6 ounce cans tuna, well drained
One 6 ounce can sweet peas, drained
4 cups elbow macaroni, pre-cooked
2 cups cheddar cheese, shredded
3 cups potato chips, crumbled

Pre-heat the oven to 375°. Using the butter, grease a high sided earthenware casserole. Combine the mushroom soup with the milk, chicken stock and seasoning, and whisk until smooth. Blend in the tuna and the peas then fold in the elbow macaroni. Now carefully fold in the cheese, pour into the casserole and cook covered for 30 minutes. After that time, remove the cover, sprinkle on the potato chips and cook for another 10 minutes until the chips are a light golden brown.

Maxwell Street Gefilte Fish

SERVES 4 TO 6

INGREDIENTS

I large head green cabbage
I quart light fish stock, chilled
5 thick slices challah bread, crusts remove

I tablespoon olive oil
2 large garlic cloves, minced
1/2 small onion, minced
2 tablespoons parley, minced
2 tablespoons fresh dill, minced
2 pounds exceedingly fresh white fish or pike fillets
3 large whole eggs, separated
2 teaspoons sea salt
1/2 teaspoon white pepper
Dash Tabasco, cayenne and nutmeg

Pre-heat the oven to 375°. Fill a large soup pot with lightly salted water, bring to a boil then blanch the head of cabbage for 5 to 10 minutes until you can remove 12 whole leaves easily. Remove to a strainer and let cool. Shred the challah slices, place in a bowl, ladle on 3/4 cup fish stock, mix with your hands and let rest until needed. In a small skillet heat the olive oil and saute the garlic and onion for 3 to 4 minutes until softened, remove from the heat, and stir in the parsley and dill. On a clean cutting board using a sharp chef's knife, chop the white fish until fine and slightly homogenous then place into a large mixing bowl. To the bowl add the soaked challah, onion mixture, 3 egg yolks, salt, pepper, Tabasco, cayenne and nutmeg. Mix with a plastic spoon until well combined then whisk the remaining egg white in a separate bowl until slightly stiff and fold into the mixture. Spread the blanched cabbage leaves out onto a clean work surface, pat dry then using a spoon divide the mixture among each one of the leaves, about 1/2 cup each. Form each cabbage leaf into a tight ball, place into a 10 by 16-inch non-stick high sided baking pan, cover with the remaining fish stock and bake covered with aluminum foil for 30 to 40 minutes. Serve with side of beet horseradish dressing.

RETRO SALADS

Hey man, I admit it. I love those old classic 70s style psychedelic colored salads and dressings that magically appeared at Continental type restaurants around the city. In their lifetime who hasn't experienced an old, crabby waitress monotonously reciting the salad dressing selection over and over again at the same table!

In my younger years as an apprentice cook, I was given the job of salad maker at a few prestigious club like restaurants. It wasn't because of my savvy salad making ability, but for the sheer fact "how can a kid screw up a salad?" Trust me, don't ask. I used to get a little crazy with food dyes back then to perk up dressings and make them look well, "happy." Everyone knows the famed history of the Caesar and the Cobb, but what wild eyed salad guy invented the rest is beyond me. All I know is that they are all really good.

Chef's note: I've scaled these dressing recipes down from a gallon size to about 2-3 cups which might lead you to re-season and adjust the consistency with a little cool water. That's just the way it is. Also don't be put off by the use of prepared mayo, it's the safest and easiest way to avoid the dreaded "botulism!"

DRESSINGS

Greeky Oil and Vinegar

YIELDS ABOUT 2 TO 3 CUPS

INGREDIENTS

- 3/4 cup light olive oil
- 1 cup red wine vinegar
- 2 1/4 teaspoon garlic powder
- 1 1/2 teaspoons onion powder
- 2 1/4 teaspoons dried oregano
- 2 1/4 teaspoons dried basil
- 1 1/2 teaspoons Dijon mustard
- 1 1/2 teaspoons sea salt
- 1 1/2 teaspoons black pepper

Place all the ingredients into a mixing bowl and whisk vigorously until well combined. Store in an airtight jar in the refrigerator until needed.

Creamy Garlic

INGREDIENTS

1 cup mayo, full fat
1 cup sour cream, full fat
1/4 cup garlic puree
1/2 teaspoon Lawry's season salt
1/4 teaspoon black pepper
1/2 teaspoon sugar
1 1/2 teaspoons Worcestershire sauce
1 1/2 teaspoons lemon juice
Dash Tabasco, garlic powder and onion powder

Place all the ingredients into a mixing bowl and whisk vigorously until well combined. Store in an airtight jar in the refrigerator until needed

Ranch Dressing

YIELDS ABOUT 2 TO 3 CUPS

INGREDIENTS

1 cup mayo, full fat
1 cup sour cream, full fat
3/4 cup buttermilk
1 tablespoon lemon juice
2 tablespoons red wine vinegar
1 1/2 teaspoons garlic, minced
1 tablespoon Worcestershire
1 tablespoon parsley, minced
1 tablespoon chives, minced
2 teaspoons Dijon mustard
3/4 teaspoon celery seeds

Place all the ingredients into a mixing bowl and whisk vigorously until well combined. Store in an airtight jar in the refrigerator until needed

American French

INGREDIENTS

1/2 can regular Campbell's tomato soup
3 tablespoons cider vinegar
1/2 cup canola oil
1/3 cup sugar
1/2 teaspoon Lawry's garlic salt
1/8 teaspoon black pepper
1 1/2 teaspoons celery seeds
1/2 teaspoon paprika
1 1/2 teaspoons dry mustard
Dash of Tabasco, Worcestershire,
   cayenne and garlic powder

Place all the ingredients into a blender, cover and frappe until the dressing comes together. Store in an airtight jar in the refrigerator until needed.

Blue Cheese

INGREDIENTS

1 cup mayo, full fat
1 cup sour cream, full fat
2 tablespoons red wine vinegar
1 teaspoon Worcestershire
1/2 teaspoon sea salt
1/4 teaspoon black pepper
1/2 teaspoon garlic powder
1/2 teaspoon dry mustard
Dash of Tabasco and lemon juice
1 cup blue cheese, crumbled

Place all the ingredients except the blue cheese into a mixing bowl and whisk until smooth. Fold in the blue cheese and store in an airtight jar in the refrigerator until needed.

Thousand Island

INGREDIENTS

1 cup mayo, full fat
1/2 cup ketchup
1/4 cup sweet pickle relish
1/4 cup black olives, chopped
1/3 cup green olive with pimento, chopped
1 1/2 teaspoons red wine vinegar
1 1/2 teaspoons sugar
1 teaspoon garlic, minced
1/2 teaspoon sea salt
1/4 teaspoon black pepper
2 tablespoons parsley, chopped
2 hard boiled eggs, chopped
Dash of garlic powder, onion powder, Tabasco
   and Worcestershire

Place the mayo and ketchup into a mixing bowl and whisk until smooth. Now add the remaining ingredients except the hard boiled eggs, stir to combine then gently fold in the eggs. Store in an airtight jar in the refrigerator until needed.

Green Goddess

INGREDIENTS

1 cup mayo, full fat
1 cup sour cream, full fat
1/4 cup green onion, minced
1/4 cup parsley, minced
2 tablespoons chives, minced
1 tablespoon garlic, minced
2 teaspoons anchovy paste
2 tablespoons lemon juice
1/2 teaspoon sea salt
1/4 teaspoon black pepper
Dash of Tabasco, Worcestershire and
   tarragon vinegar

Place all the ingredients into a mixing bowl and whisk vigorously until well combined. Store in an airtight jar in the refrigerator until needed.

Classic Caesar

INGREDIENTS

1 whole large egg
1/2 cup light olive oil

2 whole anchovy fillets
2 large garlic cloves
1 teaspoon whole black peppercorns
1/2 teaspoon celery salt
1/4 cup parmesan cheese, grated
1 teaspoon Dijon mustard
2 tablespoons lemon juice
3 tablespoon red wine vinegar
2 dashes Tabasco and Worcestershire

Place all the ingredients except the egg and olive oil into a blender. Place the whole egg in its shell into a small saucepan filled with water, bring to a boil and simmer for exactly 1 1/2 minutes then crack into the blender. Cover the blender run it at medium speed and through the hole in the top slowly pour in the oil until the dressing comes together. Store in an airtight jar in the refrigerator until needed.

SALADS

Classic Chef's

SERVES 4

INGREDIENTS

1/2 head iceberg lettuce, chopped
1 medium avocado, halved and sliced
1 cup sliced hothouse cucumber
4 Roma tomatoes, quartered
6 sliced rings of green bell pepper
6 sliced rings of red onion
2/3 cup canned garbanzo beans
2/3 cup pickled beets, cut julienne
2 large hard boiled eggs, crumbled
1/4 cup fresh bacon bits

1 recipe dressing of choice

Place all the ingredients into a large salad bowl, add the dressing that you like, toss and serve.

Mrs. Julienne

INGREDIENTS

3 cups iceberg lettuce, chopped
3 cups Romaine lettuce, chopped
1 cup Polish ham, julienne
1 cup turkey breast, julienne
1/2 cup Swiss cheese, julienne
1/2 cup cheddar cheese, julienne
2 plum tomatoes, quartered
1 small cucumber, sliced
1 cup black olives, sliced
2 hard boiled eggs, sliced

1 recipe dressing of choice

Place all the ingredients into a large salad bowl, add the dressing that you like, toss and serve.

Hollywood Cobb

Follow the directions on page for Fancy Chopped Salad.

Chicken Caesar

SERVES 4

INGREDIENTS

2 small heads Romaine lettuce, cleaned
   and chopped
2 cups seasoned Italian croutons
1 1/2 pounds chicken breast
1/2 cup freshly grated parmesan cheese

1 recipe Caesar Dressing

Using a sharp chef's knife, cut the chicken breasts in half and marinate in Caesar dressing for 4 to 6 hours. After that time, grill the breasts for 5 to 6 minutes on each side then chill. Place the lettuce, croutons, and cheese into a mixing bowl and toss to combine. Cut the breasts into bite-size pieces, add to the salad then mix in some Caesar dressing and serve.

Grecian with Gyros

Follow the directions on page 296 for Greek Salad with Feta. In a large non-stick skillet, fry up 12 pieces of gyros meat until lightly browned on both sides then chop and garnish the Greek salad.

Chicago's Very Own "The Wedge" with Thousand Island Dressing

Follow the directions on page 199 for The Wedge.

Beefsteak Tomato, Red Onion and Gorgonzola Salad

Follow the directions on page 198 for the Beefsteak Tomato Salad.

Garbage Can Salad

Follow the directions on page 200 for the Garbage Can Salad.

Street sandwiches are an integral part of the working man or woman's lunch ritual and the varieties are endless in the city. Whether you brown bag it or prefer to sit at the lunch counter, these old stalwarts will get you through the day.

Fried Bologna and Cheese

SERVES 4

INGREDIENTS

4 tablespoons unsalted butter
4 thick slices ring bologna
4 slices American cheese
8 slices Wonder bread

Melt the butter in a large non-stick skillet and when hot, fry the bologna for 2 to 3 minutes on each side until it takes on a nice golden brown. Top the bologna with the cheese and cover the skillet with a sauce pot cover. Let the cheese melt for 20 seconds then serve on white bread with a dash of black pepper Tabasco, pickles and chips.

Grilled BBQ Bologna

SERVES 4

INGREDIENTS

4 thick slices ring bologna
1 tablespoon Barbecue spice or Rib Rub
1 cup barbecue sauce
8 slices Wonder bread

Pre-heat and clean the grill. Season the bologna slices with the barbecue spice or rib rub, spray the grill with some non-stick cooking oil and grill the bologna on each side for 2 minutes. Slather on the barbecue sauce, cover the grill for 2 minutes then serve on white bread with a side of pickled jalapenos, coleslaw and French fries.

Kiszka and Egg Sandwich

INGREDIENTS

4 tablespoons unsalted butter, melted
1 small kiszka bung
4 whole large eggs
8 slices caraway rye bread, toasted

Creamy Red Beet Horseradish Dressing

In a large non-stick skillet heat the butter, slice open the bung and fry the kiszka for 4 to 5 minutes until lightly crisp and brown. Beat the eggs in a bowl, add them to the skillet and stir fry with the kiszka until the eggs are cooked. Spread the toast with the beet relish, spoon on the kiszka/egg mixture and serve.

Fried Egg and Ham

SERVES 4

INGREDIENTS

4 tablespoons unsalted butter
1 pound fresh ham steak, quartered
4 whole large eggs
Dash of sea salt, black pepper and Tabasco
8 slices Wonder bread, lightly toasted and buttered

Melt the butter in a large non-stick skillet and when hot, sauté the ham pieces for 2 minutes on each side until lightly golden brown. Stack the ham slices toward the back of the skillet and in the remaining oil and juices, cook the eggs over easy style. Season the eggs with the salt, pepper and Tabasco, place a ham piece onto 4 slices of the toast, top with an egg and the remaining bread.

Sicilian Bulls-eye

INGREDIENTS

Four 2-inch thick slices Balese Italian bread
1 recipe Sweet Red Peppers and Garlic, see page 234
4 tablespoons unsalted butter
2 tablespoons olive oil
4 whole large egg yolks
1/4 teaspoon sea salt
1/8 teaspoon black pepper
1/4 cup Pecorino Romano cheese, grated

Carefully using a 1 1/2-inch cookie cutter, cut a whole directly in the center of each piece of bread. In a medium sized non-stick skillet, heat the butter and oil and when it sizzles, sauté the bread for 2 to 3 minutes until lightly brown then flip over and crack the egg yolk into the center of each bread slice. Season with the salt, pepper and cheese, cover the pan with a lid and cook for 1 minute until the yolk sets and serve with a topping of the sweet red peppers and garlic.

Catholic's Friday Pepper and Egg

See Who's Got the Beef
Chapter for recipe!

My Father-in-Law Frank DeCarl's Sunday Morning Pepper, Sausage, Egg and Potato Frittata Sandwich

See Who's Got the Beef
Chapter for recipe!

Ham on Rye

SERVES 4

1 pound baked ham, sliced
1 cup horseradish mustard
8 slices Polish rye bread

Slather both sides of the rye bread with the mustard, top with the ham pieces and serve with a side of dill pickles and a schooner of beer.

Blue Collar Man's Fancy Liverwurst

SERVES 4

1 pound fresh liverwurst spread
1 medium red onion, sliced
2 large hard boiled eggs, sliced
Horseradish mustard
8 slices dark rye bread

Spread the liverwurst on to 4 slices of the bread and top with slices of red onion and egg then the remaining bread spread with horseradish mustard.

French Dip

INGREDIENTS

3 cups beef stock
1/4 teaspoon garlic powder
1/4 teaspoon onion powder
1/4 teaspoon oregano
1/8 teaspoon dried thyme
1/8 teaspoon black pepper
1 small bay leaf
Dash of red pepper flakes, Tabasco and Kitchen bouquet

4 Italian hogie rolls
1 pound thinly sliced deli roast beef

Combine the ingredients for the au jus in a saucepan, bring to a boil and simmer for about 10 minutes. Heat the slices of beef in the juice for a minute and then serve on the sliced rolls with a side of extra juice for dipping.

Downtown Deli Reuben Melt

SERVES 4

INGREDIENTS

8 slices dark rye bread or pumpernickel
1 cup Thousand Island dressing
2 cups jarred sauerkraut, squeezed
8 slices deli Swiss cheese
1 1/2 pounds thinly sliced quality
    corned beef or pastrami
6 tablespoons unsalted butter
Dash of Lawry's garlic salt

Place the bread slices onto a serving platter and spread each piece with the Thousand Island dressing. Onto 4 slices stack 1 piece of cheese, a heaping of sauerkraut, 1/4 of the corned beef and another slice of Swiss. Top with the remaining bread. In a large non-stick skillet, heat the butter and when hot, place the sandwiches in the pan and cook for 2 minutes on one side. Carefully flip the Reubens over, lightly flatten with a spatula, cover with a pot cover and let the sandwiches cook for 3 to 4 minutes more until crispy golden brown and the cheese is melted. Season the tops with the garlic salt and serve.

Monte Cristo

SANDWICHES

8 thick slices white bread, (Texas toast)
4 thick slices Krakus ham
4 thick slices deli Swiss cheese
4 thick slices deli turkey breast

BATTER

1 1/2 cups all-purpose flour
2 teaspoons baking powder
1/2 teaspoon sea salt
2 whole large eggs
1 1/2 cups whole milk
1/8 teaspoon white pepper
Dash of yellow food coloring

Powdered sugar and raspberry jam for garnish
1 quart Canola oil for frying

Combine all the batter ingredients in a mixing bowl until smooth. Top 4 slices of bread with a piece of ham, Swiss cheese and turkey then the remaining bread. Carefully cut the sandwiches into quarters and put a toothpick through each quarter. Heat the oil in a deep fat fry until the temperature reaches 360°, dip the sandwich quarters into the batter until well covered and deep fry for 3 to 4 minutes until golden brown. Remove from the hot oil, drain on paper towels, discard the toothpick, sprinkle with powdered sugar and serve with the jam.

Patty Melt

INGREDIENTS

2 pounds ground round
1 teaspoon sea salt
1/2 teaspoon black pepper
Dash of Tabasco
1 cup Thousand Island dressing
4 thick slices Monterrey Jack cheese
8 slices dark deli rye
6 tablespoons unsalted butter

SWEET ONION TOPPING

1 tablespoon canola oil
1 tablespoon unsalted butter
1 large sweet onion, halved and thinly sliced
Pinch of sugar
1/4 teaspoon Lawry's garlic salt

To make the onion topping, heat the oil and butter in a small skillet, and stir cook the onions until slightly opaque about 7 to 8 minutes. Sprinkle on the sugar and garlic salt, then continue to stir cook until the onions are light golden brown then remove from the fire. Season the meat with the salt, pepper and Tabasco and form into 4 equal size oval patties. Pre-heat the broiler to high. Heat the butter in a large non-stick skillet and saute the patties on each side for 2 to 3 minutes until medium cooked then remove to a serving platter. Quickly place 4 slices of bread into the hot skillet, top with the onion mixture, a cooked patty and a slice of cheese. Place the pan underneath the broiler to let the cheese melt. While the pan is in the broiler, spread the Thousand Island dressing on the remaining pieces of bread then place on top of the melted cheese. Broil for 1 minute more until the top is crisp. Flip the sandwich over before serving.

Tuna Melt

SERVES 4

INGREDIENTS

1 Recipe Classic Tuna Salad
4 thick slices Challah or potato bread, pre-toasted
4 tomato slices, about 1/4 -inch thick
8 thin slices deli cheddar or American cheese

Pre-heat the broiler to medium. Evenly divide the tuna salad among the toasted bread being sure to leave a 1/2-inch border all around. Spread the tuna out evenly so it covers the bread. Top the tuna with a slice of tomato then overlap 2 pieces of cheese onto each so it completely covers the tuna. Place the sandwiches onto a small baking pan and broil for 2 to 3 minutes until the cheese has melted and begins to brown.

Deluxe Turkey, Bacon and Avocado Club

SERVES 4

INGREDIENTS

12 slices Wonder bread, toasted
12 slices bacon, pre-cooked
12 thick slices oven roasted turkey breast
4 slices American cheese
2 medium sized avocados, peeled and sliced
8 cleaned lettuce leaves
8 thick slices beefsteak tomato
1 heaping cup mayo, full fat

Spread a little mayonnaise onto each slice of toasted bread. Onto 4 of the slices lay on some turkey, American cheese, tomato and lettuce. Top with another piece of toast then layer on some bacon, avocado, tomato, lettuce and a bit more turkey. Top with the remaining piece of bread. Insert 4 long frilled toothpicks into the top of each sandwich, cut into quarters and serve with a side of coleslaw, sweet pickles and French fries.

Master Recipe for Tuna, Chicken or Egg Salad Sandwich

SERVES 4

SANDWICH BASE
1 cup mayonnaise, full fat
1 tablespoon Dijon mustard
1 tablespoon lemon juice
1/2 cup celery, minced
1/2 teaspoon sea salt
1/4 teaspoon black pepper
Dash of Tabasco, Worcestershire and
    garlic powder

FILLING
12 ounces canned tuna, well drained
12 ounces roasted chicken breast, cubed
Or 8 large hard boiled eggs, chopped

Place all the base ingredients into a mixing bowl and stir to combine. Place the filling of your choice into another mixing bowl and a little over half of the mayonnaise mix to that bowl and combine. If more mayonnaise is needed, add a little bit more. Serve the salad on top of fresh white bread with lettuce and tomato along with pickles and potato chips.

Da Mayor's Steak Sandwich Deluxe!

SERVES 1 MAYOR
AND HIS WIFE

As a young cook, I've made this excellent sandwich for Your Honor while working at Lake Point Tower Club. Skirt steak is a juicy, robust center cut steak that takes well to marinating and grilling. The onion rings are an added bonus.

INGREDIENTS
Two 6 to 8 ounce boneless rib eye steaks

4 slices pumpernickel bread
1/2 cup Thousand Island dressing
Sliced tomatoes
Lettuce leafs
Dill pickle spears

1 Recipe Steak House Onion Rings,
    see page 204
1 Recipe Celery Seed Cabbage Slaw

MARINADE
3/4 cup canola oil
1/4 cup balsamic vinegar
2 tablespoons Dijon mustard
1 large garlic clove, minced
1 teaspoon dried oregano
1 teaspoon dried basil
1 teaspoon sea salt
1/4 teaspoon black pepper

Combine all the marinade ingredients, pour over the steaks, and refrigerate covered over night. The next day fire up the grill and when hot, grill the steaks for 4 to 5 minutes on each side until medium rare. Lightly toast the pumpernickel bread on the grill, spread with the Thousand Island dressing, then place the steak on to that. Garnish the plate with the slaw, onion rings, tomato, lettuce leaf, and dill pickle.

Celery Seed Cabbage Slaw

A cool mouth puckering refreshing salad that goes well with any sandwich.

INGREDIENTS

2 pounds red or green cabbage, cored and shredded

1/2 cup canola oil
2 tablespoons sugar
3 tablespoons red wine vinegar
1 1/2 teaspoons stone ground mustard
1 1/2 teaspoons celery seeds
2 teaspoons prepared horseradish
1/2 teaspoon sea salt
1/2 teaspoon black pepper
2 red delicious apples, cored and thinly sliced, optional
1 tablespoon lemon juice, optional
1 medium red onion, thinly sliced, optional

Place the shredded cabbage into a large mixing bowl, and in another small bowl, whisk together the remaining ingredients except the optional items. Pour 6 to 7 tablespoons of the dressing over the cabbage, and toss together using your hands. (This is the amount I recommend for this amount of cabbage.) Cover the slaw with a piece of plastic wrap and refrigerate for an hour before serving. Mix the optional items in before you're ready to serve.

Soul Man's Meat Loaf Sandwich

SERVES 4

Every working stiff has got his or her own favorite sandwich they take to the trenches and eat up on a beam or at their messy desk. Cold meat loaf sandwich is one of those dishes that doesn't need any fancy intro, just dig in and eat!

INGREDIENTS

2 tablespoon canola oil
3 medium garlic cloves, minced
I medium onion, diced
I medium green pepper, diced
2 pounds ground beef, 85% lean
1/2 pound ground pork
2 tablespoons steak sauce
2 large eggs
1/2 cup milk
I cup bread crumbs
1/2 teaspoon sea salt
1/4 teaspoon black pepper
1/4 teaspoon onion powder
1/4 teaspoon garlic powder

TOPPING

I cup ketchup
1/4 cup brown sugar
2 tablespoons Worcestershire
I tablespoon yellow mustard
I teaspoon Tabasco
Dash of red pepper flakes

Pre-heat the oven to 375°F. Heat the olive oil in a small skillet, and saute the garlic, onion, and green pepper for 3 to 4 minutes until soft then cool. Place the rest of the ingredients, except the topping into a large mixing bowl, and using your hands, knead and mix, then add the onion mixture and knead and mix again. Form the meat into a football shape and place into a Pyrex baking pan. Place the pan onto the middle rack of the oven and cook for 45 minutes, remove from the oven, and then carefully pour off the grease. Combine the topping ingredients in a small bowl, then using a spoon, heavily paint on top of the meat loaf. Return the pan to the oven to cook for another 30 minutes. Remove from the oven, and when cool, cover and refrigerate over night. The next day cut the meat loaf into thick slices and serve on white bread with a slice of red onion, dill pickle, chips, and a soda. (Some people like to add mustard.)

Maxwell Street Pork Chop Sandwich

Every visitor to Chicago should experience a pork chop sandwich that was invented by Jim's Original on Maxwell and Halsted. Late night blue's musicians needed a soul food fix that didn't break the bank so Jim's turned them on to griddled bone-in thin pork chops that are topped with a savory sweet onion mix, mustard, and served on just plain white bread with a few sport peppers to liven it up. Yeah, the sandwich is a little greasy so let me give you some advice how to eat it. "Hold the sandwich with the long side of the bone in the back and eat around it."

INGREDIENTS

4 bone-in thin pork chops, 6 to 7 ounces each

White Bread
Yellow or spicy mustard

SWEET ONION TOPPING

1 tablespoon canola oil
1 tablespoon unsalted butter
1 large sweet onion, halved and thinly slice
Pinch of sugar
1/4 teaspoon Lawry's season salt

Traditionally this is cooked on a flat top griddle, but you can use a large non-stick skillet instead. Put 2 tablespoons of canola oil in a large non-stick skillet and when hot, fry the pork chops until lightly browned about 3 to 4 minutes on each side. Remove to a serving platter. Leaving all the grease in the pan, add the remaining canola oil, butter, and sliced onions, and stir cook the onions until slightly opaque about 7 to 8 minutes. Sprinkle on the sugar and season salt, then continue to stir cook until the onions are lightly golden brown. Using a wooden spoon, push all the onions to one side of the pan, return the pork chops to the skillet, and cover with the sweet onions to infuse their grease and taste into the meat. Cook until thoroughly warmed through and serve on white bread with a splash of mustard.

Poochies Famous Char Salami

FOLLOW THE RECIPE FOR MAXWELL STREET PORK CHOP SANDWICH ABOVE AND SUBSTITUTE 4 THICK SLICE OF KOSHER SALAMI FOR THE PORK CHOPS.

Poochies on Dempster in Skokie serves excellent hot dog, fries, and cheddar burgers. They came up with the ingenious idea of making a char salami that's definitely worth a try.

Messy Bar B Qued Beef

SERVES 4

My wife Pam makes a killer barbecue beef sandwich that is always a hit with the neighbors. This is a real down and dirty recipe that is sweet and peppery, so be forewarned to pass around a lot of extra napkins.

INGREDIENTS

3 pounds deli shaved rare roast beef
I package soft cheapo hamburger buns

BARBECUE SAUCE

I cup tomato sauce
1/3 cup coca cola
1/3 cup cider vinegar
I tablespoon regular mustard
2 tablespoons steak sauce
2 tablespoons Worcestershire
I 1/2 teaspoons lemon juice
I teaspoon soy sauce
1/2 teaspoon garlic salt
1/2 teaspoon black pepper
I teaspoon dry mustard
3 tablespoons brown sugar
Dash of Tabasco
Dash of hickory liquid smoke
I teaspoon canola oil

In a medium sized non-stick sauce pot place all the ingredients for the barbecue sauce, bring to a slow simmer, stir with a whisk, and cook on a slow fire for 20 minutes. After 20 minutes add the shredded beef, stir to combine with the sauce, slightly cover, and cook slowly again for another 25 minutes. Ladle the beef and sauce onto the hamburger buns and serve with pickles and chips.

Sears' Skillet Sloppy Joe

I've always loved Sloppy Joe's with a side of maci cheese, and now that I have three growing boys, it's an easy and economical meal to make. Packaged Sloppy Joe mixes are way too salty for my taste so please give this dish a try. For your information, this recipe comes from Sears Roebuck and Company who used to include the information in a box when they started selling electric skillets some 40 years ago! Everyone go to sears today and get busia a new skillet!!

INGREDIENTS

2 tablespoon canola oil
2 medium garlic cloves, minced
1 small onion, diced
1/2 small green pepper, diced
1 large stalk celery, diced
2 pounds ground beef, 85% lean
1 teaspoon chili powder
1/4 teaspoon sea salt
1/4 teaspoon black pepper
4 teaspoons brown sugar
2 teaspoons dry mustard
1 teaspoon paprika
1/2 cup chili sauce
1/2 cup ketchup
2 cups water
4 tablespoons vinegar
2 tablespoons Worcestershire
Dash of Tabasco
Hamburger buns, chips, and sweet pickles

Heat a medium non-stick skillet, add the oil and sauté the garlic, onion, pepper and celery for 2 to 3 minutes. Crumble in the ground beef and stir cook with a wooden spoon for 4 to 5 minutes until it looses its color pink, and then pour the meat mixture into a strainer to rid it of excess water and fat. Return the meat back to the skillet with the rest of the ingredients, stir to combine, and simmer slowly for 20 to 25 minutes. Spoon out the Sloppy Joes on soft hamburger buns and serve with chips and sweet pickles.

COUNTER CULTURE   **101**

14 REALLY COOL ETHNIC SANDWICHES KEPT SECRET UNTIL NOW!

There's no question that Chicago loves their ham and cheese sandwiches, but sometimes you've just got to break away from the norm. Small ethnic joints around the city conjure up great lunch specials to showcase their cultural diversity and present their interpretation of what a sandwich should be.

Classic Cubano Press

SERVES 4

This is the real deal that started the panini craze around the country. Pick yourself up a small sandwich press to crisp the bread.

INGREDIENTS

4 Cuban rolls or soft French baguette
1/2 cup unsalted butter, softened
1 pound sweet cured ham such as Jabon Dolce or Krakus, medium sliced
1 pound lechon asado (roasted Cuban pork loin), medium sliced
1/2 pound baby Swiss, thinly sliced
1/4 pound Genoa salami, thinly sliced
Sliced dill pickles, yellow mustard and mayo, full fat

Heat the panini press and slice the rolls in half. Generously butter the inside of the rolls and layer on to the bottom of each the pickles, mustard, mayonnaise, salami, pork, ham and cheese. Put the tops back on the rolls, spread with a little butter and then place the sandwiches inside the press for 2 to 3 minutes on each side until the cheese starts to melt and the bread takes on the grill marks.

Milanesa de Pollo Torta

SERVES 4

Mexican markets around the city prepare all kinds of "tortas" or lunch sandwiches that are pre-wrapped and can be had for a buck. Give this one a try.

INGREDIENTS

4 small sized chicken breasts
1 cup Italian dressing

4 round Mexican Bollio rolls, split
2 cups shredded Monterey Jack cheese
2 cups lettuce, shredded
1 large tomato, sliced
1 medium red onion. sliced
2 medium avocados, peeled and sliced

CHIPOTLE-MAYO DRESSING

1 cup mayo, full fat
2 tablespoons canned chipotles in adobe, chopped
1 tablespoon lemon juice
1/4 cup sweet relish
Dash of salt, pepper and Tabasco

Using a sharp chef's knife cut the chicken breasts in half, marinate in the Italian dressing and refrigerate for 4 to 6 hours. To make the Chipotle dressing, combine all the ingredients in a mixing bowl and whisk together until smooth. Heat a grill and when hot, grill the chicken breasts for 3 to 4 minutes on each side until completely cooked through and set aside. Split the rolls and then place on to the grill to lightly crisp on each side for a minute. Spread the dressing on to both sides of the rolls and then layer all the remaining ingredients to make a nice Mexican sandwich.

COUNTER CULTURE **103**

Puerto Rican "Jibarito"

Originally invented at the famed "Borinquen Restaurant" in the city.

INGREDIENTS

2 large green plantains
1/2 cup olive oil

1 pound cooked shaved ham, pork roast
   or roast beef
4 slices American cheese

FILLING

2 tablespoons olive oil
3 large garlic cloves, minced
1 medium onion, sliced thin
1 large red pepper, quartered and sliced thin
1/2 teaspoon sea salt
1/8 teaspoon black pepper
1/8 teaspoon cumin
Dash of Chipotle powder
2 tablespoons red wine vinegar

GARNISH

Mayo
Lettuce leaves
Sliced tomato
Chopped cilantro

Pre-heat the oven to 400°. Peel the plantains and using a sharp chef's knife cut lengthwise into 1/4-inch wide strips (you will need 8 equal slices). Place on to a non-stick baking pan, brush each side with the olive oil and bake in the hot oven for 20 minutes until slightly brown then remove. In a large non-stick skillet, heat the remaining olive oil and saute slowly the garlic, onion and peppers for 10 minutes. Remove from the fire and season with the salt, pepper, cumin, chipotle and red wine vinegar. Place four small squares of aluminum foil on to a counter top and top each one with a piece of cooked green plantain. Lay on top of that the lettuce leaves, tomato and cilantro. Layer on some of the shaved ham and cheese, spread on some mayo and then top with the pepper onion mixture. Lay on the remaining plantain slices, tightly wrap the packages and place in the hot oven for 5 to 7 minutes to infuse.

Vietnamese Banh Mi

The French have most definitely influenced the Vietnamese diet with savory little sandwiches filled with pate or cured meats.

INGREDIENTS

Four 10-inch French baguettes
8 thin slices Vietnamese style pork roll
8 slices Vietnamese style salami, ham or turkey
4 thin slices French pate
1/2 cup mayo, full fat
4 tablespoons soy sauce
1/2 cup cilantro sprigs
1 cup thinly sliced English cucumber
Asian chili oil

BANH MI SLAW

3/4 cup white vinegar
2 tablespoons sugar
1 teaspoon sea salt
1 cup water
1/2 cup julienne carrots
1/2 cups julienne daikon radish
2 spring onions, julienne cut

To prepare the slaw heat the vinegar, sugar, salt and water in a saucepan, bring to a boil and remove from the fire. Stir in the vegetables and when cool, refrigerate the slaw in the liquid overnight. Pre-heat the oven to 400°. Slice the baguettes open lengthwise and crisp in the oven for about 4 minutes. Slather the mayonnaise inside the roll, sprinkle on the soy sauce and chili oil, and then layer on the pork, salami, pate, cucumbers and cilantro sprigs. Serve the sandwich with a side of slaw.

Cuban Breaded Steak

A favorite with the Miami crowd.

INGREDIENTS

Four 6 ounce sirloin steaks, pounded thin
Four 5-inch Cuban rolls or soft French rolls

GARNISH

Sliced avocado
Sliced tomato
Chopped cilantro

MARINADE

2 tablespoons olive oil
4 large garlic cloves, minced
1 medium onion, minced
1/2 teaspoon sea salt
1/4 teaspoon black pepper
3/4 cup orange juice
3/4 cup lime juice

4 whole large eggs
2 cups finely ground saltine or club crackers

Using a meat mallet slightly pound the steaks until nice and thin. Combine all the marinade ingredients in a mixing bowl and marinate the steaks for 4 to 6 hours. Place at least 2 inches of canola oil into a large iron skillet and heat to 350°. Beat the eggs in one mixing bowl and then place the breadcrumbs in another. Remove the steaks from the marinade, dip into the eggs and then generously coat with the crumbs. Chicken fry the steak in the hot oil for 2 to 3 minutes on each side until golden brown and cooked through. Repeat with the remaining steaks. Place on to the rolls and garnish. **The remaining marinade can be reduced quickly in a saucepan by half to coat the cooked steaks.**

Ricobenes Famous Steak Sandwich

SERVES 4

Ricobenes a local favorite serves up a great breaded Italian style steak sandwich.

INGREDIENTS

Four 6-inch Italian deli rolls split
4 boneless rib-eye steaks, 6 ounce each
1 cup Italian dressing
2 cups Geri's tomato sauce, warmed
2 cups shredded mozzarella cheese
1 cup giardiniera

BREADING

2 cups fresh breadcrumbs
1/3 cup grated Romano cheese
1 1/2 teaspoons dried oregano
1 1/2 teaspoons dried basil
1/4 teaspoon Hungarian sweet paprika
1/4 teaspoon sea salt
1/8 teaspoon black pepper

4 large whole eggs

GARLIC BUTTER SMEAR

1 stick unsalted butter, softened
1 tablespoon garlic puree
2 tablespoons parsley, minced

Lightly flatten the steaks with a meat mallet and marinate in Italian dressing overnight. Pre-heat the oven to 450°. Combine all the garlic butter ingredients in a small bowl, combine all the breading ingredients in a mixing bowl and beat the eggs in another bowl. In a large cast iron skillet, heat about 2 inches of canola oil to 350°. Split the rolls and liberally brush the insides with the garlic butter. Remove the steaks from the marinade, wipe off the excess, dip in the eggs and then the breading mixture, and fry in the hot oil for 3 to 4 minutes on each side until golden brown and the meat is cooked. Place the fried steak on to a buttered roll, top with the tomato sauce, giardiniera, shredded cheese and the top half of the roll. Place all the sandwiches on to a baking sheet, and bake in the hot oven for 5 minutes until the roll is crisp and the cheese is melted.

Pueblan Vegetarian Cemitas

SERVES 4

Not all Hispanic food is centered around tacos or tortilla shells. There are dozens of recipes for cemitas and I find this one to my liking and I think you will too.

INGREDIENTS

4 Cemita rolls or seeded Kaiser rolls, toasted
2 cups refried beans, warmed
2 medium sized avocados, peeled and sliced
1 medium red onion, sliced
1 large tomato, sliced
1 cup Mexican papalo leaves or cilantro
4 whole chipotle peppers in adobo
1 1/2 cups quesilla cheese, shredded
Olive oil, salt and pepper

Split the rolls, spread on the warm refried beans and gently stack the rest of the ingredients on top of that. Sprinkle on a little olive oil, salt and pepper and serve.

Orleans Style Muffelletta

SERVES 4

The quintessential Italian influenced New Orleans classic sub sandwich.

INGREDIENTS

One 10-inch round seeded Italian Pane
    Toscano or Siciliano
2 cups muffelletta salad chopped, see page 253
1/4 pound each of thinly sliced; Italian ham,
    Mortadella, Genoa salami, Provolone, and
    Mozzarella

Carefully cut the entire half of the loaf lengthwise and using your fingers, scoop out some of the interior of the loaf to accommodate the meats and salad. Spread some of the chopped olive salad onto the bottom half of the loaf, and then decoratively layer the meats and cheeses on top of the salad. Spread some more of the olive salad on top of the meats, top with the remaining bread, wrap tightly in plastic wrap for 20 minutes to absorb and infuse. Cut into 4 equal pieces and serve.

Veracruz Pambazo Chilango

SERVES 4

Pambazo, meaning browned bread. This is the Hispanic version of the Sloppy Joe. This sandwich is savory stuffed then topped with a spicy sauce.

INGREDIENTS

4 soft Telera rolls or Kaiser rolls
2 tablespoons olive oil

FILLING

1 pound bulk chorizo
1 1/2 cups diced boiled potatoes
1/2 cup onion, diced
1/2 cup red bell pepper, diced

SPICY SAUCE

2 tablespoons canola oil
3 large garlic cloves, minced
1 small onion, minced
1 1/2 pounds plum tomatoes, chopped
2 large guajillo chilies, seeded and de-veined
1/8 teaspoon ground cumin
2 whole cloves
2 whole all-spice
1/2 teaspoon oregano
One 2-inch piece cinnamon stick
2 cups chicken stock

GARNISH

Shredded queso fresco
Crema fresca
Chopped lettuce
Sliced jalapenos

To begin the dish you must first make the sauce. In a saucepan heat the oil and saute the garlic, onion and chilies for 2 to 3 minutes. Add the rest of the sauce ingredients, bring to a boil then simmer slowly for 30 minutes. Mash the sauce through a fine mesh strainer into a clean pot, re-season and reduce if necessary. (The sauce should be thick enough to coat the back of a spoon.) To prepare the filling, brown the chorizo in a non-stick skillet until it turns lightly brown and releases its oil. Drain off any excess grease and then add the potatoes, onion and red pepper. Saute together for another 3 to 4 minutes. While the filling is cooking brush the tops of the rolls with the olive oil and crisp under a broiler. To prepare the sandwich slice the rolls in half. Place inside each roll a hefty portion of chorizo mixture, sprinkle on the garnish, top with the other half of the roll and then place on to a plate. Using a serving spoon, ladle on top of each sandwich the hot spicy sauce. Eat with a fork and knife.

Crispy Cat Po-boy

Another New Orleans favorite.

INGREDIENTS
Four 6-inch deli rolls, split
Four 8 ounce pieces catfish fillets
1 tablespoon Creole seasoning
1 cup tartar sauce, see page 259

GARLIC BUTTER SPREAD
1 stick unsalted butter, softened
2 tablespoons olive oil
2 tablespoons asiago cheese, grated
Dash of garlic salt, pepper, paprika and Tabasco

BREADING
3 large whole eggs
1/2 cup whole milk

1 1/2 cups corn flour
3 tablespoons cornstarch
1 tablespoon Creole seasoning

GARNISH
Shredded lettuce
Sliced tomatoes
Red onion slices
Pickled jalapeno slices
Sport peppers

Season the catfish with the Creole spice and set aside. Combine all the garlic butter ingredients in a small mixing bowl and set aside. Whisk the eggs with the milk and place into a bowl. Also combine the corn flour, cornstarch and Creole seasoning in another bowl. Pre-heat your broiler to high. Liberally spread the garlic butter on each side of the rolls and toast for 2 to 3 minutes until the bread is crispy. In a large cast iron skillet, heat 2 -inches of canola oil to 350°. Dredge the catfish fillets into the corn flour mixture, shake off the excess, dip into the egg wash and then back into the corn flour mixture again. Place in the hot oil and cook for 2 to 3 minutes on each side until golden brown then drain on a paper towel. To make the sandwich, place a fried catfish fillet on to the toasted bread, dollop on the tartar sauce, and then layer on the garnish.

Greek "Keftedes" Meatball Hero

SERVES 4

The Greeks love their yaya's meatballs almost as much as they love their gyros!

INGREDIENTS

1 1/2 pounds ground beef, 90% lean
1/2 pound ground lamb
2 tablespoons olive oil
4 large garlic cloves, minced
1 small onion, minced
3/4 cup fresh breadcrumbs
1/3 cup whole milk
2 large whole eggs
1/4 cup chopped fresh mint or dill
2 tablespoons parsley, chopped
1 teaspoon dried Greek oregano
1/2 teaspoon sea salt
1/4 teaspoon black pepper
Dash of nutmeg, allspice, garlic powder,
   onion powder and Tabasco
1/2 cup parmesan cheese, grated

SALAD GARNISH

1 small red onion, diced
4 medium Roma tomatoes, diced
2 tablespoons parsley, chopped
2 tablespoons olive oil
Dash of sea salt, black pepper and garlic powder

1 Recipe Tzatziki Sauce, see page 295

Pre-heat the oven to 400°. In a small skillet heat the olive oil and saute the garlic and onion for 3 to 4 minutes until softened. Remove from the fire and completely cool. Place the ground meats into a large mixing bowl, add the rest of the ingredients including the sautéed onions and mix and knead with your hands until thoroughly combined. Using a meatball scoop, divide the mixture into 18 to 20 pieces. Using lightly floured hands, roll the balls into a meatball shape, place on a baking sheet lined with parchment paper and bake in the oven for 25 minutes until lightly browned. While the meatball s are cooking, toss together the salad ingredients. When the meatballs are cooked, heat 4 pita shells, place 3 or 4 meatballs in the center, spoon on top some of the Tzatziki sauce and then the salad, and serve.

Falafel

SERVES 4

This Middle Eastern sandwich is a big hit with the vegetarian crowd and it comes together in a snap.

INGREDIENTS

1 recipe Fabulous Falafel, see page 316

4 heated Pita pockets

GARNISH

1 recipe Jerusalem Salad with Tahini dressing,
   see page 314

Lebonese Chicken Shawarma

I was recently up in Ontario and was surprised as to how many shawarma places there are in Canada. Everything is shawarma this, shawarma that. It really gets on your nerves, but on the other hand it's really good! Shawarma usually consists of beef, lamb or chicken that is very thinly sliced, marinated, skewered , topped with an onion and lemon, and then slowly roasted on a vertical spit similar to a gyros machine. As the meat turns on the spit, the embers of the fire cook the outer portions until crispy. The shawarma chef then takes a really sharp, long knife and cuts off paper thin slices of cooked meat into a special holding skillet. The cooked meat is then served on a heated pita bread usually garnished with lettuce, tomato and homemade tahini sauce. I've had shawarmas all over the world, and there are dozens of ways to season the meat depending on what country you're in. Now I don't expect you to go out a buy a gyros machine to cook this recipe, the marinated meat can easily be grilled or broiled to hold in the succulent juices. Also, if the meat isn't seasoned to your liking you can go on the internet and purchase authentic shawarma spice that can be added to your own marinade.

INGREDIENTS

4 medium chicken breasts, thinly sliced

TAHINI DRESSING

1/2 cup Tahini
1/4 cup plain yogurt
1 teaspoon garlic, minced
2 tablespoons lemon juice
1 tablespoon olive oil
1 tablespoon chopped parsley
Pinch sea salt, pepper and Tabasco

MARINADE

1 cup plain yogurt
1/4 cup lemon juice
2 tablespoons olive oil
1 tablespoon garlic puree
2 teaspoons sea salt
1/4 teaspoon black pepper
1/4 teaspoon cayenne
1/4 teaspoon nutmeg
1/4 teaspoon cardamom
1/4 teaspoon cloves
1/2 teaspoon cinnamon
3/4 teaspoon all-spice

In a mixing bowl combine all the marinade ingredients, add the chicken and marinate overnight. Combine all the dressing ingredients and refrigerate overnight too. The next day heat a grill or broiler to high heat. Spray the grill or broiler pan with vegetable spray, lay on top the marinated pieces with some of the marinade still attached and broil for 3 or 4 minutes until the chicken is cooked through and slightly crispy around the edges. Cut the cooked pieces into long strips served on a warm pita with tahini sauce, then garnish with lettuce and tomato.

Easy "Pork al Pastor"

Simply put "Mexican gyros" another Chicago favorite that grabs the attention of local foodies. Similar to shawarma, thin cuts of pork, mutton or cabrito are highly seasoned with ground chilies, garlic and onion, then sweetened with a splash of pineapple juice. The marinated meat is then stacked like Oreo cookies on a vertical spit and slowly rotated and char roasted leaving the exposed ends to caramelize which are then thinly sliced, gyros style. A few years back I got turned on to this recipe by a cool chick I used to work with by the name of Mary Sue Milliken of the "Too Hot Tamale" fame. Again, as in the preceding recipe, I don't expect you to go out and buy a gyros spit, so I've adjusted the recipe to give you a more Chicago feel and easier preparation.

INGREDIENTS

2 to 3 pounds thinly sliced pork chops

Fresh tortilla shells and salsa to serve

LIQUID MARINADE

1 1/2 cups pineapple juice
2 tablespoons canola oil
4 large garlic cloves, minced
1 medium onion, minced
1 habanero chili, minced

MARINADE

1 tablespoon Gebhart's chili powder
2 teaspoons ground chipotle chili powder
1 1/2 teaspoons sea salt
1/2 teaspoon black pepper1 teaspoon garlic powder
1 teaspoon onion powder
1 teaspoon dried oregano
1/2 teaspoon ground coriander
1/4 teaspoon ground cumin

Place the pork chops on to a cutting board and remove any excess fat. Using a sharp chef's knife, cut the meat into thin strips. In a bowl combine the dry marinade and thoroughly season the cut up meat. Let rest in the refrigerator for 3 to 4 hours. After that time, mix together the liquid marinade, pour on top of the meat, thoroughly combine and let that rest for 3 or 4 hours. The next day heat a large griddle or non-stick skillet until hot, add 1 tablespoon of olive oil to the pan and using a kitchen tong, grab a good portion of the marinated pork and add it to the skillet. Stir fry the meat for 2 to 3 minutes until the pork turns a nice, crispy brown and caramelizes from the pineapple juice. (Don't over crowd the pan as the meat will just steam.) Serve with freshly warmed tortilla shells and salsa.

PIEROGI MANIA!

PIEROGI

RECIPES

Old Polish saying: (Swiety jacek z pierogami!) Meaning: St.Hyacinth and his pierogi!

Lately I keep having this reoccurring dream that Ray Kroc visits me in my sleep and wants to replace the French fries on his menu and put pierogis in its place! Could you imagine how many billions he would have sold?   All kidding aside, the Poles beloved pierogi has finally found it's place onto the American table as a truly wonderful dish. Some call it a stuffed dumpling and others call it a variation on the ravioli, but the Polish people have always known it as a pierogi!

Now I'm not going to get into some long-winded sermon about the history of pierogi, because we all know what it is. And I don't want to get any e-mails from busias around the country that say that I stole their recipe because there are hundreds of recipes for pierogi dough and hundreds of fillings for this delectable little treat.   Also, depending upon where you live in the country, humidity and elevation can play havoc on your dough, so it really becomes a little bit of this and a little bit of that kind of pierogi making process. The easiest way to start a Polish revolution is to proclaim who has the best peirogi, but in essence they're all good.

I've always considered Polish cuisine to be a well- rounded cultural experience, but it seems that peirogi has found its way onto other ethnic tables as well. Different cultures have adapted such fillings as goat cheese and mango, or even pineapple, ham, and cheese but I'm a traditionalist when it comes to pierogi. Busias that I've known have always favored dough that was made out of old potatoes, because it reminds them of what their mothers used to make in Poland. When I give cooking lessons on the road, younger Poles that I meet reminisce about busia's pierogi and the time it took to make them properly. Chefs around the country have created more fashionable, thinner pierogi dough that's more pasta like and easier to roll out, but the process is still time consuming. I've included in this chapter one of the easiest doughs to make and a wide range of popular fillings that have never been put in print and that should satisfy any discerning pierogi connoisseur.

Along with the hundreds of recipes for pierogi, come the words dziatki, galeczki, galuszki, haluski, kluski, knedle, kolduny, kopytka, przasniki, sliziki, and zacierki, which all in some form or another translate to dumplings and noodles or anything farinaceous. History books show that a lot of potato and noodle dishes were brought to Poland from other countries so these words can be found in Hungarian, Ukrainian, and Slavic cookbooks as well. The Poles also have a preference for dumplings and most people are surprised at how light they can be. I've also added a recipe for Lazyman's Cheese and Potato Dumplings along with a recipe for Tavern Pan Sinkers for those of you who need a quick dumpling fix with a minimum of time and effort expended.

Chef's Tips for Perfect Pierogi

1. Clean your kitchen counters of all unnecessary stuff and remove any distractions.

2. Familiarize yourself with the recipe and procedure.

3. Prepare and refrigerate the pierogi dough recipe at least 4 to 6 hours in advance. It is imperative that the gluten in the flour has time to relax and mellow out before you begin rolling out the dough. (I personally recommend refrigerating the dough for 24 hours.)

4. If you are using any non-fruit based fillings, prepare and refrigerate for at least 4 to 6 hours in advance. (All fruit based fillings should be prepared at the last minute to prevent bleeding.)

5. Assemble the tools you'll need: 1 large pot of lightly salted (sea salt only) boiling water, 1 rolling pin, 1 kid's teaspoon, 1 soft pastry brush, a 2 1/2 - inch round metal pastry cutter, 1 thin metal cake spatula, 1 metal dough scraper, 1 can shaker of flour, a small bowl of water, and assorted small sheet pans lined with parchment paper.

6. After the dough and filling have rested, remove them from the refrigerator and cut the dough into three equal pieces. (Do not re-knead the chilled dough.) Place the other two pieces back into the refrigerator until needed.

7. Now lightly flour a clean work surface, and place the cut piece directly on to it. Lightly flour the rolling pin, then gently pat the piece into a flat cake. Now using gentle force, begin rolling out the dough from the center in all directions until the dough is evenly 1/8 to 1/4 - inch thick. (If the dough sticks, it is okay to dust it with a little bit more flour, but not too much.) Using the soft pastry brush, quickly remove any excess flour from the surface of the dough.

8. Starting 2 inches inside the edge of the dough that is closest to you, place little mounds of filling (about 1 heaping teaspoon each), 3 inches apart. Now gently, from both sides, grasp the 2-inch edge and fold it over onto the mounds of filling. Carefully using your fingertips, enclose the filling leaving a 1/2 - inch space between each mound. Using the metal pastry cutter, cut the pierogi so that you're forming half circles. Now very carefully, using the thin cake spatula, lift each peirogi and place onto parchment lined sheet pans. (I recommend using the spatula because it makes lifting the pierogi a lot easier.)

9. Now that the formed pierogis are on the sheet pan, check to make sure that all of them are sealed and no filling is falling out. If the seal won't hold, brush it with a little water and pinch together again.

10. At this point, Chef Mike recommends that you cover the sheet pan loosely with plastic wrap, and place it directly into the freezer. Not only does this ensure that your pierogis will keep their shape, but also gives you the opportunity to finish rolling and filling the other dough.

11. When all your pierogis are formed and have firmed up in the freezer, it is time to cook them. Bring a large pot of lightly salted water to a boil, then reduce to a simmer. Now carefully float about 6 to 8 pierogis at a time in the water and cook for about 4 to 5 minutes, or until they rise to the surface, which means they are done. Using a slotted kitchen spoon, gently remove the pierogi from the water and place onto a serving platter being careful not to stack them on top of each other to avoid them from sticking.

12. Now place a large sized non-stick skillet over medium heat, add 4 tablespoons of unsalted butter, and 2 tablespoons of olive oil. When the butter starts to sizzle, add the drained pierogi making sure to leave a little space around each one, and gently brown on one side for about 3 to 4 minutes. Using a kitchen tong, carefully flip the pierogis over and brown on the other side. Before serving, sprinkle on some freshly ground black pepper, and serve with savory Polish topping, sour cream, and applesauce.

New Sour Cream Pierogi Dough

MAKES ABOUT 40 PIECES

The "nouvelle" pierogi dough. A basic but excellent dough that is lightened by the use of sour cream. Most chefs that I've made this for agree that it's their favorite version! The dough produces a beautifully soft, well-textured pierogi with just the right amount of bite.

INGREDIENTS

5 cups all-purpose flour
One 16 ounce container sour cream, full fat
2 tablespoons olive oil
3 whole large eggs
2 teaspoons sea salt

To mix the dough in a food processor, place the eggs, salt and oil in the work bowl fitted with a metal blade. Run the machine continuously for 1 minute. Remove the cover and add the sour cream plus 4 1/2 cups flour. Re-cover and run the machine until a soft but sticky ball forms inside the bowl. Using the extra flour, pour 1 tablespoon of flour on to a work surface. Remove all of the dough from the bowl and place it on top of the floured surface. Sprinkle on top of the dough 1 more tablespoon of the reserved flour and gently knead it into the dough until it is all absorbed. Repeat the process again using 2 more tablespoons of the reserved flour. The dough should be soft and pliable and if not, work in 1 more tablespoon of flour. Divide the dough into 2 equal portions and gently, using your knuckles, push the dough into two 6 X 6 squares. Flip each square over and using a soft pastry brush, remove any excess flour from the dough. Place each square into its own Ziploc bag, lay on a small sheet pan and refrigerate overnight. Reserve the excess flour for rolling out the dough.

Fresh Cabbage Filling

MAKES ABOUT 2 CUPS

INGREDIENTS

1 slice hickory smoked bacon, diced
2 tablespoons olive oil
2 teaspoons garlic puree
1 small onion, finely diced
1 medium head green cabbage, de-cored and diced
1/2 teaspoon sea salt
1/4 teaspoon black pepper
2 tablespoons chicken stock
2 dashes of Tabasco

In a large skillet over medium high heat, cook the bacon until it renders its fat and turns lightly brown not crisp. Pour the bacon into a small strainer set over a bowl to collect the excess fat. Return the skillet to the fire and then add the olive oil. When the oil is hot, add the garlic and onion and cook stir for about 1 minute. Now add the cabbage and cook stir for about 3 to 4 minutes until the cabbage starts to wilt. Reduce the heat to low, add the rest of the seasonings including the bacon and cook slowly, covered for about 20 minutes.

Sauerkraut and Mushroom Filling

MAKES ABOUT 2 CUPS

INGREDIENTS

1 slice hickory smoked bacon, diced
2 teaspoons garlic puree
1/2 small onion, finely diced
1/4 pound green cabbage, shredded
1/2 pound sauerkraut, drained and rinsed, twice
1/2 pound domestic mushrooms, sliced
1 tablespoon all-purpose flour
1 bay leaf
1 teaspoon Polish spice
1 tablespoon tomato paste
1 cup chicken stock

In a medium skillet over medium high heat, cook the bacon until it renders its fat and turns lightly brown not crisp. Using a slotted kitchen spoon, remove the bacon into a small bowl and discard all but 2 tablespoons of the fat. Return the pot to the fire, add the garlic and onions and cook for 1 minute. Now add the green cabbage, sauerkraut and mushrooms and cook stir for 3 to 4 minutes until the vegetables are slightly softened. Stir in the flour then add the rest of the ingredients including the bacon and bring to the boil. Reduce the heat to low, cover tightly and cook for about 45 minutes to 1 hour.

Potato and Cheese Filling

MAKES ABOUT 2 CUPS

INGREDIENTS

1 cup farmer's or ricotta cheese
1 cup leftover mashed potatoes, cold
3/4 teaspoon sea salt
1/4 teaspoon white pepper
1/4 teaspoon garlic powder
1/4 teaspoon onion powder
1/8 teaspoon freshly ground nutmeg
1 large egg yolk

Place all the ingredients except the farmers cheese into a large mixing bowl and using a heavy wooden spoon thoroughly combine the egg and seasoning with the potatoes until smooth. Now using a plastic spatula, gently fold the farmers cheese into the potato mixture until fully and evenly incorporated.

Bacon, Cheddar Cheese and Potato Filling

MAKES ABOUT 2 CUPS

INGREDIENTS

2 pieces bacon, minced
I cup cheddar cheese, finely grated
I cup leftover mashed potatoes, cold
1/4 teaspoon sea salt
1/4 teaspoon white pepper
1/4 teaspoon garlic powder
1/4 teaspoon onion powder
1/8 teaspoon freshly ground nutmeg
I large egg yolk

Heat a small skillet over medium heat and add the minced bacon. Cook stir with a wooden spoon until the bacon renders its fat and turns lightly brown and crisp. Pour the bacon into a small strainer set over a bowl to collect the excess fat. Cool the bacon and set aside. Now place all the ingredients, except the cheddar cheese into a large mixing bowl, and using a heavy wooden spoon thoroughly combine the egg, bacon and seasoning with the potatoes until smooth. Using a plastic spatula, gently fold the cheddar cheese into the potato mixture until fully and evenly incorporated.

Fresh Blueberry Filling

MAKES ABOUT 2 CUPS

INGREDIENTS

2 pints fresh blueberries, stemmed and
   cleaned
I teaspoon Vanilla Sugar
Dash of lemon juice

Place the blueberries into a medium sized mixing bowl and then sprinkle on the vanilla sugar and lemon juice. Grasp the bowl by the sides and gently toss the berries and sugar together until well combined. Let the mixture rest for 5 minutes, pour on to a nonstick sheet pan and distribute the berries so that each one is sitting directly on the sheet pan. Place the pan in the freezer for 10 to 15 minutes until the berries are slightly frozen and firm. (Proceed to roll out your pierogi dough and only remove as many berries as you need to fill the circles in front of you. This method will help to prevent the juices from discoloring your pierogi dough.)

Fresh Plum Filling

INGREDIENTS

12 fresh ripe Italian plums, pitted and
    quartered
1 to 2 teaspoons Vanilla Sugar
Dash of lemon juice
Large dash of cinnamon

Place the quartered plums into a medium sized mixing bowl and then sprinkle on the vanilla sugar, lemon juice and cinnamon, and using your hands, gently toss so the plums are well coated. Let the mixture rest for 5 minutes before using.

Lazy Man's Cheese and Potato Pierogi Dumpling

MAKES ABOUT 36 PIECES

If you have limited time or you just can't stand working Pierogi dough, this is the recipe for you. Cheese, potatoes and savory seasonings are combined to produce an easy but tasty alternative to the more labor intensive Pierog. Serve it with a side of Kapusta and sausage for a heavenly treat.

INGREDIENTS

1 cup farmers, cottage or ricotta cheese
1 cup mashed potatoes, left-over
3/4 teaspoon sea salt
1/4 teaspoon white pepper
1/4 teaspoon garlic powder
1/4 teaspoon onion powder
1/8 teaspoon nutmeg
3/4 to 1 cup all-purpose flour
1/4 cup unsalted butter, melted

Two quarts lightly salted water plus 1 tablespoon olive oil

The night before making the pierogi, place the cheese of your choice into a medium sized fine mesh strainer set over an empty bowl. Cover with plastic wrap and store in the refrigerator overnight to drain excess liquid. The next day put the mashed potatoes into a large mixing bowl and using a heavy wooden spoon, thoroughly incorporate all of the seasoning except the flour and butter until the mixture is smooth. Now add the drained cheese to the bowl and thoroughly combine until well mixed. Place a medium sized fine mesh strainer over the potato bowl and working with a quarter cup measuring scoop, add exactly 3/4 cup flour to the strainer and then sift on to the cheese potato dough. Now using the heavy spoon, thoroughly incorporate the flour into the mixture until smooth. At this point, the dough should be smooth and soft. If it still feels sticky, add 1 to 2 more tablespoons of flour into the dough. Remove the dough from the bowl and place on to a lightly floured work surface. Heat 2 quarts of lightly salted water to boiling, add the olive oil and then reduce to a slow simmer. Now using your hands, lightly flatten the dough to a 6 X 6- inch square. Using a sharp chef's knife, make five vertical cuts through the dough equally spaced. Then repeat the process and make five horizontal cuts through the dough equally spaced. You should have 36 one-inch squares. Using lightly floured hands, pick up a piece of cut dough and very carefully with your thumb and forefinger indent the center of the dough on both sides. Working in batches of six, place directly into the salted simmering water. Let the dumplings cook just until they float to the surface and then remove with a slotted kitchen spoon to a platter. Repeat with the remaining dough. Heat the melted butter in a large nonstick skillet over medium heat and add the pierogi one by one shaking the skillet often. Saute for about 2 minutes on one side until lightly browned then using a kitchen tong, flip the pierogi over and brown on the other side for another 2 minutes until lightly browned. Place a cover over the skillet for exactly one minute then remove and season the tops with freshly ground black pepper to serve.

Tavern Pan Sinkers

MAKES ABOUT 20 TO 24 PIECES

I love Mom and Pop taverns, you know the ones that are full of chachkis, and that serve (help-yourself) lunch at the end of the bar. Years back, I helped a few ailing local joints boost their lunch sales by creating Tavern Sinkers, a great alternative to the laborious Kopytka. Potatoes, bread and seasoning are combined, quickly poached and then sauteed in melted butter and covered with savory topping to produce a real working mans gut sinker. Trust me, cops and yuppies love them!

INGREDIENTS

1 cup dry mashed potatoes, chilled
1/2 cup all-purpose flour
1 teaspoon farina
1 thick slice homemade white bread, crumbled
1 large whole egg
2 tablespoons unsalted butter, melted
Large dash of Tabasco
1/2 teaspoon sea salt
1/4 teaspoon black pepper
Large dash of nutmeg
Large dash of garlic powder
Large dash of onion powder

4 tablespoons unsalted butter, melted
1 Recipe Savory Polish topping

2 quarts lightly salted water
1 tablespoon olive oil

Heat 2 quarts of lightly salted water to boiling, add the olive oil and then reduce to a slow simmer. In a large mixing bowl, combine the potatoes, flour, farina, bread, egg, butter, Tabasco and seasoning. Using your hands, mix the dough until well blended. Turn the mixture out on to a lightly floured work surface and knead the dough until it becomes semi-stiff to the touch. (It's okay to add a little more flour to the dough, but not too much. The mixture will always feel pasty.) Using floured hands, pinch off about a walnut size piece and roll it into a ball. Now place the ball on to a clean work surface and roll until it forms a 2 1/2 -inch long finger. Repeat with the rest of the dough, cook in the salted, simmering water until they float to the surface and then cook for 2 minutes more. Remove the dumplings with a slotted kitchen spoon to a platter. In a large nonstick skillet, heat the butter, add the dumplings and cook over medium low heat for 2 to 3 minutes on each side until golden brown. When the dumplings are browned, sprinkle on the savory Polish topping and serve immediately.

Savory Polish Topping

MAKES ABOUT 1 CUP

INGREDIENTS
- 1/4 cup unsalted butter, melted
- 1 slice hickory smoked bacon, minced
- 2 large garlic cloves, minced
- 1 small onion, finely diced
- 1 cup fresh breadcrumbs

INGREDIENTS
- 2 hard boiled eggs, diced
- 2 tablespoons parsley, minced
- 1/4 cup dill, minced
- Dash of sea salt and black pepper

In a large non-stick skillet, heat the butter, add the bacon and cook for exactly 1 minute. Add the garlic and onion and cook for another 2 minutes until the onion is slightly soft. Now add the rest of the ingredients and gently toss the skillet until the mixture is well blended.

Da Wife's Plate "O" Potato Pancakes

SERVES 4

Polish soul food at its best! Who can resist a heaping platter of freshly made crispy-edged, lightly seasoned potato pancakes. Don't forget to pass around the applesauce and sour cream.

INGREDIENTS
- 4 large baking potatoes, peeled and chopped
- 1 small onion, peeled and chopped
- 2 large whole eggs
- 1 teaspoon sea salt
- 1/2 teaspoon black pepper
- 1/4 teaspoon baking powder
- Dash of Tabasco
- 2 teaspoons garlic puree
- 4 tablespoons parsley, minced
- 2 tablespoons all-purpose flour

SEASONED OIL
- 2 slices hickory smoked bacon, minced
- 3 large garlic cloves, chopped
- 6 black peppercorns, crushed
- 1 cup canola oil

First make the seasoned oil by heating a small skillet and sauteing the bacon until it starts to render its fat and turns lightly golden brown. Add the garlic and black peppercorns to the skillet and stir cook for exactly 1 minute. Add the canola oil, bring to a simmer and then remove from the fire. Let the mixture cool for 1 hour and strain until needed. Pre-heat the oven to 400°. Place the potatoes and onions into the work bowl of a food processor fitted with a steel blade, cover and process until finely chopped and smooth. Place the potato pulp into a medium sized fine mesh strainer over a large bowl to drain off any excess water. (Use a spatula to carefully push down on the potato mixture to remove the excess liquid.) In a separate bowl, whisk together the eggs, salt, pepper, baking powder, Tabasco, garlic, flour and parsley. Using the spatula, quickly combine the potato-onion puree with the egg mixture until fully incorporated and set aside. Heat a large griddle over medium high heat and when hot, spoon on some of the seasoned oil. Using a soup spoon, take about 2 tablespoons of the pancake mix, place on to the griddle, lightly flatten with the back of the spoon and cook for a minute or 2 until golden brown on one side. Using a spatula, flip the pancake over, lightly flatten, brown on the other side and then remove to a parchment lined sheet pan. When all the potato pancakes are browned, place the sheet pan in the hot oven to crisp for about 10 to 15 minutes. Remove to a serving platter and serve with sour cream and apple sauce.

CHI-TOWN PIZZA

PIZZA

RECIPES

Man, ask any Chicagoan what's the greatest triumph to the Chicago food scene over the past century and the answer is undoubtedly deep dish pizza, hot dogs, and Italian beef in that order, and I agree. Nowhere outside of the states will you ever find a more fervent devotion to the Italian pizza pie, and that translates to "a lot of dough," so to speak. Here's a little pizza history.

Food historians note that the tomato was introduced to the Italians around 1522, hundreds of years before it was ever actually used on a baked pizza. The true beginnings of pizza making can be clearly traced to a small baking shop in Naples named Port Alba, circa 1830. In 1889, King Umberto I made a visit to Naples with his wife, Queen Margherita, and decided to sample the much talked about new dish. Not one for dining with the peasant folks, the Queen requested that the pizza be brought up to the palace. Raffaele Esposito, owner of the famed pizzeria Pietro Il Pizzaiolo, and his wife, Pasqualina Brandi, prepared an assortment of pizzas in honor of the Queen's request and hurried up to the palace with them in a make-shift heated container. The Queen was elated with the pies and chose as her favorite the simplest one, which consisted of tomatoes, mozzarella and fresh basil. The dish was quickly crowned Pizza Margherita, and the Espositos went down in history as inventing pizza delivery. It took royalty to bring pizza to the forefront; however Napolitanos had been eating pizza for hundreds of years before that.

The actual first pizzeria in the United States was opened in 1905 in New York City by Gennaro Lombardi, who first made his baking-pan style pizza pie for family and friends. However, the real demand wasn't fueled until G.I.s who were returning home from tours in southern Italy after World War II (1941-1945) needed a pizza pie fix. These determined soldiers scoured the Italian neighborhoods and their bakeries in hopes of replicating the beloved pizza that they enjoyed while overseas. It wasn't until the 1950s that the rest of America caught on. Celebrities of Italian heritage such as, Frank Sinatra, Jimmy Durante, Joe DiMaggio and Dean Martin all sang the praise "when the moon hits your eye, like a big pizza pie, that's amore." From that point on, red-checkered tabletop pizzerias began to flourish around the country, serving thin crust pizzas.

Many of the pizzerias on the Northwest and South Side of Chicago have held on to the thin crust pizza making tradition, but the true innovators of Chicago style deep dish were Ike Sewell and Ric Riccardo, who in 1943 opened a restaurant called Pizzeria Uno. Their restaurant specialized in a concoction that we now know as Chicago style deep dish pizza. The concept was simple. The pizza starts with a thin layer of dough laid in a deep, well-seasoned pizza pan with its sides pulled. It's then topped with a heavy layer of mozzarella cheese, your choice of meat or vegetables and then a layer of seasoned crushed tomatoes. Baked for a good 40 minutes and served directly from the pan at your table, this is no ordinary pizza because it is then eaten with a knife and fork. I guarantee you that 1 to 2 slices are more than substantial for any hearty appetite. In 1974, Rocco Palese of Nancy's pizza fame, refined the deep dish style further by introducing the stuffed pizza. Based on one of his mother's recipes for Italian Easter pie, Rocco added a thin layer of dough above the cheese and below the tomatoes to create a somewhat firmer pizza. Other innovators such as Edwardo's and Giordano's took the concept even further by introducing spinach-stuffed style pizzas.

To give an opinion on who has the best pizza in Chicago would be foolish since there are thousands of pizzerias, with as many crusts, dough, toppings, and sauces all prepared with an abundance of affection. An interesting fact is that at this time Chicagoans are going through a transition period in regards to the pizza that they prefer. Old-fashioned thin crust pizza is replacing the heavier stuffed types. The south and northwest sides are leading the revolution by producing a non-rimmed, thin pizza that is crisp edged and slightly foldable. The pre-baked, mass-marketed cracker crust days are over. I personally think that a big part of the allure of eating pizza is not only the pie, but the joint where you're eating. My wife and I have always favored the small storefront types with the dim lighting, Chianti bottles and fake grapes hanging from the ceilings. We always laugh because it reminds us of past parties we've attended in our cousin's basements. Not only is it the anticipation of the pizza to arrive, but the ritual and atmosphere which make it a complete experience. My family enjoys sitting at a booth, munching on some antipasto salad, and re-arranging the mandatory shakers of cheese and hot pepper to make way for the pizza that is always cut into canape size squares. Ah! And don't forget the wafting smell of oregano, basil and garlic that seems to permeate all your senses and get the juices flowing! I also have fond memories of eating homemade pizza at my Italian in-laws' home, and I have come to the realization that if the experience feels like mama's kitchen, that's the way it should be.

In the process of writing this book, I was constantly confronted by every pizza aficionado I know as to who has the best pizza, New York or Chicago? The answer is very simple; both are equally good, but we are dealing with two different schools of thought. New Yorkers brag about their deep-rooted pizza history and foldable chewy slices that are usually pre-prepared and held under heat lamps until ordered. (a big no-no in Chicago). You might catch us walking around with a hot dog and a beer but never a folded slice! Also, New Yorkers got their first taste of an authentic Neapolitan-style pizza cooked in ancient coal-fired ovens that were brought over by Italian immigrants. This method imparts a smoky taste and slightly charred crust that as of yet just hasn't been duplicated in Chicago. Some have tried but many have failed. On the other side of the coin, my beloved Chicago has evolved from a thin crust cracker-like tradition into a deep dish kind of town. Long waits, loosened belts, and fork and knife are the norm to enjoy this delectable, made-to-order, soul-satisfying creation. Next time you get on a plane at O'Hare, look and see what the out-of-towners are bringing on board for lunch; you guessed it -- deep dish!

Throughout my travels, I am always asked if I have recipes for that great pizza you get in Chicago. In my earlier years, I worked for a couple of pizzerias on the Northwest side and then refined my pizza-

making techniques while learning from my mother-in-law and her twin sister, who taught me the art of the pan pizza (Sicilian style). It's with this knowledge that I give you the following really great Chicago-style pizza recipes that you can make at home.

Classic Chicago Pizza

Most aficionados outside of Italy will concede that Chicago has the best pizza. New York style is good with its crisp-edged foldable and greasy slices, but most of their pies are pre-cooked and heat-lamp warmed, which is a big no-no in Chicago. The West coast offers up a crunchy and light 8-inch goat cheese and smoked salmon infused concoction that would never be served at any respectable tavern around this city. As noted in the introduction, classic Chicago style pizza was actually a by-product of some of the city's oldest and still surviving Italian bakeries dating back to the early 1900s. Pizzerias in the Windy City are usually small mom and pop joints that daily knock out to order a variety of crisp-crusted and spicy, delectable pizzas traditionally cut into canape style squares rather than wedges.

Typically, Chicago has five different styles of pizza:

1. Extra thin and crispy baked without a dough border. A south side tradition.

2. Northwest side, which is thin and crispy with a 1/2-inch thick crust and a hand-pressed border.

3. Pan pizza a/k/a Sicilian style a/k/a bakery style pizza, which has a 1-inch thick crust and is usually baked in a 12 x 16 inch heavy-duty rectangular sheet pan. The springy, chewy crust has a soft and subtle texture and is sparsely topped with spicy tomato sauce, olive oil and mozzarella cheese. This weekend bakery specialty is usually cut into 4 x 4 inch squares with large kitchen shears and is typically eaten at room temperature.

4. Chicago-style deep dish, which is baked in a high-sided non-stick pan, layered with mozzarella cheese and Italian sausage, then topped off with plum tomatoes and fresh Romano cheese. This is usually 1 1/2 inches thick.

5. Stuffed pizza, which consists of two layers of dough that are stuffed with savory ingredients, typically spinach or broccoli and mozzarella cheese, topped with homemade pizza sauce and Romano cheese and then baked.

Pizzerias around Chicago also have their own in-house specialty items such as double dough or thick crust pizzas. There is a concoction called the double-decker which is a pizza baked on top of another pizza. Also there are seasoned crusts and cheese-filled crust dough, and another variation is a specialty from 26th street which consists of a pizza baked with a crust on top. I also enjoy a Calabrese Stromboli and a sausage and cheese-filled calzone.

Favorite Pizza Combinations

Everyone has a favorite combination of pizza toppings, so I thought I would give you a list of the most popular around Chicago.

Chi-town Favorite - Cheese, sausage, mushroom, green pepper and onion.

Chicago Seven - Cheese, sausage, mushroom, onion, green pepper, black olives and pepperoni.

Pizza Monster - Cheese, sausage, pepperoni, bacon, ground beef, mushroom, onion, green pepper, green olives and black olives.

That S.O.B. - Cheese, sausage, onion and bacon.

Luke's Special - Cheese, Italian beef and hot giardinera.

BBQ Chicken - Grilled chicken breast, red onion, red pepper, black olives, Colby cheese, mozzarella and barbeque sauce.

Taco - Seasoned ground beef, green onion, black olives, tomatoes, cheddar cheese, mozzarella, salsa, sour cream and jalapenos.

Western BBQ - Cheese, sausage, pepperoni, bacon, onion and barbeque sauce.

Vegetarian - Spinach, mushrooms, onion, green pepper, tomato, zucchini, broccoli and garlic.

Spinach Supreme - Spinach, ricotta, mozzarella and Italian spices.

Ingredients

Great Pizza can only be achieved by using superior products. My ingredient list is pretty straightforward and will help guide you through the readily available foodstuffs you should use.

Flour - Undoubtedly, the backbone of any great pizza is the quality of the flour that is used to make the crust. Typically, pizza restaurants around Chicago use a bleached all-purpose flour that consists of a protein level of about 10.5 to 12.5 %. Flour is usually categorized as either strong or weak. A higher protein level results in higher gluten levels which make the dough strong and elastic when mixed with water. Bread flour is usually rated between 12 to 14 % protein, which is similar to the flour used in Italy by pizza makers. They prefer to use 00-grade hard flour that makes a great pizza, although the dough must be mixed in a heavy-duty mixer for a very long time. I have found that using bread flour will result in dough that is not very tender nor is it easy to roll out.

For the home pizza maker, I recommend using all-purpose flour which typically has a protein level of 10.5 to 11.5 %. I find that all-purpose flour is easier to work with than bread flour and it will give your pizza a nice, mellow, chewy crust. I've had a lot of good luck using King Arthur brand all-purpose flour at 11.7% or Gold Medal unbleached at 10.5%.

Yeast - Yeast is the fuel that gives pizza dough that subtle rise when mixed with flour, water and a little sugar. Yeast, a living organism, counter attacks and eats the natural sugar that is present in flour, and this creates carbon dioxide or natural gas which expands the gluten structure that gives the dough its lift and flavor.

There are many types of yeast on the market, but I prefer to use regular Red Star granular in the jar that should be stored in the freezer to keep fresh. I recommend that you use a scant 1/2 teaspoon of yeast per every cup of flour used in pizza dough. I like to make the dough the night before to let it rise slowly in the refrigerator over night. (Trust me, it makes all the difference.) Modern technology has made it easier to use yeast so there is no need for pre-proofing. Water temperature is very important to the yeast when mixing a batch of fresh dough. The proper temperature should be between 105°F and 115° F. If the water is too cold or too hot, the yeast can be destroyed. Also another good piece of advice is to check the expiration date on a package or jar to make sure that the yeast is fresh.

Water - Throughout the years, a lot of fuss has been made as to which city has the best water for making pizza dough. The truth of the matter is that if your water department purifies your tap water using chlorine and/or fluoride, it could greatly affect the flavor of your pizza dough, and also may inhibit proper development of the yeast. If in doubt, I recommend buying a gallon of spring water to use to make the dough.

Tomatoes - Depending on where you live in the country, canned tomato products can vary widely in taste and texture. Some canneries add too much liquid to the tomatoes and others harvest the tomatoes before they're ripe. I've experimented with jarred spaghetti sauces and have found that most are too bitter to use on pizza! Many chefs I know in Chicago prefer to use a tomato product called Six in One which is a combination of whole and crushed tomatoes; however, I've had a lot of success in using canned plum tomatoes by San Marzano, Contadina, Muir Glen, S&W and Progresso. The larger companies seem to have better quality control when processing their product. Most of my Italian friends grow their own plum tomatoes during the summer, which they like to use instead of canned, but the tomatoes have to be peeled, seeded and passed through a food mill before you can use them. This is a lot of work. Homemade pizza sauce should always be simmered slowly with a few aromatic Italian herbs to heighten the tomato flavor.

Cheese - Pizzerias in Chicago use two types of cheese. The first is mozzarella that is made from cow's milk. All grocery stores sell whole milk or part-skim, low-moisture mozzarella. Taste testers prefer the richness of the whole milk over the skim variety. I recommend that you buy a one- pound chunk and hand grate or finely chop in a food processor to get the cheese at an even-sized cooking consistency. One-pound grated will yield about 4 heaping cups. The other cheese that is most often used is Pecorino Romano, which is made from sheep's milk. Romano cheese is similar to Parmesan, but has a sharper and less salty taste. I also recommend that you buy a small whole chunk and grind it yourself in a food processor. If you are a real cheese head, try combining equal parts of mozzarella and provolone when making your pizza for added flavor.

Beautiful!!

Sicilian Bakery Pie

Feta Salad

Hot Steaks

Pachki

Meatball Pho

Fried Shrimp

Vic's Vesuvio

Greek Plate

Stromboli

Chicago Style Dogs

Carne Asada Taco Plate

Fran's Beef Casserole

Stuffed Pizza

Posole

Busia's Pierogi

Cheesecake

Mike's Ribs

Pam's Challah

Polish Plate

Good Italian Beef

Egusi Stew

My Kid's Buffet

Fries and Char Polish

Farmer's Market

Bi Color Corn

Bade Farms

October Sunshine

Indian Corn

Illinois Gourds

Breaking Bread

Hot Cherry Bombs

McIntosh and Honey Crisp

Nice Peaches!

Farmer's Market

Beans and Cucs

Sweet Peppers

Blueberry Lady

Corn Stalks

Preserves

Fingerlings

Huge Oyster Mushroom

Root Vegetables

Cherry Tomatoes

Maxwell Street Market

Menu 3

Food Stall

Hispanic Produce

Chili Spice

Crispy Masa

Best in the City

Excellent Meat Fillings

Antojito Frying Station

Tamarindos

Maxwell Street Market

Foxy Chica Zapatas

Cool Kid!

Maxwell Street Overview

Chicago Blues

Classic Maxwell Street

Good Stuff

Mother Mary

Balloons

Praise

Milwaukee Avenue Rye Bread

Risen Dough

Let's Go

Flatten

Fold and Crimp

Repeat

Crimp Ends

Let Rise

Slash Top

Crispy Baked

Making Balice Bread

Good Puffy Dough

Don't Flatten

Cut Dough

Slightly Stretch

Crimp and Crease

Perfect Middle Fold

Ready to Bake

Spritz

Excellent Job!

Making Chicago Style Ribs

Pork Spare Ribs

Underbelly Fat

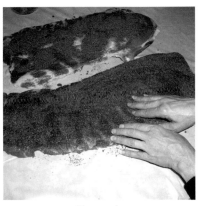

Remove Fat

Mike's Rib Rub

Cover Slabs

Massage In

Indirect Cooking

Nice and Basted

My Rib Buffet

Sicilian Bakery Pan Pizza

Punch Dough

Roll Out

Puffy Edges

Sauce Top

Romano Cheese

Mozzarella Cheese!

Apply Topping

Pre-baked

Sicilian Bakery Pie

Making Cabbage Pierogi

Flatten Dough

Roll Out

Place Filling

Fold Over Dough

Cut and Crimp

Sheet Pan and Repeat

Easy Simmer

Quick Pan Fry

Busia's Favorite

Auntie Fran's Italian Beef

Beef Set Up

Brown Meats

Juice Seasonings

Flavor Meats

Add Stock

Before Baking

After Baking

Slice Er Up!

Outstanding Beef Sandwich!

Chicago Style Deep Dish

Oil Pan

Roll Dough

Crimp Edges

Fork Bottom

Layer Cheese and Sauce

Sausage and Seasonings

Oven Baked

Cool in Pan

Deep Dish Slice

Stromboli 1, 2, 3

Roll Dough

Sauce and Cheese

Layer Meats

Grasp

Roll Over

Slash, Oil, Season

Oven Baked

Really Nice!

Ready to Eat

Toppings - When it comes to toppings, I have to admit that I'm a purist and I have never gone for the wackiness of pineapple, sun-dried tomatoes or goat cheese. To satisfy an ever increasing pizza-demanding and health- conscious audience, pizzerias around Chicago have incorporated dozens of added ingredients which you will handsomely pay for. To give you an example, here's a list of favorite toppings that can be found on local menus: cheese, sausage, ground beef, roast beef, pepperoni, bacon, Canadian bacon, ham, anchovy, shrimp, tuna, grilled chicken, artichoke hearts, eggplant, olives, mushrooms, green peppers, onion, garlic, zucchini, broccoli, tomatoes, spinach and ricotta, pineapple, giardiniera, pepperoncinis and jalapenos. If you get the urge to add any of the vegetables, I highly recommend that you cut them into uniform size pieces and saute them up in a little bit of olive oil until slightly softened, and then cool before adding them to the pizza.

Seasonings - There are only three seasonings that I recommend for Chicago style pizza, and if used judiciously, they can really make your pizza shine. The three vespers are dried oregano, basil and freshly ground black pepper. I usually sprinkle the three on top of the cheese sparingly before I bake the pizza to give it that extra kick.

Oil - There is always a lot of confusion as to what is the proper oil to use when making pizza dough. So let me set the record straight. Some olive oils are too heavy to use in the making of pizza dough and could actually give the dough a heady, weird aftertaste if the oil isn't fresh or of good quality. I like to use a Bertolli brand extra light, Colavita, or Filippo Berio. If you would like to save money, you can always brush your pizza pans with a good canola oil which has a clean and consistent taste.

Pizza-Making Equipment

If you're going to play the game, you have to have the right equipment! Pizza making does require some special tools, but don' fear because measuring cups, mixing bowls, and pans can be found at all major stores and restaurant supply houses.

Pizza dough can easily be made by hand, but if you can afford them, I recommend two other tools, a food processor and a mixer.

Cuisinart, 11 cup capacity - Probably the easiest machine to make dough, and here's how it works. Combine flour, yeast, salt, honey, and oil into the work bowl of the food processor fitted with a metal blade. With the machine running, pour the warm water through the feed tube and process until the dough forms a ball, about 30 seconds. Remove the dough from the machine, knead slightly on a counter top and it's ready to rise.

Kitchen aid heavy - duty stand mixer, 5 qt. capacity - If you've got the "dough," I recommend buying a stand mixer with the dough hook attachments. You can easily knock out a dozen batches of dough in under an hour to freeze for later use.

For baking, there's a wide assortment of pans you can use.

Baking Stones - 14 x 16 inch pizza baking squares are great if your oven has the space to accommodate them. The porous material of the stone heats up very quickly while drawing the moisture out of the dough, leaving a crisp bottom crust.

Pizza Peel - If you're going to use the stone, you will need a peel to construct and slide the pizza off of it. Sixteen-inch wood peels work best and should always be heavily dusted with cornmeal before adding the dough to ensure a good slide onto the stone.

Baking Parchment Paper - Let Mikey give you a cool chef's tip. If you're worried about sliding the dough off of a pizza peel, first roll your dough out onto a large, lightly floured piece of parchment paper, then slip the pizza peel underneath the paper, and then slide the prepared pizza, parchment paper and all, on to the baking stone. When the pizza's cooked, slide the peel underneath the parchment paper again and safely remove from the oven.

Pizza Screen - An excellent invention for the home pizza maker. The round screens are made of heavy-gauge wire mesh with a thick metal tape border. The screen is first brushed with oil, then the dough is shaped on top. The mesh actually holds the dough into place, and the best part is that you can place the screen directly onto an oven shelf or baking stone to cook.

Pizza Pans - Everyone owns at least one good, round, old pizza pan that they use for Saturday night pizza. I recommend finding one that is 14 - 16 inches round, slightly heavy-duty type metal, and preferably the kind with a million different holes drilled into the bottom that allows direct heat to reach the crust.

Deep Pizza Pans - A must for baking deep-dish pizza. Cake pans are too flimsy so try to find a 1 1/2 - 2 inch deep heavy-gauge dark-metal pan. (Best bought at a restaurant supply house, and the darker the pan the better.) Pans with a removable bottom are great to release a stuck pizza pie.

Note!!! New deep-dish pizza pans must be seasoned before being used. First, wash the new pan with warm soapy water, then dry. Pour a tablespoon of vegetable oil into the bottom of the pan and using a paper towel, rub the oil evenly around the bottom and the sides. Now place the pan into a preheated 350° oven for 45 minutes, then remove, cool and wipe out the oil with another paper towel. Before using the pan again, apply another tablespoon of oil.

Plastic Measuring Bucket - Let me turn you on to another cool chef's trick. I like to let my dough rise in a small, lightly oiled, 4 quart, see-through measuring bucket with a tight fitting lid. After you mix your dough, place it into the measuring bucket, clamp on the lid, and just leave the bucket on the counter to let the dough rise until doubled. Since the bucket is marked, it takes all the guesswork out of when the dough is ready.

Chef Mike's Top Ten Pizza Pointers

1. Re-read my pizza intros and procedures before beginning.

2. Use only high-quality all-purpose flour and make sure the yeast is fresh and has not expired. Also, be sure to properly measure your ingredients.

3. Always let the dough rest overnight and rise in the fridge to relax the gluten. The next day remove the dough from the refrigerator for at least 2 to 3 hours to come to room temperature before using.

4. Use a high-quality tomato product when making the pizza sauce.

5. Never buy pre-grated cheese. Always grate your own fresh.

6. Have all your toppings prepared and cut ahead of time, ready to dress on top of the pizza.

7. Clean off your countertops and have all your pizza utensils ready to rock and roll.

8. Calibrate and pre-heat your oven for at least 20 minutes to ensure proper crispness.

9. Don't open the oven door while the pizzas are cooking.

10. Remove the hot cooked pizza to a large cooling rack for 3 to 4 minutes before cutting.

To be honest with you there are more pizza recipes around then there are Italians living in Norridge and Elmwood Park, and that translates to a lot of handed down Mama's recipes. If there's one thing that I have learned over 25 years of professional cooking is that consistency and proper measuring are key to any baked product. With a little care and patience, you to can become a pizza maker and impress your family and friends. This chapter contains the master recipes that I have been using for years with great success. I've updated them to conform to current industry standards and the proportions are accurate, so don't fool with them too much.

Basic Pizza Dough

MAKES 2 14-INCH PIZZAS

INGREDIENTS

4 cups all-purpose flour
1 1/2 cups warm water 105 to 115F
1 teaspoon sea salt
2 teaspoons yeast
1 1/2 teaspoons honey
2 tablespoons olive oil

To make the dough by hand

In a large mixing bowl combine the flour, salt and yeast. Make a well in the center the of the flour mixture, then pour in the water, honey and oil. Using a wooden spoon vigorously stir the flour mixture into the well, beginning in the center and working towards the sides of the bowl until the flour mixture is incorporated and just begins to hold together. Now turn the dough out on to a lightly floured work surface and using the heel of your hands, knead the dough gently by pushing it slightly away from you on the counter. Fold it back over itself and keep kneading for 8 to 10 minutes until the dough is smooth and elastic. If the dough seems sticky sprinkle on a little extra flour. Form the dough into a ball, place into a lightly oiled plastic container, and cover until risen and doubled in size, about 1 1/2 to 2 hours.

Food Processor Dough

Place the flour, salt, yeast, honey and oil in the processor bowl with the metal blade attached, attach the lid, and process 5 seconds to mix the ingredients. Now slowly with the machine running, pour the water through the feed tube until the dough forms a single ball, about 30 seconds. If the dough seems too sticky and won't come together add a little bit more flour through the feed tube until it does. If the dough seems too dry add 1 to 2 tablespoons more of water until the dough comes together. Remove the ball to a lightly floured work surface, hand knead for 1 minute then place into an oiled plastic container and cover until risen and doubled in size, about 1 1/2 to 2 hours.

Heavy-Duty Stand Mixer Dough

In the mixer bowl add the flour, salt, yeast, honey and oil. Attach the flat beater, put the machine on to low speed, and with the machine running, slowly add the water until it forms a shaggy mass around the paddle, about

I minute. Now replace the flat beater with the dough hook, and knead at medium speed until the dough is smooth and elastic and forms a round ball, around 4 to 5 minutes. If the dough seems sticky and won't form a ball add a little bit more flour until it does. If the dough seems too dry add 1 to 2 tablespoons more of water until the dough comes together. Remove the ball to a lightly floured work surface, hand knead for 1 minute, then place into an oiled plastic container and cover until risen and doubled in size, about 1 1/2 to 2 hours.

Sicilian Bakery Pan Dough   MAKES 1 GENEROUS 12 BY 16-INCH PAN

INGREDIENTS

6 cups all-purpose flour
2 1/4 cups warm water 105 to 115F
2 teaspoons sea salt
2 1/2 teaspoons yeast
1 tablespoon honey
1/4 cup olive oil

Knead the dough according to any of the methods above, and then place into an oiled plastic container, and cover until risen and doubled in size, about 1 1/2 to 2 hours.

Deep Dish Pizza Dough   MAKES 1 14-INCH DEEP DISH PAN

INGREDIENTS

3 1/2 cups all-purpose flour
1/2 cup corn meal
1 1/4 cup warm water 105 to 115F
1 teaspoon sea salt
2 teaspoons yeast
2 teaspoons honey
5 tablespoons canola oil

Knead the dough according to any of the methods above, and then place into an oiled plastic container and cover until risen and doubled in size about 1 1/2 to 2 hours. (A dash of egg shade food color can be added to the mixing dough to give it a deeper golden hue.)

Calzone Dough

INGREDIENTS

4 cups bread flour
1 1/2 cups warm water 105 to 115 F
1 teaspoon sea salt
2 teaspoons yeast
1 1/2 teaspoons honey
2 tablespoons olive oil

Knead the dough according to any of the methods above, and then place into an oiled plastic container and cover until risen and doubled in size, about 1 1/2 to 2 hours.

PIZZA SAUCES

I like to use three different types of sauce when making pizza. Each one is completely different depending on what pie you have a taste for. Pizza sauce should always be simmered slowly with a few aromatic Italian herbs to heighten the tomato flavor. I prefer to use tomato puree instead of canned plum tomatoes for my sauce because I don't like chunky bits of tomato topping on my pizza, but feel free to substitute a 28 ounce can of Italian style plum tomatoes if you like. Just remember to lightly crush the plum tomatoes before adding them to the pot.

Pizzeria Pizza Sauce

INGREDIENTS

One 28oz. can tomato puree
2 tablespoons olive oil
1 teaspoon sea salt
1 teaspoon dried basil
1 teaspoon dried oregano
1 teaspoon parsley flakes
2 tablespoons Pecorino Romano
   cheese
Dash of red pepper flakes

Place all of the ingredients into a small non-stick cooking pot and simmer slowly for 20 minutes. Cool before using.

Sicilian Spicy Pizza Sauce

MAKES ABOUT 3 CUPS OR
ENOUGH SAUCE FOR TWO 14-INCH PIZZAS

INGREDIENTS

1 tablespoon olive oil
2 small garlic cloves, minced
1 anchovy fillet, chopped
1/3 cup dry red wine
One 28oz. can tomato puree
1 teaspoon dried basil
1/2 teaspoon dried oregano
1/2 teaspoon garlic powder
1/2 teaspoon onion powder
1/8 teaspoon black pepper
Dash of red pepper flakes
2 tablespoons pecorino Romano cheese

Heat the oil in a small sauce pan, and sauté the garlic and anchovy for 2 minutes, then add the rest of the ingredients and simmer for 20 minutes slowly. Cool before using.

Seasoned Plum Tomato Pulp

MAKES 2 1/2 TO 3 CUPS

Plum tomato pulp is generally used in deep dish or stuffed pizza. I highly recommend that you track down a brand of canned plum tomatoes imported from Italy called San Marzano. They are the ultimate Italian canned tomato product and can be found at Italian food markets around the city.

INGREDIENTS

Two 28 ounce cans Italian style plum
  tomatoes
2 tablespoons olive oil
3 large garlic cloves, minced
1 teaspoon dried basil
1 teaspoon dried oregano
2 tablespoons parsley, chopped
1/2 teaspoon sea salt
1/4 teaspoon black pepper
Dash of red pepper flakes

Drain the tomatoes into a colander to remove all excess juices and seeds, then carefully using your hands, lightly crush and open the tomatoes and drain again. Heat the oil in a small saucepan, and sauté the garlic for 1 minute, then add the rest of the ingredients and simmer slowly for 12 to 15 minutes. Cool before using.

Pizza Sausage

No Chicago style pizza would be complete without the addition of a spicy Italian sausage that is sold at meat markets throughout the city. Italian sausage is usually sold in two forms in the casing, either mild or hot. All you have to do is remove the ground sausage from the casing and apply it in quarter size pieces to the top of your pizza before it goes in the oven. For you paesans or out-of-towners who complain that you can't get good Chicago style pizza sausage, here's a great recipe.

INGREDIENTS

2 1/2 pounds pork butt, cubed
1 1/8 teaspoon sea salt
1 1/2 teaspoon pepper
1 1/2 teaspoon fennel seeds
A large pinch of red pepper flakes

Combine all the ingredients in a mixing bowl, and then run through a medium plate on a meat grinder or process until semi-chunky in a food processor. Refrigerate or freeze until needed.

Now that you have the master pizza recipes, it's time to get into the kitchen and cook some pizzas. All you need to do is have all the basic ingredients together and ready before you begin.

Basic "Chi-town Favorite" Pizza

MAKES 2 14-INCH PIZZAS

Every pizza joint in the city bakes this all-time classic combination of onion, green pepper, mushroom and sausage. It's been a favorite of mine for years and it's easy to prepare.

INGREDIENTS

1 recipe Basic pizza dough
1 recipe Pizzeria pizza sauce
1 pound mozzarella cheese, shredded
1/4 cup pecorino romano cheese, grated

2 tablespoons olive oil
1 medium onion, diced
1 medium green pepper, diced
1/2 pound domestic mushrooms, sliced

3/4 pound Italian sausage, casing removed
Dried oregano, dried basil, black pepper

Pre-heat the oven to 475°F. In a small skillet heat the olive oil and sauté the onion and green peppers for about 3 to 4 minutes, then add the mushrooms and continue cooking until all of the liquid has evaporated. Brush each pizza pan with olive oil. On a lightly floured surface, divide the dough into 2 equal pieces. Gently flatten the cut dough with your hand, flip it over, and using the heel of your hands, press the dough into a rough circle about 1/4-inch thick. Now using a rolling pin, roll the dough into the desired shape and place on top of the pans. Using your fingers, crimp the edges of the dough to create a decorative border, then cover the pans with a kitchen towel to rest for 20 minutes. (The longer you let the dough rest, the thicker and higher your crust will be.) Using a kitchen spoon divide the pizza sauce equally among each pizza, then sprinkle on the romano. Equally spread the vegetable mixture over each pizza, then sprinkle on the mozzarella cheese. Using your fingers, place quarter size pieces of sausage over the pies. Season with the herbs and bake on the bottom rack of the oven for 10 to 12 minutes until the crust and cheese are golden brown.

Sicilian Bakery Pan Pizza MAKES 1 GENEROUS 12 BY 16-INCH PAN

"Pan style pizza" was originally created by local Italian bakeries who didn't want to throw out extra dough that was left over at the end of the day. Some bakeries let the dough rise 1 to 2 inches high and then top with savory Italian ingredients to the delight of their customers.

INGREDIENTS

1 recipe Sicilian bakery pan dough
1 recipe Sicilian spicy pizza sauce
1 pound mozzarella cheese, shredded
1/3 cup pecorino romano cheese, grated
Dried oregano, dried basil, black pepper
1/4 cup olive oil

Pre-heat the oven to 450°F. Brush the baking pan with olive oil. Place your pan dough on a lightly floured work surface but do not punch it down. Now using a small rolling pin, gently push the dough into a rectangular shape until you feel it is the size of the pan. Carefully lift the dough into the pan, and using your fingers push the dough into all the corners. (If the dough is difficult to handle don't worry, if you let it rest for 4 or 5 minutes it will be easier to mold.) Cover the pan with a kitchen towel and let it rest for 30 minutes. (The longer you let the dough rest, the thicker and higher your crust will be.) Using a kitchen spoon spread the pizza sauce evenly over the dough being sure to leave a 1/2-inch border. Sprinkle on the romano and mozzarella cheeses, and then lightly season with the herbs. Now drizzle on the olive oil and bake on the second rack from the bottom for 20 to 25 minutes until the crust is golden brown.

Chicago Style Deep Dish with Sausage

The "Big Mac Daddy" of pizza in Chicago. Deep dish was invented with the blue collar working man's appetite in mind, so be forewarned when you pull up to the dinner table. Loosen your belt and keep your chair back an extra 3 inches.

INGREDIENTS

1 recipe Deep dish dough
1 recipe Seasoned plum tomato pulp
Olive oil for brushing
3/4 pound mozzarella cheese, shredded
1/3 cup pecorino romano, grated
1/2 pound Italian sausage, casing removed

Pre-heat the oven to 475°F, and position two oven racks in the lowest and middle settings. Brush a deep dish pan with olive oil evenly coating the bottom and sides. Place the ball of dough into the pan and using your fingers, stretch the dough to completely cover the bottom, and then crimp the dough until it comes an 1 1/2 to 2- inches up the sides of the pan. (If the dough is difficult to handle don't worry, if you let it rest for 4 or 5 minutes it will be easier to mold.) Cover the pan with a kitchen towel and let it rest for 15 minutes. After 15 minutes, prick the bottom of the dough with a fork about every 1/2-inch and bake on the bottom rack for 4 to 5 minutes. Remove the pan from the oven, and drizzle a little more olive oil on top of the pricked dough. Now quickly but evenly cover the pre-cooked dough with the mozzarella cheese and then cover with the tomato pulp spreading it around with a kitchen spoon. Sprinkle on the romano cheese and top with quarter size pieces of sausage meat. Bake on the lower rack of the oven for 5 minutes, then transfer the pan to the middle oven rack for about 45 minutes until the crust is golden brown and the sausage is cooked through. Let the pie rest for 5 minutes before cutting it.

Stuffed Pizza with Spinach

The vegetarian cousin to deep dish pizza. The Sicilian name is actually "Sfinciuni" which means to have a top and a bottom then something savory baked in between. Spinach has become the classic around town but there are also variations such as broccoli stuffed.

INGREDIENTS

1 recipe Basic pizza dough
1 recipe Seasoned plum tomato pulp
1/2 pound mozzarella cheese, shredded
1/4 cup pecorino romano, grated
1/2 pound fresh spinach, cleaned, dried,
   and coarsely chopped
1 tablespoon olive oil

Pre-heat the oven to 475°F, and position two oven racks in the lowest and middle settings. Brush a deep dish pan with olive oil evenly coating the bottom and sides. On a lightly floured work surface divide the dough into two pieces, one slightly larger than the next. Using the heel of your hand, slightly flatten the larger piece into a large circle 1/8-inch thick. Then using a small rolling pin, roll it into a 13 to 14 inch circle, and carefully press the dough into the oiled pan leaving about a 1-inch overlap over the lip of the pan. (Be sure to press the dough into the bottom and sides of the pan, then trim off any excess with a sharp knife.) Now roll the second piece of dough into a 12-inch circle and set aside. To assemble the pizza, combine the mozzarella, romano, spinach and olive oil in a separate bowl, toss to mix, then pour into the dough lined pan. Lay the second piece of dough over the spinach mixture and crimp the dough's edges together to create a tight decorative border. Using a sharp knife, cut a 2-inch slit into the top of the dough for steam to escape. Now carefully using a kitchen spoon, spread about 2 cups of tomato pulp over the top of the dough and bake the pie on the lower shelf for 10 minutes. Transfer the pan to the middle rack and cook for another 25 to 30 minutes until the dough is light brown and the pizza is puffy.

Mom DeCarl's Calzone

My mother-in-law Geri has been making homemade calzones for her friends and family for years without using a recipe, and this would aggravate all of us to no end. We finally tied her down and tickled her with basil leaves until she gave it up.

INGREDIENTS

1 recipe Calzone dough

FILLING

1 pound ricotta cheese, well drained
1/2 pound mozzarella, shredded
3/4 cup Pecorino Romano, grated
1 large whole egg
2 to 3 tablespoons parsley, minced
2 teaspoons garlic, minced
1/8 teaspoon black pepper
Dash of red pepper flakes
1 tablespoon olive oil

Pre-heat the oven to 475°F. Cover a large heavy-duty sheet pan with a piece of baking parchment paper and lightly dust with a fine sprinkling of semolina or cornmeal. On a lightly floured work surface divide the dough into 4 equal pieces, then roll each one into a tight ball and cover with a kitchen towel to rest for 12 to 15 minutes. While the dough is resting, thoroughly combine all of the filling ingredients then refrigerate until needed. Using your hand, lightly flatten each dough ball and then flip them over. Now using a small rolling pin, roll out each piece into an 8 to 9-inch circle. (If the dough sticks dust flour underneath it.) Using a spoon, place 3/4 cup of the cheese filling in the center bottom half of the dough round, and using the spoon spread the filling in an even layer across the bottom half of the dough round leaving a 1-inch border uncovered. Fold the top half of the dough over the cheese covered bottom half making a half moon pie. With your fingertips, lightly press around the curved side of the dough to seal the pieces. Carefully place each calzone onto the prepared baking sheet. Now using a razor blade cut three 1 1/2-inch long slits diagonally across each calzone to release the steam while baking. Brush the top of each calzone with a little olive oil and a sprinkling of romano cheese then bake on the second to bottom shelf for 15 to 20 minutes until lightly brown and crisp. Remove the calzones to a baking rack and cool before serving about 5 minutes.

Chef's Tip If you would like a spicier calzone, sauté up in a little olive oil, 1 small onion diced, 1 medium red pepper diced and 1/2 pound bulk Italian sausage until fully cooked through. Strain out all the grease, cool, and then add to the filling mixture.

South Side Stromboli

Stromboli, which means puffed and ready to explode like a volcano is a Sicilian bread that came to Chicago via New York. Bakeries layer the dough with wonderful Italian cured meats, peppers and olives, then roll it up, bake and cool slightly before wrapping up in paper. The packages are popular in Italian neighborhoods as a quick breakfast before school. My boys like it as a cold afternoon "pick me up" before heading out to football practice.

INGREDIENTS

1 recipe Basic pizza dough
1 cup Pizzeria pizza sauce
3 tablespoons Pecorino Romano, grated
1 1/2 cups mozzarella cheese, shredded
8 deli slices Krakus ham
8 deli slices Italian Cappicola
8 deli slices Italian salami or large
   pepperoni
6 jarred red pepper slices in olive oil
   and garlic
3/4 cup pitted Italian olive salad, well
   drained and chopped, optional
6 deli slices provolone cheese

STROMBOLI SPICE

4 tablespoons Pecorino Romano, grated
1 1/4 teaspoon dried oregano
1 1/4 teaspoon dried basil
1/4 teaspoon black pepper
1/4 teaspoon garlic powder

Olive oil for brushing

Pre-heat the oven to 425°F. Cover a large heavy-duty sheet pan with a piece of baking parchment paper and lightly dust with a fine sprinkling of semolina or cornmeal. Place the pizza dough on a lightly floured work surface but do not punch it down. Now using a small rolling pin, gently push the dough out to a rectangular shape that measures 15 long by 13 inches wide about 1/4-inch thick. Starting 2-inches away from the bottom closest to you and leaving a 1-inch border around the edges, lightly spread a 3-inch band of pizza sauce horizontally across the lower half of the dough. Sprinkle the romano cheese over the tomato sauce band followed by the mozzarella cheese. On top of the cheese starting from the right to the left, layer the ham in overlapping slices until the cheese is covered. Again starting from right to left, layer on the cappicola and then the Italian salami. Repeat the process with the peppers and olive salad followed by the provolone. (You could spoon a little bit of the pepper oil over the provolone cheese before rolling up the Stromboli.) Now carefully using someone else to help, roll up the Stromboli in jelly roll fashion starting from the bottom by grabbing the 2 inches of excess dough and folding it on to the filling. Continue rolling the entire loaf until the seam is on the bottom of the dough, and then carefully lift the Stromboli and place it diagonally on the prepared sheet pan. (Do not crimp the 2 ends.) In a small bowl combine the Stromboli spice. Using a razor blade, evenly slash the top of the Stromboli 8 times making quarter inch deep cuts. Liberally brush the top of the dough with 1/4 cup olive oil, and then sprinkle on the spices. Bake in a hot oven on the second shelf from the bottom for 20 to 25 minutes until the Stromboli is lightly golden brown. Remove to a wire rack for 20 minutes to cool before slicing.

 Chef's Tip If you like your Stromboli on the light and doughy side, cover it with a kitchen towel for 20 minutes after you've rolled it up, slashed and seasoned before baking.

DAS "WIENER" SHALL RULE

HOT DOG
RECIPES

I have to admit that my northwest side upbringing has turned me into a hot dog fast food junky. Since so many stands line the street corners of the city, who could possibly resist their alluring temptation? I have memories from early childhood of whimsical dancing dogs up on rooftops and steamed window facades that bear such names as Super Dawg, Fat Johnny's, Weiner Circle, Hot Diggity Dog, Jimmy's Red Hots, Gene and Jude's, Taste Haste, Demon Dogs and Fluky's. Norwood Park, which was my neck of the woods, was like another Bermuda Triangle as it was home to such joints as Super Dawg, Taste Haste and Parse's. These places were fondly referred to as The Father, Son, and The Holy Ghost due to the fact that their mystical allure would bring in droves of patrons from miles away. In the Windy City, the boundaries of your neighborhood determine what your favorite joint is, and the easiest way to get into an argument is to proclaim that your favorite haunt is "the best." It has been 110 years since Chicago was first introduced to the wiener and its history goes back further than that. Let's take a look at some of the past and more current facts about the dog.

In 1987, Frankfurt, Germany celebrated the 500th birthday of the frankfurter, claiming ownership of the invention. However, they were not alone. Vienna, Austria also threw its towel into the ring claiming that the word wiener or "Wein" comes from their city, which is proof that the little sausage was introduced there. These two cities have also been joined by Coburg, Germany in the battle for invention rights, as many believe that butcher Johann Georghehner (circa 1650) who lived there created the "little-dog" sausage or "dachshund" and then traveled to Frankfurt to sell it. All eastern European countries at this time were producing some kinds of sausages that were typically served with a side of rustic whole meal bread. This controversy still continues with claims of who sold the first hot dog on a bun. Some say it was a German immigrant operating a pushcart stand in New York in the 1860s, while others claim it was Charles Feltman, a German Butcher, who opened an actual free-standing hot dog stand in Coney Island in 1871 and sold a whopping 3,500 hot dogs on a milk roll during his first year.

A historical fact that many are sure of is that the hot dog buns of today are much different from the milk rolls of the 1860s. One popular tale is that a Bavarian concessionaire who sold frankfurters handed out white gloves to his customers so that they wouldn't get grease on their fingers while eating their little treasure. When the gloves became too costly, he asked his baker brother-in-law for a solution, and thus the long soft roll that we now know as the hot dog bun was created! Critics balk at the glove story but agree that the bun was a European invention that evolved over time.

The actual name hot dog, however, did not come into play until April of 1901. The story goes that on a freezing cold day at the New York city polo grounds, concessionaire Harry Stevens, who sold ice cream and cold soda, was foundering with the bad weather. He sent all his vendors to local sausage shops and bakeries to gobble up all the wieners and buns they could find. By that afternoon, portable hot water cookers were set up to cook the sausages, and the vendors cheerfully shouted, "Get your hot wieners, come get your dachshund wieners!" A young sports cartoonist by the name of Tad Dorgan took notice of this new found food sensation while sitting in a press box at the game. In need of an idea to meet his deadline, he quickly drew a cartoon of "barking sausages nestled in buns," and he captioned his cartoon "Hot Dogs." Needless to say, the cartoon drew a lot of attention and the name "Hot Dog" was born! Many years later, Dorgan was quoted saying "he was ashamed that a journalist such as himself didn't know how to spell dachshund." Again critics argue the story, and newly found research points to Yale University circa 1890, where dog wagons sold hot dogs outside the dorms, thus coining the name hot dogs.

It amazes people to find out that Chicago got its first taste of a "frankfurter on a bun" in 1893 at The Chicago World Fair/Columbian Exposition. The all-beef frankfurter was brought to the fair by two sausage-making immigrants from Austria-Hungary named Samuel Ladany and Emil Reichel. The no-nonsense, no-drip wiener fit into Victorian Age etiquette as a perfect accompaniment to stroll the fair with. Shortly afterwards, the two young lads opened a small sausage shop on Halstead and quickly turned their business into a

Chicago empire called Vienna Beef. This company has slowly flourished around the country and currently boasts that they supply roughly 80% of all hot dog stands in the city of Chicago.

The hot dog industry flourished in the 1920s and 30s with push cart vendors selling the cheap and filling meal on a bun to working class people around the city. Push carts became very popular with immigrant owners, and each vendor, depending on his country of origin, added his own special condiments to the dog. With a stroke of genius in 1929, a green grocer by the name of Abe Drexler decided to convert the family's Maxwell Street vegetable cart into a hot dog stand. Abe's oldest son, Jake "Fluky" Drexler, who was a local sports hero, joined the family business and opened Fluky's on the corner of Maxwell and Halstead Streets. Fluky's claim to fame was its "Depression era" sandwich, which was a hot dog with mustard, relish, onions, pickles, peppers, lettuce and tomato, with a side of French fries for only 5 cents. This hot dog stand became an instant success not only for the quality of the products they used, but also for their reputation of having a warm and generous heart by feeding the underprivileged and out of work. Fluky's is also known for inventing neon green relish and coining the term "dragging the dog through the garden," which means dressing the hot dog with condiments and vegetables in a precise order.

Ten years later in 1939, another character by the name of Big Jim Stefanovic, an immigrant from Romania, took over his aunt's street stand on Halstead and Maxwell Street and introduced Chicago to a spicier variation of the hot dog. Jim's original broke away from the norm using his own family recipe, and is credited for inventing the Maxwell Street polish, that is a polish sausage link that is scored on the surface with diagonal cuts, charred or grilled until the skin is a crisp, red mahogany color, and then topped with a spicy mustard, sweet grilled onions and hot peppers. Jim's was also known for their bone-in pork chop sandwiches, an item often requested by the blues musicians who lived in the bohemian area and missed mama's home cooking.

It's at this time in Chicago's history that actual free-standing hot dog establishments started cropping up around the city, sadly replacing the popular street carts. Local food historians place the blame for their demise on greedy food inspectors and rival gangs who controlled city blocks.

The west side wasn't the only area to procure such classic joints. SuperDawg off of Milwaukee Avenue and Devon has been serving a steady clientele since 1948. Owner Maurie Berman, a true visionary, wanted to create a chic retro space-like atmosphere featuring car hop service, simple food and two ever-gleaming characters, Florrie and Morrie, who are the loving hot dog couple perched up on the roof. Maurie's vision was to attract an ever increasing audience that had moved north up Milwaukee Avenue (which incidentally was the end of the street car line servicing the local Whealan Pool). Maurie's dogs were different in the fact that he used a plump kosher dog that snapped when eaten, and he also garnished them with a kosher style green tomato pickle. Other innovations of his were to use crinkle cut French fries and to serve his dogs in a small, convenient whimsical box that read "Inside Your Dog Lounges Comfortably on a Bed of Super Fries" with a picture that depicts Superdawg Morrie relaxing on a lounge chair. Small innovations, but everlasting memories that have turned this institution into a classic American icon. As a side note, Superdawg's storefront was the back drop for the hit T.V. show Crime Story starring local actor, Dennis Farina, a retired Chicago cop.

I'm often asked when I'm on the road what makes Chicago style hot dogs so great. Is it the hot dog itself, the bun, the toppings, or is it the atmosphere of the joint? I usually give my stock answer that "the best hot dog is wherever you happen to be when you need one." I know that this answer is simplistic so let me explain the real secret behind the classic Chicago hot dog. In Chicago, there are some 2,000 hot dog stands that are spread out all over the city, and they all follow a secret code of ethics that dictates how a Chicago style dog is "dragged through the garden" or constructed. All the components must neatly be in place before commencing with this ritual.

1. Chicago joints use an all-beef, natural casing, hickory-smoked hot dog that snaps when eaten and is usually steamed. The most notable brand used is Vienna Beef but there are others equally as good, such as Fluky's, Best Kosher, Red Hot Chicago and Hebrew National that are well worth trying too. As a side note, some stands prefer to cook their dogs in a hot water bath that never comes to the boil. Also not every stand uses the same size hot dog. The most desired is 8 to 1, meaning 8 to a pound. Some joints use 10 to 1.

2. Next comes the bun, which is equally important as the dog. Chicago likes to use a "steam warmed" high gluten, poppy seed bun, preferably the S. Rosen Mary Ann Brand. The bun is actually larger and a little firmer than regular store bought buns. Some hot dog aficionados prefer not to steam the bun if it's exceedingly soft and fresh!

> **Once your dog is fully steamed and your bun is warm, all you need to do is "drag it through the garden." (Major sexual connotation here!)**

3. Squeeze a little regular mustard on top of the dog; French's is good.

4. Spoon on some neon green pickle relish. Claussen and Vlasic are good substitutes.

5. Sprinkle on some finely chopped, diced onions.

6. Tuck four thinly sliced tomato wedges into the side of the dog,

7. Place on the other side one fat, kosher-style dill pickle spear.

8. Lay down the middle two or three sport peppers. Small jarred pequinos are an alternative.

9. Lightly sprinkle on top a dash of celery salt.

10. **Never, ever, ever, ever think about putting ketchup on a Chicago- style hot dog. You will not only embarrass yourself but will be subject to having Jim Belushi come to your house and kick your ass!!!**

> *That's the system for making a classic Chicago-style hot dog. It's been that way for well over 75 years and I doubt it will ever change.*

It's sad to say that because of urban renewal many neighborhood stands have closed down. It's not so much the loss of the dog itself, it's really the loss of the personality and charm of the owner that is irreplaceable. I'm often asked if Chicago-style hot dogs can be duplicated in other cities. The answer is most definitely yes. Every major city has at least three or four quality sausage makers that turn out all-beef natural casing hot dogs everyday. It's interesting to note that a few years back a huge newspaper in Chicago rated every hot dog available for sale to the general public. The oldest and largest hot dog selling company in the city came in eighth place out of thirteen brands named. So maybe the most recognized name isn't always the best. Also, quality high gluten, poppy seed hot dog buns can be found in any major grocery store, and neon green relish is really just dyed for the novelty of it. The rest of the stuff is easy to come by. Quality ingredients and attention to details make a good dog PURE AND SIMPLE.

What makes the hot dog so unique in Chicago is the experience of finding a local joint with a personality of its own. For me, the memories associated with eating hot dogs is what makes them so special, whether as a youngster sitting in the open-air bleachers at Wrigley Field or hanging with my high school buddies at Taste Haste in the dead of winter eating a hot supreme tamale and sipping a cold one. It's the images and sensory overload such as the hickory-scented and celery-salt induced smells and clanging of steam table lids that add to the excitement and make the experience unforgettable.

What makes the Chicago-style hot dog is the "style" that is Chicago: big shoulders, big city, big portions. No pretenses here! An old Polish tavern owner I know once described Chicago-style hot dogs as "gut bombers served with greasy strings." Whether it's a jumbo dog, double dog, chili cheese dog, char Polish, char cheddar dog, garden on a bun, superdawg or whoopskidawg, I love them all. The great Maurie Berman of Superdawg fame paraphrased his love for the hot dog like this, "On a poppy seed bun we tenderly place the loveliest, juiciest creation of pure beef dog, formally dressed with all the trimmings, escorted by the often imitated, but never equaled, super fries." God Bless America!

"Really Anal Hot Dog Trivia That You Just Need To Know!!!"

HOT DOGS - Frankfurters come from Germany and wieners come from Austria. Da Bears, Da Bulls, Da Polish Sausage come from Chicago!

A hot dog is actually an emulsified sausage, basically meaning that you must achieve a completely homogenous mixture of meat and fat to make a proper sausage before it's stuffed. In plain English, choice cuts of beef are trimmed of visible fat and finely ground with herbs and spices, then swirled in a massive Cuisinart type contraption until completely smooth, and held together at the right temperature. If the mixture gets too warm because of the friction, the meat will actually separate from the fat, failing to create the proper emulsion. A lot of this technology was attributed to modern food- processing exhibits demonstrated at the Columbian Exposition. Most modern sausage-making plants now use computerized equipment that controls every aspect of this process and can usually produce a truck load of dogs ready to be shipped in a matter of a few hours.

NEON GREEN RELISH - Relish has been used on Chicago style hot dogs since 1929. Relish as we know it is a finely ground mixture of cucumbers, peppers, onions and spices that are marinated, finely chopped and then processed under a canning term called "hot pack." When the final ingredients are ready, they are poured into hot sterilized jars, covered and simmered in a hot-water bath for 10 minutes to kill the bacteria. One of the drawbacks for a hot dog stand owner is that relish, if not properly stored, turns a light pale greenish-yellow color, becomes watery and easily sours, which is not very appealing. Rumor has it that old man Fluky, the green grocer, was never fond of old-time relish and wanted to liven up his classically garnished hot dogs. Experiments were made and experts were brought in to work on this dilemma, and the final outcome was "cold pack" neon green relish. "Cold pack" is a pickling term that means no heat is used to brine or process the pickle or relish. Exceedingly fresh ingredients and spices are combined in large pickling barrels at a very cool temperature, and are left for a period of 3 - 4 weeks to cure until the product develops a satisfactory flavor. This method is similar to the way kosher-style pickles are brined. Even "cold packed" pickles or relish tend to lose their greenish color over time, and keeping with the kosher tradition, Fluky's made sure that no preservatives were added to the batch. So a compromise was reached and an all natural green food dye was added to brighten up the relish. It may seem trivial now but I think that Abe, the green grocer, was a true food artist, maybe envisioning the hot dog as a palate, so to speak, with the mustard complementing the neon green relish field, offsetting the tomato patch and upping the ante with the kosher pickle and peppers. Pure genius!

SPORT PEPPERS - In the 1920's, African Americans from the south were steadily making their way to Maxwell Street's west side. Not only did they bring their down home blues but also some other cherished items from home that were new to Chicago. "Mississippi style" sport peppers cured in vinegar brine have been a table condiment for hundreds of years on the delta. The pepper itself, called Louisiana or Mississippi sport, is actually a Tabasco cultiver or hybrid (capsicum annum) that's milder in taste. The sports were used as substitutes in vinegar packed whole fruits when disease threatened the Tabasco pepper crop. The plant is a compact, bushy mass growing about 2 to 4 feet tall yielding an average crop of 100 upright 11/2 -inch size peppers that are small, slender, green and firm in texture. The scoville or pepper heat index rates this hybrid at about 3,000 to 4,500 but it mellows out during processing. It usually takes about 75 days in the proper delta sun to reach full maturity, but the crop is harvested right before it goes to red. Pepper experts say that the first year is tough for planting but the second year produces a better yield. Sport pepper plants are interchangeable with cascabella or the Sante Fe grand variety. For your information, the last two varieties are more cone shaped, yellow toed, and thickly fleshed with a bit more of a peppery kick.

CELERY SALT - Another southern soul tradition. There was a time in this country when tomatoes, cucumbers, peppers and lettuce were so vine ripened and lusciously beautiful that nothing more than a sprinkling of regular table salt and pepper was the added dressing. You've got to remember that back in the 1920s and 30s fancy olive oils, vinaigrettes and Caesar dressing didn't exist. At the time, the Depression-era dog was a more vegetable or salad-based "garden on a bun" and since people were used to dressing their salads with salt and pepper, the habit carried over to their hot dogs, too. Celery salt is a combination of really fine salt and dried powdered celery that was mostly used for spicy tomato-based cocktails and drinks which were popular in the south. As an interesting side note, many hot dog stands in Chicago are removing celery salt from their menus because yuppies find that it is not politically correct or heart healthy. Yeah Right!

DIRTY WATER - Dirty water is a term that is used by hot dog shop owners that describes their utilization of the previous day's cooking water. When hot dogs are steeped in a water bath for long periods of time, they create a flavorful kind of cloudy water that is loaded with a natural hickory and smoky hot dog essence. Some feel this is worth saving to cook the next day's hot dogs in to enrich their taste. Some joints also use the dirty water to steam the buns.

Hey Mikey, Whud Up wit that Char Ting!

Good Question. Hot dog joints around the city advertise on their menus char dogs, char Polish, and even char burgers. The concept is very simple. To char means to lightly brown a surface over high heat to seal in the natural juices of the product. Since hot dogs and Polish sausages are generally encased in an all natural casing, it's really the outer skin that gets browned and sealed before the actual inner ingredients are cooked. The char, in essence, gives the product a distinctive smoky flavored crunch and snap when bitten into. The one drawback to charring is that if the dog is not properly prepped or pre-scored, it might explode under the intense heat, so slow-as-you-go is the rule of thumb.

Chicago joints use two different types of commercial equipment depending on the size of the operation. The first and most popular piece of equipment is the char broiler, which is usually fueled by gas that heats up lava rocks, ceramic coals or steel radiant tents. Lava rocks actually imitate the properties of coal or wood embers when heated. One drawback is that lava rocks are a pain in the butt to keep clean so steel radiant inserts are usually used. A lot of people ask me what actually gives char broiled meat its barbeque taste? The answer is simple. When hot dogs, sausages or burgers are grilled over lava rock, the natural meat juices and fats drip down onto the rocks creating a small fire and wisp of smoke that bounces back up and seasons the food. Lava rock broilers also emit a carbon residue that builds up over time, and if not properly cleaned can cause a fire.

The second most commonly used piece of equipment is the tabletop gas griddle. Basically, a griddle is a thick plate of metal that has 4 or 5 gas heating elements underneath the plate that control the actual cooking surface. The cooking surface is divided into different zones so an assortment of food items can be cooked at the same time but at different temperatures. The beauty of this equipment is that all natural juices stay on top of the plate until either scraped or burned off, which means you never lose any of the natural seasonings. A good example is to visit a Denny's and see that they cook eggs next to bacon, hash browns next to peppers and pancakes next to ham. McDonald's is another proponent of the griddle. To char on a griddle, most joints buy plates that are slightly grooved which helps the excess grease drain off and prevent flare ups. Throughout my career, I've used both pieces of equipment and I actually prefer the smoky flavor of the lava rock broiler. It might be a little messy but the added flavor is well worth it.

Homemade Sport Peppers

MAKES 1 QUART

Mississippi sport peppers are those hot tart little beauties that are irresistible when placed on a Chicago dog or Polish. Seedlings or plants can be bought off the internet if you search it out and grow beautifully with a little care. I recommend doubling the liquid ingredients so you have enough to fully cover the peppers.

INGREDIENTS

1 pound mature sport peppers
1 1/4 cup white vinegar
1/4 cup water
1/2 teaspoon sugar
1/2 teaspoon sea salt
2 garlic cloves, sliced
1 quarter sized piece fresh horseradish root

Place the sport peppers into a colander, de-stem and thoroughly wash until well cleaned. Place the garlic and horseradish in the bottom of a 1 quart Ball preserving jar. Carefully stuff all the peppers into the jar being sure to leave 1-inch head space from the top of the jar. Bring the vinegar, water, sugar and salt to a boil, stir and then carefully pour into the jar over the pepper. Tightly seal the jar with a cover, wipe down the sides and when completely cool store in the refrigerator for one month before using.

"Classic" Chicago Style Hot Dog

SERVES 4

The original dog that put Chicago on the culinary map. Running the hot dog through the garden ,as they say, is an important ritual so have everything in place and don't even think about pulling out the ketchup.

INGREDIENTS

8 natural casing all beef hot dogs
8 high gluten poppy seed buns
1/2 cup yellow mustard
1/2 cup green relish
1/2 cup finely chopped onions
16 thinly sliced tomato wedges
8 kosher style dill pickle spears
16 sport peppers
Celery salt

Fill a medium sized pot half way with water, bring to the boil and then reduce the flame to the lowest setting. Place the hot dogs in the water and let them warm through for about 12 to 15 minutes. If you would like, you could place a steamer basket over the hot dogs and lightly warm the buns through. (1 to 2 minutes for the buns is enough.) When the hot dogs are warmed through, line the buns in a row on a platter and place a hot dog into each one. Now going in order drag the dog through the garden, that is, spoon some yellow mustard onto each dog, then add some relish to each, sprinkle on some chopped onion, garnish the right side of the dog with tomato wedges, garnish the left side with the kosher pickle spears and then lay the sport peppers down the middle. Sprinkle some celery salt on each dog and then serve with a side of fresh cut French fries.

Garden on a Bun

The working man's interpretation of when the doctor advises that you need more fiber in your diet dog! Another Chicago original but loaded with fresh vegetables.

INGREDIENTS

8 natural casing all beef hot dogs
8 high gluten poppy seed buns
1/2 cup yellow mustard
1/2 cup green relish
1/2 cup finely chopped onions
16 thinly sliced tomato wedges
1 cup finely shredded lettuce
8 thinly sliced green pepper rings
8 thinly sliced cucumber rings
8 kosher style dill pickle spears
8 sport peppers
Celery salt

Fill a medium sized pot half way with water, bring to the boil and then reduce the flame to the lowest setting. Place the hot dogs in the water and let them warm through for about 12 to 15 minutes. If you would like, you could place a steamer basket over the hot dogs and lightly warm the buns through. (1 to 2 minutes for the buns is enough). When the hot dogs are warmed through, line the buns in a row on a platter and place a hot dog into each one. Now going in order drag the dog through the garden, that is, spoon some yellow mustard onto each dog, then add some relish to each, sprinkle on some chopped onion, garnish the right side of the dog with the tomato wedges and the left side with the cucumber rings. Now carefully sprinkle down the middle, the shredded lettuce and then garnish the top with the pepper rings, pickles, sport peppers and celery salt. Serve with a side of fresh cut French fries.

"Messy Chili Cheese Dog"

Sometimes called a "Cincinnati cheese Coney." Our version is similar, but the difference is the taste of the chili. (Their chili is sweet and our mustard is smooth, not grainy.) This dish gets sloppy very quickly so eat fast with plenty of napkins at hand.

INGREDIENTS

8 natural casing all beef hot dogs
8 high gluten poppy seed buns
1/2 cup yellow mustard
2 to 2 1/2 cups Chi-town chili recipe, hot
1/2 cup finely chopped onions
1 heaping cup sharp cheddar cheese, finely grated

Fill a medium sized pot half way with water, bring to the boil and then reduce the flame to the lowest setting. Place the hot dogs in the water and let them warm through for about 12 to 15 minutes. If you would like, you could place a steamer basket over the hot dogs and lightly warm the buns through. (1 to 2 minutes for the buns is enough.) When the hot dogs are warmed through, line the buns in a row on a platter and place a hot dog into each one. Now going in order, spoon some yellow mustard onto each dog, divide the chili equally on top followed by the onions and grated cheese. Serve with a side of fresh cut French fries.

Francheezie

This is an East coast style dog that somehow snuck its way into a few local hot dog stands.

INGREDIENTS

4 jumbo natural casing all-beef hot dogs
4 slices American cheese
4 slices hickory smoked bacon
4 large hot dog buns

Using a sharp chef's knife cut a slit down the middle of each hot dog. Cut the American cheese into long strips and then generously stuff inside the cut slit of the dog. Wrap the entire hot dog with the bacon strip and skewer with toothpicks to secure. Deep fry the hot dog at about 350° for 2 to 3 minutes until the dog and bacon crisp to a nice golden brown. Serve on the bun with the usual Chicago style hot dog condiments.

Ya Hey Der Beer Brat

A tribute to all my fishing buddies up in Wisconsin. The initial beer bath actually acts as a baste, sweetening the brat and giving the skin a nice snappy crunch when cooked. The sweet and sour holding sauce is more of a condiment to slather on after it's cooked. Brats are usually served with a brown German style Dusseldorf mustard, pickle, German potato salad and baked beans.

INGREDIENTS

4 Sheboygan style fresh brats
4 crispy submarine style French rolls
1/2 cup Dusseldorf mustard

BEER BATH BASTE

One 12 ounce bottle Pilsner or Pale Ale beer
1 small onion, diced
2 large garlic cloves, minced
Dash of salt and pepper

HOLDING SAUCE

2 tablespoons Canola oil
1 large onion, halved and thinly sliced
2 tablespoons dark brown sugar
2 tablespoons cider vinegar
1 tablespoon Worcestershire
1/4 teaspoon sea salt
1/8 teaspoon pepper
1 teaspoon paprika
1 small bay leaf
1 cup chicken stock

Using a toothpick poke about 8 to 10 holes in each one of the brats and then place into a medium sized saucepan. Pour the beer, onions and garlic into the pot, gently bring to the simmer and then immediately remove the pan from the fire. When the liquid has cooled cover the pan and refrigerate over night. The next day make the holding sauce by heating the oil in medium sized saucepan. Add the onions and stir cook for 4 to 5 minutes until lightly sauteed and slightly brown. Now add the rest of the ingredients until the sauce takes on good taste about 7 to 8 minutes, remove from the fire, cover and keep warm. Fire up a charcoal grill and when the flames die down to a medium heat, slowly grill the brats for 8 to 10 minutes turning frequently while basting with the remaining beer bath. When the brats are cooked through and golden brown, move them to the cool side of the grill. Place the buns directly on the grill for 30 seconds on each side to crisp and then put a brat on each bun, slather on the mustard and top with the holding sauce.

Perritos Mexicanos

SERVES 4

Another fine addition from our brothers over the border!

INGREDIENTS
4 jumbo natural casing all-beef hot dogs
I cup fresh queso
4 slices hickory smoked bacon
4 large corn tortillas

CONDIMENTS
I cup shredded lettuce
I cup diced tomatoes
I cup salsa
I cup guacamole
I cup sour cream
I cup canned jalapeno slices
Yellow mustard

Using a sharp chef's knife cut a slit down the middle of each hot dog. Stuff the dog with the fresh queso and then carefully wrap in the bacon. Place the corn tortillas on a clean counter, put each dog on top, roll up tightly in a cigar shape and secure each with a toothpick. Deep fry the dogs at about 350° for 2 to 3 minutes until the hot dogs, bacon and tortilla shells crisp to a nice golden brown. Place the browned dogs onto a hot dog boat then garnish taco style with the condiments.

Supreme Chili Tamale Boat

SERVES 4

Supreme Tamale Company has been knocking out the freshest corn style tamales since the 1950's. Tamale boats can be had all over the city in different variations.

INGREDIENTS
4 Supreme tamales
2 to 3 cups Chi-town Chili Recipe
I heaping cup cheddar cheese, finely shredded
1/2 cup sour cream
1/2 cup sliced jalapenos or chopped onion

Steam the tamales for 8 to 10 minutes then remove from the wrapper and place into a hot dog boat. Top with the hot chili, sprinkle on the cheese, plop on a dollop of sour cream and garnish with the jalapenos or onions.

Da Bears, Da Bulls, Da Maxwell Street Char Polish

SERVES 4

Kudos to **Big Jim Stefanovic** of Jim's Original fame. **A Maxwell Street Polish is a polish sausage link that is scored on the surface with diagonal cuts, charred or grilled until the skin is a crisp red mahogany color, then topped with a spicy mustard, sweet grilled onions and hot peppers. Some joints around the city char grill, deep fry, and even pan griddle the sausage to give it that special taste and look so you have to decide which method best suits you.**

INGREDIENTS

4 Polish sausage links
4 high gluten poppy seed buns
1/2 cup Dusseldorf style mustard
12 sport peppers

SWEET ONION TOPPING

I tablespoon canola oil
I tablespoon unsalted butter
I large sweet onion, halved and thinly sliced
Pinch of sugar
1/4 teaspoon Lawry's seasoned salt

Fill a medium sized pot half way with water, bring to the boil and then reduce the heat to the lowest setting. Using a sharp knife score both ends of the sausage links with an "X" and then make 2 or 3 shallow diagonal cuts on the surface of each Polish. Place the sausage into the hot water and turn the fire off. (This insures that your sausage will be partially cooked before it's charred) In a small non-stick skillet heat the oil and the butter and stir cook the onions until slightly opaque for about 7 to 8 minutes. Sprinkle on the sugar and seasoned salt, then continue to stir cook until the onions are lightly golden brown. Remove the pan from the fire. (Once the onions are cooked, it is time to either char grill or pan char the sausage. I prefer to pan char to keep the succulent juices together.) In a medium sized non-stick skillet over medium heat, heat 1 tablespoon of oil, add the sausages and cook on each side for 2 to 3 minutes until the skin turns a beautiful crisp red mahogany color on both sides and the sausage starts to release its juices. When the sausages are nicely charred, pour all of the browned onions over the sausages and shake and toss in the pan so that the onions can take on the juices from the cooked sausages. Turn the heat off. Line your buns in a row on a platter, then place a piece of sausage on each bun and spoon on the mustard. Using a kitchen tong equally divide the browned onions over the Polish and then garnish with the sport peppers. Serve with a side of fresh cut French fries.

"Mother-in-Law"

A variation on the theme.

INGREDIENTS

4 Supreme tamales
2 to 3 cups Chi-town Chili Recipe
4 hot dog buns
Sport peppers or chopped onions

Steam the tamales as directed, place on a hot dog bun and top with the chili and peppers.

"Father-in-Law"

SERVES 4

Another variation on the theme.

INGREDIENTS

4 Supreme tamales
2 to 3 cups Chi-town Chili Recipe
1 cup cheddar cheese, finely shredded
4 hot dog buns
Sport peppers or chopped onions

Steam the tamales as directed, place on a hot dog bun and top with the chili, cheese and peppers.

Bag "O" Fries

SERVES 4

No righteous burger would be complete without a hot-from-the-fryer side of golden French fries. The secret to a great fry is to pick the right potato, pre-blanch and use a good clean oil. That's it!

INGREDIENTS

4 large russet potatoes, lightly washed
2 quarts rendered beef fat or peanut oil
Fine sea salt

Brown paper bags

Without peeling the potatoes, cut them into 1/2 - inch size fingers or French fries. Fill a large bowl with ice water, place the cut fries into the water to chill for 3 to 4 hours and then drain and dry. (This removes the excess starch.) Fill a deep fat fryer with the oil until it reaches 325°. Carefully throw about two to three handfuls of cut fries into the hot oil and cook for exactly 7 to 8 minutes or until a really light golden brown. Remove the pre-blanched fries to a layer of brown paper bags and pre-blanch the rest. With all the fries removed from the hot oil, raise the temperature to 375°. Now again add the pre-blanched fries in batches to the hot oil and fry for another 3 to 5 minutes until golden brown and one more place on the brown paper bags to drain and then season with the sea salt.

Merkt's Chili Cheese Fries

SERVES 4

Let's face it, sometimes you're a little short on cash so chili cheese fries are the entrée du jour. Local joints are catching on to the trend of using Merkt's sharp cheddar cheese spread to top their burgers and fries. Don't forget a stack of napkins!

INGREDIENTS

1 recipe Bag "O" Fries
2 to 3 cups Chi-town Chili recipe
1 cup Merkt's sharp cheddar cheese spread,
room temperature

Sliced jalapenos, sport peppers, kosher pickle
    spears, assorted hot sauces and ketchup

Brown paper bags

Place 1 or 2 brown paper bags onto a large serving platter. Place the chili into a small saucepan and bring to a boil and then reduce the heat.   Now working quickly, cook the French fries according to the recipe and when finished place onto the paper lined serving platter and sprinkle with the sea salt. Ladle the hot chili directly on top of the cooked French fries, and then dabble on the melted cheese over the chili in a decorative fashion. Garnish the platter with the sliced jalapenos, sport peppers, pickles, assorted hot sauces and ketchup.

CHEEZBORGER, CHEEZBORGER, CHEEZBORGER!

BURGER RECIPES

Cheezborger, Cheezborger, Cheezborger! SERVES 4

Billy Goat Tavern, home away from home to the late comic John Belushi and the late great columnist Mike Royko, has undoubtedly served more burgers to visiting tourists than any restaurant in the city. Nothing hits the spot like a good burger and they are easy to make as long as you use the best ingredients and don't over cook them on the grill. Sam Sianis, the owner is a wonderful guy, but just remember when you order no Pepsi, no Coke, no fries, no chips!

INGREDIENTS

2 pounds freshly ground chuck
2 teaspoons Lawry's seasoned salt
4 thick slices cheddar cheese
4 poppy seed hamburger buns, halved
4 ice burg lettuce leaves
1 large beefsteak tomato
1 large Vidalia onion
Sweet pickle slices

Ketchup, mustard or barbeque sauce

Pre-heat a gas or charcoal grill to medium high heat and while the grill is getting hot, form the ground chuck into 4 burgers that are 3/4 -inch thick by 4 1/2 inches round. (Try not to handle the meat too much and when the burgers are formed, slightly flatten the middle so that they will cook evenly.) Season both sides of the burgers with the seasoning salt and cover with plastic wrap. Cut the tomato and onion into 1/4-inch slices and arrange on a platter with the lettuce leaves and cheddar cheese. When the grill is hot quickly clean the grates with a steel brush, then lightly oil a paper towel and rub the grates with the oil from the towel. (This helps to prevent sticking.) Cook the burgers for 3 to 4 minutes on each side for medium rare. (Don't be tempted to press down on the burgers with a spatula while they're cooking because this removes all the succulent juices.) During the last minute of cooking top each burger with a slice of cheddar cheese, and then cover the grill for about 1 minutes to melt the cheese on the burgers. When the cheese is melted, move the burgers to the side of the grill and lightly toast the buns until golden brown. Place a burger onto each bun and top with the lettuce, tomato, onion, pickles and ketchup, mustard or barbeque sauce.

"South Side" Big Baby Burger

Way before the Whopper and the Big Mac were invented, Nicky's a small Greek diner on the south side was knocking out this famous sandwich that epitomized the quintessential $1.50 griddled burger. No lettuce, no tomato, no notin'!

INGREDIENTS

4 sesame seed burger buns
8 quarter pound beef burger patties
4 slices American cheese
Ketchup, mustard and pickle slices
Lawry's Seasoned Salt

ONION TOPPING

1 large sweet onion, halved and thinly sliced
1 tablespoon canola oil
1 tablespoon unsalted butter
Pinch of sugar
1/4 teaspoon Lawry's garlic salt

Lightly season the burgers with the seasoned salt. Heat a large stovetop griddle and when hot, sauté the onions in the canola oil and butter until slightly opaque about 7 to 8 minutes. Sprinkle on the sugar and garlic salt and then continue to stir cook until the onions are lightly golden brown. Push the onions to the side then griddle the burgers in the onion oil on both sides until lightly golden brown about 3 to 4 minutes. Place a piece of cheese onto four of the patties and then top the cheese with the other four patties and let them continue to cook until the cheese starts to melt. Warm the buns on the hot griddle, then garnish the bottom bun with a dash of ketchup, mustard, pickle slices, the twin patty and top with the golden onions to serve. **(I don't recommend grilling the burgers, because the taste sensation actually comes from the sweet onion oil that melds into the burger while it's cooking on the flat griddle.)**

Local Variations on the Burger

Chicagoan's love their burgers usually just plain grilled or broiled, but some people like to spice things up so here's a few variations on the theme that you can fool around with.

THE HICKORY BURGER - A hamburger patty grilled, then topped with cheddar cheese, crisp bacon and tangy barbecue sauce.

PIZZA BURGER - A broiled hamburger patty topped with Italian seasonings, spaghetti sauce and mozzarella cheese then baked and served on crusty Italian bread.

MEXICALLI BURGER - It's a grilled hamburger patty that is topped with spicy pepper Jack cheese, pico de gallo, guacamole and jalapeno slices.

CHILI HUCK BURGER - A broiled hamburger patty that is topped with cheddar cheese, hot chili, pico de gallo and sliced jalapenos.

THE CONTINENTAL BURGER - This is a thick hamburger patty that is broiled and topped with sweet caramelized onions, sautéed mushrooms, Swiss cheese and served on dark rye bread.

Homemade Onion Rings

Crispy and beautiful little rings of gold!

INGREDIENTS

2 large sweet Vidalia onions
2 cups buttermilk
1 teaspoon Tabasco
1 teaspoon sugar

2 cups all-purpose flour
1 tablespoon baking powder
2 teaspoons sea salt
1 1/2 teaspoons black pepper

1 quart peanut oil

Using a sharp chef's knife cut the onions into 1/2-inch thick rings. In a mixing bowl combine the buttermilk, Tabasco and sugar and marinate the onions for 1 hour. In another mixing bowl combine the flour, baking powder, salt and pepper and set aside. Heat the oil in a deep fat fryer to 400° and when hot, carefully remove a couple of the onions rings, shake off the excess liquid and dredge in the flour mixture. Deep fry the rings for 2 to 3 minutes until lightly golden brown on all sides. Drain on paper towels and serve.

No righteous burger is complete without some kind of frosty libation to help it go down with. Midwestern summers get really hot and there was a time when most places made fresh milk shakes to order. The secret is to use quality full-fat ice cream, really fresh whole milk and a frosty coated mixing cup

Basic Vanilla Milk Shake

MAKES 1 LARGE

INGREDIENTS

1 cup full fat vanilla ice cream
1/2 cup whole milk
Dash of vanilla extract
Canned Redi whip
Festive cake sprinkles

In a clean ice cold blender, process the vanilla ice cream, whole milk and vanilla extract until they are well combined and thick. Pour into a large milk shake glass and top with the Redi whip and sprinkles.

Chocolate Milk Shake

MAKES 1 LARGE

INGREDIENTS

1 cup full fat vanilla ice cream
1/2 cup whole milk
3 to 4 tablespoons quality chocolate syrup
Canned Redi whip
Maraschino cherry

In a clean ice cold blender, process the vanilla ice cream, whole milk and chocolate syrup until they are well combined and thick. Pour into a large milk shake glass and top with the Redi whip and cherry.

Chocolate Banana Milk Shake

MAKES 1 LARGE

INGREDIENTS

1 cup full fat vanilla ice cream
3/4 cup whole milk
1 small banana
4 tablespoons chocolate syrup
Canned Redi whip
Maraschino cherry

In a clean ice cold blender, process the vanilla ice cream, whole milk, banana and chocolate syrup until they are well combined and thick. Pour into a large milk shake glass and top with the Redi whip and cherry.

Strawberry Shake

MAKES 1 LARGE

INGREDIENTS

1 cup vanilla ice cream
1/2 cup whole milk
1/2 cup frozen strawberry slices in syrup
Canned Redi whip
Festive cake sprinkles

In a clean ice cold blender, process the vanilla ice cream, whole milk and strawberries until they are well combined and thick. Pour into a large milk shake glass and top with the Redi whip and sprinkles.

BARBECUE RIBS

RIB

RECIPES

A retired TWA pilot I once knew told me that if you ever get lost above Chicago in a plane to just look for the lingering barbecue smoke in the sky over the west and south sides to lead you to Midway Airport--true story!!!! Barbecue shacks and joints have been a constant mainstay on the Chicago culinary map for generations and currently there are some 50 - 60 places scattered throughout the south and west sides of the city. That's a lot of pit bossin' and queing going on! It's also the city where the Weber Grill, originally nicknamed "the Sputnik," was invented in 1951! Chicago's rib traditions were actually transported north by the Illinois Central Green Diamond Line that serviced the rural backwaters of Louisiana, Mississippi and Arkansas in the early 1920s. The Pullman porters on this line, who were for the most part African American, would distribute copies of the most influential black newspaper, The Chicago Defender, along their route down south. Robert S. Abbott, who founded the newspaper, enticed his readers with promises of better opportunities in a job market that was depleted by America's entry into World War I. African Americans from the deep south were lured to the big city with hopes of a better life and to flee the poverty and oppression of their southern homes. Historians have called this the "Great Northern Drive." Unfortunately, the reality of the cold Industrial North for these poor folks was a city crammed with smoke stacks, the stench of the stock yards and competition with other immigrants. On a God-blessed good note, African Americans endured by bringing their culture from the south and turning Chicago onto some of the best blues, art and southern cooking known to man. Lucky for us!

A lot of people are confused as to what real barbecue is all about, so let me give you a quick education. Barbecuing consists of placing a cut of meat into a closed pit and allowing it to cook indirectly by the heated smoke from a hardwood fire such as hickory or oak. Low pit temperatures of 190° - 225° held over a long period of time cause the connective tissue of the meat to tenderize and season the finished product with the distinctive barbecue smoke taste. BBQ is the total opposite of grilling, as the barbecued meats used are never cooked over an active open flame, just the heated flavored smoke. BBQ aficionados like to use the term "indirect cooking," which means if you light a fire in your grill and push the gray smoldering coals to the far right side, and cook your food over to the far left side, that's indirect cooking.

There are several problems with this type of cooking process on a large scale. First, you need massive barbecue pits, which for the most part are custom made. The infamous Carson's Ribs in Chicago has a custom pit rotisserie that handles up to 180 slabs of ribs at a time and down south, pits are even larger. The second problem is that barbecue pit bosses like to cook their ribs and meats for anywhere from 8 - 12 hours at a constant temperature between 190° - 225° to achieve that perfect barbecue taste. That takes a lot of time and requires a ton of clean-burning coals and green hickory wood to produce the perfect blue-tinted smoke. I've traveled extensively down south and was surprised to learn that many barbecue joints employ an armed cook who sleeps in the cooler overnight to keep the ribs safe and the fire stoked at a constant temperature!

You'd be hard pressed to find a classic-type offset BBQ setup in Chicago because of the building codes and ventilation restrictions. Most pit bosses here use a custom-built box made of tempered steel, covered in high gauge aluminum finish with a tempered-glass enclosed cooking chamber to show off their delectable goods (the street name is the aquarium design). The base of the aquarium houses two steel doors behind which a fire of coal and wood can be built and smoldered. Above the base are horizontal stainless steel grates that can be adjusted to accommodate different smoked products such as chickens, ribs, briskets and sausages. Think of it as a large aquarium that houses smoked meats. This is how it works: a pit boss preps and marinates his meats for a few days to preseason. When he's ready to smoke, he lights a fire in the lower chamber, usually with coal, and when the fire subsides wood chips or hickory chunks are placed on the coals to generate smoke. When he achieves a good smoke and proper temperature, the marinated meats are placed on the grates and all the doors are closed. Every half hour, the meats are turned and the fire is re-stoked to finish the cooking process. That's it! SOUNDS EASY IN YOUR WILDEST DREAMS!!!!

All right, let's get down to it! Chi-town barbecue joints specialize in a handful of items, the most popular being ribs, rib tips, hot links and chicken. (I'll tell you about the sides later.)

RIBS - Chicago-style ribs are the product of a melting pot of different tastes and cultures from down south. Our ribs have been best described as being not too smoky or charred on the outside, but the meat is cooked to a perfectly tender and springy-cushioned middle that is plump and juicy. Two types of ribs are commonly prepared in Chicago, baby-back ribs and spare ribs. Baby-back ribs come from the loin of the hog and are small in size, about 1 1/2 - 2 pounds total. These ribs are less meaty, less fatty, more tender and cook a lot faster than spare ribs. They are also more expensive due to their high demand. Spare ribs, on the other hand, come from the belly of the hog, are larger in size-- usually 2 to 4 pounds average--and are very meaty and fatty. Both slabs of meat usually yield about 11 to 14 bones or ribs. Rib tips are actually the trimmed flap pieces from the sternum and cartilage of the pre-processed rack. I'm often asked what's the best way to buy ribs, so let me give you a few pointers. Always try to buy fresh slabs with good meat coverage over the bones, and look to make sure there are no large areas of surface fat that need to be trimmed. Frozen ribs have a tendency to dry out at the rib tips making the meat dry and inedible. Cryovaced ribs are a good buy since they are packaged at the plant at the peak of freshness, and are easy to store. Ribs sold at your local butcher shop are pretty much ready to go, but there are a few extra steps you can take to make them really shine. The first is to remove any excess visible fat, as the rack should look neat and clean in appearance. The second is to remove the membrane from the underside of the rack by placing a small knife or screwdriver between the bone and the layer of skin, and pulling upward until you can peel it off the entire back (if in doubt, ask you butcher).

SAUCES AND SPICES - Most purists in Chicago don't believe in pre-seasoning a rack with a dry spice rub, instead they would rather marinate the meat for a day or two in their own homemade sauce to keep it real! I say, "Yes and No!" The purpose of a pre-season is to not only season the meat, but to break down the enzymes so that it will be more tender and flavorful. Ribs are usually cooked for up to 3 to 4 hours with just a dry rub seasoning before being slathered in the last 15 minutes with a good barbecue sauce. Typically, classic Chi-town barbecue sauce is described as being rich and thick with a good bite of sweetness and pepper, so if the racks were both marinated and cooked with the sauce, the ribs would surely burn. I find that it is easier to pre-season with a dry rub to enhance the flavor and avoid the burn (I've included a basic recipe). As far as sauces go, I prefer to make my own, but if you're not so inclined, the best substitute I have found for Chicago-style is Bulls Eye Barbecue Sauce spiced up with a little Creole seasoning for that extra kick.

COOKING THE RIBS - There's always been a lot of confusion as to what is the best way to cook ribs, and I've tried every different method so let me share Mikey's secret. Typically, ribs are cooked using the indirect method at temperatures of 225° - 250°. At this temperature, it would take about three hours to cook, depending on weather and wind conditions and how well you are able to maintain an ideal temperature. To give you an example, using the above method you would need a 22 1/2 - inch charcoal kettle grill and a rib rack that could accommodate 4 slabs of baby back ribs (that's a lot of work for four racks!). I prefer this method if you're out in a field with a large grill and a lot of time. When you light your fire using this method, your initial temperature inside the grill will be 350° and will drop down to 250° after two hours so there is no reason to replenish the charcoals. Also, a really cool chef's trick is to remove the ribs from the grill when they are done and wrap them tightly in a large sheet of aluminum foil to rest for an hour. The ribs actually relax and redistribute their juices making the meat more tender and succulent. Now for those of you who live in the real world and just want to get your ribs done conveniently, here's my secret: Pre-heat your oven to 225°. Lay your pre-seasoned racks onto large sheet pans so they're not overlapping each other and cover tightly with aluminum foil. Place the pans into the heated oven and cook the ribs for a good three hours until the meat is fork tender(purists despise this method but you've got to do what you've got to do). When the ribs are done, you have two options. The first is to let them cool, then re-wrap and freeze for up to two weeks. The second is to go outside and light your grill, and when the charcoals go gray toss on a few hickory chips and cook the prepared ribs to reheat slowly, and then baste with the sauce. This is an old restaurant technique that saves a lot of time and inconvenience, especially if you're having a large crowd.

SIDES - Ribs are good on their own, but a few cold ones and an assortment of other side dishes make the meal. Most joints I know serve a heaping portion of white bread and extra barbecue sauce along with the sides that are typically homestyle potato salad, creamy coleslaw, spicy barbecue beans, hot potato wedges, honey cornbread, and yes for dessert, drunken' apple crisp with homemade vanilla ice cream. It's interesting to note that a lot of barbecue places employ someone's mother or grandmother to lovingly prepare all these old-fashioned delectable goodies.

Rib Notes There's an old saying that "Barbecue is more than a meal; it's a way of life!" Chicago's rib culture has actually grown from its southern backwoods roots to become an integral part of our city's backyard gatherings, church socials and political get- togethers, all enticed by the smell of the que. Barbecue defies the modern age of fast food joints by the very nature of the time, love and care it takes to make it right. Food historians note that the original barbecue joints were born out of necessity by rural farmers who needed extra cash when their crops weren't supplying it. Small pits were built behind barns, a small sign was put out by the road and friends and neighbors would come out for the que. The word would spread and before you'd know it, this small side business would become a legendary smoke shack with tattered pick-up trucks parked beside Mercedes and BMWs. Over the past few years, there has been a lot of controversy about who has the best ribs, the west or the south side? This rivalry is folly because it's all good! In a nutshell, pit bossin' is a magical and mystical dance with blue smoke that conjures up visions of voodoo, old New Orleans and the slow-moving trains of the tranquil old south. My advice is to get in your backyard, gather some friends around and do the que.

CHEF MIKE'S MASTER BARBECUE RECIPES

The secret to making great ribs is to use a good quality meat, rib rub and a homemade sauce. I've been using these recipes for over 25 years that I learned while going to chef school at Triton College. The rub and the sauce are pretty straightforward Chicago style, but feel free to spice them up to your liking.

Rib Rub Spice

MAKES ABOUT 1 CUP

INGREDIENTS

1/4 cup sea salt
1/4 cup brown sugar
1/4 cup paprika
3 tablespoons black pepper
1 tablespoon garlic powder
1 teaspoon onion powder
1/4 teaspoon cayenne pepper

Place all the ingredients into a small glass jar and shake until well combined.

Mike's Barbecue Sauce

MAKES 1 HEAPING QUART

INGREDIENTS

2 tablespoons canola oil
4 medium garlic cloves, minced
4 cups ketchup
1/2 cup orange juice
1/2 cup water
1/4 cup apple cider vinegar
1/3 cup Worcestershire sauce
1/4 cup molasses
1 tablespoon soy sauce
2 tablespoons regular mustard
1/3 cup brown sugar
1 tablespoon Rib Rub
1/2 teaspoon onion powder
1/8 teaspoon red pepper flakes
1 1/2 teaspoons hot pepper sauce
A few dashes of hickory smoke

Heat the oil in a saucepan and sauté the garlic for 2 minutes. Add the rest of the ingredients, stir to combine, bring to a boil and then simmer slowly for 20 minutes. Cool overnight to let the flavors meld.

Charcoal Barbecue Ribs

This is the preferred method for good Chicago style ribs. You will need a 22 1/2-inch charcoal grill that will accommodate about four racks of ribs. If you don't have a large enough grill don't worry, just follow the oven cooked method, cut the ribs into smaller pieces and re-heat and sauce on the grill of your choice.

INGREDIENTS

4 slabs baby back ribs (about 6 pounds)
1/2 cup Rib Rub
2 cups Mike's Barbecue Sauce
2 heaping handfuls hickory wood chips soaked in water

Read the introduction to learn how to prep the ribs!

Season both sides of the ribs with the rib rub, place into a large plastic bag and refrigerate for 3 to 4 hours. Drain the soaked wood chips, place into a piece of aluminum foil, seal tightly and poke the package with a fork to create about six holes to allow the smoke to escape. Adjust the bottom vents of your kettle so that they are about halfway open. Remove the top cooking rack and place about 40 to 50 briquettes in the center of the bottom rack. Light the charcoal and allow it to burn for about 20 to 25 minutes or until the coals go to gray. Carefully push all the briquettes over to the left side of the grill and place the wood chip packet on top of them. Replace the cooking grate and put the grill lid on top with the vents 1/4 open on the opposite side of the hot coals. (This will allow the smoke to get drawn through the grill.) Clean your grill thoroughly with a wire brush. Position the ribs over the cool side of the grill and barbecue slowly by turning them every half hour. (Your initial temperature inside the grill will be about 350°, but after a few hours the temperature will drop to the ideal zone of 225 to 250°. It's okay to add a few more briquettes to maintain that temperature.) After 3 hours the internal temperature of the meat should be about 150 to 160°. At this time, liberally brush on the barbecue sauce and cook for another 10 minutes or until the ribs take on a slight char.

Chef's "Top Secret" Barbecue Ribs

SERVES 4

If you're a lazy guy like me and just don't feel like dragging yourself out to the grill for 4 hours, this is the method for you. Seasoned ribs are pre-cooked in your home oven for a few hours and then quickly re-heated and sauced in your backyard or at the Forest Preserve on a gas or charcoal grill. The trick is to re-heat the ribs slowly over a smoldering smoky fire.

INGREDIENTS

4 slabs baby back ribs (about 6 pounds)
1/2 cup Rib Rub
2 cups Mike's Barbecue Sauce
2 heaping handfuls hickory wood chips soaked in water

Read the introduction to learn how to prep the ribs!

Season both sides of the ribs with the rib rub, place into a large plastic bag and refrigerate for 3 to 4 hours. Pre-heat the oven to 225°, lay the rib racks onto a large baking sheet pan and cover tightly with a piece of aluminum foil. Cook in the hot oven on the middle rack for 3 hours until the ribs are tender. Remove the foil, let the ribs cool and wrap tightly in plastic wrap until needed. (At this point the ribs can be frozen for up to 2 weeks, just be sure to defrost before re-heating.)

When you're ready to re-cook the ribs, light a charcoal fire or pre-heat your gas grill to 250°. Drain the soaked wood chips, place into a piece of aluminum foil, seal tightly and poke the package with a fork to create about six holes to allow the smoke to escape. Place the package directly over the hot coals (if you're using gas, over the burner) and let the chips get a good smoke going for about 15 minutes. Clean your grill thoroughly with a wire brush and then slowly re-heat your ribs for 12 to 15 minutes before applying the sauce. Cook the ribs until they take on a slight char.

Firehouse BBQ Rib Tips

SERVES 4

I learned this trick while in boy scouts from an old fire captain that used to work at the station down the block from my house in Norwood Park. Rib tips are the scrumptious little tidbits that are trimmed off of processed slabs of ribs. The pre-seasoned rib pieces are pre-cooked in a hot oven, heavily sauced and then sealed in aluminum foil packages that are slow cooked over the smoldering embers of a lingering grill or camp fire.

INGREDIENTS

6 to 8 pounds pork or beef rib tips
1/3 cup Rib Rub
3 cups Mike's Barbecue Sauce

Place the rib tips in a large mixing bowl or plastic container and pick through each piece to make sure there are no loose bones or cartilage. Heavily season with the rib rub and using your hands, toss and thoroughly mix until all of the pieces are seasoned. Refrigerate for 3 to 4 hours. Pre-heat the oven to 225°, lay the rib pieces onto 2 large baking sheets and cover tightly with aluminum foil. Cook in the hot oven on the middle rack for 2 hours. Remove the pieces to a large mixing bowl and let cool. Using a roll of aluminum foil, cut out four sheets that are 12 X 12-inches each and place onto a clean work surface. Pour all of the barbecue sauce over the cooled rib tips and using your hands, thoroughly combine until all of the rib tips are covered. Divide the rib tips equally on top of each piece of aluminum foil and make a tight package by folding over each end. (All of the folds and flaps should be on top to seal in all of the natural juices so they don't leak out of the foil.) When you're ready to cook the packages, light a charcoal fire or pre-heat your gas grill to 250°. Place the sealed packages directly on top of the grill grate, cover the grill and cook for another hour until thoroughly tender and piping hot.

Grilled Barbecue Chicken

Everyone loves **BBQ** chicken ,but too hot of a fire will ruin your party fer sure Vern! A cool chef's trick is to first sear the pieces and then slow cook over a cooler side of the grill slightly covered with a disposable aluminum pan. I guarantee your **BBQ** chicken will be the hit of the block.

INGREDIENTS

Two 3 to 4 pound chickens, cut up
1/3 cup Rib Rub
2 cups Mike's Barbecue Sauce
2 heaping handfuls hickory wood chips
    soaked in water

Carefully using a sharp chef knife remove any excess or overhanging fat from the chicken and then place the pieces in a large mixing bowl. Sprinkle on all the rib rub and using your hands, toss the chicken and the spices to evenly coat and then refrigerate covered for 3 to 4 hours. Drain the soaked wood chips, place into a piece of aluminum foil, seal tightly and poke the package with a fork to create about six holes to allow the smoke to escape. While the chicken is marinating, adjust the bottom vents of your kettle so that they are about halfway open. Remove the top cooking rack and place about 40 to 50 briquettes in the center of the bottom rack. Light the charcoal and allow it to burn for about 20 to 25 minutes or until the coals go gray. You know that the coals are ready when you can hold your hand 5 inches over the grilling grate for 5 to 6 seconds. Carefully push all the briquettes over the left side of the grill and place the wood chip packet on top of them. Replace the cooking grate and put the grill lid on top with the vents 1/4 open on the opposite side of the hot coals. Leave the cover on for 5 minutes to heat up the grate, then remove and clean your grill thoroughly with a wire brush. Using a vegetable oil soaked paper towel held by a long kitchen tong, quickly give the grate an oiling to prevent sticking. Place the chicken pieces directly over the hot coals and sear for 3 to 4 minutes per side with the grill cover off. When the meat is seared, place the chicken pieces on the opposite side of the grill and cover with a large disposable aluminum pan. Do not cover the grill with the kettle lid. The residual heat from the hot side of the grill will get trapped under the aluminum pan and create an oven like effect without the fear of flare-ups or burning. When the internal temperature of the chicken reaches 160° (about 20 minutes), baste the pieces with the BBQ sauce, grill 1 to 2 minutes more and then place all the chicken into the aluminum pan to serve.

Hot Links

Hot links are those smoky, peppery, spicy little delicacies that go great with all kinds of barbecue and are welcome at any backyard party. I learned this recipe from some old country chef while traveling down South and find them utterly addictive and delicious! You'll need a small backyard smoker that you can find at any sporting goods store.

INGREDIENTS

1 1/2 pounds beef chuck, cubed
1 1/2 pounds fatty pork butt, cubed
1/2 cup ice water
2 tablespoons garlic, minced
1 1/2 tablespoons kosher salt
1 tablespoon course ground black pepper
2 teaspoons cayenne pepper
1 tablespoon Hungarian sweet paprika
2 teaspoons sugar
1 teaspoon dried marjoram
1/2 teaspoon ground sage

Grind the beef chuck and pork butt through a 3/8-inch sausage grinding plate and place into a large mixing bowl. Sprinkle on the rest of the ingredients and carefully using your hands, knead the mixture until everything is well blended. (At this point a pinch of all spice, cardamom, cloves, coriander and cinnamon can be added into the mix for a sweeter sausage, but is not necessary.) Cover the bowl and chill the mixture for a few hours to let the flavors meld. When the meat is ready, stuff into medium sized hog casings and tie into 5 or 6-inch links. Pre-heat your outdoor smoker to a temperature between 175° and 250°, and hot smoke the sausages using hickory sawdust until the sausages reach and internal temperature of 155° to 160° or about 2 hours. When the sausages are smoked, cool them down and grill slowly along with the chicken or the ribs for 10 to 12 minutes being careful not to let them burn. The links can be seasoned on the grill with a little spice rub or a brushing of barbecue sauce.

No self-righteous barbecue would be complete without an assortment of cool and refreshing salads or a few homemade side accompaniments. These recipes are old standards and seem to be everyone's favorites to round out a backyard bash.

Honey Corn Bread

MAKES ONE 9-INCH PAN

INGREDIENTS

4 tablespoons unsalted butter, melted
1 1/3 cup yellow cornmeal
3/4 cup flour
1/4 cup light brown sugar
2 tablespoons honey
1 1/2 teaspoons baking powder
1/2 teaspoon baking soda
1 teaspoon sea salt
2 large eggs
1 cup buttermilk

Pre-heat the oven to 400°. Using 2 tablespoons of the butter, lightly coat the bottom and sides of a 9-inch baking pan or black iron skillet. In a medium sized mixing bowl combine the cornmeal, flour, brown sugar, baking powder, baking soda and salt, and stir with a whisk until well blended. In another bowl beat together the eggs, buttermilk, remaining butter and honey, then add to the flour mixture and stir until the mixture comes together in a light batter. (Don't over mix or the corn bread will be tough.) Using a spatula pour into the baking pan and bake in the hot oven on the middle rack for 30 minutes until the crust is a nice golden brown. Let the corn bread chill slightly before cutting.

Verna's Old Fashioned Potato Salad

SERVES 3 TO 4

Everyone loves chili! This is a basic Midwestern recipe that's not too spicy but will most definitely warm your belly up.

INGREDIENTS

2 pounds potatoes, red or new
1 cup mayo, full-fat
1 1/2 tablespoons Dijon mustard
1/4 teaspoon sea salt
1/4 teaspoon celery salt
1/4 teaspoon black pepper
Dash of Tabasco, Worcestershire, and garlic powder
2 large hard boiled eggs, diced
1 large green onion, diced
1 large celery stalk, diced

Scrub the potatoes until clean, cut in half and place in a large pot of lightly salted cold water. Bring the pot to a simmer over medium heat and simmer the potatoes for 15 to 20 minutes until easily pierced with a fork. Drain in a colander until cool and then place in a mixing bowl and refrigerate for one hour. Remove the bowl and using a small paring knife, cut the potatoes into bite size pieces and sprinkle over the hard boiled eggs, scallion and celery. Gently mix until well combined. In another bowl combine the rest of the ingredients, pour over the potato mixture and blend together. Refrigerate until needed.

Elsie's Famous Macaroni Salad

SERVES 4

INGREDIENTS

1 pound elbow macaroni, pre-cooked al dente
1 cup Miracle Whip salad dressing
1 tablespoon Dijon mustard
2 tablespoons cider vinegar
1 teaspoon sugar
1/2 teaspoon sea salt
1/4 teaspoon black pepper
3/4 cup celery, diced
3/4 cup green pepper, diced
1/4 cup red onion, diced
Dash of Tabasco, Worcestershire, and garlic powder

Place the chilled cooked macaroni into a large mixing bowl and sprinkle over the celery, peppers and onion. Gently mix together until well blended. In another small mixing bowl combine the rest of the ingredients. Pour over the macaroni and mix. Refrigerate until needed.

Gert's Creamy Coleslaw

SERVES 4

INGREDIENTS

4 cups shredded green cabbage
2 cups shredded red cabbage
1/2 cup shredded carrots
I cup mayo, full-fat
I tablespoon Dijon mustard
I tablespoon prepared horseradish
I to 2 tablespoons sugar
1/4 teaspoon sea salt
1/8 teaspoon black pepper
1/8 teaspoon garlic powder
1/8 teaspoon celery seeds
Dash of Tabasco and Worcestershire

Place the cabbage and carrots into a large mixing bowl and using your hands thoroughly combine to mix. In another small bowl combine the remaining ingredients and stir until well blended. Pour over the cabbage and carrots and mix until well combined. Refrigerate until needed.

Uncle Bob's Baked Beans

SERVES 4

INGREDIENTS

I large can Bush's Baked Beans
2 slices hickory smoked bacon, diced
I small onion, diced
3/4 cup Mike's Barbecue Sauce
1/4 cup molasses
3 tablespoons brown sugar
2 tablespoons mustard
I teaspoon Rib Rub
Dash of Worcestershire and hot sauce

In a medium sized non-stick saucepot, sauté the bacon until it turns slightly brown and begins to render its fat, then add the onion and sauté for 3 to 4 minutes. Add the rest of the ingredients and stir to completely combine. Bring to the boil, lower the heat and simmer for 20 to 30 minutes

Spicy Potato Wedges

INGREDIENTS

6 to 8 medium sized Russet baking potatoes
2 tablespoons canola oil

2 teaspoons Rib Rub
2 teaspoons Lawry's garlic seasoning
1 teaspoon onion powder
1/2 teaspoon dried oregano
1/4 teaspoon black pepper
1/8 teaspoon cayenne pepper
2 teaspoons Hungarian paprika

Pre-heat the oven to 425°. Clean and wash the potatoes leaving the skin on and pierce with a fork then microwave for 8 minutes. Cut each potato lengthwise into 6 or 8 pieces then toss with the canola oil. Combine the remaining ingredients, season the potatoes and cook on a non-stick pan skin side down for 40 minutes until tender and brown.

Mom's Hot Apple Crisp with Vanilla Ice Cream

CRUST

1 cup all-purpose flour
1/4 teaspoon sea salt
2 tablespoons sugar
1 stick unsalted butter, softened
2 tablespoons ice water

FILLING

2 pounds granny smith apples
2 teaspoons corn starch
1/3 cup sugar
1/2 teaspoon cinnamon
1 teaspoon vanilla extract
1 tablespoon brandy

1 quart vanilla ice cream

To prepare the flaky crust, place the flour, salt and 1 tablespoon of the sugar in a mixing bowl and use a mixing spoon to well combine. Using your hands, break off little pieces of the butter over the flour mixture and gently knead them into the dough until it resembles a rough mass. Add the water and continue kneading with your hands until you have a soft and pliable dough. Cover with plastic wrap and refrigerate for at least one hour. After an hour, pre-heat the oven to 375°. To prepare the filling, peel, core and cut the apples into thick slices and place in another mixing bowl. Sprinkle over the rest of the filling ingredients and using your hands gently mix until its well combined. Remove the dough from the refrigerator and roll out the pastry into a 10-inch circle. Place the fruit filling into a 9-inch deep dish pie pan and cover with the rolled out dough being sure to tuck the excess pastry in between the pan side and the fruit. Using a sharp knife, cut three air vents into the dough, brush the top with a little milk and sprinkle on the remaining tablespoon of sugar. Bake on the middle rack of the oven for 50 to 60 minutes. When the crisp is done, let it rest for 20 minutes before cutting and serve with a dollop of vanilla ice cream.

Open Face Apple Pie
$ 4.95

DAT STEAK JOINT !

STEAK

RECIPES

C hicago has always been known for being the city that works, but steak houses in this town have always been known as where Chicago eats! You might be asking yourself, why would I include such a chapter in this book about street food? The answer is simply that steakhouses rule! Early in my career when I was about 20, I was fishing around for a job in the city and I just so happened to attend a cooking class at Triton College that was being taught by a great chef by the name of Hans Auschbacher. At the time, Hans was working as the executive chef of the famous restaurant, Lawry's The Prime Rib, located in the city, and through some chance of fate, the guy was kind enough to offer me a job. Although not technically a steakhouse, Lawry's turned out some of the best prime rib and side dishes known to man and was easily one of the top-grossing restaurants in the city.

My apprenticeship under this Swiss chef was phenomenal and educational not only in the fact of his knowledge of food, but also for his ability to effortlessly cook beautiful and delicious dishes for thousands of patrons a week. Chef Hans was not only a great mentor, but he also held the moniker of being the sports chef of Chicago. Now Chef Hans was a character such as myself and sometimes we would skip work to go visit his endless list of friends at restaurants, supply houses or meat packers, or attend an occasional Cubs game in the afternoon. One of my favorite jaunts with him was to visit a restaurant named Gene and Georgetti's, a really old school (started in 1941) neighborhood steakhouse that specialized in prime steaks, chops and Italian delicacies. On memorable visits to this steakhouse, I would have the treat of lunching with his friends such as Bobby Hull, Stan Makita, Mike Ditka, Jack Brickhouse, etc. When you're 20 years old, awestruck and sitting at a table with sports legends dressed to the nines, conversation doesn't come easily, but there is one thing that everyone agrees on and that's a great steak!

Chicago has always been known as the meat-packing capital of the world and the legendary book, *The Jungle*, by Upton Sinclair, which was mandatory reading in my high school, described the trials and tribulations of the meat-packing industry in the early 1900s. A lot has changed through the years and Chicago is blessed not only with a slew of great steakhouses, but also with two great purveyors by the names of Stock Yards and Allen Brothers, which supply prime meats to restaurants all over the world. It's interesting to note that some of our oldest steakhouses, such as Eli's, Morton's, Chicago Chophouse and Gene and Georgetti's, got their start in the early 60s as delicatessens or taverns that evolved into the great restaurants they are today. Their recipe for success is simple: use exceedingly fresh ingredients, have a limited menu, serve stiff drinks and have a really hot grill.

I'm often asked by other chefs what makes Chicago beef so special, so let me give you a quick education. First, most joints use USDA Prime meat (the highest quality beef available) that is processed by meat packers around the city. Most steers that are used weigh nearly 1,200 pounds and yield about 80 good steaks suitable for broiling. The average age of a steer used is two years, so they're not too fatty, and only about 2% of all meat processed is graded prime. These steers render steaks that can best be described as having a, light cherry color and being firm, well textured and marbled with just the right amount of fat that when broiled melts into your steak, making it juicy and tender. Second, steak joints around the city have an ingenious way of tenderizing the meat through aging. Aging is a process where the sides of meat are held in a cooler between 34° and 38° degrees for a period of 2-3 weeks. Held at that temperature the natural enzymes in the meat act as a tenderizer, breaking down the connective tissue and rendering the meat soft and supple. Last but not least, most restaurants use an extremely hot broiler that cooks at about 1,200° which seals the natural juices into your steak.

When I'm on the road, I'm always asked by weary travelers where the best place in the city is to just get a good Chicago-style meal and a great steak. My answer is simple: go to Gibsons on North Rush! I love Gibsons, I wish I was the chef at Gibsons, I wish I was a steak being broiled at Gibsons! Everything about this place is world class. Although a fairly young restaurant, Gibsons epitomizes the best in our city with the quality of their fare, their oversized portions and the loving generosity of a spirited staff that treats patrons as equally special. The dining room has a clubby-type appeal that attracts local celebs, politicians and sports figures with its warm and comforting ambience. Two more reasons I have high praise for this restaurant is that soup and salad is included with the entrée and the professional wait staff encourages you to split orders, which is a really nice touch for a big city restaurant. BRAVO!

Now I could easily go into some long lament about prime steaks such as T-bone, rib-eye, porterhouse or filet and I could also really confuse you with trivia about grading, selecting and butchering cattle, but I ain't gonna do it! What I would like you to do is visit your old-fashioned butcher shop around the corner and take the time to talk to the owner who will more than happily answer any questions you have. For all the rest of you armchair quarterbacks and pyro grill masters such as myself, please contact www.allenbrothers.com or www.stockyards.com. These are two great local firms that will gladly send you a beautiful catalog to salivate over and get your beef juices flowing! As my wife is typing this chapter for me, she is encouraging me to include some recipes I've collected over the years that typify the great side dishes you would get at any steakhouse around the city. The following is a well-rounded group of recipes I learned from Chef Hans that can be prepared to enliven your steak dinner party!

Since I can't come to your house and cook a steak for you, I thought I would give you a good collection of starters and sides that will enliven your party.

Classic Shrimp Cocktail

SERVES 4

Gulf shrimps majestically served with a tangy cocktail sauce!

INGREDIENTS

24 extra large chilled Gulf shrimps, pre-cooked, peeled and de-veined
2 cups shredded lettuce

COCKTAIL SAUCE

1 cup ketchup
3 tablespoons prepared horseradish
2 large garlic cloves, minced
2 tablespoons parsley, minced
3/4 teaspoon sea salt
1/4 teaspoon black pepper
2 tablespoons lemon juice
2 teaspoons Worcestershire
1/2 teaspoon Tabasco
Dash of celery salt and garlic powder

Place all the sauce ingredients into a small mixing bowl and thoroughly combine, cover and refrigerate for at least 3 to 4 hours. To serve place equal amounts of shredded lettuce into the bottom of four cocktail coupes, hang over the lip six chilled shrimps, dollop the center with the cocktail sauce and garnish with a few parsley sprigs.

Louisiana Style
"Lump Crab Remoulade" Cocktail

An old recipe that's making a comeback around town.

INGREDIENTS

2 heaping cups pre-cooked lump
 crabmeat
2 cups shredded lettuce
2 small ripe avocados
2 hard boiled eggs, lightly chopped
2 lemons, quartered

REMOULADE SAUCE

1 cup mayo, full-fat
1 heaping tablespoon Creole mustard
1 tablespoon red pepper, minced
1 tablespoon green onion, minced
1 tablespoon dill pickle, minced
1 tablespoon capers, minced
2 tablespoons parsley, minced
1 tablespoon lemon juice
1/4 teaspoon sea salt
1/8 teaspoon black pepper
Dash of Tabasco, Worcestershire and garlic powder

Place all the sauce ingredients into a small mixing bowl and thoroughly combine, cover and refrigerate for 3 to 4 hours. Carefully pick through the crabmeat to make sure there are no shell remnants and place into a mixing bowl. Using a plastic spatula, mix into the crab a little under half of the remoulade sauce and thoroughly combine. Peel, pit and halve the avocados. To serve equally divide the shredded lettuce among four cocktail coupes and then place a halved avocado into the center of each. Using a soup spoon gingerly scoop some of the crabmeat into the center of the avocado, garnish with a few lemon wedges and sprinkle on top the chopped egg. Serve with a side of saltine crackers.

Lobster Calypso Cocktail

Most definitely the cocktail for a high roller!

INGREDIENTS

2 pounds cold water lobster tails, pre-cooked
   and kept in shell
2 medium oranges
1 medium grapefruit
2 small lemons

CALYPSO SAUCE

1 cup mayo, full-fat
2 tablespoons ketchup
1 tablespoon lemon juice
1 tablespoon orange juice
1 tablespoon cognac
2 teaspoons Dijon mustard
1 teaspoon Worcestershire
1/4 teaspoon sea salt
1/8 teaspoon black pepper
Dash of Tabasco

Place all the ingredients for the sauce in a small mixing bowl and thoroughly combine, cover and refrigerate for 3 to 4 hours. Peel the oranges, grapefruit and lemons, carefully cut into segments and place in a mixing bowl to combine. Using a sharp chef's knife cut the lobster tails lengthwise in half and remove the lobster meat. Cut each quarter of the tail meat into thin slices and then re-pack back into its shell, red side up. Equally divide the fruit salad among four cocktail coupes, then place a stuffed tail onto each. Garnish the coupe with a few parsley sprigs and a drizzling of calypso sauce over the lobster. **(Don't overdo the sauce!)**

Shrimp De Jonghe

An original Chicago favorite that was invented by Pierre De Jonghe who served it at his classical restaurant in the early 20s. I've seen many interpretations of this dish throughout the years, but this recipe comes about as close as you're going to get to the original.

INGREDIENTS

24 extra large raw peeled and
   de-veined shrimp
1/2 cup unsalted butter, melted
2 tablespoons dry sherry or white wine

DE JONGHE BUTTER

1/2 pound unsalted butter, softened
1/4 cup Panko breadcrumbs
1/4 cup parsley, minced
2 tablespoons garlic, minced
2 tablespoons dry sherry or white wine
1 tablespoon lemon juice
1 tablespoon Dijon mustard
1/4 teaspoon sea salt
1/8 teaspoon black pepper
1/2 teaspoon sweet paprika
Dash of Tabasco, nutmeg and cayenne

1 cup Panko breadcrumbs for breading

To make the De Jonghe butter use a plastic spatula to combine all the ingredients in a mixing bowl, roll into a 2-inch diameter log, cover in plastic wrap and freeze for 2 hours. Toss the shrimps with the melted butter and wine and then cover until needed. Pre-heat the oven to 425°. Using a tablespoon of olive oil lightly coat the bottom of an oven-proof, medium sized oval gratin dish. Lightly dip the marinated shrimps into the breadcrumbs on both sides and then arrange in the gratin dish being sure to leave a little space between the shrimps. Remove the butter from the freezer and using a sharp chef's knife, slice off thin pieces of butter and scatter on top and around the breaded shrimp. Place the gratin dish immediately in the oven and bake for 10 to 12 minutes until the butter has melted and the shrimp is a light crispy brown. (If the shrimps aren't brown enough, you can always place the dish under the broiler for a minute.)

Creole Style BBQ Shrimps

SERVES 4

I learned how to make this delectable messy Louisiana specialty way back when and find it utterly delicious and mouthwatering before the steak comes.

INGREDIENTS

2 pounds large whole fresh shrimp in the shell

BBQ SAUCE

2 cups unsalted butter
4 tablespoons olive oil
1 tablespoon garlic, minced
2 small bay leaves
2 teaspoons dried rosemary leaves
1/2 teaspoon dried basil
1/2 teaspoon dried oregano
1/4 teaspoon sea salt
1/8 teaspoon black pepper
1/8 teaspoon cayenne pepper
2 teaspoons paprika
1 tablespoon lemon juice
Dash of Worcestershire

Pre-heat the oven to 450°. Place all the ingredients for the barbecue sauce into a medium sized cast iron skillet set over medium heat. Stir with a wooden spoon to combine and when it comes to a simmer, add the shrimps being sure that they are covered evenly by the melted butter. (A little bit more butter can be added if needed.) Cook the shrimps on the stove until their shells turn pink, then flip them over and place the skillet in the hot oven to cook for 10 minutes. Remove the pan from the oven and using a kitchen tong, equally divide the shrimps into 4 serving bowls, ladle on the remaining hot butter juices and eat.

Classic "Escargots"

I'm always amazed at how many requests I get for this recipe. Savory snails steeped in a luscious garlic butter have always exuded a touch of class at any high-end steak joint.

INGREDIENTS

1 large tin canned snails
1/2 cup white wine
1 cup chicken stock
1 bay leaf
2 sprigs fresh thyme
Dash of sea salt and pepper

2 tablespoons unsalted butter, melted
1 1/2 pounds cepes or porcini
    mushrooms, quartered

HERBED BUTTER

1 pound unsalted butter, softened
6 large garlic cloves, finely minced
1 tablespoon white wine
1 teaspoon brandy
1 teaspoon lemon juice
1 teaspoon sea salt
1/8 teaspoon black pepper
Pinch of nutmeg and cayenne
Dash of Tabasco
1/2 cup parsley, chopped

Drain the snails in a strainer and then rinse under cold water for a minute. Place the snails in a small saucepan with the wine, stock, bay leaf, thyme, salt and pepper and bring to a simmer, turn the heat off and let the snails cool in the liquid. Prepare the herbed butter by placing all the ingredients into a bowl and stir with a spatula to combine. Cover and refrigerate. Pre-heat the oven to 400°. Drain the snails of all liquid and set aside until needed. Place a medium sized heavy-duty cast iron skillet over medium heat and when the pan turns white hot, add the 2 tablespoons of butter and saute the mushrooms for 3 to 4 minutes until all liquid is evaporated. Now add the snails and cook stir with a wooden spoon for a minute more and then remove the pan from the fire. Remove the herbed butter from the refrigerator and using a tablespoon, scoop 1/3 of it out of the bowl and place directly on top of the snail-mushroom mixture. Put the skillet in the hot oven and cook for 8 to 10 minutes until the butter bubbles without burning.

Fried Calamari

Everyone loves fried squids! The secret is to have all your ingredients ready to go and make sure that your oil is hot hot hot!

INGREDIENTS

2 pounds squid rings and tentacles, cleaned
2 cups half and half
1 tablespoon Creole spice
1 1/2 cups all-purpose flour
1/2 cup fine yellow cornmeal

1 quart canola oil
Lemon wedges for garnish

In a medium sized bowl whisk together the half and half and Creole spice, then add the squid and marinate in the refrigerator for 3 to 4 hours. In another large bowl combine the flour and cornmeal and heat the oil to 400° in a deep fat fryer. When the oil is hot dredge the calamari pieces into the flour mixture and deep fry them for 2 minutes until lightly golden brown. Drain on paper towels and serve with the lemon wedges.

Baked Clams Casino

An old Playboy Club favorite studded with peppers, pimento and bacon.

INGREDIENTS

24 to 30 fresh Littleneck clams, scrubbed
   and cleaned
1 small bag rock salt

CASINO FILLING

2 tablespoons unsalted butter
3 large garlic cloves, minced
1/2 cup onion, minced
1/2 cup green pepper, minced
1/2 cup pimento or red pepper, minced
2 tablespoon parsley, minced
1 tablespoon lemon juice
1/8 teaspoon black pepper
Dash of Tabasco

5 bacon slices for garnish

Pre-heat the broiler to high. (Alternatively the clams can be baked in a 500° oven for 7 to 8 minutes.) Evenly spread the rock salt onto a large baking sheet and set aside. To make the filling heat the butter in a non-stick skillet, add the garlic, onion and peppers and sauté for 3 to 4 minutes. Add the rest of the seasoning and set aside to cool slightly. Stack the bacon pieces one on top of each other and using a sharp kitchen knife, cut into really fine strips. Carefully using a clam shucker open the clams, discard the top shell and place the clams onto the rock salt. Top each clam with about a teaspoon of the pepper mixture and then sprinkle on a good topping of the bacon strips. Place the baking sheet underneath the broiler for 4 to 5 minutes until the bacon is brown and crisp. Serve with a side of lemon wedges.

Baked Clams Oregenato

A warm and inviting Italian classic that every paesan loves.

INGREDIENTS

24 to 30 fresh Littleneck clams, scrubbed
    and cleaned
1 small bag rock salt

GARLIC BUTTER BASTE

3/4 pound unsalted butter
2 tablespoons garlic, minced
1 tablespoon white wine
1 teaspoon lemon juice
2 tablespoon parsley, minced
Dash of Tabasco, cayenne and red pepper flakes

OREGENATO TOPPING

1 heaping cup Panko breadcrumbs
1/3 parmesan cheese, grated
1/4 cup parsley, minced
1/2 teaspoon dried basil
1/2 teaspoon dried oregano
1/4 teaspoon sea salt
1/8 teaspoon black pepper

Pre-heat the oven to 450°. Spread the rock salt onto a large baking sheet and set aside. Place all the butter baste ingredients into a small saucepan, bring to a quick boil to cook for 1 minute, stir and then remove from the fire to steep. Combine all the oregenato ingredients in a small bowl and set aside. Carefully using a clam shucker open the clams, discard the top shell and place the clams onto the rock salt. When the butter baste is cooled, stir with a soup spoon and then pour a little bit over each clam to moisten. Now using your fingers top each clam with a good dusting of the oregenato mixture patting down slightly to make sure that it adheres. A little more garlic butter can be poured over the crumb topping. Place the pan in the hot oven and cook for 8 to 10 minutes until the breadcrumbs are a nice golden brown. Serve with a side of lemon wedges.

Baked Oysters Rockefeller

This is the real deal that I learned how to prepare a long time ago from a great Creole chef at Lake Point Tower Club.

INGREDIENTS

16 to 20 fresh Gulf oysters, scrubbed
   and cleaned
1 small bag rock salt

ROCKEFELLER FILLING

4 tablespoons unsalted butter
4 large garlic cloves, minced
1/2 cup onion, minced
1/2 cup green onion, minced
1/2 cup celery, minced
1/2 cup parsley, minced
Four 10 1/2 ounce packs frozen spinach, thawed
   and well-drained
1 teaspoon lemon zest, minced
1/4 teaspoon sea salt
1/8 teaspoon black pepper
Dash of Tabasco, Worcestershire, garlic powder,
   onion powder and cayenne
2 tablespoons Pernod liquor
1/2 cup heavy cream
1/3 cup parmesan cheese, grated
1/3 cup fresh breadcrumbs
1 whole large egg

Evenly spread the rock salt onto a large baking sheet and set aside. To make the filling place the spinach onto a cutting board and using a sharp knife, chop the spinach until it is exceedingly fine in texture with no large pieces visible. Remove any excess liquid from the board. In a medium sized saucepan, heat the butter and saute the garlic, onion, green onion and celery for 4 minutes until well cooked, but not brown. Add the parsley and spinach to the pan and saute for 2 to 3 minutes more until all liquid is evaporated. Now add the lemon zest, salt, pepper, seasonings and heavy cream to the pan and cook until the mixture resembles a thick creamed spinach. Immediately remove from the fire. Off the heat and when the mixture is slightly cooled, stir in the Pernod, cheese and breadcrumbs and mix to combine then refrigerate for a good 3 to 4 hours. Pre-heat the oven to 450°. Shuck the oysters, discard the top shell and any excess liquid then place onto the rock salt. Remove the spinach from the refrigerator, beat the egg with a whisk and then stir into the mixture with a wooden spoon until well combined. Carefully top each oyster with a generous dollop of the Rockefeller, flatten slightly and bake in the oven for 12 to 15 minutes until the sauce bubbles and becomes lightly golden brown. Serve with a side of lemon wedges.

Savory Stuffed Mushrooms

My in-law's Sicilian style mushroom appetizer that goes great with a martini or a Manhattan!

INGREDIENTS

1 pound hot Italian sausage, casings removed

32 medium-sized white domestic mushrooms
   with stems
2 tablespoons olive oil
2 large garlic cloves, minced
1/2 small onion, minced
1/2 red pepper, minced
1/3 cup black olives, pitted and diced
Parmesan cheese and olive oil for sprinkling

Remove the stems from the mushrooms and using a sharp knife finely chop the stems only. Set the caps aside until later. Heat the oil in a non-stick skillet, add the garlic, onion and red pepper and saute for 2 minutes. Now add the diced mushrooms stems and saute for 3 to 4 minutes until any liquid evaporates. Remove the pan from the fire and stir in the black olives. When the mushroom mixture is cool, combine with the bulk sausage until well mixed. Pre-heat the oven to 450°. Using a small spoon, scoop a tablespoon of stuffing into the mushroom caps and place on a parchment lined baking sheet. It is important to be sure the stuffing is completely in the mushroom cap. Liberally sprinkle on the cheese and oil and bake in the oven for 15 or 20 minutes until the tops are golden brown and bubbling.

Smoked Salmon Garnished

Some upscale steak joints tempt you with this light and classic appetizer that's always an appealing starter.

INGREDIENTS

1 pound thinly sliced smoked salmon
1/3 cup shallots, minced
1/3 cup baby capers
1/3 cup gherkins, chopped
2 large hard boiled eggs, chopped
2 small lemons, halved

Carefully lay four or five pieces of the smoked salmon onto chilled dinner plates. Place a half of lemon directly in the center of each plate on top of the salmon. Decoratively sprinkle the capers over the top of the salmon and garnish each plate with a little pile of the shallots, egg and gherkins. Serve with a side of toast points.

STEAKHOUSE SALADS

No dinner would be complete without a cool and refreshing salad to wake up the palate. Most joints like to keep it simple using the freshest ingredients that they can get their hands on. No bottled dressings here! To save time I'm giving you proportions that can be mixed up in a large serving bowl or platter, and then presented to your guests so they can help themselves.

Warm Spinach Salad

SERVES 4

This is an old continental favorite that is usually prepared tableside by some waiter in a cheap suit at some high-end fru fru joints.

INGREDIENTS

2 pounds fresh baby spinach leaves
1/4 pound country bacon, diced
2 tablespoons olive oil
1 small onion, diced
4 tablespoons raspberry vinegar
Dash of sea salt and black pepper

Thoroughly clean, wash and dry the spinach and then place into a large round serving bowl. Sauté the bacon in a skillet until it lightly begins to crisp then drain the grease, add the oil and onion and sauté for 2 minutes more. Remove the skillet from the fire, stir in the vinegar, a dash of salt and pepper and then carefully drizzle all of it over the fresh spinach leaves in the bowl. Using two kitchen spoons toss the spinach in the hot dressing until all the leaves are coated and serve.

Classic Caesar Salad

Easily the most popular salad at any restaurant around the city.

INGREDIENTS

2 small heads Romaine lettuce, cleaned and
   chopped
2 cups quality garlic or Italian croutons
1/2 cup freshly grated parmesan cheese

CAESAR DRESSING

1 whole large egg
2 anchovy fillets
2 large garlic cloves, minced
1 teaspoon whole black peppercorns
1/2 teaspoon celery salt
1/4 cup parmesan cheese
1 teaspoon Dijon mustard
2 tablespoons lemon juice
3 tablespoons red wine vinegar
2 dashes Tabasco and Worcestershire
1/2 cup olive or canola oil

To prepare the dressing place the anchovies, garlic, peppercorns, celery salt, cheese, mustard, lemon juice, vinegar, Tabasco and Worcestershire into the bowl of a food blender. Place the whole egg into a small saucepot filled with water, bring to a boil and simmer for exactly 1 1/2 minutes. (This kills any bacteria in the egg.) Remove the egg from the water and crack into the blender with the other ingredients, cover and pulse the blender a few times. Now remove the center cap from the cover and with the machine running, slowly pour in the oil until the dressing is well blended and smooth. Refrigerate for at least three to four hours before using. Place the lettuce and croutons into a large serving bowl, toss with the dressing and sprinkle on the remaining parmesan cheese.

Beefsteak Tomato, Red Onion and Gorgonzola Salad

SERVES 4

Really ripe and luscious Midwestern beefsteak tomatoes are essential to making this salad, so don't get cheap.

INGREDIENTS

2 to 3 large beefsteak tomatoes
1 medium red onion, peeled
1 small wedge gorgonzola cheese

GARLIC RED WINE DRESSING

2/3 cup extra virgin olive oil
4 tablespoons garlic red wine vinegar
1 teaspoon garlic, minced
1/2 teaspoon sea salt
1/4 teaspoon black pepper

Coarse ground black pepper for garnish

Place all of the dressing ingredients into a small jar, vigorously shake and refrigerate for one hour. Using a thin sharp chef's knife cut the tomatoes into quarter inch slices and decoratively overlap on a large serving platter. Cut the red onion into thin slices, separate the rings and arrange on top of the tomatoes. Cut the gorgonzola into bite-size pieces, sprinkle over the top of the tomato salad and then drizzle on the dressing. Garnish with some coarse ground black pepper.

Chicago's Very Own "The Wedge" with Thousand Island Dressing

SERVES 4

Don't ask me who invented this presentation, but I find it pure genius. It's also the laziest way to present a salad that I've ever seen!

INGREDIENTS

1 small head ice-burg lettuce
1 cup bacon, pre-cooked and chopped
1 cup hard boiled eggs, chopped
1 cup tomatoes, diced

THOUSAND ISLAND DRESSING

1 cup mayo, full fat
1/4 cup chili sauce
1/3 cup sweet pickles, minced
1/3 cup green olives with pimento, chopped
2 tablespoons parsley, minced
1 tablespoon lemon juice
1 teaspoon garlic, minced
1/2 teaspoon sea salt
1/4 teaspoon black pepper
Dash of garlic powder, onion powder and Tabasco

Combine all the ingredients for the dressing in a small bowl and stir until well combined. If the dressing is too thick, add 1 to 2 tablespoons of water. Refrigerate for three to four hours before using. To serve the salad cut the lettuce into four quarters and place each wedge piece onto a long serving platter. Re-stir the dressing and pour a good sized dollop over each wedge. Sprinkle over the top of each lettuce wedge the bacon, eggs and tomatoes to serve.

Garbage Can Salad

This is a Sicilian concoction that is comprised of a little menza menza or whatever you want to put into it. Some joints around the city charge up to $18.95 for this salad, but it's well worth it.

INGREDIENTS

1 small head iceberg lettuce, cleaned and chopped
3 Roma tomatoes, quartered
1/2 small cucumber, sliced
1 small red onion, sliced
1 large rib celery, sliced
4 radishes, sliced
1 cup pepperoncinis
One 6 ounce jar marinated artichokes in brine, drained
1 heaping cup Italian olive salad
1/2 cup garbanzo beans
1/3 pound provolone cheese, cut julienne
1/3 pound salami, cut julienne
3/4 pound medium sized shrimps, pre-cooked, shelled and de-veined

ITALIAN DRESSING

3/4 cup extra virgin olive oil
1/3 cup red wine vinegar
1 tablespoon garlic, minced
1 1/2 teaspoons dried Italian seasoning spice
1/2 teaspoons sea salt
1/4 teaspoon black pepper
Pinch of red pepper flakes

Combine all the dressing ingredients in a small jar, shake vigorously to mix and refrigerate for one hour. Place all the ingredients for the salad in a really large mixing bowl and using your hands toss to combine. Re-shake the dressing and lightly dress the salad, mix again and pour onto a large decorative platter to serve.

Fancy Chopped Salad

SERVES 4

Often known as the classic Cobb salad, it's usually served with cold cooked breast of chicken or turkey. I've enlivened the salad dressing to give it that extra kick.

INGREDIENTS

1 pound leftover cooked chicken or turkey
    breast, cubed
4 thick slices bacon, cooked and crumbled
2 large plum tomatoes, diced
1 large avocado, peeled, pitted and diced
1 small red onion, chopped
2 hard boiled eggs, chopped
1/2 small head iceberg lettuce, chopped
1/2 small head Romaine, chopped
1/4 pound Roquefort cheese, crumbled

COBB DRESSING

1/4 cup grainy mustard
2 large garlic cloves, minced
2 tablespoons lemon juice
2 tablespoon red wine vinegar
1 tablespoon honey
1/4 teaspoon sea salt
1/8 teaspoon black pepper
1/2 cup extra virgin olive oil

Place all the ingredients for the dressing a jar, shake vigorously to mix and refrigerate for one hour. Place all the salad ingredients into a large mixing bowl and using your hands toss to combine. Re-shake the dressing and lightly dress the salad, mix again and pour into a large decorative bowl to serve.

No steak dinner would be complete without some type of appetizing side that usually comes in a gargantuan head-size portion! The following represent the top six sellers that are served around the city which I think you'll enjoy.

Stuffed Jumbo Baked Potato

SERVES 6 TO 8

This potato dish just jumps out of the oven and says, "Eat me!"

INGREDIENTS

4 large baking potatoes, cleaned and dried
3 strips hickory smoked bacon, cooked and chopped
1/2 cup sour cream, full fat
1/4 cup unsalted butter, softened
1 cup sharp cheddar cheese, grated
1 whole large egg
2 tablespoons chives, minced
1/2 teaspoon sea salt
1/4 teaspoon black pepper
Dash of nutmeg, garlic powder and Tabasco

TOPPING

Sprinkling of paprika
1/3 cup grated parmesan cheese

Pre-heat the oven to 375°. Using a kitchen fork lightly pierce the tops of the potatoes and bake on the middle rack for about 1 hour until the potatoes are tender. When cooked remove the potatoes, slightly cool, cut in half and carefully scrape out all of the potato pulp into a mixing bowl. (You will need four perfect potato boats to re-stuff so be careful.) Add the remaining ingredients to the potatoes except the topping and thoroughly combine with a spatula until the mixture is chunky smooth. Using a kitchen spoon carefully re-stuff four of the boats piled high and place onto a baking sheet. Increase the oven temperature to 400°, sprinkle on the topping and bake for another 15 minutes until the tops are lightly golden brown.

Creamed Spinach with Mushrooms

A really soul satisfying side dish that goes great with a slice of prime rib.

INGREDIENTS

4 pounds fresh spinach leaves, cleaned and pre-
    blanched
4 tablespoons unsalted butter
2 slices hickory smoked bacon, minced
1 pound domestic mushrooms, sliced
6 large garlic cloves, minced
2 cups heavy cream
1/2 teaspoon sea salt
1/4 teaspoon black pepper
1/8 teaspoon nutmeg
Dash of Tabasco and Maggi

Drain the blanched spinach leaves of all excess liquid, chop and set aside. Heat the butter in a medium sized non-stick skillet, add the bacon, mushrooms and garlic, and sauté quickly until the mushrooms start to release their liquid. When the liquid starts to dissipate, add the rest of the ingredients including the spinach, stir to combine, reduce the heat and simmer slowly until the cream and spinach thicken about 8 to 10 minutes.

Steak House Onion Rings

SERVES 4

Bigger, badder and bolder then the average onion ring!

INGREDIENTS

2 cups all-purpose flour
I tablespoon baking powder
I 1/2 teaspoons sea salt
One 12 ounce bottle of beer
I large egg
2 medium Spanish onions, peeled and
  cut into 1/2 -inch slices
6 cups rendered beef fat or peanut oil

Brown paper bags

In a medium sized mixing bowl combine I 1/2 cups of the flour, baking powder and salt. Make a well in the center, pour in the beer and egg, and whisk until a smooth batter forms. In another bowl separate the onion slices into rings, and then dust with the remaining flour and toss. Fill a deep fat fryer with the oil until it reaches 375°. Dredge about 6 to 8 of the onion rings into the batter, shake off the excess, then using a kitchen fork carefully place into the hot oil. Fry the rings for about 2 minutes on each side or until lightly golden brown, and then remove to a layer of brown paper bags.

Cheesy Potato Gratinee

SERVES 4

A more refined version of your mom's scalloped potatoes au gratin!

INGREDIENTS

2 tablespoons unsalted butter, softened
2 large garlic cloves, minced
3 cups half and half
1/2 teaspoon sea salt
1/4 teaspoon black pepper
1/8 teaspoon nutmeg
Dash of cayenne, garlic powder and Tabasco
2 1/2 pounds Idaho potatoes, peeled and cleaned
1/2 pound finely grated cheddar cheese

Pre-heat the oven to 350°. Lightly butter a medium sized oval earthenware casserole and then evenly sprinkle on the minced garlic. In a mixing bowl combine the half and half and seasonings. Slice the peeled potatoes paper thin and place directly into the milk mixture. Sprinkle the cheese over the potatoes, thoroughly mix and pour directly into the prepared casserole. Bake for I 1/2 to 2 hours until the top is golden brown.

Classic Grilled Asparagus with Hollandaise Sauce

SERVES 4

Every young chef should learn this classic recipe. It's an old steakhouse specialty that's very popular when prepared correctly.

INGREDIENTS

1 1/2 pounds jumbo asparagus, cleaned
   and trimmed
1/4 cup olive oil
1/2 teaspoon Lawry's season salt
1/4 teaspoon black pepper

HOLLANDAISE SAUCE

2 large egg yolks
2 tablespoons water
1 1/2 stick unsalted butter, melted
1/4 teaspoon sea salt
2 tablespoons lemon juice

Pre-heat a charcoal grill. Bring 1 quart of lightly salted water to the boil and cook the asparagus until al dente, remove to a platter and sprinkle on the olive oil, season salt and pepper. Place the egg yolks and water into a medium sized mixing bowl and then set onto a medium warm baine marie full of water. Whisk the yolks and water until thick and fluffy about 2 to 3 minutes then remove the bowl from the fire. Now carefully drizzle in the melted butter while whisking, until it forms a thick sauce, season with the salt and lemon juice and keep warm. Quickly grill the asparagus for 2 to 3 minutes until it takes on some grill marks. Arrange on a platter and dollop with the Hollandaise sauce.

American Fries

SERVES 4

No, these are not French fries, these are cowboy style steak and meat fries!

INGREDIENTS

2 tablespoons unsalted butter
2 tablespoons olive oil
3 medium garlic cloves, minced
1 medium onion, diced
1 large red or green pepper, diced
4 cups pre-boiled potatoes, cubed
1/2 teaspoon sea salt
1/4 teaspoon black pepper
1/2 teaspoon dried oregano
1/4 teaspoon dried basil
1/4 cup parsley, chopped

Heat the butter and oil in a large non-stick skillet and when hot sauté the garlic, onions and peppers for 3 to 4 minutes. Add the potatoes to the pan and continue sauteing and tossing for another 8 to 10 minutes until the potatoes are light golden brown. Add the remaining seasoning, toss and serve.

KING CHICKEN VESUVIO
UNWRAPPED

CHICKEN

VESUVIO

If I only had a dollar for every time I've been asked this question, "Who invented Chicken Vesuvio?" Chicken Vesuvio, or Kotopoulo Psito Lemonata Me Patates, meaning roasted chicken with lemon, herbs, wine and potatoes is actually a morphed, mystical invention popularized by two famous Chicago restaurateurs, one Italian and one Greek. (For all you nay-sayers and disbelievers, sit down, take a deep breath and read the entire introduction before jumping to any conclusions.) When I was a kid, I grew up just a little bit shy of Cumberland and the 94 which was the gateway to the suburbs in the early 60s. Norridge, my home, was all about the best of Italian culture and cooking. Also, down the road on Harlem Ave. by Lawrence, was a new emerging population of Greek restaurant owners whose philosophies were very similar to the Italian culture and work ethic. It was at this time in the early 60s that two great restauranteurs emerged and changed the way people thought about going out to eat. Nic Giannotti, a paesan from Naples near Mount Vesuvius, opened an Italian Steakhouse called Giannotti's on Mannheim Road in The Air Host Hotel. Some people remember a lounge downstairs from the restaurant called Orlando's Hideaway where they served quality highballs and cocktails. Nic's claim to fame was his warm and generous heart and the exceptional way in which he stayed true to the Italian sense of family. Nic was an adventurer who liked to visit other eating establishments, and he was also known to frequent the restaurant shopping district of Randolph and Halsted seeking out fresh produce and quality meats. At the same time, a Greek by the name of Petros Kogiones from Nestani, Greece, opened a landmark grocery and restaurant called Petros Dianna on Halsted. Petros was reputed to have kissed more women than any man alive, and had earned the name, King of the Opaa. From what I've been told, the two restaurateurs had a friendly rivalry going relating to who could create the best dish and who had the best chef. In the midst of this feud, chefs were hired and fired and swapped, as were recipes. Over the years, these chicken recipes evolved and came together and eventually became Chicken Vesuvio as we know it. The old paesans claim that it's the eruption of spices that assault your mouth that gave the dish it's name, and the Greeks insist that the invention came from the classic Greek marinade of spices they use on their poultry and lamb. French chefs that I know in the city point to the classic dish called Picatta Maitre D'Hotel (meaning veal in lemon butter) that utilizes the technique of flash-frying, then de-glazing the skillet with a splash of white wine, lemon juice and stock to create a savory sauce which blankets the succulent veal or perhaps a chicken cutlet. Other sources claim that when the hot, oven-cooked chicken, potatoes and peas are stacked on a serving platter, they are reminiscent of Mount Vesuvius erupting. Whatever the origin, both restaurants specialized in high quality food products and soon earned international acclaim that brought such stars as Frank Sinatra, Dean Martin, Don Rickles and Sammy Davis Jr. to the Chicago area. The word got out and soon everyone was doing a Vesuvio. In my career, I've worked with many French, Italian and Greek chefs, and while Vesuvio is always a lively topic of conversation, you would be hard pressed to find the recipe in any printed cookbook. Earlier in my career I actually worked with a Greek chef who was a line cook at a Chicago restaurant called Vesuvio back in the 1950s, but he couldn't recall the recipe being invented there, only that it was popularized at such old acclaimed restaurants as Caruso's, Riccardo's, Club Corsica, Club El Bianco and Gene and Georgetti's. It was this chef's opinion that the dish came together accidentally as a melding of classical technique seasoned with a variety of cultural spices. In this case, too many chefs did not spoil the broth! It has recently come to my attention that a recipe for a dish called Pollo alla Vesuviana was first published in a 1954 Italian cookbook by the Culinary Arts Institute of Chicago. This printed recipe calls for the use of Marsala wine and deep-fried potatoes, a far cry from the recipe I've listed here. Some chefs add more garlic, some chefs add more wine, and I say, "Who's to judge, it's all Vesuvio!"

King Chicken Vesuvio!

Often imitated but never duplicated, this is the real deal. Most restaurants use a 10-inch high sided nonstick skillet with a tempered handle so it can be placed directly in the hot oven to cook. Feel free to get a little heavy on the spices to give it that special kick!

INGREDIENTS

3 medium Russet potatoes, cleaned and peeled
1/4 cup olive oil

One 3 to 4 pound frying chicken, cut up
1/2 cup all-purpose flour
1/2 cup dry white wine

VESUVIO SPICE

2 cups chicken stock
2 teaspoons cornstarch
6 large garlic cloves, minced
3/4 teaspoon garlic salt
1/8 teaspoon black pepper
Dash of red pepper flakes
1 teaspoon dried basil
3/4 teaspoon dried oregano
1/4 teaspoon dried thyme
Large pinch dried rosemary
Large pinch dried sage
Dash of Tabasco and Maggi

2/3 cup fresh green peas, lightly cooked
6 roasted red pepper slices
2 tablespoons parsley, chopped

Pre-heat the oven to 425°. Cut each potato into 6 equal pieces. Heat the olive oil in a 10-inch skillet and when hot, sauté all the potatoes until lightly golden brown on all sides about 5 to 6 minutes, remove from the skillet and set aside. Pour a little more olive oil in the skillet, dredge the cut chicken pieces into the flour and then sauté the floured pieces in the hot oil for 5 to 6 minutes or until well browned on each side. While the chicken is browning combine all the ingredients for the Vesuvio spice until well blended. When the chicken is well browned, remove any excess grease from the skillet and then scatter the potatoes over the top of the chicken. Give the skillet a quick toss, add the white wine and let it come to the boil. Now pour the Vesuvio spice mixture over the potatoes and chicken, let that come to a boil and then place the entire pan into the hot oven to cook for 30 minutes. After 30 minutes sprinkle on the remaining fresh peas, peppers and parsley and let the chicken cook for another 10 minutes. Pour hot onto a serving platter.

Greeky Chicken and Lemon Potatoes!

SERVES 4

The Italians have most definitely crowned chicken Vesuvio as their own, but in defense of my Greek friends I only find it fitting to include this beautiful dish that can be found at any quality Greek joint around the city. This recipe is in three parts so read it carefully.

INGREDIENTS

5 large potatoes, peeled and quartered

CHICKEN SPICE

2 large cloves garlic, minced
1/2 teaspoon sea salt
1/4 teaspoon black pepper
1 teaspoon dried oregano
1/2 teaspoon garlic salt
2 tablespoons olive oil
1/3 cup fresh lemon juice
1/4 cup dry white wine

POTATO SPICE

1/2 teaspoon sea salt
1/4 teaspoon black pepper
1/2 teaspoon garlic salt
2 teaspoons dried oregano
1/2 cup fresh lemon juice
2 tablespoons olive oil
1 teaspoon Hungarian sweet paprika

2 small fresh chickens (about 3 pounds each), quartered

COOKING STOCK

2 1/2 cups chicken stock
1 teaspoon cornstarch, dissolved
3 large dashes Tabasco
3 large dashes Maggi
1/4 cup parsley, chopped

Pre-heat the oven to 425°. Bring a medium sized pot of salted water to a boil, add the potatoes and cook for exactly 4 minutes. Drain and then place them into a large mixing bowl, sprinkle on the potato spice and mix to coat. Place the chicken pieces onto a clean work surface and using a sharp boning knife, trim away any excess fat. Place the chicken in a large bowl, sprinkle on the chicken spice and mix to coat. Give the potatoes a quick toss in the bowl and then pour directly into a medium sized non-stick roasting pan and place in the hot oven to cook for 30 minutes. After 30 minutes, remove the roasting pan from the oven and using a kitchen tong flip the potatoes over. Now place the chicken pieces directly on top of the potatoes and pour over the excess marinade. Put the pan back in the oven to roast another 30 minutes. Remove the pan from the oven again and pour the cooking stock over the chicken and potatoes and roast for another hour being sure to baste the chicken every 15 minutes with the cooking liquid. When the chicken is nicely browned, remove the pan from the oven and carefully arrange the chicken pieces and potatoes decoratively onto a serving platter.

WHO'S GOT THE BEEF?

ITALIAN

RECIPES

One of the most hotly contested arguments in Chicago centers around a concoction that's called an Italian beef sandwich. In the annals of Chicago history, never have I witnessed such fervent devotion and rivalry pitting beef stand against beef stand and brother against brother. The fight has even been taken to the computer airwaves where local Chowhounds spar on their keyboards as to who has the best juice or giardiniera. Pilgrimages have been made and war has been declared as to who has the best, so I've decided to throw my hat into the ring and set the record straight.

Before I begin, let me explain to you out-of-towners what a "beef sandwich" is. An Italian beef sandwich is basically a classic French dip (very thin slices of lean roast beef served on a hard roll with a side of beef au jus for dipping) with a few major differences. First, the meat is highly seasoned with Italian herbs such as oregano, basil, garlic and pepper, then slow roasted with a little liquid until medium rare. After roasting, the meat is cooled and thinly sliced or shredded, and the leftover juice is seasoned again to be transformed into a flavorful simmering gravy. The sliced meat is then steeped in this gravy until heated through, and then served on a semi-soft, 6-inch Italian roll with a dipping of spiced juice and a topping of either sautéed sweet red peppers or hot pepper giardiniera. That's it! Sounds easy, only in your dreams!

History

Chicago-style beef sandwiches didn't just appear on the Midwestern horizon; it's actually been a work in progress since the early 1920s. The influx of southern Italian immigrants moving to the near west side around the turn of the century not only brought a profusion of herbs and spices indigenous to their land, but the hearty and spicy foodstuffs they were familiar with. Most of these newly arrived Italians were known as the "contadini" or peasant farmers, so it's logical that many would turn their work ethic toward becoming grocers and meat packers. (Scala, Caputo, Antognolli, Valli, V Formusa, Ferrara, and Fontanini are a few of the biggest purveyors in the Midwest.) The hot dog push cart industry was going strong throughout the wards during this time, and the Itallans, looking for their own identity and to satisfy their ethnic patrons, set up small stands that served grilled or cured Italian sausage on a roll, thus mimicking the new found hot dog on a bun. They also served "spiadini," skewered meats that were lightly marinated in a little olive oil, garlic and Italian spices. These meats were usually pork, lamb or veal, which although at the time were far less expensive than beef, could also cause rampant bouts of triconosis that would send the fear of God through any self-respecting Italian. (My in-laws, who were originally from Taylor street and of that era, have told me horror stories about it.)

To give you a better perspective of that era, Italians from the old country were not used to Americans' widespread use of fatty beef, since beef in Italy was far leaner and much more scarce. One of the most famous beef dishes from the Italian culture is "bisteca a la fiorentina," which is similar to an American T-bone or porterhouse that is simply grilled and served with a sprinkling of salt, black pepper and lemon. One problem is that a real fiorentina requires a special breed of beef found only in the Chiana Valley of Florence.

The Italian meat purveyors had to forge ahead with the newly found abundant beef and find varied and interesting ways to appeal to an ever increasing Italian audience. With that said, after all the choice cuts of meat from the cow--steaks and chops--were sold for a premium, the purveyors could acquire the less desirable cuts from the chuck and rump at bargain basement prices. However, this meat was perishable and needed to be used quickly. The answer was simple. It came in the form of old Italian dishes such as "poposo," "bollito misto," "stufato," and "manzo alla lombarda." The classically written book, "The Food of Italy," by Waverley Root, describes these recipes as dishes that consist of boiling or braising meat in liquid to achieve not only a highly flavorful broth, but a mouth-watering, tender meat that can be eaten with a spoon. The resulting tender meat juice and gravy were prized as an accompaniment to dress a dish of pasta or to be sopped up with a hard roll or piece of Italian bread.

Another problem that the Italians of the west side faced was that most were forced to live in tenement housing under not so ideal cooking conditions. To maximize the flavor of the less desirable chunks of beef, people had to resort to slow braises and heavy spicing. The meat was cooked in large covered casseroles overnight, mostly by an obliging neighborhood baker whose ovens were still hot from a day of bread baking.

In the Depression Era of the 20s and early 30s, many Italian immigrants were just trying to earn a living and feed their large families by providing ethnic foods to their paesans in the neighborhood. The most notable of these was Pasquale Scala, who emigrated from Naples around 1912. Originally a wine maker, Scala abandoned that profession once in the U.S. to make a more lucrative living curing meats at Luca Baking Company on Polk and Western. Besides the cappicola and mortadella, Scala made a great Italian sausage that people would buy and sometimes cure themselves in their own cold closet. (They'd have pepperoni in a couple of months.) He expanded his clientele and began providing luncheon plates to local joints and taverns and eventually to the larger catering halls. Starting out with the sausage sandwich and seasoned meats, the Italian beef sandwich was born out of the necessity of stretching a cut of roast beef. The thinner the meat was sliced, the more people you could feed at a neighborhood restaurant, wedding, banquet or party.

Papa Scala must have been a culinary genius because it's at this time that he started experimenting with the curing and spicing of different cuts of choice beef. One of the most popular was the beef round that was covered with Italian spices, slow roasted and thinly sliced. An increase in the Italian population brought more people to the gatherings. To meet this demand, catering halls were opening up in the neighborhood, the most prominent being that of the Ferrara family. In a recent phone interview, Nella Ferrara, owner of Ferrara Baking and Candy Company, reminisced about their original catering hall, where old Italian weddings--called "peanut weddings" in reference to their frugality--were held. All that was served was wedding cake and Italian beef and sausage sandwiches on crusty Italian rolls. Her family supplied the beautiful cakes and rolls from their bakery and Scala supplied the meats. I'm proud to say that I have some in-laws who had their receptions at Ferrara Catering Hall and the stories they tell bring you back to simpler times.

The spicy Italian beef took off and Scala eventually set up shop supplying all the major stands, including Al's, Marge's and Carm's. The key word here is "stand," as these places were so small you literally had to stand and lean forward to eat these juicy concoctions so the drippings wouldn't ruin your clothes. Currently, there are a few dozen Italian beef stands scattered throughout the city and the suburbs, all turning out freshly-made Italian beef sandwiches to an appreciative audience.

Beef stands are truly a Chicago icon, not only for their tasty delicacies but also for creating their own jargon which out-of-towners sometimes find puzzling. Before you enter a beef joint, you've got to know the lingo. Chicago-style Italian beef is commonly just called "beef" by the locals. When you go into a joint, you've got a couple options when ordering. The first is whether you want your sandwich "dry" or "wet." "Dry" means without a lot of juice and "wet" means the whole sandwich is deep sixed into the spicy juice, which leaves the roll soggy, tender, and utterly delicious. Next comes the topping of your choice, which is usually sweet red peppers or hot pepper giardiniera. The peppers aren't mandatory, but I highly recommend them as you don't want to insult the beef stand owner. There's also another option for your sandwich and that's called a "beef combo." A "combo" is a beef sandwich that sits on top of a spicy fennel-infused grilled Italian sausage link. The "combo" is the way to go if you really want to experience culinary nirvana. The interplay of the crusty roll with the spiciness of the grilled sausage, the tenderness of the thinly sliced beef, the perfect garlic and Italian-spiced juice that runs down your arms, and the hot giardiniera oil all add to the dimension and the depth of flavors. So next time you visit Chicago, stop in at a beef joint, proudly walk up to the counter and tell the guy these sweet words, "I want a combo juicy with sweet and hot, fries and a lemon ice to go!" I want to leave you with one last piece of advice. The proper way to eat an Italian beef sandwich is to roll up your sleeves, tuck a napkin in your shirt and eat standing up, leaning slightly forward.

The Science of da Beef

All right, Mikey, now we know the history of Chi-town beef, so let's get to the meat of the matter. (No pun intended!) Okay, we're going to start with Beef Class 101, so hold on to your seats. An interesting fact that I've got to let you know is that a mature steer beef cattle normally weighs about 1,200 pounds, yielding between 55 and 60% of its weight in meat (about 350 pounds per side of beef; you know, the thing that Rocky was training on during the movie.) According to strict regulations set forth by the National Association of Meat Purveyors, the carcass is divided up into five sections: the chuck, rib, loin, round and brisket plate flank. Once the meat is cut into these sections, it is processed into steaks, chops, roasts, ground beef, etc. When we're talking about Italian beef meat, we are interested in three sections of the steer. Those are the round or arse, the sirloin or lower back and the chuck area or neck. I know a lot of beef stand owners who, depending on their cash flow and cooking prowess, utilize meat from all three sections. But be forewarned, not all of the aforementioned cuts take to just one cooking technique. Let me explain. Chicago beef stands typically serve their beef in a highly flavored juice; however some places like to thinly slice their meat, some thickly slice their meat and others shred it. (It's all good; it just depends on how much work you want to do.)

To get really technical, the NAMP puts numbers on its specific cuts of meat that are recognized as the standard world wide. (To help you along, I'll give you the specific name and number so you can impress your butcher when you request these cuts.) If you are the kind of guy who likes really thinly sliced meat, you are looking at two cuts from the sirloin called No. 184 top sirloin butt and No. 185 bottom sirloin butt. These two cuts of meat from the sirloin are excellent pieces that are not too fatty and are usually sold for boneless sirloin steaks. The top butt usually weighs about 12 to 14 pounds on average, whereas the bottom butt averages 8 to 10 pounds. Some say that the top butt is of higher quality than the bottom; however, with escalating meat prices, I would always buy the more economical cut. I've experimented a lot with this cut of meat and find it a good choice for making homemade French dip, Philly cheese steak or roast beef.

Two other popular cuts of meat that I recommend are the old standard No. 168 and No. 169 beef round/top (inside). No. 168 is basically an untrimmed top round. Roast top round of beef au jus has been around since the early 1900s when a French immigrant by the name of Philippe Mathieu created the classic French dip sandwich at his famous restaurant in Los Angeles, Philippe the Original. Beef top round is extremely lean and easy to slice, producing maximum yield if slow roasted in an oven. This cut of meat typically weighs about 18 to 22 pounds. Italian delis usually sell this precooked beef sliced to order and gladly give you a quart of beef jus for free. Another cut from the round that can be used is No. 167 beef round knuckle, averaging about 12 pounds in weight. This is also a lean and flavorful cut of meat that can be used to make your "sammies."

Chef Mike's Wisdom!!! It's at this time that I have to inform you that the above mentioned cuts of beef are all good choices for making a beef sandwich, assuming the meat is seasoned, slowly oven roasted to an internal temperature of 130 to 135°F medium rare, then cooled and thinly sliced. But be forewarned, these are big chunks of meat that need to be not only cooked perfectly, but also will have to be thinly sliced by hand on a good heavy-duty deli type electric slicing machine. That's a lot of work for a home cook who just wants to knock out a good beef sandwich. You would also need a pretty good size oven and baking pan to accommodate these big chunks of meat. If you don't want to go to the trouble of roasting your own meat, go to the Italian store, buy 3 to 4 pounds of thinly sliced rare Italian beef, and just add it to my juice recipe that appears after this intro.

Cook it Right! As I mentioned earlier, not all cuts of beef take to the same methods of cooking. The above cuts, Nos. 184, 185, 168, 169, and 167, all do very well if plainly seasoned and oven roasted. The first tip I want to share with you is to have these primal cuts of meat cut in half so they are easier to handle, cook and slice. If in doubt, ask your butcher. The second tip is to pre-sear and pre-season your meat before roasting to seal in the natural juices. It's also wise to let the roast sit on the countertop for at least 1 hour after searing and before cooking to take the chill off. The third is to pre-heat your oven to 325°, and place the meat fat side up on a baking rack in a shallow roasting pan. I recommend cooking each one of these cuts of meat an average of 20 minutes per pound to reach an internal temperature on a meat thermometer of 130 to 135° for medium rare. (Always rely on your meat thermometer rather than the kitchen clock when cooking your roast.) Chef's Tip: Remove the roast from the oven when an instant read thermometer registers 5° below the temperature of desired doneness. Let the meat stand for 15 to 20 minutes covered with a piece of foil as it will continue to cook as it sits. At this point, the roast must be completely chilled overnight before slicing. Do not discard the brown bits that have accumulated on the bottom of the baking pan. Just deglaze the pan with a little white wine or water, scrape up all the bits with a spatula and pour into a bowl to be added to your Italian beef juice. When the meat is cooled, slice thinly across the grain. You can easily store the meat in one pound packs in the freezer for up to 3 months.

Old World Paesan Beef Stand Science

I know I've given you a lot of specific information about the most popular beef cuts that can be thinly sliced. There are a few others that I'm purposely not going to mention because they are unmanageable or too fatty for a home cook to prepare.   Cattle prices, just like the stock market, fluctuate hourly depending upon supply and demand, and if you're not privy to that information, basically you're shit outta luck! My family members are big fans of homemade beef sandwiches, but the biggest hassle always seems to be the slicing of the meat. Small home slicing machines just don't cut it, and really good restaurant quality machines are a hassle to clean and store, so I had to find a solution. In researching this project, I spent a lot of time talking to old paesans who, for the most part, are avid cooks and experts at turning out meals in grand proportions. All agree that there's no question that the cooking methods of beef sandwiches have drastically changed over the years because the reality is that Italians used to cook their lower end cuts of beefs or meat in covered casseroles overnight for as long as 12 hours. My wife's Auntie Fran, who's a wonderful Italian cook, agrees that sliced prime cuts of meat are great, but when you have to set a varied Italian buffet to accommodate 50 people, you find efficient and economical cuts that can be stretched to feed a crowd.

My Italian in-laws always had huge holiday parties that would start outside, and then everyone would gravitate toward the basement where card tables and folding chairs were set up in neat rows around the room. My mother-in-law, Geri, and her sister, Fran, were the masters of the Italian buffet, serving such homemade delicacies as meatballs and sausage, hand-rolled manicotti, roasted chicken and potatoes, freshly made antipasto and olive salads and the list goes on from there. The piece d' resistance of the buffet was a huge old white, enamel-on-steel 18 quart Rival tabletop roaster, filled to the brim with hot, juicy, homemade Italian beef, peppers and sausage, that was ceremoniously brought down stairs from the garage where it was slowly simmering from the night before. No one dared to touch what was in the roaster, as that job was left to the sole proprietorship of the hostess. As a chef, I was always fascinated as to who devised that spicy beef, sausage and juice-laden concoction, and it also amazed me how it was produced without a measurement or recipe.

Now that I am in with the family, let me tell you their secret--No. 113 -116, meaning chuck pot roasts! Yes, I said chuck pot roasts, which include 7- bone roasts, arm pot roast, blade roast and chuck eye roast. It makes a lot of sense because cuts from the chuck are highly tasty and juicy with a good amount of connective tissue fat that melts away and makes the meat intensely flavorful and tender if cooked in liquid for a long time. Chick, one of my wife's uncles, just so happened to be a butcher, and it was his nana's job to make the Italian beef casserole which she would obligingly do, but she hated to cut the meat, due to her frail hands from being a seamstress.   Uncle Chick knew that if meat from the chuck was cooked long enough and slowly enough, it could be easily broken apart or shredded with a long roasting fork or kitchen tong, ideal for Nana to do. A few years back he told me that in the 50s and 60s, the Rival cooking ware company would drop off white electric roasters and electric skillets to tavern owners and butchers to use to cook such items as beer brats, polish sausage and kraut, fresh ham and or Italian beef dishes like sausage and peppers. The owners of these establishments were happy to use these new-fangled slow cookers and did the marketing for the company by handing out samples of items made in their wares. Chick's Italian beef was pure genius because the meat and sausages could be browned in the same casserole, then all that was needed was a good dose of Italian seasonings, garlic, peppers and liquid to cover-- that was it, no slicing or special equipment needed. Since the unit was electric, all you had to do was plug it in, set the temperature, cover the cooker and in 8 to 12 hours you would have an unbelievably moist, juicy, and flavorful beef that was just falling off the bone. When my in-laws would have their basement parties, my mother-in-law and her sister always stood proudly over the white rival cooker, working in unison on the buffet line placing equal amounts of beef, sausage, peppers and juice on each roll, making sure everyone got an equal share. This was always the first dish to empty. If you grew up in an Italian family, you know exactly what I'm talking about. Now I'm not telling you to run out and buy a huge 18 quart cooker, I just want to give you all the options in making Italian beef as easily as possible. Yeah, thinly sliced beef is great, but shredded beef could be a lot more tender and more economical to make. I'm going to leave it up to you to experiment with smaller cuts of meat from the chuck that can be bought at any grocery store. Just trim off any excess fat. Chef's Tip: Try an 8-14 pound No. 116E chuck under blade roast.

Italian Beef Juice and Gravy

Alright, I've given you all the information you need to produce a really good beef sandwich, depending on how much work you'd like to do. Don't be as concerned with the slicing of the meat as with the flavor of the juice. The juice has always been the key to making a great beef sandwich. It can't be too greasy and it should have the subtle taste of garlic, fennel, Italian herbs such as basil and oregano, and also have the depth of beef juice flavor that rounds out the total experience of the Italian beef sandwich. Regardless of which recipe you use, my advice is that when making the gravy or juice, it's always a good idea after it's done cooking to remove the meat with a large slotted spoon to a serving platter, then carefully strain the beef gravy through a fine mesh sieve into a clean bowl and refrigerate uncovered overnight. (Be sure to push all the juices out of the garlic, peppers and onions.) Cover and refrigerate the meat separately. The next day there will be a hardened fat layer on top of the juice. Just discard this layer, re-heat the juice slowly, re-season add your meat back to it and serve.

Auntie Fran's Slow Cooker Italian Beef

SERVES A SMALL CROWD

Every Italian has their own favorite Italian beef recipe. I learned this from my wife's Auntie Fran. It's utterly delicious and comes together in a snap. It's a great recipe for a small family and is less messy and time consuming than using a larger cut of meat. I recommend cooking this in a four to five quart slow cooker or earthenware casserole. Feel free to get a little heavy on the seasoning mix!

INGREDIENTS

One 4 to 5 pound pot roast or rump roast
5 links hot Italian Sausage
2 tablespoons canola oil

4 large garlic cloves, sliced
1 medium onion, sliced
1 large red or green pepper, sliced
1/3 cup hot pepper giardiniera with oil
1/3 cup pepperoncinis, sliced
Dash of Worcestershire
1/4 cup dry white wine
1 cup diced tomatoes
4 to 5 cups beef stock
1 tablespoon corn starch

SEASONING MIX

1 teaspoon dried basil
1 teaspoon dried oregano
1/4 teaspoon sea salt
1/8 teaspoon black pepper
Pinch of red pepper flakes
Pinch of fennel seeds, paprika, garlic powder and onion powder

Heat a medium sized skillet, add the canola oil and brown the roast for 4 to 5 minutes on all sides then remove to a serving platter. In the same oil sauté the Italian sausage links until well browned on all sides then remove to the platter. Combine all the ingredients for the seasoning mix and when the meat is cool enough to handle, evenly rub the spice mix into the browned roast.

If using a slow cooker, scatter the garlic, onion, peppers, Worcestershire, white wine and tomatoes over the bottom of the cooking chamber. Place the seasoned meat directly on top of the vegetables, then stuff the sausage links on either side of the roast. Carefully add about 4 cups of beef stock to the crock pot just enough to cover the meat but not overflowing. (Add enough that you feel comfortable with in cooking and reserve the rest to add later if needed.) Cover the cooker and set the temperature to low or high. Low will cook the meat in about 10 to 12 hours, whereas high will cook the meat in 5 to 6 hours or until the meat is tender and can be either shredded or sliced.

If using an earthenware casserole, pre-heat your oven to 325°, and layer the casserole the same way as above. Cook in the hot oven, covered for 3 to 4 hours.

To serve the beef, remove the roast from the casserole to a serving platter and carefully shred or thinly slice. Return the meat back to the casserole, re-season if necessary, then using a kitchen tong equally divide on to some hard rolls and serve with some sweet peppers or giardiniera.

Authentic Chicago Style Italian Beef SERVES A SMALL CROWD

This is as good as a recipe as you're going to find for real Chicago style Italian beef without having to go to the stand. The cut of meat used is up to you, just be sure to borrow someone's meat slicing machine and slice it thin. This is a 2 part recipe so be sure to follow the directions and feel free to get heavy on the spices.

INGREDIENTS

One 8 to 10 pound your choice of top sirloin
    butt, bottom sirloin butt, beef round top
    inside, or beef round knuckle
1/4 cup canola oil

MEAT SEASONING MIX

2 tablespoons Italian seasoning spice
1 teaspoon sea salt
1/2 teaspoon black pepper
1/2 teaspoon garlic powder
1/4 teaspoon onion powder

BEEF JUICE

2 tablespoons canola oil
3 to 4 pounds meaty beef bones
8 links hot Italian sausage
8 garlic cloves, sliced
1 large onion, chopped
2 large green or red peppers, chopped
1/2 cup hot pepper giardiniera
1/2 cup pepperoncini peppers, sliced
2 teaspoons dried basil
2 teaspoons dried oregano
1/2 teaspoon fennel seeds
1/2 teaspoon sea salt
1/4 teaspoon black pepper
1/2 teaspoon red pepper flakes
2 teaspoons paprika
1/2 teaspoon garlic powder
1/4 teaspoon onion powder
1 tablespoon Worcestershire sauce
1 tablespoon Kitchen bouquet
2 tablespoons corn starch
1/2 cup dry white wine
10 cups beef stock
2 cups diced tomatoes

Re-read the introduction for the Cook it Right section. Pre-heat the oven to 325°. Heat the oil in a large skillet and when hot, brown the roast on all sides for a good 3 to 5 minutes. Remove to a serving platter. When the meat is cool enough to handle, combine the seasoning mix and evenly rub over the roast. Place the roast onto a baking rack on top of a baking pan and cook for 2 to 2 1/2 hours or until the internal temperature reaches 130 to 135°. Rely on your meat thermometer not the cooking time!!! At this point the meat has to chill over night before slicing. The next day thinly slice the roast against the grain and reserve any end scraps that can be used in making the juice. Refrigerate the sliced meat until needed.

To prepare the juice heat the oil in a large stock pot and when hot, sauté the beef bones for 4 to 5 minutes or until nicely browned. (Do not burn the beef bones.) Remove the bones to a serving platter. In the same hot oil sauté the Italian sausage links and reserved end scrapes for 4 to 5 minutes or until browned on all sides, then remove to the serving platter. Add to pot oil the garlic, onion, and peppers and sauté for 2 to 3 minutes. Now add all your dry seasonings to the pot, sauté for 1 minute to infuse the herb oils, then add the rest of the ingredients including the bones, sausage links, and beef scraps. Bring the juice to a gentle simmer, reduce the heat and cook for a good 3 to 4 hours or until the gravy has good taste. Be sure to skim off any grease that floats to the top, remove the sausage links to a serving platter and discard the beef bones. When cool enough to handle carefully strain the juice through a fine mesh strainer being sure to push down and get the juices from the garlic, peppers and onions.

To serve the beef re-heat and re-season the juice, add the sausage links cut in half and 3 to 4 pounds of the sliced beef, simmer slowly for 2 to 3 minutes. Using a kitchen tong equally divide the beef, sausage and gravy on to some hard rolls, and serve with some sweet peppers or giardiniera.

Just Good Beef Sandwich Gravy!

MAKES ABOUT 2 QUARTS

Hey Paesan, don't feel like cooking your own beef? No Problem. This is an excellent tasty recipe for Italian beef au jus. All you gotta do is follow the juice recipe that is directly above, go to the Italian store and buy 6 to 8 pounds thinly sliced Italian beef, and then add the beef to the juice. Voila! Italian Beef!

Beef and Sausage Combo

SERVES 4

The ultimate Chi-town combo! Succulent plump fennel induced Italian sausage lightly grilled, then bedded on a 6-inch soft Gonnella roll and finally topped with the majestic spiced beef, dipped of course!

INGREDIENTS

4 Italian sausage links
1 pound Italian beef in gravy
Four 6-inch Italian rolls
Sweet red peppers or hot pepper giardiniera

Pre-heat a charcoal grill and when hot, grill the Italian sausage links for 8 to 12 minutes until nicely browned and slightly charred. While the sausages are cooking, place the beef and juice into a medium sized sauce pot and gently bring to a slow simmer. Make a slit in the Italian bread, place a sausage link in the center of each roll, then using a kitchen tong place a good amount of Italian beef directly on top of the sausage. Carefully using a kitchen tong, grasp each sandwich and deep six it into the hot beef juice so that the bread absorbs the gravy. Serve with the peppers.

Geri's Tomato Sauce

People are always so closed mouth about their Mom's recipe for spaghetti sauce, but I say what good is it going to do you if you take it to the grave! My mother-in-law Geri makes all different kinds of spaghetti sauces and she gladly turned me on to this one that I think you will like. Feel free to adjust the spices to your liking and always use the best tomato products you can get your hands on.

INGREDIENTS

2 tablespoons olive oil
2 meaty pork neck bones
4 links hot Italian sausage
4 medium garlic cloves, minced
1 small onion, minced
Three 6 ounce can tomato paste
Two 15 ounce cans tomato sauce
One 28 ounce can crushed tomatoes
One 28 ounce can cold water
1/4 cup dry red wine
1 teaspoon sugar
Pinch of baking soda
1 teaspoon dried basil
1 teaspoon dried oregano
1/4 teaspoon sea salt
1/4 teaspoon black pepper
Pinch of red pepper flakes
1/4 cup Pecorino Romano cheese

Heat the oil in a large non-stick sauce pot and fry the pork bones and Italian sausage until nicely browned but not burned. Remove to a small plate, then add the garlic and onions to the pot and stir cook for 2 to 3 minutes. Add the tomato paste and using a wooden spoon, fry the paste in the hot oil until it turns a darker red hue. Add the sugar and baking soda and stir for another minute, then add the rest of the ingredients, bring to a boil and reduce the heat to a slow simmer. At this point, add back to the pot the pork bones and sausage and slowly cook for 1 1/2 to 2 hours being sure to skim the residue that rises to the top.

Mama D's Meatball Sandwich

Hey, mama always knew how to fix Dad's balls.

INGREDIENTS

2 tablespoons olive oil
2 large garlic cloves, minced
1 small onion, minced
1 pound round beef, 85% lean
1/2 pound ground pork
1/2 cup fresh breadcrumbs
1/2 cup Pecorino Romano cheese
1/4 cup parsley, minced
1/2 teaspoon sea salt
1/4 teaspoon black pepper
1 large whole egg
4 ounces whole milk

TOPPING

2 cups Geri's Tomato Sauce
1/4 cup Pecorino Romano cheese
1/2 cup hot Italian giardiniera
Four 6-inch Italian rolls

Pre-heat the oven to 375°. In a small skillet heat the olive oil and saute the garlic and onion for 3 to 4 minutes until nicely softened. Set aside to cool. In a large mixing bowl, place all the rest of the ingredients for the meatballs, add the onion-garlic mixture and thoroughly knead until combined. Now using a 1/4 cup size measuring cup, evenly scoop out about 18 to 20 meatballs. Carefully using lightly floured hands gently roll the meatballs into a nice round shape, place onto a non-stick sheet pan and bake in the hot oven for 25 minutes only. When the meatballs are cooked place them into a medium sized saucepot and cover with Geris tomato sauce. Bring to a gentle simmer and cook slightly covered for another 10 minutes to warm through. While the meatballs are cooking, slit the rolls and lightly crisp. To serve place four meatballs onto each roll, cover with some extra sauce, sprinkle on some extra cheese and giardiniera.

Baked Sausage Sandwich Paesan

Hey, nice spicy package there Vito Corleone!

INGREDIENTS

4 Italian sausage links, mild or hot
1 1/2 cups Geri's Tomato Sauce, warmed
1/4 cup Pecorino Romano cheese
1 cup mozzarella cheese, grated
Four 6-inch Italian rolls

CORLEONE'S PEPPERS

2 tablespoons olive oil
2 large garlic cloves, sliced
1 small onion, sliced
1 small red pepper, sliced
1 small green pepper, sliced
Dash of sea salt, black pepper and
    red pepper flakes

Pre-heat the oven to 400°. To prepare the peppers heat the oil in a medium sized non-stick skillet, add the garlic and saute for one minute. Now add the onions and peppers and saute for 3 to 4 minutes until slightly browned and soft. Season with the salt, pepper and flakes, pour into a bowl and cover with a plate to steam. To the same skillet, add 2 more tablespoons or olive oil and saute the sausages for 4 to 5 minutes until nicely browned on all sides. Lower the heat, cover the pan and cook for another 4 to 5 minutes. (A good tip is to pierce the sausages while cooking to release their flavorful juices and caramelize.) After the sausages are browned, pour off all the grease from the pan and add the peppers back to the skillet with the sausages. Continue sauteing for another 3 to 4 minutes. Remove the pan from the fire and slit the rolls halfway through. Place a sausage link onto the roll and then place on a sheet pan. Ladle the sauce over the links, top with some of the peppers, layer on the cheese and bake in a hot oven for 4 to 5 minutes until the cheese is melted and the rolls are crisp.

Cheesy Beef with Red Sauce

Hey, some guys just can't get away from Sunday gravy so Tore and Luke's Beef Stand invented this Chicago classic!

INGREDIENTS

1 pound Italian beef with gravy
1 1/2 cups Geri's Tomato Sauce
1/4 cup Pecorino Romano cheese
2 cups mozzarella cheese, grated
Four 6-inch Italian rolls
1/2 cup hot pepper giardiniera

Pre-heat the oven to 400°. Carefully slit the rolls not all the way through and place on a baking pan. In one sauce pot bring the tomato sauce to a gentle simmer and in another sauce pot, bring the beef and juice to a gentle simmer. Using a small ladle spoon some of the beef juice into the roll to lightly moisten. Carefully using a kitchen tong divide the warn beef among the 4 rolls. Again using the ladle, generously apply the tomato sauce to the top of the beef. Using a soup spoon, pour some of the hot giardiniera on top of the tomato sauced beef. Sprinkle over the top the Romano cheese, then sprinkle on top of that the grated mozzarella. Place the pan into the hot oven for 4 to 5 minutes and bake until the cheese is melted and the rolls are crisp.

Cheesy Beef and Meatballs on Garlic Bread SERVES 4

A delectable sandwich created at the famous Dino's Pizzeria on Higgins! They also serve a half beef and spaghetti sandwich, no joke. The garlic bread is first crisped in the oven and then piled high with the two meats.

GARLIC BREAD

Four 6-inch Italian rolls

1 stick butter
2 tablespoons olive oil
4 large garlic cloves, minced
1/2 teaspoon garlic powder
1/8 teaspoon paprika
1/4 cup parsley, minced

1 Recipe Mama D's Meatballs
1 pound Italian beef with gravy
1/4 cup Pecorino Romano cheese
2 cups mozzarella cheese, grated
1/2 cup hot pepper giardiniera

Pre-heat the oven to 400°. Carefully slit the rolls not all the way through and place on a baking pan. To make the garlic butter, place the butter, olive oil and garlic in a small skillet. Bring to a quick boil until the garlic sizzles and the butter is melted and remove from the fire. Add the rest of the ingredients and stir until well combined. Gently re-heat the meatball recipe in one sauce pot and in another sauce pot gently re-heat the beef. Using a pastry brush liberally brush the inside of the sliced rolls with the garlic butter and then place in the hot oven and bake until slightly crisp about 3 to 4 minutes. Remove from the oven and using a kitchen spoon, lay three or four meatballs down the center of the roll. Using a kitchen tong evenly divide the beef on top of the meatballs. Again using a kitchen spoon, pour a little red sauce on top of the beef, sprinkle on the Romano cheese, top with the giardiniera and mozzarella and bake in the hot oven for 4 to 5 minutes until the cheese is melted.

89 Cent Gravy Sandwich

SERVES 1

Sometimes after a night of partying and getting juiced up, you come to the realization that you only have a buck in your pocket. Some beef joints will take late night pity on you and serve up a crusty roll drenched in the spicy hot juice to give you back that edge to face your irate old lady!

INGREDIENTS

One 6-inch Italian roll
1 cup beef juice, hot

Carefully slit the roll and place into a soup bowl. Pour over the hot beef gravy and eat.

99 Cent Red Sauce and Pepper Sandwich

SERVES 1

Hey, you might be broke, but if you're a proud Sicilian you would never order just the gravy sandwich. This street food is a lot more cosmopolitan and sophisticated then the above, but it will cost you an extra dime!

INGREDIENTS

One 6-inch Italian roll
1 cup Geri's Tomato Sauce, hot
3 or 4 sweet red peppers slices
1 tablespoon Pecorino Romano cheese

Pre-heat the oven to 400°. Carefully slit the roll not all the way through and place on a baking pan. Pour the tomato sauce down the center, lay the peppers on top of that, sprinkle on the cheese, fold and bake in the hot oven for 4 to 5 minutes until the cheese is melted and the roll is crisp.

Friday Pepper and Egg Sandwich

SERVES 4

Every Catholic knows that you can't eat meat on Friday, so this local favorite would be found in most Italian neighborhoods. The secret is to use really fresh ingredients and be sure to make it to order. Some guys put ketchup on the top although most Sicilians find this practice sacrilegious.

INGREDIENTS

Eight 1-inch thick slices Balice Italian bread
1 Recipe Sweet Red Peppers and Garlic
Dash of red pepper flakes
2 tablespoons unsalted butter
2 tablespoons olive oil
6 whole large eggs
1/4 teaspoon sea salt
1/8 teaspoon black pepper
1/3 cup Pecorino Romano

Pre-heat the oven to 400°. Roughly chop 8 to 10 red pepper slices, place in a bowl until needed and cover with a little bit of the oil and garlic slices that they were originally cooked in. Sprinkle on top of the peppers a dash of red pepper flakes. Whisk the eggs, salt, pepper and cheese in a medium sized mixing bowl until well combined. Place the bread slices onto a baking pan and crisp slightly in the hot oven for 2 to 3 minutes. Using a 12-inch round non-stick skillet, heat the butter and the oil over medium heat and when hot, add the chopped peppers and saute briskly until the oil in the skillet takes on a slight red hue. Now add the eggs and continue cooking stirring with a wooden spoon until the eggs and peppers are scrambled and light and fluffy. Divide evenly among the sliced crisp bread and serve.

My Father-in Law Frank DeCarl's Sunday Morning Pepper, Sausage, Egg and Potato Frittata Sandwich

My beautiful father-in-law Frank was never allowed in the kitchen because he had four daughters and a wife who ruled that domain. But every once in a while he would sneak out of the house and go buy the ingredients to make this frittata for the girls. We would all sit around at the small kitchen table, listen to WGN radio and watch Frank spin his magic with this delightful dish. The feast is a family affair so place the hot skillet on a trivet in the center, next to the sliced bread and almond coffee cake.

INGREDIENTS

One loaf Balese Italian bread
1 Recipe Sweet Red Peppers and Garlic

3/4 pound hot fennel Italian sausage,
    casing removed
2 tablespoons unsalted butter
2 large garlic cloves, minced
1 medium onion, diced
1 medium red pepper, diced
1 1/2 cups potatoes, pre-boiled and diced
6 whole large eggs
1/4 teaspoon sea salt
1/8 teaspoon black pepper
Pinch of nutmeg
1/3 cup Pecorino Romano cheese

Place a 12-inch non-stick skillet over medium high heat, add the bulk sausage and sauté for 4 to 5 minutes until it releases its oil and takes away the color pink. Using a slotted kitchen spoon, remove the cooked sausage to a small bowl and leave only 1 tablespoon of the cooking oil in the skillet. Return the skillet to the fire, add the butter, garlic, onion and pepper, and sauté for 2 to 3 minutes. Now add the potatoes and sauté them with the vegetables for another 3 to 4 minutes until they are slightly brown. While the vegetables are cooking whisk together the eggs, salt, pepper, nutmeg and cheese in a mixing bowl. Add the sausage back to the skillet and thoroughly combine. Carefully pour the egg mixture over the vegetables and sausage and using a plastic spatula, distribute the egg mixture evenly. Cook the frittata slowly undisturbed for 3 to 4 minutes until the edges begin to turn lightly brown. Top the skillet with a flat pan cover for one minute to let the eggs firm up. Now is the hard part. Firmly grasp the pan's handle with your right hand, push down on the pan cover with your left hand and then quickly, in one motion, flip the skillet over so that the frittata falls onto the flat cover. Return the skillet back to the fire, then gently slide the frittata back into the skillet and cook for another 3 to 4 minutes uncovered. Slide onto a platter, cut into eight wedges, place on top of a piece of bread and top with the sauteed sweet red peppers and garlic to serve.

The Three Parmesans

Most joints around the city will offer up some kind of variation on the Parmesan. You just have to decide whether you're an eggplant, veal or chicken kind of guy or gal!

INGREDIENTS

2 medium eggplants
1 tablespoon sea salt
1 cup all-purpose flour

EGG WASH

2 whole large eggs
1/3 cup whole milk

BREADING

1 1/2 cup fresh breadcrumbs
1/2 cup Parmesan cheese, grated
1 teaspoon dried oregano
1 teaspoon dried basil
1/4 teaspoon sweet paprika
1/4 teaspoon sea salt
1/8 teaspoon black pepper
Dash of garlic powder and onion powder

2 cups Geri's Tomato Sauce
2 cups mozzarella cheese, grated
4 soft Gonnella rolls, split

Pre-heat the oven to 400°. Cut the egg plants cross wise into 1/2-inch thick slices, sprinkle on the sea salt then place into a colander to drain for 1 hour. After 1 hour place the slices onto paper towels and gently squeeze out as much excess water and salt as you can. Place the flour into a bowl, the eggs and milk into a bowl and beat. Now place the breading into its own separate bowl. Pour about 2 inches of canola oil into a cast iron skillet and when hot, flour the egg plant slices, dip in the egg wash then into the breadcrumbs and fry in the hot oil for 2 to 3 minutes on each side until golden brown. Remove to a paper towel lined serving platter. Place the egg plant slices onto a non-stick sheet pan, douse with Geri's tomato sauce, sprinkle on the mozzarella and bake in the hot oven for 7 to 10 minutes until the cheese is melted and golden brown. Serve on a slightly crisp roll with a dollop of giardiniera. Veal and Chicken Parmesan are prepared in the same manner without the pre-salting and draining. 5 to 6 ounce scaloppinis of veal or chicken can be obtained from your local butcher.

Sicilian Breaded Steak Sandwich

SERVES 4

A local favorite with paesans made famous at "Ricobenes" restaurant in the city.

INGREDIENTS

Four 6 to 8 ounce boneless rib eye steaks
1 tablespoon Lawry's garlic salt

Place the steaks onto a work surface and season with the garlic salt. Smash the steaks slightly with a meat mallet and then prepare as in the preceding recipe for chicken or veal parmesan. Please note that the steaks will usually cook in the hot oil so there is no need to place them in the oven. Most places just slather on the spaghetti sauce and a sprinkling of Romano cheese.

Fresh Lemonade

YIELDS 2 QUARTS

Most beef joints on the Northwest side offer their rendition of homemade lemonade or Italian ice to quiet the burn of the hot giardiniera oil. Thin skinned lemons supply the most tang for your buck so search them out at your local Italian store.

INGREDIENTS

7 large thin skinned lemons
1 cup sugar
2 quarts ice cold water

Using the palm of your hand roll the lemons on top of the kitchen counter to excite the fruit to release its natural juices. Cut the lemons in half and squeeze out the juice using a juicer. Strain into a large glass pitcher adding some of the yellow inside pit. Pour in the sugar and using a kitchen spoon, stir until the sugar is dissolved. Add the cold water, stir again and refrigerate until needed. Serve in a tall glass over ice with a straw.

Homemade Italian Ice

MAKES 1 QUART

During the hot summer months only, Italians like to congregate at two local institutions for their fix of Italian ice. Carm's and Mario's down in the Taylor Street area have people lined up for hours to buy a scoop or a quart. It's easy to make. All you need is a small ice cream maker that will fit in your freezer.

INGREDIENTS

1 quart cold water
1 to 1 1/4 cups sugar
3/4 cup fresh squeezed lemon juice
1 tablespoon grate rind of the lemon

In a clean saucepan combine 1 cup of the water and the sugar, bring to a gentle boil until the sugar is thoroughly dissolved and then remove from the heat. When cool, add the rest of the water, lemon juice, rind and stir to combine. Pour into a tabletop ice cream maker and churn until the paddle can beat the mixture no more. Place the churning bowl into the freezer until the lemon ice is semi-hard and set. Scoop into little cups and eat with a plastic spoon.

Really Smooth Lemon Ice

MAKES 1 QUART

This sweet Italian ice recipe is one I learned from Chef Warren Leruth, of New Orleans fame. It is a lot smoother due to the fact that egg whites are whipped into the mix. Feel free to fool around with the amount of sugar as this one's really tart and sweet.

INGREDIENTS

1 envelope unflavored gelatin
1/4 cup cold water

1 quart cold water
2 cups sugar

3/4 cup fresh squeezed lemon juice
1 tablespoon grated rind of lemon

2 egg whites
2 tablespoons sugar
3/4 teaspoon sea salt

Soften the gelatin in 1/4 cup cold water. Place the remaining water and sugar into a saucepan, bring to a simmer and boil for exactly 5 minutes. Remove from the heat, cool and then add the lemon juice and rind. Pour the gelatin into the mix and then process in an ice cream maker until semi-frozen but slushy. In a mixing bowl beat the egg whites until soft peaks form, add the sugar and salt, and continue beating until you obtain stiff peaks. Carefully using a spatula fold together the slushy ice mixture and egg whites and then churn in the ice cream maker until the ice has smooth consistency. Scoop into little cups and eat with a plastic spoon.

Uncle Tony's Jumbo Cannoli

MAKES 18 TO 20 PIECES

Uncle Tony from Elmwood Park has always been known for having the sweetest cannoli recipe. Whenever there was a wedding, all the Italian girls would dance around doing the Tarantella and singing "Uncle Tony's Jumbo Cannoli, Uncle Tony's Jumbo Cannoli"

CANNOLI SHELLS

2 cups all purpose flour
1/2 teaspoon sea salt
2 tablespoons shortening
1 tablespoon sugar
1/2 cup sweet wine

1 quart canola oil

FILLING

2 pounds ricotta cheese, well drained
3/4 cup confectionary sugar
1/4 cup candied orange peel
1/2 teaspoon cinnamon
1 1/2 teaspoons vanilla extract

DECORATION

1 cup chopped pistachio nuts
1 cups finely chopped semi sweet chocolate
Confectionary sugar

To prepare the dough place the flour, salt, shortening and sugar onto a clean kitchen surface and mix together with your fingers. Make a well in the center, add the sweet wine and using your hands, mix the dough together until it forms a nice soft ball. (Add a little more wine if needed.) Place the dough in a clean plastic bag and let it rest on the counter top for about an hour. In a mixing bowl combine the ricotta, sugar, candied orange peel, cinnamon and vanilla extract until smooth and well mixed. Cover the filling with plastic wrap and refrigerate until needed. To form the shells divide the cannoli dough into two equal pieces. Now using a rolling pin or a pasta maker, gently roll out one of the pieces on a lightly floured work surface until it forms a long band about 5 inches wide by however long you can make the strip. Using a 4-inch round pastry cutter, carefully cut the rolled out dough and place the cut circles onto a clean baking pan. Gather up the leftover dough, knead slightly and then place it back into the bag to re-use. Now again, roll out the other piece of dough and cut until you have around 18 to 20 pieces. Heat the canola oil in a deep fat fryer until it reaches 375°. To prepare the shells lightly beat 1 large whole egg with a little water in a small bowl and set aside. Carefully place a cannoli frying tube horizontally onto the center of one of the cut pieces of dough, and then fold the top half of the dough over the mold. Place a little egg wash on the lip and then fold the bottom half over the top. (This forms a seal for the shell. Also, try not to get any of the egg wash on the cannoli mold.) Repeat this process with as many molds as you have. I highly recommend that you only fry two cannoli shells at a time. Using a kitchen tong or a long handled pliers, gently place the molds into the hot oil and fry them until they are a deep golden brown, about 1 minute. Remove to a parchment lined sheet pan to cool. Repeat with the remaining shells and let them cool completely before filling. Place the filling into a pastry bag, then gently grasp one of the cooked shells in your left hand and pipe some of the filling into each one of the shells until it is slightly visible at both ends. Lightly sprinkle on each end some of the chopped pistachios and chocolate and then place the filled cannoli onto a decorative serving platter. Sprinkle with powdered sugar to serve.

Cousin Chic's Frozen Eclairs

MAKES 18 TO 20 PIECES

Our cousin, Frank, from Melrose Park, was a dentist for some 40 years, but always had the desire to become a pastry chef. He learned how to make frozen eclairs from his mother, Ann and used to bring them around whenever we had a special occasion.

ECLAIR DOUGH

3/4 cup water
6 tablespoons unsalted butter
Pinch of sea salt
1 cup all-purpose flour
4 whole large eggs, room temperature

CREAM FILLING

1 1/2 cups whole milk
1/2 cup sugar
4 large egg yolks
3 tablespoons cornstarch
1 teaspoon vanilla extract

CHOCOLATE GLAZE

6 tablespoons water
6 tablespoons light corn syrup
1 cup sugar
8 ounces semi sweet chocolate, chopped

Pre-heat the oven to 375°. To prepare the dough place the water, butter, sugar and salt into a heavy saucepan with a handle and bring to a boil. While the liquid is on the heat, add all of the flour and stir with a wooden spoon until the mixture comes away from the sides and forms a ball. Remove from the heat and add the eggs one at a time, beating well to incorporate each one into the dough before adding the next. The mixture should be smooth. Line a large, heavy-duty baking sheet with a piece of parchment paper. Fit a pastry bag with a 3/4 to 1-inch tip and fill the bag with the hot paste. Holding the bag at a 45 degree angle with the tip 1/4-inch away from the pan, pipe a 3-inch log onto the parchment paper. Continue piping 3-inch logs 2-inches apart from each other until all of the dough is used up. Place the baking pan onto the center rack of the oven and bake for 20 minutes. Decrease the heat to 325° and bake for 15 minutes more until golden brown. Remove the shells from the oven and let them cool completely and then place in a plastic bag and freeze until needed. To prepare the filling combine 1 cup of the milk and all the sugar in a medium saucepan and bring to a boil. In another mixing bowl whisk together the remaining milk, cornstarch and vanilla. Carefully pour about 1/4 cup of the hot milk into the mixing bowl and whisk until smooth. Place the hot milk back onto the fire and reduce to medium. Pour the egg-milk mixture into the hot milk and whisk constantly until the pastry cream begins to thicken. Keep whisking until the pastry cream comes to a boil, taking care that the whip reaches all corners of the pan. Continue whisking for about a minute more and then pour the pastry cream into a glass bowl and refrigerate. When you are ready to fill the eclairs, fit a pastry bag with a 1/4 -inch tip and fill the bag with the cooled pastry cream. Using a small paring knife, make a small round hole into the bottom of each one of the eclair shells. Carefully pipe the filling into the hole until the shell is full and then place onto a wire rack. To make the glaze combine the water, corn syrup and sugar in a small saucepan, bring to a boil and remove from the heat. Add the chocolate to the hot syrup and stir until it melts and is completely smooth. When the glaze cools down slightly and is semi-thick, dip the tops of the eclairs into the glaze and then place on a serving platter to cool. Serve immediately or freeze for later use.

MYSTICAL GIARDINIERA

Definition!!!

(ah-lah jahr-dee-nyay-rah) From the Italian giardiniere (gardener), a culinary term that refers to dishes served with pickled or cured mixed, sliced vegetables.

No self-respecting beef sandwich would be complete without the mystical topping of sautéed sweet red peppers or hot pepper-infused giardiniera. Italian giardiniera has been around the Chicago area since the late 1800s. Early Italian importers used to ship in huge barrels of cured olives, peppers, artichokes, vegetables and capers steeped in vinegar and quality olive oil. It was back in those times that barrel vendors ruled the streets and if you wanted fresh produce or cured condiments "menza menza" (meaning a little bit of this and a little bit of that), the street cart owner would oblige by doling it out for a nickel or two at their discretion. Whatever was left at the bottom of the barrels was either sold as a tonic cure or used as an oil and vinegar antipasto condiment to be served with Italian cured meats. All Mediterranean countries have been preserving the fruits of the hot summer for centuries due to the lack of modern refrigeration, and crocking or jarring has evolved into a lucrative business. The system is pretty simple: vegetables and fruit are picked at their optimum ripeness, then cut and packed into jars. The jars are then filled with a pickling solution of vinegar, syrup or oil and then sterilized and stored in the pantry to be used year round.

Giardiniera falls into two categories. The first is called "sotto aceti," which uses vegetables that are pickled in seasoned vinegar, allowing its acidity to keep the food from spoiling. Some good examples would be dill pickles, sport peppers, hot cherry peppers, Greek pepperoncini , Hungarian style banana peppers and pickled jalapenos. This has always been the preferred Italian method for preserving vegetable antipasto. The second method is called "sotte'oli," which is a term used for vegetables that are packed in oil. Old paesans mastered this technique by experimenting in the cold wine cellars of their basements. Typically they would pickle caponata, eggplant, olive salad and mushrooms in crocks. But be forewarned, oil is not a preservative! "Sotte'oli" vegetables are always preprocessed and cured in a seasoned vinegar solution to prevent bacteria and mold, then the finished product is covered with a quality olive oil or vegetable oil to seal in the natural flavors.

There are literally dozens of giardinieras on the market, ranging from the simple cherry peppers in vinegar to the more complex eggplant and peppers in oil. All originally were made by hand and used as a cold side condiment to accentuate a plate of Italian meats and cheeses or as a dazzling array of finger food antipasto. I'm often asked why hot pepper giardiniera is an exclusive Chicago tradition and how it became the favorite topping for Italian beef sandwiches. The answer is simple. The thousands of Sicilians who immigrated to Chicago in the early 1900s had always had an affinity for pairing Italian meats with spicy condiments, vegetable salads and vegetable antipasto. One of the oldest and most popular southern Italian dishes is called "bolitti misti," which is large pot of assorted meats simmered in an aromatic broth and classically served with condiments such as "mostardi di frutta," a mixture of fruits candied in a heavy syrup spiced with a hot mustard oil. (similar to a Midwestern boiled dinner). Once the meat and vegetables in the pot are cooked to perfection, they are removed to large platters, sliced, and topped or drizzled with broth from the pot and served with a condiment of the mustard fruits. This union produced an irresistible hot, spicy and soul-satisfying sensation that was addictive and created a precedent to the Italian beef and giardiniera combination. For your information, French dip sandwiches consist of thinly sliced roast beef that is layered onto a hard roll then drizzled with beef juice, whereas Philly cheese steak is thin slices of beef that are quickly browned and sautéed, and served on a roll with Cheese Whiz. Our beloved Italian beef sandwich is pre-seasoned, roasted, thinly sliced and then simmered in a highly seasoned Italian broth, plopped onto a crisp roll, sopped with the juice and topped with the hot pepper giardiniera. This is truly a Chicago invention. Through my research, I have found that E. Formella and Sons, an Italian company out of Bridgeview, Illinois, has actually been making homemade giardiniera since 1909. An even older company by the name of V. Formosa on Grand Avenue has been importing Marconi brand giardiniera since 1898. As you can see, giardiniera has a long culinary history on the Chicago food scene.

These little gems have come a long way, and I actually prefer to make my own using the freshest ingredients. As much as I love the convenience of jarred pepper giardiniera, I find that all are not created equal, and some brands are mushy, salty or way over processed. I was surprised to find that giardiniera actually started out as a simple cured green olive, celery, fennel and pepper salad, but was reinvented more simply due to escalating olive and vegetable prices. Also, in American culinary terminology fancy giardiniera refers to a vegetable mixture of carrots, cauliflower, peppers, celery, onions and assorted pickling spices that are simmered in a sugary vinegar solution with a touch of turmeric added, a far cry from what you would put on an Italian beef sandwich.

Choosing which Chicago-style giardineira is used for beef is actually a two-step process. First is the choice of the peppers used. Typically the peppers are common to the botanical family of "solanacea" (night shade family) and are of the variety of either Jalapeno M, Mirasol, Serrano del Sol hybrid, Mesilla finger hots or Italian roasters hybrid. Their Scoville or heat index rating is measured between 5,000 to 15,000, meaning they are medium hot. The firm-walled, fiery seeded peppers typically grow about 3 - 4-inches long and mature between 70 and 80 days under the proper temperature. To give you some perspective on the spiciness, a ripe red pepper is rated at about a 1.1 heat index, whereas a Jalapeno M is rated at about a 5.5 heat index on the Scoville scale. Depending on where they're grown--anywhere from Illinois down to the south, these super hybrid peppers will mature green in the summer and be picked at their maximum ripeness before turning red. **(For your information, major agricultural universities vigorously hybrid or propagate seedlings to create new, spicier and disease-resistant strains of pepper plants on a consistent basis. Pepper plants of this family are notorious for becoming magnets for insects and plant disease and require extra special care and maintenance. A good hot pepper giardiniera can be made by using any pepper with a Scoville heat index between 5,000 and 15,000, whether it be green, red, or yellow.)**

The second step determines how you want the giardiniera processed. Some manufacturers brine the cut peppers and vegetables in a vinegar, salt and herb solution and some brine them in a salted water solution. The brine basically cooks the peppers to make them more palatable. They are then drained and covered with soy bean oil, which is heavy and has a pronounced flavor and aroma. Some manufacturers I've talked to actually take it a step further and process the peppers by pasteurizing the sealed jars; however, this tends to make the peppers mushy.

I didn't want to leave you hanging in this book without a recipe for homemade giardiniera since companies and delis are very hush hush as to how they make it. My in-laws used to make homemade giardiniera, but it was always a little bit of this and a little bit of that and there was no written recipe. If you have a better recipe, please send it to me and I will send you an autographed book. My advice to you is to search out homemade giardinieras that are usually available at Italian delis, or feel free to fool around with the recipes that I have given you here.

As noted earlier, giardiniera or preserved Italian vegetables have evolved over the years and I wanted to give you a true perspective as to where it started and where it ended. I have listed them in order of importance to the classic beef sandwich! Be sure to check out the Paesan Sub Grinder Chapter for more interesting Italian salads.

Sweet Red Peppers and Garlic

MAKES 1 QUART

Commonly known or ordered as "sweet" at beef joints! The secret is to use extremely fresh red or green peppers and to saute them up slowly in a good light olive oil. Be sure to remove the cooked pepper salad from the refrigerator 20 minutes before topping on your beef!

INGREDIENTS

6 large red or green peppers
3 large garlic cloves, sliced
1/2 cup light olive oil
1 teaspoon dried oregano
Dash of garlic powder
1/2 teaspoon sea salt
1/4 teaspoon black pepper

Cut the peppers in half, core and remove all the pits and seeds. Cut each half into 8 long strips. Heat a large high-sided non-stick skillet, add the oil and garlic and let the garlic steep in the hot oil for exactly 1 minute. Now add the peppers and saute over medium heat for 3 to 5 minutes being sure to toss the peppers so that they are all covered with the hot oil. Reduce the heat to low, season with the salt and pepper only and continue tossing and sauteing for another 10 minutes. When the peppers just take on a touch of brown on their skin and are softened, add the oregano and garlic powder then toss the skillet a few more times to redistribute the seasoning. Immediately pour the hot peppers into a Pyrex bowl and cover with a piece of plastic wrap to steam and infuse the flavors. When the peppers are cooled, toss gently, store in a glass container and refrigerate until needed.

Classic Beef Stand Giardiniera

Commonly known as "hot" when ordered at the beef stand. Most joints I know use this standard recipe mix to stretch out a pre-processed jar of hot peppers. Some people like more vegetables and some people like more peppers so feel free to adjust the amount to your liking. You can also substitute for the fresh vegetables in this recipe 2 cups of pickled "vegetable" giardiniera that is drained and chopped.

INGREDIENTS

One 16 ounce jar hot pepper giardiniera in oil
   without vegetables added
1 heaping cup celery, diced small
1/2 heaping cup carrots, diced small
1/4 heaping cup cauliflower, diced small
1/2 red pepper, diced small
1 teaspoon Italian herb spice
Dash of red pepper flakes
1 cup Italian green olives, pitted and quartered

Heat a medium saucepan full of lightly salted water and when it comes to the boil, add the diced celery, carrots, cauliflower and pepper and cook for exactly 1 minute. Drain into a colander, rinse with cool water then dry completely. Place all of the diced vegetables, seasonings and olives in a mixing bowl and combine. Pour over the top the hot pepper giardiniera with all the oil, and again toss to thoroughly combine. Place the mix into a 1 quart mason jar and refrigerate for 3 to 4 days before using.

Homemade Hot Pepper Giardiniera

MAKES 1 QUART

If you're a paesan gardener who likes to grow his own peppers, this is a really quick, good and authentic Italian recipe to use. All the below mentioned peppers are similar in size about 3 inches long, firmly textured, easily sliced and have a medium heat Scoville rating of 5,000 to 15,000, the key to a happy faced beef eater!

INGREDIENTS

1 pound your choice mature green hot
    peppers - (Jalapeno M, Mirasol, Serrano del Sol
    hybrid, Mesilla finger hots, or Italian roasters
    hybrid), sliced
1 heaping cup celery, diced
1/2 heaping cup carrots, diced
1/4 cup cauliflower florets, diced
1/4 cup red pepper, diced
6 large garlic cloves, minced
1 cup white vinegar
1 cup water
2 tablespoons sea salt
1/4 teaspoon black pepper
1/4 teaspoon red pepper flakes
1/4 teaspoon garlic powder
1 teaspoon dried oregano
1/2 teaspoon dried basil
Soy bean or canola oil to cover

Place the peppers, celery, carrots, cauliflower, red pepper and garlic into a medium sized mixing bowl and combine. In another saucepan heat the vinegar, water, salt, pepper, pepper flakes, garlic powder and Italian spice until it comes to the boil then remove immediately from the heat. When the brine cools down to luke warm, pour it over the vegetables, mix with a spoon cover and refrigerate for 2 days to mellow. **(On the third day, strain the vegetables through a find mesh strainer and place into a mason jar. Add about 1/2 cup of the strained marinade to the jar, then add enough oil to just cover the peppers and vegetables. Refrigerate and shake the jar every couple of days before using. Two weeks mellowing time seems to work the best.)**

ITALIAN SUB GRINDERS

GRINDER
RECIPES

My mother-in-law, Geri, recently visited and read through my Italian Beef and Giardiniera chapters. She was highly impressed and enthusiastic about the content, which got me reminiscing about all the great sandwich shops I've visited on the northwest side of Chicago through the years. I have to admit I dig mom-and-pop joints--tiny grocery stores crammed to the gills with Italian foodstuffs, homemade sausage, prime meats, pastas, oils, vinegars, a variety of fresh salads and the ominous deli counter. Growing up around Harlem Avenue in the early 70s was a cool time, as it was a portal through some of the best Italian neighborhoods in the city. Small markets, bakeries, butchers, Italian restaurants, pizzerias and taverns lined the street which would become my adolescent playground and Mecca. I attended Holy Cross High School which was a good ten miles from my home, and this situation led to years of missed bus rides, long walks and learning the art of finding obliging bakers and deli owners who would take pity on this young boy, frozen to the gills and awaiting a lift. Lucky for me, I hung out with some really cool paesans like Tony Greco, Frank Palumbo, Ralphie Bartuch and Chic Pinto. All had secret street names like Joey Bag-o-doughnuts, Tony da king of Belmont Avenue, Aqua Velva Bobby, Frank the Greek, etc. and for some strange reason, they always had an aunt or uncle who owned or worked at one of these family-run shops.

About a year ago, I received an award in Chicago for my cookbook, The New Polish Cuisine and having time to kill on a cold, gloomy, wintry Thursday, I decided to park my rental and take a reminiscent bus ride up Harlem Ave. I was amazed as to how many things had changed, but I was also enthralled as to how many of the old places were still around, including Parse's Hot Dogs, Dino's Pizza, Hansen's Fish Pier, Oven Fresh Bakery, Maurice Lenell Cookies, Gino's Italian Imports, Nottoli Sausage Shop, Riviera Italian Foods, Il Giardino, Luke's, Angelo Caputo's and Bari Foods. Now mind you, this is only about a 45-minute ride and the bus driver must have thought I was nuts, because I kept moving from side to side trying to see what was still around. Once I stopped hyperventilating, I went to go sit by the driver, an old black gentleman who had been driving that route for years, and we were now engaged in major conversations about all the old joints and where was the best place to eat. He quickly pointed out that the "Poles" were working their way further up north while the "Paesans" were standing their ground around Belmont, Irving and Grand, my old stomping ground and a hot bed of Italian culture. The driver related to me that once you cross over Belmont Ave., you are leaving deli country behind and entering into major Italian bread and pastry making territory: D'Amato's Bakery, La Briola Baking, Allegretti's Baking, Palermo Baking, Mazzeo Baking, Calabrese Baking, Casa Nostra Baking, Domino's, and Claudio's Pastry Company. Man, this guy's been working on the bus too long to remember all these names, but who knows better about street food than a seasoned bus driver?

Italian delicatessens and bakeries are a true testament to the American working spirit, as most are passed down from generation to generation. Some will specialize in one item such as homemade sausage or beef sandwiches, while others will expand into a small but comfortable grocery store procuring as many homemade foods as they can handle. In my mind, the first true test of an authentic Italian deli is the aroma that emanates from it the minute you walk in the door. Garlic, basil, oregano, fresh bread, salamis and the sweet smell of Romano cheese all provide a true sensory Italian nirvana that has to be experienced. The second test is something I learned from my Italian wife, Pam, and that is basically to savor the moment and not be rushed. She says, "Mike, shut up, don't touch anything and you just push the cart." as we make our way down the aisles through the store. My wife, who's a true Sicilian, is very, very particular about her selection of fresh fruits, vegetables, proper crust on bread consistency and deli items. Sometimes I'll catch her holding grapes up to the lights to see how many seeds are in there, smelling red peppers, pinching endless loaves of bread and checking tomato product cans for dents, because (God forbid) you don't want to get salmonella poisoning! I can give her all that because she's a good shopper, but the one thing that has made me totally nuts over 20 years of marriage is her Sicilian encyclopedic knowledge of the Italian deli counter. This has to be something that is genetically handed down because it still confuses me.

Let me put this in some kind of visual perspective: So check this out. Saturday morning, prime time, 11:00 A.M. Italian deli counter time. Before us like an altar is a 20- foot long, glass-enclosed deli counter loaded with Italian goodies, with about six employees fervently slicing, wrapping, yelling at the same time and sometimes busting balls over an order. To the far left of the case are all Italian pastries, cookies, canollis, small cakes, biscotti, gucidatta, Napoleon slices etc. Just left of center you'll find homemade antipasto such as olive salad, zucchini and peppers, pasta salad, macaroni salad, broccoli with garlic, calamari salad with pesto, stuffed baked eggplant, artichoke salad, roasted peppers, seafood rice salad etc. To the right of that are deli meats and cheeses such as salami, pepperoni, mortadella, ham, capicolla, prosciutta, sopressata, coppa, mozzarella, romano, provolone, American cheese, etc. Also in that same area will be pounds of freshly-made sweet and hot Italian sausage and Chicago's favorite--finger-skinny, Barese-style sausage that is seasoned with red wine, cheese and parsley. To the far right are prepared items such as meatballs, sausage and peppers, lasagna, chicken and veal parmesan etc. I think you get the idea. To enrich your visual picture, on top of the counters are usually two or three scales, the ticket numbering machine (because there's always a line) and you are usually surrounded by plexiglass bins filled with assorted self-serve breads and rolls supplied by local bakers. It's at this time in this journey that I have to stop because the chapter's dragging on and I think you're getting my drift. Not to leave you hanging, though, let me give you some really cool history and information that I think you'll enjoy.

Chicago-style Italian subs consist of three main ingredients: homemade bread, cured meats and savory toppings! The words submarine, grinder, hero, hogie, poorboy and torpedo are all terms or regional variations for the popular sandwich that is made by splitting a long torpedo-shaped roll in half lengthwise and filling it with meats and condiments. The term "sub sandwich" was created in the 1940s when the commissary of the U.S. Submarine Navy base in Groton, Connecticut, was ordering 500 hero sandwiches a day from Benedetto Capaldos, an Italian deli owner in New London. Security and manpower were so tight at the time that the navy enlisted local patriotic shop owners to feed the troops. The sandwiches mimicked the shape of the sub and torpedo, quickly gaining popularity with the men. The term "Italian Sub Grinder" also came out of World War II, when Italian immigrants set up shops close to shipyards and made sandwiches for the paesan workers whose job it was to grind down protruding bolts on new warships. These Italian workers were known as "grinders." At ten to fifteen cents per sandwich, the shop owners had a pretty sweet deal going, thus leading to the invention of the sub sandwich!!!

Chicago Style Italian Breads - Quick fact: there are some 30,000 bakers in Italy as I write, and about 100 of those are government-certified artesian bakers who prefer to work in small scale, dedicating their livelihood and family recipes to keep up the true Italian tradition. Bread typically in Italy is rough country loaves with thick chewy crusts and flatbreads of foccacio that are seasoned with assorted olives, pesto, peppers, tomatoes and herbs. Not to get too boring and to propel you to the front of the class in the world of baking, there are three universal breads that are classified as thin crisp crusted. These are Vienna, French and Italian, which are all very popular in Chicago, due to their light, crispy, and airy texture. History notes that the Viennese are the true inventors of French and Italian baguettes, but controversy reigns as to what is the proper recipe. Local professional bakers claim that Italian bread contains no salt, sugar or oil, whereas French bread does, but that's not always the case!!!. Modern baking practices dictate that salt is used for seasoning, structure and strengthening of the gluten, that sugar is used for color, sweetness, flavor and food for the yeast, and that oil is used for moisture and flavor. Italian delis around Chicago carry a lot of different breads, but the most popular, in order from lightest to chewiest, are:

Italian Hard Rolls - Exceedingly thin crusted, lean, airy, soft interior, the ultimate Italian roll. Best eaten within 8 hours of baking.

Pane Filone - Fat cigar-shaped bread. A white bread with crisp, thin crust and soft interior that was originally developed in Austria, then brought down to Milan by the ever-charging Napoleon troops. A perfect bread for the upper-class set. Heavenly, lighter and airier than most Italian loaves, this is the perfect bread to make into crisp Italian rolls for subs or sausage sandwiches.

Saltless Pane Toscano - The original saltless bread from Tuscany. Originally baked in a round shape, it possesses a dark golden color and has a thick crust and a moist, light, airy crumb. This robust loaf has a sourdough- like chew without the sour taste.

Seeded Pane Siciliano - The most beloved bread of the Sicilians. This semolina infused and sesame seed crusted loaf is the Mac daddy of Italian bread. Pane Siciliano is made with a rich durum wheat flour (semolina) that imparts a sweet, nutty, peanut flavor and texture to this country hearth-baked artesian loaf. This bread is often shaped into "occhi di santa lucia" (eyeglasses) in loving tribute to the patron saint of vision.

Balice Bread (aka ciabatta, crocodile, stirato, pane de bari) - Balice (now Mazzeo Baking Company), one of Chicago's first Italian artesian bakers, put this local favorite on the culinary map. Balice ciabatta loaf, also known as "slipper bread," is a flat, long, stretched, chewy loaf that when baked produces a porous, airy interior that is ideal for dipping into olive oil and making deli sandwiches.

To say who makes the best Italian bread in Chicago is redundant, because in addition to the 20 brands that are available in Italian stores, there are hundreds of independent bakers scattered throughout the city. Fresh bread is at its peak consistency a few hours after it has been baked, so if you get the last loaf on the shelf, it will not be the best. Gonnella Bread Company, which has been operating in Chicago since 1886, has been knocking out loaves of 3-foot long French baguettes for years, and it is undoubtedly the best recognized for family-style Italian eating because it's a light, airy, chewy loaf that everyone loves. Not to be left out of the pack, Turano Baking Company also turns out beautiful sandwich rolls and breads recognized for their consistent quality and taste to the delight of droves of customers. I've mentioned a lot of Italian baking companies who turn out wonderful loaves of bread on a daily basis, but it's up to you to decide who makes the best. If you can't get to the Chicago area, I'm including here three really good and popular recipes for making Chicago-style Italian bread.

Please note that these recipes work best if made in a KitchenAid stand mixer with dough hook and paddle!!!.

Daily White Filone

This is a quick and easy recipe to make. The rolls and loaves come out beautifully if they are allowed to rise properly.

INGREDIENTS

2 cups water
5 teaspoons sugar
2 1/2 teaspoon sea salt

6 cups bread flour
4 teaspoons yeast
1 egg white and a little yolk
2 tablespoons canola oil

In a small saucepan combine the water, sugar and salt, bring to a boil, stir and then remove from the fire and cool until 105° to 115°. In the mixer bowl add the flour, yeast, egg white and oil. Attach the flat beater, put the machine on to low speed and mix for 1 minute. While the machine is still running slowly add the water until it forms a shaggy mass around the paddle. Now replace the flat beater with the dough hook, and knead at medium speed until the dough is smooth and elastic and forms a round ball, around 3 to 4 minutes. If the dough seems a little sticky and won't form a ball, add a little bit more flour until it does. If the dough seems too dry, add 1 to 2 more tablespoons of water. Remove the ball to a lightly floured work surface, hand knead for 1 minute then place into an oiled bowl and cover until risen and doubled in size about 1 1/2 to 2 hours. Turn the risen dough out onto a lightly floured work surface. Deflate the dough and divide into 24 equal pieces or into 2 equal pieces if making loaves. Cover the pieces with a kitchen towel and let rest 10 minutes. To form the rolls using lightly floured hands, roll each piece into a nice ball and place onto a parchment lined sheet pan that is dusted with semolina flour. To form into loaves, use your hands to punch the dough back and flatten it out. Fold a piece of dough over onto itself away from you. Square the edges and push them an inch or so near the middle and then roll the loaf up into a tight log, sealing the dough at each turn with the tips of your fingers. Pinch each end to seal and place onto a parchment lined sheet pan that is dusted with semolina. Repeat with the remaining loaf then cover with a kitchen towel and let rise until doubled. Pre-heat the oven to 410° and adjust the oven rack to the middle. (You have to inject a little steam into the oven while the bread is baking so the loaves will crisp up, so fill a spray bottle with some cool water.) When the oven is hot, open the door and mist the walls of the oven with a good 10 sprits from the spray bottle then close the door. Lightly spray the rolls or loaves then place directly into the hot oven and bake for 5 minutes. Quickly open the door, spray 10 more times then close the oven door. Repeat after another 5 minutes. The rolls take about 15 to 20 minutes to bake and the loaves around 30 minutes.

Sesame Seeded Pane Siciliano

MAKES 2 ROUND LOAVES

The Sicilians make this bread in a myriad of shapes and sizes, and it can often be found around Chicago's markets in a loaf or round shape. For a deeper rich flavor, let the starter sit overnight in the refrigerator before proceeding with the recipe.

STARTER

2 cups fine semolina flour
2 cups warm water (105 to 115F)
4 teaspoons yeast

3 cups bread flour
1 tablespoon sugar or malt syrup
2 tablespoons olive oil
1 tablespoon sea salt

2 to 3 tablespoons sesame seeds for sprinkling

At least 3 to 4 hours before making the dough, place the semolina, water and yeast into the bowl of a kitchen aid mixer, stir with a spoon, tightly cover with plastic wrap and leave in a semi-warm place to let the starter rise, bubble and ferment. When the starter is ready place the bowl on the machine and attach the paddle. Add the remaining ingredients except the sesame seeds, turn the machine on and let the dough mix until it forms a shaggy mass around the paddle. Now replace the flat beater with the dough hook and knead at medium speed until the dough is smooth and elastic, around 3 to 4 minutes. If the dough seems too sticky and won't form a ball, add a little bit more flour until it does. If the dough seems too dry, add 1 to 2 more tablespoons of water. Remove the ball to a lightly floured work surface, hand knead for 1 minute and then place into an oiled bowl and cover until risen and doubled in size about 1 1/2 to 2 hours. Turn the risen dough out onto a lightly floured work surface. Deflate the dough, divide into 2 equal pieces, cover with a kitchen towel and let rest for 10 minutes. To form a loaf using your hands, grasp the dough and form it into a rough shaped ball. Now gently using both hands, fold the dough underneath itself to create a tight ball. Repeat with the other piece and then place them onto a parchment lined sheet pan that has been dusted with semolina. Cover the loaves with a kitchen towel and let rise until doubled. Pre-heat the oven to 425° and adjust the oven rack to the middle. (You have to inject a little steam into the oven while the bread is baking so that the loaves with crisp up, so fill a spray bottle with some cool water.) When the oven is hot, open the door and mist the walls with a good 10 sprits from the spray bottle and then close the door. Lightly spray the loaves, sprinkle on top the sesame seeds and bake for 5 minutes. Quickly open the door, spray 10 more times and then close the oven door. Repeat after another 5 minutes. The loaves take about 30 minutes to bake.

Balice Bread

Often referred to as a dense ciabatta bread. This Mazzeo Baking Company original is a favorite item at local Italian markets. A rustic, chewy, slipper shaped bread that is porous with big eyes and produces an elastic dough that must be pulled into its unique shape. Italians love it for its chewy, peasant like texture that will most definitely take your dentures out so chew cautiously!

STARTER

1 cup bread flour
2 1/2 teaspoons yeast
1 cup warm water (105 to 115F)

1 1/4 cup water (105 to 115F)
1 tablespoon sea salt
5 1/2 cups bread four

At least 3 to 4 hours before making the dough, place he starter ingredients into the bowl of a kitchen aid mixer, stir with a spoon, cover tightly with plastic wrap and leave in a semi-warm place to let the starter rise, bubble and ferment (about 2 to 3 hours). When the starter is risen, place the bowl on the machine and attach the paddle. Add the remaining ingredients, turn the machine on and let the dough mix until it forms a shaggy mass around the paddle. Now replace the flat beater with the dough hook and knead at medium speed until the dough is smooth and elastic, around 3 to 4 minutes. (This dough is slightly wet and sticky, that's the way it should be). A little bit more flour can be added to the bowl when mixing, but not too much. Remove the ball to a lightly floured work surface, hand knead for 1 minute then place into an oiled bowl, cover with a towel and let rise until doubled, about 1 1/2 to 2 hours. When the dough has risen, pour it onto a lightly floured work surface without deflating it. Dust the top of the dough with a little flour patting the dough into a rectangular shape. Place a piece of parchment paper onto a baking pan and dust it with semolina. Now carefully using floured hands, lift the dough from each end stretching it to twice its size. Fold the dough over itself letter style to return it to a rectangular shape. Cover with a kitchen cloth and let rest 10 minutes. After 10 minutes, cut the dough into 2 equal pieces. Again using lightly floured hands, lift a piece from each end stretching it out in a long slipper shape and then place it onto the parchment paper. Repeat with the other piece. Lightly dust the loaves with a little bit more flour, cover with a kitchen towel and let rise for another 45 to 60 minutes until puffy. Pre-heat the oven to 400° and adjust the oven rack to the middle. (You have to inject a little steam into the oven while the bread is baking so it will crisp, so fill a spray bottle with cool water.) When the oven is hot, open the door and mist the walls with a good 10 sprits from the spray bottle and then close the door. Lightly spray the loaves and bake for 5 minutes. Quickly open the door, spray 10 more times then close the door. Repeat after another 5 minutes. The bread takes about 40 minutes to bake.

DELI SANDWICH WORKS

Sub Sandwiches and Meats. I've given you some detailed information about the breads used around Chicago delis, which is a key sandwich component, but the meats also play a big part. Every city seems to have its favorite combination of deli meats and breads which they playfully like to name, such as the Vito, Big John, Kitchen Sink and so on. But this is Chicago, so don't get cute with the names or the deli guy will slap you really hard! Chicago's got its share of Italian delis and I think that three places merit recognition for making great deli sandwiches. They are Bari, Riviera Italian Imported Foods and Tony's Italian Deli. Their premise is very simple: use the freshest bread available, use only prime cured Italian meats and cheeses that are sliced to order and use exceedingly fresh oil and vinegar, spices and interesting spicy vegetable giardiniera as toppings. Italian delis around the city utilize about a good two dozen cured and smoked Italian meats and cheeses that all seem to jive together to create one outstanding meal. **The secret to a good Italian deli sandwich is not only the quality of the goods, but also how thin the meat is sliced and whether or not the sandwich is made to order!** Local foodies tend to like their sandwiches on the spicy side, and one of the best-loved combination sandwiches you can get is called "a basic Italian sub." This sandwich is served on a ciabatta roll and consists of capicolla, mortadella, salami, mozzarella, lettuce, tomato, onion, oil and vinegar and Italian spices.

The system is pretty simple: walk up to the deli counter, take a number, wait your turn and when your number's up, politely request that you'd like a fresh sandwich made. They will promptly tell you to turn around and pick your own roll out of the bin. Now here's where it gets a little bit tricky. Some joints don't have a menu and this is no time to hold up the line. If you want to impress the deli guy just tell him, "Hey, make me something spicy and Italian!" They'll be more obliged to give you some really choice cuts such as capicolla, pepperoni, salami, provolone and mortadella. And you can take it a step further by telling them to spice it up with some giardiniera, roasted red peppers or oil-drenched eggplant salad. By all means, please, when you're in an Italian deli, don't become a white Presbyterian slacker who just wants a turkey sandwich with mayo with the crusts cut off. You will be shamed away from the deli counter to go learn some proper Italian culture and etiquette!!! Another good piece of advice is to be careful when you eat an Italian deli sandwich. The sandwiches are usually made with a topping of oil and vinegar and vegetables, then wrapped tightly in waxed paper, marked on the outside and given to you over the counter like the handing off of a football. There's one beautiful problem: this football has a very fresh garlicky, onion aroma. It oozes juices that have a tendency to smell up any taxi cab, airplane, rental car or hotel room and stains your clothes like you have never seen! You will definitely draw attention to yourself! Here's a list of some favorite combination subs that you will find around the city.

Italian Sub - Capicolla, mortadella, salami, provolone, lettuce, tomato, onion, oil and vinegar.

Extra Special Italian - Prosciutto, salami, pepperoni, mortadella, provolone, lettuce, giardiniera, tomato, onion, oil and vinegar.

Siciliano - Prosciutto, sopressata, ham, coppa, mozzarella, sweet red peppers, lettuce, tomato, onion, oil and vinegar.

Muffaletta - Homemade olive salad, salami, capicolla, mortadella, and mozzarella cheese served on ciabatta bread.

American - American cheese, ham, turkey, bologna, lettuce, tomato and mayo.

Turkey Sub - Turkey breast, mozzarella, lettuce, tomato and mayo.

Ham and Cheese - Krakus ham, American cheese, lettuce, tomato, mayo and mustard.

Tuna - Homemade Italian-style tuna, lettuce, tomato, onion, oil and vinegar.

Italian Vegetable - Artichoke salad, roasted peppers, eggplant, mushrooms, onion, fresh mozzarella and balsamic vinaigrette.

Old Paesano - Breaded eggplant, broccoli rabe, roasted red peppers, fresh mozzarella and olive oil.

Savory Toppings - When the Sicilians started moving to the Chicago area in the early 1900s, not only did they bring their appetites for the lust for life, but also their appetite for everything spicy. What most Americans would consider a simple salad of hot dog topping pales in comparison to what Italians use as a condiment. Mustard, mayo and relish can't hold a candle to extra hot pepper giardiniera, roasted red peppers, sport peppers, sweet cherry peppers, pepperoncinis, marinated artichoke salad, eggplant salad, mixed olive salad. The list goes on and it just gets me excited thinking about it! Italian delis in the city utilize these condiments and toppings not to mask the goodness of the sandwich, but to accentuate and heighten the overall experience. It's just beautiful layers of flavors! Most delis I know usually carry the basics such as fresh sliced tomatoes, lettuce, red onions, jarred pepperoncinis, the mandatory oil and vinegar dressing and a savory spice mixture of oregano and basil that is usually sprinkled on top of the sandwich. I've eaten a lot of Italian sandwiches in my life and have found that the simpler the topping the better, as long as it's exceedingly fresh. I try to stay away from places that use a pre-mixed Italian dressing because it loses its taste and integrity. I prefer just a simple drizzling of extra virgin olive oil and really good red wine vinegar accompanied by a quick sprinkling of Italian herb mix. Another cool trick is to just drizzle on a little giardiniera oil that will perk up any sandwich. I've included in this chapter a good selection of homemade giardiniera and salads that you can use either as an accompaniment or to top your sandwiches. Also, if you're looking for a spice recipe to dust your sandwich, check it out in this book under South Side Stromboli spice. A little sprinkling will do you good!

DELI SANDWICH GIARDINIERA TOPPINGS - PART DUE!

If you got to this point in the chapter, I want you to sit down, take a deep breath and read this very carefully. The word "giardiniera" not only has to do with hot peppers but it also includes dozens of vegetable, olive and fruit based condiments that go well with anything Italian. Just as the beef sandwich gets my total respect, I also have to give cudos to its close brother the Italian deli sandwich. In fact, I've devoted a whole chapter in this book to it. Most Italian delis around the city make beautiful antipasto salads so I thought I would throw you a bone to try your own.

Chef's Note & Tip The first four recipes in this chapter involve a canning process that most are familiar with, but some are not. Nana's old recipes would dictate that after the jars are filled and sealed, they must be processed in a hot water bath for a good 10 minutes to cook the vegetables. I'm a modern day chef who likes to put up small batches as the vegetables are at their peak ripeness, and I feel that the water bath technique actually renders the vegetables mushy. Since I can't come to your house and show you how to jar, it is strongly advisable that you seek out a paesan who has jarred and canned before to help you through the process. If in doubt, please pick up a copy of the Ball Blue Book: The Guide to Home Canning and Freezing.

Homemade Sport Peppers

MAKES 1 QUART

Mississippi sport peppers are those hot, tart little beauties that are irresistible when placed on a Chicago dog, Polish or sandwich. For more information on this pepper, please go back to the hot dog trivia section in this book.

INGREDIENTS

1 pound mature sport peppers
2 1/2 cups white vinegar, 5%
1/2 cup water
1 teaspoon sugar
1 teaspoon sea salt
3 small garlic cloves, sliced
1 quarter size piece fresh horseradish
  root, optional

Place the sport peppers into a colander, de-stem and thoroughly wash until well cleaned. Place the garlic and horseradish into the bottom of a 1 quart Ball preserving jar. Carefully stuff all the peppers into the jar being sure to leave one inch head space from the top. Bring the vinegar, water, sugar and salt to a boil, stir and then carefully pour over the peppers. (You will have extra liquid but that's the way the recipe works.) Tightly seal the jar with a cover, wipe down the sides and when completely cool, store in the refrigerator for one month before using.

Spicy Jarred pepperoncinis, Hungarian or Banana Peppers

MAKES 1 QUART

Hey Paesan! I know what you're growing in your backyard, but what are you going to do with all them peppers? This is an easy and basic recipe that's not too salty and matures well over time if stored in a cool place. For an interesting treat, try combining in the same jar Hungarian, banana, sweet red or cherry peppers along with a jalapeno for a colorful display.

INGREDIENTS

1 pound mature peppers
1 1/2 cups white vinegar, 5%
3/4 cup water
1 1/2 teaspoons sea salt
1 1/2 teaspoons sugar
4 small garlic cloves, peeled
1 small bay leaf
6 black peppercorns
1 to 2 all-spice berries, optional

Place the peppers into a colander, de-stem and thoroughly wash until well cleaned. Using a small kitchen knife slit the tip of each pepper. Place the garlic, bay leaf, peppercorns and berries in the bottom of a 1 quart Ball preserving jar. Carefully stuff all the peppers into the jar being sure to leave one inch head space from the top. Bring the vinegar, water, salt and sugar to a boil, stir and then pour over the peppers. Tightly seal the jar with a cover, wipe down the sides and when completely cool, store in the refrigerator for one month before using.

Mom DeCarl's Spiced Pickled Vegetables

Geri always likes her vegetables on the tart and crispy side without the added sweetness or the heat which gives her angina. This is a basic and simple DeCarl recipe that can be spruced up to your liking.

INGREDIENTS

1 cup red or green peppers, cubed
1 cup celery, large diced
1 cup peeled baby carrots
1 cup cauliflower florets
1/2 cup pearl onions, peeled
1 1/2 cups white vinegar, 5%
3/4 cup water
1 1/2 teaspoons sea salt
1 1/2 teaspoons sugar
4 small garlic cloves, peeled
1 small bay leaf
4 black peppercorns
1 medium sized dried red chili pepper

In the bottom of a glass Ball jar place the garlic, bay leaf, peppercorns and red chili. Cut up the vegetables, rinse under cold water, drain and then decoratively stuff into the jar being sure to leave one inch head space. In a saucepan heat the vinegar, water, salt and sugar until boiling, stir and then carefully pour over the vegetables. Seal the jar tightly, wipe down the sides, let it come to room temperature and refrigerate for a week before using.

"Fancy Mix" Sweet Pickled Vegetable Giardiniera

MAKES 1 QUART

This recipe is as old as they come. Fresh picked vegetables are steeped in a slightly sweet vinegar pickling brine that makes them extra crispy and refreshing as a side condiment to any sandwich.

INGREDIENTS

1 cup peeled baby carrots
1 cup cauliflower florets
1 cup red peppers, cubed
1 cup celery, large diced
1/2 cup pearl onions, peeled

BRINE

2 cups white vinegar, 5%
1/2 cup water
1/3 cup sugar
1 1/2 teaspoons sea salt
1/2 teaspoon pickling spice
Dash of turmeric
2 small dried red chili pods

Cut up the vegetables, rinse under cold water, drain and then decoratively stuff into a wide mouth mason jar leaving 1/2-inch head space. In a small saucepan heat all the brine ingredients, stir to dissolve and bring to the boil. Let the spices infuse for 1 minute and then pour over the vegetables leaving 1/2-inch head space. Seal the jar tightly, let it come to room temperature and refrigerate for a week before using.

Marinated Artichoke and Fennel Salad

MAKES 1 QUART

I've seen this refreshing salad at delis around town and a few local cops recommend it as a topping for any Italian deli sandwich. Be sure to ask for a little extra juice for the bread.

INGREDIENTS

2 to 3 Six ounce jars marinated artichokes in seasoned brine, drained and brine reserved
2 small fennel bulbs, cleaned
1 cup Recipe Sweet Red Peppers and Garlic
1 cup green Italian olives, pitted and quartered

DRESSING

3/4 cup extra virgin olive oil
5 to 6 tablespoons reserved artichoke brine
1 tablespoon garlic, minced
2 anchovy fillets, minced
1/4 teaspoon sea salt
1/8 teaspoon black pepper
Dash of red pepper flakes, garlic powder and onion powder
2 tablespoons parsley, minced

Place all the ingredients for the dressing into a small jar, cover and shake to combine. Leave on the counter at room temperature to steep for 1 hour. Using a sharp chef's knife cut the fennel bulbs in half, remove the hard core and discard. Cut the fennel diagonally into thin slices and place into a medium sized mixing bowl. Cover with enough of the dressing to make it a little bit wet mix, cover and refrigerate for 2 hours. After 2 hours, add the rest of the vegetable ingredients and mix. Refrigerate for a couple hours before serving.

Sicilian Style Marinated Eggplant Salad MAKES 1 QUART

Everyone loves this darn salad which seems to take so long to make, but is oh, so good on top of any Italian sandwich! Be sure to remove the jar from the refrigerator an hour before using.

INGREDIENTS

2 to 3 pounds small eggplants
3 tablespoons sea salt
4 large garlic cloves, minced
3 tablespoons fresh oregano, chopped
3/4 cup white wine vinegar
1/4 to 1/2 teaspoon red chili flakes
1 cup extra virgin olive oil

Peel the eggplants, cut into 1/2 -inch slices and then cut into 1/2-inch strips. In a large mixing bowl combine the eggplant strips with the salt and cover with a heavy kitchen plate for 2 hours to help the eggplants release their liquid. After 2 hours, pour the eggplant into a colander and gently using your hands, squeeze the eggplant so that it releases all its liquid and then discard the liquid. Place the eggplant into a mixing bowl and add the garlic, oregano, vinegar and chili flakes. Combine and marinate for 1 hour. After 1 hour, gently arrange the eggplant pieces into a wide-mouth mason jar or small Italian crock being sure to press down gently with a spoon to pack the mixture tightly. Add all of the olive oil making sure that it covers the eggplant completely. Cover and keep at room temperature for a few hours. After a few hours make sure that the eggplant is completely covered with the oil. If not add a little more oil to cover. **Refrigerate the crock or keep in a cool place for preserving. If kept submerged under the oil, the eggplant should last for a few months.**

Anthony's Excellent Party Olive Salad MAKES 1 HEAPING QUART

My son, Anthony, likes to make this olive salad around the holidays when grandma visits so he can get an extra fiver in his size 12 stocking!

INGREDIENTS

1 cup green Manzanella olives with
  pimento
1 cup Greek style black olives
1 cup pepperoncinis, split
1/2 cup small sport peppers, drained
1 cup celery, sliced thin
1 cup carrots, thinly sliced
One 10 ounce jar marinated artichokes
  in seasoned brine, drained
1 cup Recipe Sweet red peppers and
  garlic
2 tablespoons small capers, optional

DRESSING

1 cup extra virgin olive oil
4 tablespoons red wine vinegar
2 tablespoons lemon juice
1 1/2 tablespoons garlic, minced
2 teaspoons dried oregano or dry Italian spice
1/4 teaspoon sea salt
1/2 teaspoon black pepper
1/4 teaspoon red pepper flakes
Dash of garlic powder and onion powder

Place all the ingredients for the dressing into a small glass jar, cover, shake to combine and let steep on the counter for 2 hours. After 2 hours, combine the remaining ingredients in a large mixing bowl and pour on enough dressing to coat. Mix, cover and refrigerate for 5 to 6 hours before serving.

Old Fashioned Taylor Street "Kitchen Sink" Olive and Vegetable Salad MAKES 1 HEAPING QUART

Paesans from Taylor Street just can't leave well enough alone, so they invented this party favorite that perks up any buffet table.

INGREDIENTS

2 cups Italian green olives with pimento
2 cups Recipe Mom DeCarl's Spiced Pickled
Vegetables, lightly chopped
Two 6 ounce jars marinated artichokes in
  seasoned brine, drained
One 15 ounce can chick peas, drained and rinsed
1 cup Recipe Sweet red peppers and garlic
1 medium red onion, halved and sliced thin
1/2 cup small sport peppers, drained

DRESSING

3/4 cup extra virgin olive oil
1/3 cup red wine vinegar
1 tablespoon garlic, minced
1 1/2 teaspoons dried Italian seasoning spice
1/4 teaspoon sea salt
1/4 teaspoon black pepper
1/8 teaspoon red pepper flakes
Dash of garlic powder and onion powder

Place al the ingredients for the dressing in a small jar, cover, shake to combine and let steep on the counter for 2 hours. After 2 hours, combine the remaining ingredients in a large mixing bowl and pour on enough dressing to coat. Mix, cover and refrigerate for 5 to 6 hours before serving.

New Orleans Style
Italian Muffalletta Salad

Pronunciation (muff-uh-let-ta) As I stated earlier, giardiniera has come a long way and this Sicilian concoction is a prime example of the quintessential majestic topping for the famed **New Orleans** sandwich created early in the 20th century. It consists of a 10-inch round Italian loaf that is filled with **Genoa salami, baked ham, mortadella and provolone** and then generously topped with this condiment. I like to keep the olives whole and serve it on the side as a salad. When chopped, it makes a good and simple garlic bread topping or an interesting garnish for pizza and beef sandwich.

INGREDIENTS

1 heaping cup green Italian olives in oil and
    herbs, pitted
1 heaping cup Manzanilla olives with pimento
2 cups vegetable giardiniera, drained and lightly
    chopped
4 large garlic cloves, minced
2 tablespoons parsley, minced
2 teaspoons small capers
1/4 teaspoon dried oregano
1/8 teaspoon sea salt
1/8 teaspoon black pepper
1/8 teaspoon red pepper flakes
1/2 cup olive oil

Drain the green olives and place into a large mixing bowl with the rest of the ingredients. Carefully using your hands, toss the salad to combine, place into a mason jar and let marinate in the refrigerator for 2 days before using. **(2 to 3 tablespoons of the drained olive or vegetable juice can be added to the jar for a spicier version.)**

CALUMET FISHERIES, SMELTS AND FRIED PERCH

FISH

RECIPES

Lately, for some strange reason I've had the northern woods on my mind, specifically the Wisconsin area. If you're a city kid who grew up in the 50s, 60s or 70s, you most definitely endured long, slow summer rides up to lakes such as Hayward, Eau Claire, Dells, Rhinelander, Steven's Point, Elkhart or Geneva. Halfway through the trip you most undoubtedly stopped to cool off at a Dog N' Suds, Tastee Freeze or A & W Root Beer for the frosted mug special. Now I'm not going to candy coat it, but back then we used to rough it! Accommodations usually were of the self-serve type, whether it was an old trailer park, wigwam tent city, strip Motel 8 or rickety old cabins that lined Wisconsin's majestic lake regions. Ahhh! The glorious moon shimmering on the lake, wieners cooked on a stick, Nehi grape soda pop, your first real make-out session and a cheapo Zebco rod and reel to catch that big pike perch. Boy, I sure miss those good old times.

Something mystical and magical appeared on the Chicago horizon around the 50s in the form of fisheries (small mom-and-pop fish stores that processed, fried or smoked your catch). You see, all that abundant fish you caught up north, meticulously wrapped in newspaper and stored in dry ice coolers wouldn't fit in your old avocado-green Remco frost-laden freezer space above the refrigerator. And God forbid that your ice cubes or T.V. dinners tasted like that fresh catch!

I come from a long line of Midwestern anglers and my Grandpa John Gronek used to own a company called Land Em' that manufactured rods, reels, fishing nets and hand-knit smelt nets. Chicago is home to a good dozen or so fisheries, a few that actually back up to the city's river ways and the rest on the outskirts of town. When I was a kid, my Grandpa used to take me around to local joints such as Hagen's, Calumet Fisheries, Lawrence Fisheries or Goose Island Shrimp to sell his wares and get his fresh catch smoked. Fisheries are unique in the fact that they all started on a shoe string in far out locations and most had a hand-built smoke house, perfected on a trial and error basis. Shop owners I know reminisce about the days when local anglers and hunters would excitedly call ahead from Wisconsin, Michigan or Florida and tell them to prepare for their magnificent prize or catch to be processed and smoked. Fisheries are unique in the fact that they've perfected the technique of smoking and frying exceedingly fresh seafood and are a favorite with local anglers.

Seafood joints around the city run a relatively clean operation that usually consists of a small glass-covered display case that houses fresh filleted fish and seafood such as shrimp, catfish, lake perch, walleye pike, smelt, scrod, oysters and clams. Other display cases feature such items as smoked chubs, trout, sturgeon, salmon, white fish and sable. Alongside are the typical house-made shrimp cocktail and assorted salads such as coleslaw, potato, macaroni and seafood. Behind the counter you usually see a few deep-fat fryers and a pinewood dredging table for seasoning and breading the fish. The operation is pretty straightforward. You tell the fish guy what you'd like fried, they weigh it on a scale (most joints sell by the pound), they dredge it and batter it in their special blend and fry those babies up for a good 3 to 4 minutes until golden brown and piping hot. Regulars enjoy a side of fries, deep fried mushrooms or hush puppies and a few salads to go along with homemade cocktail or tartar sauce.

When I was in high school there was a really heavy snow storm that shut down the bus lines, so my buddies and I had to walk 5 miles home. And on this particular snowy Friday evening, we happened upon a local fish house that took pity on us and warmed us up and treated us each to a small, greased-bottom brown bag of fried perch and hush puppies in exchange for our bus money. I can still remember standing on the snowy sidewalk cradling that bag of piping hot goodness with the steam warming my face and the hot fish burning the tips of my fingers. That long tortuous walk home after that meal didn't seem so bad and it showed the generous nature and kindness of these local shop owners. I have many good memories of eating at these establishments through the years; I'm proud to say that Chicago is keeping up the tradition with the arrival of Dirk's Fish & Gourmet, Fish Guy Market and Snappy's Shrimp. I've included in this chapter some local recipes that I've enjoyed. I want to leave you with a good piece of advice: fish houses around the city will be glad to smoke your fresh catch for a mere pittance just as long as you didn't buy it from Costco!

Curried Crab Salad Dip

SERVES 4

1 1/2 pounds fresh lump crabmeat, cleaned
1/2 cup mayo, full-fat
2 teaspoons quality curry powder
2 teaspoons mango chutney
1 medium sized apple, finely diced
1 large celery rib, finely diced
1 green onion, minced
Dash of lemon juice, Tabasco, celery salt,
   pepper, garlic powder and Worcestershire
   sauce

Place the cleaned crabmeat into a small mixing bowl. In another bowl thoroughly combine the remaining ingredients until smooth, gently fold in the crab and serve in a cold decorative serving bowl with assorted crackers or fancy breads.

Baby Shrimp, Horseradish Egg Salad Dip

SERVES 4

1/4 pound baby shrimp, pre-cooked
8 hard boiled eggs, chopped
1/2 cup mayo, full-fat
1 tablespoon white prepared horseradish
1 1/2 teaspoons Dijon mustard
1/8 teaspoon sea salt
1/8 teaspoon black pepper
Dash of lemon juice, Tabasco, Worcestershire
   and garlic powder
1 tablespoon chopped chives

Place the shrimp and chopped eggs into a small mixing bowl. In another bowl thoroughly combine the remaining ingredients until smooth, gently fold in the eggs and shrimp and serve in a cold decorative serving bowl with assorted crackers or fancy breads.

5pm Mid West Sky

Anthony Stromboli Pie

Antipasto

Antipasto 2

Apple Pie

Asian Spice

Babka

Bean Soup

Beans and Rice

Beef Stand

Beet Soup

Bi Bim Bap

Cacciatore

Caesar Salad

Carnitas

Catfish

Char Polish

Cheese Burger

Cheesy Beef Pie

Chi Town Chili

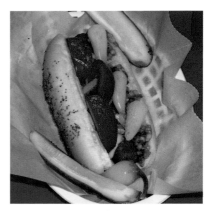

Chicago Hot Dog

Chicken Gyro

Chicken Klutski

Chicken Shawarma

Chix and Dumplings

Classic Gyros

Colored Lentils

Corned Beef

Creole Bowl

Deli Salads

Deli Specials

Dennys 1

Duck Eggs

Excellent Chorizo and Pappas Gordita

Excellent Fries

Extra Hot and Spicy

Fajitas Plate

Falafil

Feet

Filet and Strip Steak

Fishes

Florrie and Morrie

Fried Perch

Fried Pork Rinds

Frittata

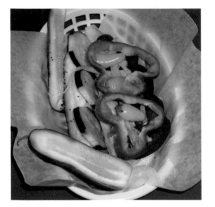

Garden on a Bun

Geris Casserole

Giannottis Vesuvio

Good Hotdog

Goulash

Greek Jarred

Greek Plate 2

Greek Salad

Greeky Chicken

Gumbo Pot

Happy Pizza

Harolds Chicken

Hocks

Homemade Pickles

Hot Fresh Herbs

Hot Sauce

Hotel Breakfast

In Tribute Flowers

Indian Beans

Indian Samosa

Italian Beef Sandwich

Italian Breads

Italian Cheese

Italian Herbs

Italian Rolls

Jalapeno Cheese Burger

Jerk Chicken

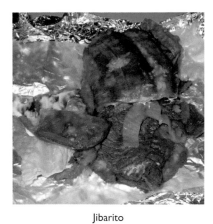

Jibarito

Kasias

Kimchee

Kiss the Clown

Lot o Rice

Lot o Ryes

Lots of Olive Oil

Manly Steaks

Meatball Sandwich

Meatballs

Mexicali Plate

Cajun Grilled Polish

Chilled Sodas

Homemade Soups

Mexican Spices

Milwaukee Ave. and Devon

Minestrone

Monte Cristo

Mousse Treats

Nice Floral

Nice Italian Sausage

Noodles

Noodles and Cabbage

October Decor

Olives

Oxtails

Pam Ordering Beefs

Pams Italian Bread

Pepper Steak

Petit Fours

Pho Bo

Pickled Goodies

Pickled Jalapenos

Polish Beer

Polish Pastry

Pork al Pastor

Portable Eats

Potato Pancakes

Potato Salad

Poundcakes

Produce 1

Produce 2

Produce 3

Produce 4

Ryes 1

Salsas

Sausage and Kraut

Sausages at Andy's Market

Sausages Hanging

Sweet Tamale

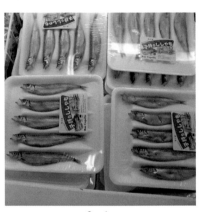

Smelts

Soup

Spicy Feet

Spinach Pies

Split Pea Soup

Sport Peppers

Stuffed Cabbage

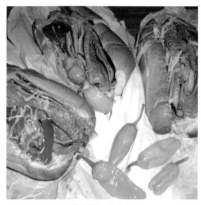

Sub Sandwich

Supreme Tamales

Sweet Delores

Sweet Plantains

Szechuan Green Beans

Tea Cups

Tomato Pickles

Tomato Salad

Truck o Corn

Veal and T-Bone

Vietnamese Eggroll

Weiners

Workin the Line

Xmas Stocking Pizza

Yaki Soba

Seafood Salad Supreme

INGREDIENTS

1 pound medium shrimp, pre-cooked and shelled
1 pound squid rings and tentacles, pre-cooked
1/2 pound lump crabmeat
20 mussels, steamed and shelled
1 small red onion, halved and thinly sliced
1 small fennel bulb, halved and thinly sliced
1 small red pepper, halved and thinly sliced
1 cup Italian black and green olives, pitted and quartered
2 cups bowtie pasta, cooked al-dente

DRESSING

1/2 cup light olive oil
1/4 cup fresh lemon juice
3 medium garlic cloves, minced
1/2 teaspoon sea salt
1/4 teaspoon black pepper
Pinch of red pepper flakes
2 tablespoons parsley, minced
2 tablespoons small capers, optional

Place all the seafood and salad garnish into a large mixing bowl and combine. In another small bowl combine all the dressing ingredients, whisk thoroughly and pour over the salad. Gently toss the seafood salad until it is thoroughly combined and evenly mixed. Cover and refrigerate for at least 4 hours before serving.

New England Clam Chowder

Everyone loves a good clam chowder and this is a really quick and easy recipe. I prefer using canned chopped clams in this soup for their taste and consistency. If you like your chowder on the fishy side, feel free to substitute the canned clam juice for the chicken stock.

INGREDIENTS

4 tablespoons unsalted butter
1/4 cup bacon, minced
4 large garlic cloves, minced
1 medium head of leek, diced
3 medium celery stalks, diced
3 medium carrots, diced
1 teaspoon dried thyme
2 small bay leaves
6 tablespoons all-purpose flour
8 cups chicken stock
1/4 teaspoon sea salt
1/4 teaspoon black pepper
Dash of nutmeg
Dash of Tabasco
Dash of Maggi
1 pound potatoes, peeled and diced 1/2-inch cubes
20 ounces diced canned clams, drained
1/2 to 1 cup heavy cream
1 tablespoon chives, minced
1 tablespoon parsley, minced

Heat the butter in a medium sized sauce pot and add the bacon. Cook stir with a wooden spoon until the bacon renders its fat and turns lightly brown. Add the garlic, leek, celery and carrots and cook stirring until slightly softened about 2 minutes. Add the thyme and bay leaves, cook 1 minute then add the flour and cook a minute more. Now add the rest of the ingredients except the heavy cream, chives and parsley, bring to a boil, reduce the heat and simmer slowly for exactly 45 minutes. Now add the heavy cream, chives and parsley and cook for another 10 to 12 minutes until nicely thickened and smooth. Serve with a good shot of Tabasco and some oyster crackers.

Pan Fried Lake Perch with Tartar Sauce SERVES 4

"Ya Hey Der" to all my great lakes fishing buddies. Sometimes in life it's best to leave well enough alone and this is one of those recipes. Fresh caught perch lightly breaded and fried until crisp and hot is the way to go! The savory and chunky tartar sauce is the perfect foil. So knock back a few cold ones and tell Ma about the big one that got away.

INGREDIENTS

2 to 2 1/2 pounds fresh perch fillets, cleaned
2 teaspoons seafood seasoning spice
2 whole large eggs
1 cup whole milk
1 cup all-purpose flour
1 1/2 cups fresh breadcrumbs
1 tablespoon Seafood seasoning spice
1 quart canola oil or vegetable shortening
   for frying

TARTAR SAUCE

3/4 cup mayo, full fat
1 tablespoon Dijon mustard
2 tablespoons green onion, minced
2 tablespoons Polish dill pickle, minced
2 tablespoons capers, minced
2 tablespoons parsley, minced
1 tablespoon lemon juice
1/8 teaspoon sea salt
1/4 teaspoon black pepper
2 dashes Worcestershire sauce
2 dashes of Tabasco
Dash of celery salt
Dash of garlic powder
2 hard boiled eggs, diced (optional)

At least 2 hours before cooking the perch, prepare the tartar sauce by placing all the ingredients into a medium sized mixing bowl and combine until well blended. Cover and refrigerate. To prepare the perch place all the fillets into a large mixing bowl, season the fillets with 2 teaspoons of seafood seasoning and toss to coat. In another small bowl beat the eggs with the milk until frothy and then set aside. Place the flour into a medium sized mixing bowl and then in another mixing bowl, combine the fresh breadcrumbs with the remaining seafood seasoning until well mixed. Now place all four of the bowls on the counter next to your stove. Heat the oil in a deep iron skillet until the temperature reaches 375°. (I highly recommend using a frying thermometer to gauge the temperature. It is imperative that the temperature remains in the 375° range for proper cooking.) Combine the seasoned fillets with the flour and toss until well coated. Grasping a floured fillet by it's tail, carefully dip it into the egg wash and then working quickly dredge it into the breadcrumbs making sure that it is evenly and thickly coated. Now gently lower it into the hot oil. (I highly recommend working in batches, 4 to 5 pieces at a time so that the oil temperature does not dip below 375°.) Cook the perch for about 3 to 4 minutes until the coating forms a deep brown color and they float to the top. It's a good idea to remove one and test it before removing all of them from the skillet. When the fish is cooked, carefully remove it with a skimmer to a paper-lined basket. Repeat with the remaining fillets and then serve with the tartar sauce.

Grandpa John Gronek's Fried Shrimp
with Spicy Cocktail Sauce

SERVES 4

My Grandpa John Gronek originally from Wausau, Wisconsin, owned a company many years ago called, "Land Em", one of the biggest manufacturers of the smelt net. Through the years he taught me the fine art of fishing and the best way to fry up those little babies. Whether it be perch, shrimps or smelts, as long as they were fresh, he loved em' all. Fried shrimps are a favorite on the northwest side of Chicago, and spicy cocktail sauce, French fries and a cold beer is all that is needed to complete this truly simple dish.

INGREDIENTS

2 1/2 to 3 pounds large shrimp,
   headless, peeled and de-veined
1 tablespoon Seafood Seasoning Spice
4 whole large eggs
1/4 cup whole milk
1 cup all-purpose flour
2 cups Japanese breadcrumbs (Panko)
1 tablespoon seafood seasoning spice
1 quart canola oil or vegetable
   shortening for frying

SPICY COCKTAIL SAUCE

1 cup ketchup
3 tablespoons prepared horseradish
2 large garlic cloves, minced
2 tablespoons parsley, minced
3/4 teaspoon sea salt
1/4 teaspoon black pepper
2 tablespoons lemon juice
2 teaspoons Worcestershire sauce
1/2 teaspoon Tabasco
Large dash of celery salt
Large dash of garlic powder

At least 2 hours before cooking the shrimps, prepare the spicy cocktail sauce by placing all the ingredients into a medium sized mixing bowl and combine with a whisk until well blended. Cover and refrigerate. Place the shrimps in a large mixing bowl, season with 2 teaspoons of seafood seasoning and toss to coat. In another small bowl beat the eggs with the milk until frothy and then set aside. In another bowl combine the Panko breadcrumbs and seafood seasoning until well mixed. Now place all three of the bowls on the counter next to your stove. Heat the oil in a deep iron skillet until the temperature reaches 375°. (I highly recommend using a frying thermometer to gauge the temperature. It is imperative that the temperature remains in the 375° range for proper cooking.) Sprinkle the flour over the shrimps and using your hands, toss until all the shrimps are lightly coated. Now working quickly, grasp a shrimp by its tail and dredge into the egg milk mixture and then dredge into the Panko breadcrumb mixture. Now gently lower the shrimp into the hot oil. (I highly recommend working in batches, 10 to 12 pieces at a time so that the oil temperature does not dip below 375°.) Cook the shrimps for about 2 to 3 minutes until the coating forms a deep brown color and they float to the top. It's a good idea to remove one and test it before removing all of them from the skillet. When the fish is cooked, carefully remove it with a skimmer to a paper-lined basket and serve with the cocktail sauce. Repeat with the remaining shrimps.

Bag "O" Fries

SEE PAGE 158 FOR RECIPE

No righteous perch dinner would be complete without a hot from the fryer side of golden French fries. The secret to a great fry is to pick the right potato, pre-blanch and use a good, clean oil. That's it!

Hush Puppie

MAKES ABOUT 30 PIECES

For your information the origin of the hush puppy comes from an old southern tale. The hounds that followed their owners on hunting or fishing expeditions would start yelping as soon as they caught a whiff of the fish frying. In response to the dogs, the hunters would drop bits of wet cornmeal into the frying pan and toss the tidbits to the dogs with a rebuke "Hush, puppy!"

INGREDIENTS

2 cups white or yellow cornmeal
1 cup all-purpose flour
2 to 3 tablespoons sugar
2 teaspoons baking powder
1/4 teaspoon baking soda
1 teaspoon sea salt
1/2 teaspoon Creole spice
1/4 cup finely minced green onion or chives
2 large whole eggs
1 1/4 cups milk
1 tablespoon canola oil

1 quart canola or vegetable oil for frying

Place the oil in a deep fat fryer and heat to 375°. In a medium sized mixing bowl combine the cornmeal, flour, sugar, baking powder, baking soda, salt, Creole seasoning and onion. In another bowl combine the egg, milk and canola oil and mix until smooth. Pour over the dry ingredients and using a wooden spoon mix together until just combined. Using a tablespoon, scoop a spoonful of the batter into the hot oil and fry for 2 to 3 minutes until lightly brown and crispy on all sides. (Don't overcrowd the fryer.) Remove with a slotted spoon to a paper lined basket and serve.

Old Fashioned Potato Salad

SERVES 3 TO 4

INGREDIENTS

2 pounds potatoes, red or new
1 cup mayo, full-fat
1 1/2 tablespoons Dijon mustard
1/4 teaspoon sea salt
1/4 teaspoon celery salt
1/4 teaspoon black pepper
Dash of Tabasco, Worcestershire, and
garlic powder
2 large hard boiled eggs, diced
1 large green onion, diced
1 large celery stalk, diced

Scrub the potatoes until clean, cut in half and place in a large pot of lightly salted cold water. Bring the pot to a simmer over medium heat and simmer the potatoes for 15 to 20 minutes until easily pierced with a fork. Drain in a colander until cool and then place in a mixing bowl and refrigerate for 1 hour. Remove the bowl and using a small paring knife, cut the potatoes into bite size pieces and sprinkle over the hard boiled eggs, scallion and celery. Gently mix with your hands until well combined. In another bowl combine the rest of the ingredients until well blended, pour over the potato mixture and mix until smooth. Refrigerate until needed.

Famous Macaroni Salad

SERVES 4

INGREDIENTS

1 pound elbow macaroni, pre-cooked al dente
1 cup Miracle Whip salad dressing
1 tablespoon Dijon mustard
2 tablespoons cider vinegar
1 teaspoon sugar
1/2 teaspoon sea salt
1/4 teaspoon black pepper
3/4 cup celery, diced
3/4 cup green pepper, diced
1/4 cup red onion, diced
Dash of Tabasco, Worcestershire and garlic powder

Place the chilled, cooked macaroni into a large mixing bowl and sprinkle over the celery, peppers and onion. Gently mix together. In another small mixing bowl combine the rest of the ingredients and stir until well blended. Pour over the macaroni and mix until well combined. Refrigerate until needed.

Creamy Coleslaw

INGREDIENTS

4 cups shredded green cabbage
2 cups shredded red cabbage
1/4 cup shredded carrots
1 cup mayonnaise, full-fat
1 tablespoon Dijon mustard
2 tablespoons sugar
1 tablespoon prepared horseradish
1/4 teaspoon sea salt
1/4 teaspoon black pepper
1/4 teaspoon celery seeds
Dash of Tabasco, Worcestershire, and garlic powder

Place the cabbage and carrots into a large mixing bowl and thoroughly combine to mix. In another small bowl combine the remaining ingredients and stir until well blended. Pour over the cabbage and carrots and mix until well combined. Refrigerate until needed.

Luscious Lemon Squares

MAKES ABOUT 20 PIECES

After indulging in some rich and spicy fried seafood, nothing is better than a cool homemade lemon square to cleanse the palate and enliven your spirit.

CRUST

1 stick unsalted butter, softened
1/4 cup sugar
1 cup all-purpose flour
Pinch of sea salt

FILLING

2 large whole eggs
3 1/2 tablespoons fresh lemon juice
Grated rind of one lemon
1 cup sugar
Dash of sea salt
2 tablespoons all-purpose flour
1 tablespoon cornstarch

Pre-heat the oven to 350°, line a 9 by 9-inch square baking pan with parchment paper and then set aside. To make the crust, cream the butter and sugar and then add the flour and salt. Mix until well combined. Press the dough into the bottom of the prepared pan and bake for 20 minutes. Remove the pan from the oven and lower the temperature to 325°. Place the rest of the ingredients into a mixing bowl and using a whisk, beat vigorously until thoroughly combined. Pour the filling into the pre-baked shell and bake for another 25 to 30 minutes. Chill the squares for at least 24 hours before cutting into pieces.

CHICKEN SHACK BASKET

CHICKEN

RECIPES

G rowing up on the northwest side of Chicago was always an adventure, and being Catholic meant always spending time with family on Sunday and taking the mandatory afternoon drive to some destination and restaurant. My dad, Marion, who was an attorney, had this big old four-door, dark blue LTD Brougham that we nicknamed the Polish cruiser. Since our home was centrally located near a major expressway, cruising was easy. All we had to do was pick up Busia and off we went to some venerable institution such as White Fence Farm, The Milk Pail, Dellrheas, or Hienie McCarthy's that specialized in deep-fried chicken. Let me give you some insightful information so that you can relive this experience along with me. These places, which typically started in the late 40s or 50s, are located out in the far suburbs, like way out in the country, and are housed in old road houses, taverns or barns that were formerly attached to an adjacent farm. These restaurants are fancifully trimmed with old farm-type décor, stuffed heads and fish motifs (a taxidermist's dream), and specialize in volume production, long waits, loud families, heavy-set waitresses dressed in the shaker type uniforms and predictably straight-down-the road "comfort food" just the way Busia liked it (nothing too spicy for her). Although the main attraction was fried chicken, my dad's frugality would kick in because these institutions placed on each table (at no charge) the mandatory never-ending relish tray that consisted of a three bean salad, coleslaw, pickled beets, cottage cheese and deep-fried, powdered sugar-coated corn fritters. Once you'd decided on white or dark meat, all you had to do was wait with the hundreds of others, and let's face it, how many kiddy cocktails could a kid drink? Good fried chicken, a side of mashed with chicken gravy and canned corn--what more could a guy ask for?

I've got to admit it, I'm a fried chicken and biscuit junky! In the early 1970s when the fast food craze started to kick in around the city, chicken joints such as KFC, Brown's and Church's, followed by Pop-eye's, opened their doors to feed droves of people broasted chicken hot out of the vat and into a whimsical greasy-bottomed bucket that you could carry home or take to the Forest Preserves. For you chicken aficionados, there's a big difference between broasted and deep fried. Broasted is actually a registered trademark name of the Broaster Company located in Beloit, Wisconsin, which has been operating since 1954. Their process is to marinate chicken pieces in their own special blend of herbs and spices, then cook the chicken in a sealed pressure cooker that leaves the chicken up to 40% moister and 70% less fatty than typical fat frying. The secret to this system is that the chicken is actually cooking from the inside out using its own natural juices, thus limiting the absorption of cooking oil from the outside.

Chef's Tip I urge you not to be foolish and try this broasting technique at home with your own pressure cooker. Cooking oil heats up very fast and can literally cause your ,pressure cooker to implode and spray you with hot grease dumb ass!!

The process of frying chicken consists of filling a heavy cast iron skillet with at least 2 inches of shortening heated to 350°, then seasoning the chicken pieces and lovingly frying them up, cooking them from the outside in. As to who invented fried chicken, it can clearly be traced to the southerners. As to who turned Chicago on to great fried chicken, all we have to do is look to the soulful cooking from our brothers on the southside of the city. I have to give kudos to a genius of a guy by the name of Harold Pierce, owner of Harold's Chicken Shack, which most call a Southside poultry empire founded in the 1950s. The story goes that Harold was not much of a fast-food lover, but he saw the necessity of feeding the college students and his fellow neighbors who lived around the University of Chicago. At the time, fast-food chains were purposely ignoring the south and west sides because they thought it was too risky (a huge and damaging corporate mistake!!). Harold's vision was to dole out huge portions of southern fried chicken served on Wonder Bread with French fries, coleslaw and a heavy slathering of bright red hot sauce or honey-sweet barbecue sauce, all for about $3.00. The grape soda is extra! Harold is undoubtedly a prince among men for taking on the fast food chains and he now has more than 50 plus locations scattered around the city. Harold's chicken is great but parking can be a hassle, and some suburbanites aren't used to ordering through a thick, bullet-proof glass revolving door. In spite of these inconveniences the freshness, taste and portion size of the chicken makes Harold's well worth a try. (Don't forget to get a side order of fried okra, gizzards and livers hot outta da grease, as they say!!!.) In my book, Harold's is the king but there are easily another 200 chicken joints scattered throughout the city that also knock out a great deep-fried USDA chicken every day. Long time mom-and-pop joints such as The Chicken Inn, Chicken Hut, Chicken Shack, Uncle Remus, Phil and Lou's, Farmer Brown's and Sir Chicken have also been feeding a loyal patronage for years. Over the past few years, I've also enjoyed a taste of the Caribbean in jerk grilled chicken at places like Daddyo's, Café Pilar, Tropic Island and J.R.'s. (Ya Man, Good Stuff!)

If you really want to experience the ultimate in southern hospitality and foods that go along with country fried chicken, please visit two great restaurants on the Southside called Priscilla's Ultimate Soul Food Café and Gladys' Luncheonette. These establishments serve up gargantuan portions of fried chicken, candied yams, sweet spiced rice, turnip greens, mac and cheese, corn muffins and banana pudding that will fix you right up, bubba! If you don't feel like heading out, try some of the following recipes as they'll get you pretty close to that southern fried feeling.

CHEF'S TIPS FOR PERFECT FRYING!

1. Try to find birds that average 3 to 4 pounds.

2. Remove any excess fat.

3. Marinate overnight in buttermilk to soften the bird.

4. Always season the bird, not the flour for a fuller spicier taste.

5. A 12 inch iron-cast skillet works best if filled with 2 inches of vegetable shortening.

6. Crisco vegetable shortening works best for all frying.

7. Always drain your fried chicken on a wire rack instead of brown bags.

Spicy Fried Chicken

SERVES 6 TO 8

This is the classic "slap your pappy til he's happy" fried chicken recipe! Pre-brining your chicken in buttermilk will make the bird more flavorful and tender. Feel free to use an electric skillet if you have one, but don't leave it by an open window too long as the smell will drive your neighbors crazy.

INGREDIENTS

One 4 to 5 pound chicken, cut up
2 cups buttermilk
2 teaspoons Tabasco
2 cups all-purpose flour

CHICKEN SEASONING

4 teaspoons sea salt
2 teaspoons black pepper
1 teaspoon cayenne
2 teaspoons sweet paprika
1 teaspoon garlic powder
1/2 teaspoon onion powder

1 cup all-purpose flour
Crisco vegetable shortening

The night before making the chicken combine the buttermilk and Tabasco in a mixing bowl. Using a sharp boning knife, remove any excess fat polyps and hairs from the chicken and then place into the buttermilk until completely covered. Cover the chicken with plastic wrap and refrigerate overnight. The next day combine all the chicken seasoning into a small jar, cover and shake until well combined. About an hour before you're ready to cook the chicken, remove the pieces from the buttermilk shaking off as much excess liquid as you can. Place the pieces into a large mixing bowl, season heavily with the chicken spice and toss. Fill a 12-inch heavy-duty cast iron skillet with about 2 inches of the shortening and bring to a temperature of 350°. Place the flour and chicken pieces into a brown paper bag, tightly seal and give it a good shake. Carefully place the pieces into the hot oil and when the oil comes to an aggressive boil, cover the skillet for 5 minutes to let the chicken crisp. After 5 minutes remove the cover and flip the pieces over. Continue this process uncovered for a total of 20 minutes cooking time. Remove the chicken to a wire rack to drain.

Luscious Buttermilk Biscuits

Down in the south they like to eat their chicken with waffles and sweet honey, but us Northern folk love our soft, tender and buttery hot out-of-the-oven buttermilk biscuits. Light, flaky and airy is the way to go so try not to over knead the dough.

INGREDIENTS

2 cups all-purpose flour
2 teaspoons baking powder
1/2 teaspoon baking soda
1 1/2 teaspoons sugar
1 teaspoon sea salt
6 tablespoons unsalted butter, softened
3/4 cup buttermilk
1/4 cup butter melted for brushing

Pre-heat the oven to 425°. Sift the flour, baking powder, baking soda, sugar and salt into a large mixing bowl. Add the softened butter and using a pastry cutter, cut the butter into the flour mixture until it resembles course cornmeal. Pour in the buttermilk and stir with a wooden spoon until the dough comes together. Turn the dough onto a lightly floured work surface and knead gently until it comes together. (If the dough is sticky add a little bit more flour.) Using your hands, pat the dough into an 8-inch round circle about 1/2-inch thick. Using a 2-inch round biscuit cutter, cut the dough into rounds and then gently place onto a lightly greased baking sheet. Liberally brush the tops with the remaining melted butter and bake on the middle rack for 12 to 15 minutes until golden brown. Remove the pan from the oven and serve hot.

Crispy Corn Fritters

Sweet corn fritters were made famous by White Fence Farm up on the North Shore, and I find them utterly addictive and delicious as an accompaniment to fried chicken. A light dusting of powdered sugar is all that is needed to spruce up these golden beauties.

INGREDIENTS

1 cup fresh or canned corn kernels
1/4 cup scallions, minced
1 1/2 cups all-purpose flour
1/2 cup cornmeal
1 tablespoon sugar
1 tablespoon baking powder
1/2 teaspoon sea salt
1/4 teaspoon black pepper
1/8 teaspoon cayenne
2 whole large eggs
1 cup whole milk
2 tablespoons unsalted butter, melted

Crisco vegetable shortening
Powdered Sugar for dusting

Pour 2-inches of shortening into a 12-inch heavy-duty cast iron skillet and bring the temperature up to 360°. In a medium sized mixing bowl, sift together the flour, cornmeal, sugar, baking powder, salt, pepper and cayenne. In another bowl beat together the eggs, milk and melted butter. Pour over the flour mixture, stir with a wooden spoon until the batter comes together and then carefully blend in the corn kernels and scallions. Using a kitchen tablespoon, quickly dip the spoon into the hot skillet oil and then into the batter mixture scooping out a heaping tablespoon. Slide the spoonful of batter into the hot oil. Repeat the process trying not to overcrowd the skillet and cook the fritters for 2 to 3 minutes on each side until puffed and golden brown. Remove to a wire rack and sprinkle on the powdered sugar.

Fried Okra, Gizzards and Livers

Hey man, you might laugh but when you're juiced up on the sauce and you only got a buck to spare, the carnivore inside of you will eat just about anything!

INGREDIENTS

I pound fresh okra
1/2 pound chicken gizzards
1/2 pound chicken livers
I cup buttermilk
I teaspoon Tabasco
1/2 teaspoon sea salt
I heaping tablespoon Creole spice
1/2 cup all-purpose flour
I cup cornmeal

Crisco vegetable shortening

Place the chicken gizzards and livers into a strainer and rinse under cold water until no more blood appears. In a mixing bowl, combine the buttermilk, Tabasco and salt then add the gizzards and livers. Cover and refrigerate for 4 hours. While the gizzards are resting, remove the stem from the okra, cut the pod in half, place into a strainer and rinse under cold water for I to 2 minutes and then thoroughly dry on paper towels. Pour 2 inches of shortening into a 12-inch heavy-duty cast iron skillet and bring the temperature up to 350°. Remove the gizzards and livers from the buttermilk leaving them slightly wet and place into a large mixing bowl along with the okra. (It's imperative that the gizzards and livers are kept wet so that they will adhere to the flour.) Sprinkle on the Creole spice, mix with your hands ,then sprinkle on the flour and cornmeal, and thoroughly combine until all the pieces are well coated. Gently fry the pieces in the hot oil for 3 to 5 minutes until brown and crispy.

Creamy Coleslaw

Everyone loves chili! This is a basic Midwestern recipe that's not too spicy but will most definitely warm your belly up.

INGREDIENTS

2 pound head of green cabbage, cored and
   shredded
1 green pepper, finely chopped
1 small carrot, shredded
3/4 cup mayo, full fat
1 teaspoon mustard
2 teaspoons sugar
1/2 teaspoon sea salt
1/4 teaspoon black pepper
3 tablespoons cider vinegar
Dash of Tabasco, garlic powder and onion
   powder

Place the shredded cabbage, pepper and carrot into a large mixing bowl and combine with your hands. In another mixing bowl combine the rest of the ingredients, whisk until smooth and then pour over the cabbage. Using your hands again, thoroughly combine and refrigerate overnight.

"YAE MAN" CARRIBEAN JERK!

JERK

RECIPES

When I was a kid our usual vacations were long rides up to the Dells and Wausau, Wisconsin, or in the opposite direction down south to Tampa, St. Pete's. There's no question that the wholesomeness of my aunt's farm up North grounded my cooking style, but that sweet Floridian air most definitely reeled me in to the exotic side! The Caribbean, often referred to as the American Mediterranean, is vast; hundreds of small islands are mere shadows of larger land masses such as Cuba, Jamaica, Haiti and Puerto Rico. Chicago has a sizable community of Bahamians, Barbadians, Arubans and U.S. Virgin Islanders who churn out Caribbean cuisine to a crowd of adoring fans. Food writers I know love the island cuisine but find it difficult to write about because there is considerable overlapping of cultures which are hard to pin down. Let me digress. Through the years the islands have shared many a government such as the English, Dutch, French, Spanish and Portuguese. Unfortunately, along with exploration came a slew of slave trades from Africa, India and China. Fortunately for us these founding fathers and displaced souls stuck to their true culinary roots and molded a distinctive and mind-blowing cooking style called Caribbean cuisine.

Chicago has embraced the Jamaican culture since the 1950s, but it really hasn't been until lately that its cuisine has caught on and taken center stage. Fragrant spices such as allspice, cinnamon, cloves, nutmeg and mace grace such dishes as pepper pot soup, jerk chicken and stewed cow's foot with beans. Avocados, plantains, chilies, guavas, limes and papayas create a soothing salad to cool down the palate. History notes that it was the original Arawak Indians of the Caribbean that invented the "barbacoa" a simplified grill to seer and slowly cook over pimento or all-spice wood such delicacies as spit roasted fish, pork leg and chicken that were heavenly seasoned with sweet spices. I spent a lot of time cruising the islands and it's my opinion that to fully appreciate this majestic cuisine one must kick back, slip off the Dockers, chill and grill. I've worked with many great Caribbean cooks and chefs over the years and found their gentle nature and passion for life endearing. We should all be so lucky!

Nuevo Plantains

Plantains are part of the banana family, but are eaten most commonly in the green stage. When they are fully ripened and brown, they are often eaten as a sweet dessert sprinkled with honey.

INGREDIENTS

2 large green plantains
2 tablespoons honey
2 tablespoons orange juice
1 tablespoons canola oil
1 teaspoon Creole spice

Preheat the oven to 425°. Using a sharp chef's knife peel the plantains and cut into 1/2-inch slices. Combine the remaining ingredients, pour over the plantains, mix and bake on a non-stick sheet pan for 30 minutes until browned and glazed.

Quick Island Rice and Peas

The islands produce all kinds of rice and pea dishes. This simple dish is fondly known as Jamaica's coat of arms. Canned pigeon peas, turtle beans or black-eyed peas can be substituted.

INGREDIENTS

2 tablespoons unsalted butter
1 large garlic clove, minced
1/2 small onion, diced
1 whole scallion, minced
1/2 teaspoon fresh thyme leaves
1 small scotch bonnet pepper, left whole
1 1/2 cups raw long grain rice
2 cups light chicken stock
1 cup canned unsweetened coconut milk
1/2 teaspoon sea salt
1/4 teaspoon black pepper
One 15 ounce can red kidney beans, well rinsed
   and drained

In a medium sized non-stick sauce pan heat the butter and saute the garlic, onion, scallion, thyme and bonnet pepper for 2 to 3 minutes. Add the rice, stir cook for 1 minute then add the remaining ingredients except the kidney beans. Stir, bring to a simmer, cover and let cook for 20 minutes. After 20 minutes stir in the kidney beans, re-cover and cook for another 5 minutes then turn the fire off. Let the rice sit covered for another 10 minutes before serving.

"Home style" Cabbage and Noodles

SERVES 4

Every culture has their rendition of my famous Kapusta with Egg Noodles. This is Caribbean comfort food at its best.

INGREDIENTS

1 slice hickory smoked bacon, diced
2 tablespoons olive oil
2 teaspoons garlic, minced
1 small onion, diced
1 medium head green cabbage, cored and diced
1/2 teaspoon sea salt
1/4 teaspoon black pepper
4 tablespoons chicken stock
2 dashes Tabasco

1 pound extra wide egg noodles, pre-cooked al dente

In a large non-stick skillet, heat the oil and saute the bacon until it is lightly brown and renders its fat. Add the garlic, onion and cabbage to the pot and stir cook for 3 to 4 minutes until the cabbage starts to wilt. Reduce the heat to low, add the remaining ingredients except the noodles, cover and let slowly cook for 20 minutes. After that time gently fold in the noodles, re-cover, let cook 5 minutes more and serve.

Cat Fish "Escovitched"

SERVES 4

Spanish settlers in the 15th century turned the Jamaicans on to this quick street food that means "pickled fish". It's easily prepared and utterly delicious!

INGREDIENTS

2 pounds small catfish fillets
1 tablespoon Creole spice
1/4 cup all-purpose flour
1/2 cup canola oil

MARINADE

2 tablespoons canola oil
2 large garlic cloves, sliced
1 small onion, sliced
1 small red pepper, sliced
1 small green pepper, sliced
2 scotch bonnet peppers, sliced
1 small carrot, peeled and sliced
1/2 teaspoon fresh thyme
1/4 teaspoon whole all-spice seeds
1 cup white vinegar
1/2 cup water

Season the fish with the Creole spice, flour then saute in the canola oil for 2 to 3 minutes on each side until lightly golden brown. Place the cooked fillets into a high sided decorative oval platter. In another clean pot heat the remaining oil and saute the garlic, onions, peppers and carrot for 2 to 3 minutes until slightly wilted. Add the remaining ingredients and cook slowly for 5 minutes more. After that time give a good stir and carefully ladle over the fish fillets and let marinade for 30 minutes before serving. Can be eaten hot or cold.

Excellent Jerk Chicken

I learned this recipe years ago from a great young chef by the name of Jay Solomon while visiting up state New York. Jay's recipe is right on the money with the subtle sweet spices accentuated by the heat of the peppers.

INGREDIENTS

2 small chickens, 3 to 4 pound average

MARINADE

2 large garlic cloves, minced
1 small onion, minced
4 green onions, chopped
2 to 4 scotch bonnet peppers, seeded and chopped
One 1-inch chunk fresh ginger

1/4 cup canola oil
1/2 cup red wine vinegar
3/4 cup soy sauce
1/4 cup brown sugar
2 teaspoons dried thyme leaves
1 teaspoon whole cloves
1 teaspoon whole black peppercorns
1/2 teaspoon ground nutmeg
1/2 teaspoon ground all-spice
1/4 teaspoon ground cinnamon

Using a sharp kitchen shear, cut the backbone out of the chicken being sure to leave the chicken whole. Place the birds on the countertop, flatten with your hands then using the tip of a paring knife pierce little holes into the meaty part of the chickens. Place the garlic cloves, onions, pepper and ginger into the bowl of a cuisinart machine and buzz until finely chopped. Scrape out the mix on top of the flattened chickens and using your fingers, push into the slits that were previously made. Combine the remaining ingredients in a mixing bowl until smooth, pour over the chicken and let marinate covered in the refrigerator for 4 to 6 hours. Heat a charcoal grill to medium heat, throw on some hickory or mesquite chunks and slowly grill the chicken for about 45 minutes turning frequently and basting with the remaining marinade.

"Yae Man" Curried Goat

For all you hard core goat fans, I've included this recipe in The Other Ethnic Side Chapter at the back of the book so check it out!

Nigerian Egusi Stew

For all you hard core bush meat fans, I've included this recipe in The Other Ethnic Side Chapter at the back of the book so check it out!

Ice Box Lemon Lime Pie   SERVES 8

After eating jerk chicken or curried goat, you most definitely need something to cool down the palate. I find this pie to be the perfect foil for a spicy evening.

INGREDIENTS

One 9-inch pre-baked graham cracker pie shell

FILLING

1 envelope unflavored gelatin
1 cup sugar
1/8 teaspoon sea salt
4 large eggs, separated
1/2 cup lemon or lime juice
1/3 cup cool water

Combine the gelatin, 1/2 cup of the sugar and the salt in the top of a double boiler. In a separate bowl beat the egg yolks, lemon juice and water together then stir into the gelatin mixture. Cook stirring constantly with a wooden spoon over warm water until the gelatin is completely dissolved about 5 minutes. Remove from the heat and chill until the mixture is partially set. In a separate bowl, beat the egg whites until they form soft peaks. Slowly add the remaining sugar one tablespoon at a time and continue beating until the egg whites form stiff peaks. Carefully fold the whites into the lemon mix, turn into the baked pie shell and chill until firm. Serve with a dollop of cool whip.

AFRICAN-AMERICAN SOUL

SOUL

RECIPES

I have to admit that I was hesitant at first about including this chapter, not because it didn't merit attention, but more simply for the question of how street food fits into this culture. Yea, fried cat, ribs, chicken and watermelon are way too stereotypical for me. Through some mystical magical powers, I have the luxury of having my chapters reviewed by some professors at colleges around the country, who like an old school teacher, red flag my writing abilities and make me do it over again. Quite a while back, I submitted a rough draft of this introduction to a well known University of Chicago professor of African-American studies who chastised my work claiming that "it wasn't street enough and too whitey to interest African Americans." (Mind you, I got similar responses regarding my Polish cookbook from Polish groups claiming that it was too nice.) The professor explained that no self righteous brother is interested in fried catfish with mango salsa or stuffed pork chops with truffle and balsamic glaze or fancy greens with poached eggs and champagne vinaigrette! "Please, my Polish brother, get it right and keep it real. Soul, man, soul, that's what we want. Hop into the pot of hog jowls and maw and send me a revised edition." Hog jowls and maw, hoppin' John, limpin' Susan, stoup, succotash, ginger-ale salad, callaloo, grits and cheese, hoe cakes, coosh coosh, red velvet cake and blue coconut cake. Man o' man, I was all messed up. Luckily for me, I'm a fearless and adventurous guy so I took my cause to the south side for a month. Man, I can tell you if you really want to research the true beautiful beginnings of Chicago street food and the foundations of our culinary heritage, just look to the soulful brothers and sisters that dominate the south and west sides. Let me give you a little bit of their history.

The Great Northern Migration of the early 1920s brought a new class distinction within Chicago's African-American community. The settled, middle-class African- American population living at the southern end of the city considered the newly-immigrated blacks to be less educated than themselves and unfamiliar with the social etiquette that had allowed the settled population to gain acceptance from Chicago's white citizens. In a sense they were right, because the migrant workers who came up from the South brought a whole new culture with them which was completely different than what Chicago's black community was familiar with. The differences were most obvious in their food preferences, with the southerners preferring down and dirty street cuisine that is true to itself, with simple preparations that can simmer all day on the stove). The migrant workers brought with them not only the desire for steady work and a better life, but also knowledge of an agrarian culture and culinary history that defined the way they ate, shopped for foodstuffs and celebrated events. All this was to have a profound influence in their quest for urban acceptance and the infiltration of soul food as it is known in Chicago today.

I don't want to get into any long dissertation. I'll leave that to my more educated professor friends. Plainly speaking, the African-American migrant workers from the South were used to eating a lot of greens, corn products and seasonal fruits to keep their energy up for long, backbreaking workdays. They also ate boiled stews that simmered all day, because working in the fields didn't leave much time for preparing gourmet meals, and less choice cuts of meat tasted better if left to cook longer. Integrated into their diet were foods their ancestors brought over from Africa, such as black-eyed peas and sweet potatoes, so much like the African yam. One day a week they had communal eating to celebrate a day of rest or a harvest of cotton brought in, and this meant feasting on loads of fresh chicken, freshly-caught fish and vegetables picked fresh from a nearby field. All of these rural cultural habits they brought up to the urban harshness of the North. They took comfort in what was familiar to them, just like the European ethnic groups who preceded them, and the African-Americans had the extra bonus of being free from having to bend to anybody else's way of thinking.

To incorporate their Southern culture, they slowly began to open small markets and some restaurants in the southern part of the city. Most who migrated weren't educated, so they struggled with understanding how to make a business flourish and grow. But they did know about the types of food and preparation their fellow Southern migrants yearned for. Settling mostly in the Bronzeville area just south of the Loop, the newly arrived blacks had to compete with fellow African-Americans who already had established businesses, the big chain grocery stores and European immigrants. Just like the European immigrants they were competing with, these black migrants developed their own sense of ethnicity around symbols of their Southern culture: simple preparations of fresh foodstuffs and communal feasts for celebrating a holiday or gathering with friends and relatives. Many who opened markets or food stores ended up closing them within a year. However, as difficult as it was, some stayed in business by stocking hard-to-get products and specialty food items that the other migrants needed to prepare their traditional Southern feasts. Those African-Americans with the foresight and a couple of bucks were able to stick it out and open lunch rooms, chicken and fish shacks, barbecue huts and other restaurants in their neighborhood to cater to other migrant's longings for the comfort and soul of the foods from the South. It's ironic that the very thing that made these black migrants stand out as different--their Southern roots and foodstuffs--was what allowed them to infiltrate and thrive in the Chicago urban economy.

I've been lucky in my career to have worked with some really great chefs, but also hundreds of really talented cooks from different backgrounds and nationalities that have molded my culinary existence. African-American cooking is such an unexplored culinary dimension that I'm shocked that more books haven't been written about the subject. As far as I'm concerned, soul food is an integral part of street culture in the city. There's probably a half dozen or so soul food restaurants that knock out fresh daily standard fare to adoring crowds who just love their homemade buffet-style fried chicken, candied yams, turnip greens with smothered turkey, mac and cheese, corn muffins, sweet potato pie, pinto beans, rice and gravy, and the list goes on. If you're in the mood for some great soul food, go to Army and Lou's Restaurant, Queen of the Sea Restaurant, Barbara's Restaurant or Priscilla's Ultimate Soul Food Cafe. If you don't get a chance, check out my Rib, Chicken and Fish chapters in this book or try some of the following soul-filled recipes.

Soul food cooking has always been a communal affair so I find it befitting to turn you on to some really great recipes that you can cook for relatives or friends. Feeling stressed out? Why not Xerox the recipes, send them out to your cousins and have each family prepare one of the dishes for a soul food get together?

Mom's Buttermilk Biscuits

MAKES ABOUT 30 PIECES

Light, tender, rich and delicious as well as a true masterpiece of a hand-rolled dough.

INGREDIENTS

6 cups all-purpose flour
1/3 cup sugar
3 tablespoons baking powder
2 teaspoons sea salt
2 sticks unsalted butter, softened
2 1/4 cups buttermilk

Pre-heat the oven to 425°. Sift the dry ingredients into a large mixing bowl and combine. Using a pastry blender, cut the butter into the flour until it forms small pea size pieces and then add the milk and combine until the dough comes together. On a lightly floured surface, roll out the dough into a 1-inch thick square. Fold the dough in half on top of itself, give a quarter turn and roll out again into a 1-inch thick square. Repeat the process three more times and then roll out the dough into another 1-inch thick square. Using a 2 1/2-inch round pastry cutter, cut out the biscuits and place on top of a parchment lined sheet pan. Brush the tops with a little whole milk and bake in the hot oven for 12 to 15 minutes until golden brown.

Ruth's Salmon Croquettes with Beet Horseradish Dressing

MAKES 16 PIECES

Cousin Ruth from up North was never fond of fried cat, but the girl surely could knock out some great salmon patties.

INGREDIENTS

1 pound boneless skinless salmon fillet
1 cup water
1/4 cup dry white wine
Dash of lemon juice
Dash of sea salt

2 whole large eggs
2 tablespoons mayo, full fat
1 teaspoon dry mustard
1 teaspoon Seafood Seasoning Spice
2 teaspoons Worcestershire
2 teaspoons lemon juice
Dash of Tabasco
2 tablespoons parsley or chives, minced
1 cup fresh breadcrumbs

4 tablespoons canola oil
2 tablespoons unsalted butter, melted

BEET HORSERADISH DRESSING

1 cup mayo, full-fat
1 1/2 to 2 tablespoons beet horseradish
2 teaspoons Dijon mustard
1/8 teaspoon celery salt
1/4 teaspoon garlic powder
1/8 teaspoon black pepper
Dash of Tabasco and Worcestershire

Place the salmon into a small saucepan with the water, white wine, lemon juice and salt, bring to a slow simmer and cook for exactly 4 minutes. Remove the pan from the fire and let the salmon cool in the liquid for about 20 minutes. In a large mixing bowl combine the eggs, mayonnaise, mustard, seafood spice, Worcestershire, lemon juice, Tabasco and parsley and using a heavy wooden spoon combine until well mixed. Gently using your hands, pick up the salmon piece and crumble it into the mixing bowl. Lightly stir with the wooden spoon until well combined, mix in the fresh breadcrumbs and shape the mixture into 16 golf ball size patties. Heat the oil and melted butter in a non-stick skillet over low heat. Add the patties, lightly flatten and saute for about 3 to 4 minutes on each side until lightly golden brown. To make the beet horseradish dressing combine all of the ingredients in a small mixing bowl, stir until smooth and refrigerate for a few hours before using.

Red Potato Salad with Pickle, Egg, Radish and Dill

INGREDIENTS

2 pounds small red new potatoes, cleaned and halved
1/3 cup olive oil
1/4 cup apple cider vinegar
3/4 teaspoon sea salt
1/2 teaspoon black pepper
2 large garlic cloves, minced
2 medium celery stalks, finely chopped
4 green onions, white and some of the green part
   finely chopped
8 radishes, sliced
1 large dill pickle, finely chopped
4 tablespoon fresh dill, chopped
2 tablespoons parsley, chopped
2 hard boiled eggs, coarsely chopped

Steam the new potatoes in a vegetable steamer placed over 1 inch of hot water for 12 to 15 minutes until tender. Remove to a large mixing bowl and cool slightly. While the potatoes are steaming combine the oil, vinegar, salt, pepper and garlic and mix well. In another large bowl combine the remaining ingredients until well blended and then add the dressing and stir with a spoon until well mixed. Arrange the slightly cooled potatoes in one layer cut side up onto a serving platter and gently spoon all the mixed dressing onto the potatoes. This dish is best served at room temperature.

Beet, Green Bean, Tomato and Red Onion Salad

This is my updated version of the beloved Mexican breakfast soup. Pre-blanching the tripe 2 to 3 times removes a lot of the gamey smell that people find offensive.

INGREDIENTS

4 medium sized beets, unpeeled
1/2 pound green beans, trimmed
4 large Roma tomatoes
1 medium red onion, peeled
1/4 cup raspberry vinegar
1/4 cup light olive oil
Large pinch of sugar
1/4 teaspoon sea salt
1/8 teaspoon black pepper

In a small mixing bowl combine the vinegar, oil, sugar, salt and pepper and whisk until smooth. Place the beets into a saucepot, cover by 2 inches with cold water, add a pinch of sea salt, bring to a boil and simmer for 20 to 30 minutes until a knife pierces the beets easily. Remove the beets from the water, cool slightly and gently rub off the skins with a paper towel and set aside. Bring 1 quart of lightly salted water to a boil and cook the green beans until they are crisp to the taste. Immediately remove with a kitchen skimmer to a bowl containing ice cubes and water to stop the cooking process. When the beans are cool, drain thoroughly and dry with paper towels. Using a sharp kitchen knife, slice the beets 1/4-inch thick and then place into a large bowl and add the green beans. Now cut the red onions into 1/4-inch slices and quarter the tomatoes. Re-stir the dressing, add about half to the green beans and beets and gently toss to mix. Add the onions and tomatoes to the bowl and again, toss to mix. Cover the bowl with plastic wrap and refrigerate for an hour before serving.

Creamy Mac N' Cheese Bake!

INGREDIENTS

12 ounces elbow macaroni, pre-cooked al dente
12 ounces evaporated milk
2 whole large eggs
1/2 teaspoon sea salt
1/4 teaspoon black pepper
1 teaspoon dry mustard
1/4 teaspoon Tabasco
4 tablespoons unsalted butter, melted
1 cup sharp cheddar, shredded
1 cup Colby, shredded

4 tablespoons parmesan cheese
Dash of paprika

Pre-heat the oven to 350°. In a large mixing bowl combine the milk, eggs, salt, pepper, mustard, Tabasco and butter and whisk until light and creamy. Toss in the macaroni and combine until the noodles are evenly covered with the sauce. Sprinkle on the cheddar and Colby and using a wooden spoon, mix to combine and then immediately pour into a high sided earthenware casserole. Sprinkle on top the parmesan cheese and a dash of paprika and bake uncovered in the hot oven for 40 minutes until the top is bubbly and golden brown.

Spicy Collard Greens in Pot Licker! SERVES A SMALL CROWD

4 pound mixed greens such as collard,
   mustard or turnip

2 tablespoons bacon grease
4 large garlic cloves, minced
1 medium onion, minced
1 medium jalapeno pepper, minced
4 cups chicken stock
1 medium sized smoked hock
1/2 teaspoon sea salt
1/4 teaspoon black pepper
Dash of red pepper flakes
1 to 2 teaspoons sugar
Dash of onion powder, garlic powder
   and Tabasco

Wash the greens thoroughly, drain and remove the stems then cut into broad strips. Heat the bacon grease in a medium sized stock pot and when hot, saute the garlic, onion and jalapeno for 2 to 3 minutes. Add the remaining ingredients except the greens, bring to a boil and slowly simmer to infuse the stock for 30 minutes. Now add the greens to the pot, stir until well submerged and slowly simmer for 40 minutes until the greens are tender and tasty.(After the greens are cooked the pot licker juice can be reduced in a separate pan to deepen the broth).

Cabbage and Noodles

SERVES A SMALL CROWD

INGREDIENTS

1 pound extra wide egg noodles, pre-cooked

1 slice hickory smoked bacon, diced
2 tablespoons olive oil
2 large garlic cloves, minced
1 small onion, minced
1 medium head green cabbage, cored and diced
1/2 teaspoon sea salt
1/4 teaspoon black pepper
1/2 cup chicken stock
2 dashes of Tabasco

In a large sauté pan over medium high heat cook the bacon until it renders its fat and turns lightly brown. Remove the bacon grease, but leave the bacon in the pan. Return the pot to the fire then add the olive oil, garlic and onion and sauté for about 2 minutes. Now add the cabbage and cook stir for 3 to 4 minutes until the cabbage starts to wilt. Reduce the heat to low, add the remaining ingredients except the noodles and cook slowly covered for about 20 minutes. After 20 minutes stir the cabbage, add the noodles, evenly combine and place on a serving platter.

Glazed Sweet Potatoes Gratinee

SERVES A SMALL CROWD

INGREDIENTS

8 to 10 small sweet potatoes
1/2 cup brown sugar
1/2 cup white sugar
2 cups chicken stock
1/2 teaspoon ground cinnamon
1/2 teaspoon ground nutmeg or all-spice
2 whole cloves
1/4 teaspoon sea salt
1/4 teaspoon black pepper
6 tablespoons unsalted butter

Pre-heat the oven to 325. Scrub the potatoes, rinse, peel and then cut into quarters. Butter a 2 quart casserole or shallow baking pan and arrange the potatoes in the pan. Place the remaining ingredients Into a small saucepan, bring to a boil, stir to combine and then pour the glaze over the potatoes. Cover with aluminum foil then bake in the hot oven for 1 hour until glazed, brown and bubbly.

Cousin Gladys' Smothered Pepper Steaks

SERVES A SMALL CROWD

Cousin Gladys from down south, a devout Christian woman, refuses to eat pork so she devised this recipe to satisfy her soulful cravings.

2 to 2 1/2 pounds cube steak, pounded
1/2 cup all-purpose flour
1 teaspoon dried thyme
1 teaspoon Hungarian sweet paprika
Dash of sea salt, pepper and garlic powder

1/4 cup canola oil
4 large garlic cloves, minced
1 medium onion, sliced
1 large red pepper, sliced
2 cups mushrooms, sliced
1 bay leaf
1 teaspoon dried basil or marjoram
1/4 teaspoon sea salt
1/8 teaspoon cayenne pepper
1/4 cup dry red wine
3 cups beef stock
1 cup tomato puree
1 teaspoon Worcestershire
3 dashes Tabasco

Pre-heat the oven to 350°. In a medium sized mixing bowl combine the flour, thyme, paprika, salt, pepper and garlic powder and reserve 2 tablespoons to thicken the sauce. Heat the oil in a large skillet over high heat and working in batches, lightly dredge the cubed steak into the flour and then saute in the hot oil for 3 to 5 minutes on each side until golden brown. Remove the browned steaks to a medium sized earthenware casserole and brown the remaining meat. When all the steaks are browned, pour off all but 2 tablespoons of excess oil from the skillet and return the pan to the heat. Now add the garlic, onion, peppers and mushrooms and cook stir until the vegetables are slightly softened about 3 minutes. Add the bay leaf, basil or marjoram and reserved tablespoons of flour, and cook for a minute to release their oils. Add the rest of the ingredients to the skillet and bring to the boil. Pour the vegetables and stock over the cubed steak, cover the casserole tightly and cook in the oven for 2 hours until the meat is fork tender.

Uncle Rufus' Famous Chicken, Sausage and Shrimp Jambalaya Casserole

Rufus was born down Mississippi way and learned how to make this Creole dish from his mama, a great Creole cook, who worked at the famed Restaurant Antoine's.

INGREDIENTS

1/4 cup canola oil
1/2 pound kielbasa, sliced
1 pound chicken breast, cubed
1 pound medium sized shrimps, peeled raw
2 tablespoons Creole spice

4 large garlic cloves, minced
1 small onion, minced
1 medium red pepper, diced
1/2 cup green onion, diced
1/2 cup celery, diced
2 cups raw converted rice
One 14 ounce can diced tomatoes
3 1/2 cups chicken stock
2 teaspoons dried thyme
1 bay leaf
1 teaspoon Creole spice
1/2 teaspoon Worcestershire
1/4 teaspoon Tabasco

Pre-heat the oven to 350°. Place the kielbasa, chicken breast and shrimps into a large mixing bowl and liberally season with the Creole spice. Heat the canola oil in a medium sized high sided earthenware casserole and when hot, saute the kielbasa for 2 to 3 minute until lightly browned. Remove to a serving platter being sure to leave the residual oil in the pot. Now saute up the chicken breast for 2 to 3 minutes until lightly brown and set aside. Saute up the shrimps in the same manner and set aside. Now add 2 more tablespoons of oil to the pot and saute the garlic, onion, pepper, green onion and celery for 2 to 3 minutes. Add the rice to the pot with the vegetables and stir cook for another 2 to 3 minutes. Add the rest of the ingredients including the sausage, chicken and shrimps, bring to a slow simmer stirring all the while to combine. Cover tightly and bake in the hot oven for 40 to 45 minutes until the liquid is absorbed and the rice is fluffy. Fluff with a kitchen spoon before serving.

Auntie Phyllis' Orange Marmalade Dinner Ham

SERVES A SMALL CROWD

Everyone loves a beautifully glazed ham as a centerpiece for their buffet table.

INGREDIENTS

One 10 to 12 pound lightly smoked
   ready to eat ham, bone-in

HAM GLAZE

3 large garlic cloves, minced
One 9 oz. Jar Major Grey's Mango Chutney or
   bitter orange marmalade
1/4 cup Dijon mustard
1/2 cup light brown sugar
1/2 cup fresh orange juice
1/2 teaspoon black pepper

Pre-heat the oven to 350°. (I recommend cooking the ham 10 to 12 minutes per pound so set your clock accordingly.) Place all the ingredients for the ham glaze into a small bowl, whisk together and set aside. Using a sharp chef's knife peel the skin from the ham and trim the fat, leaving a 1/4 - inch layer. Using the tip of a sharp knife, score the fat into diamond pattern all around then place the ham onto a rack set over a roasting pan. Place the ham into the hot oven and cook for exactly 30 minute. After 30 minutes remove the ham from the oven and baste it with the chutney glaze. Return the pan to the oven and bake, basting frequently with the rest of the glaze for another 1 1/2 hours. When the ham is cooked, remove it from the oven and let it rest 15 minutes before carving.

The Best Banana Cream Pie

MAKES TWO 9-INCH PIES

This is a really cool and delicious counterpart to spicy soul food. The recipe is pure chef text book and it will give you the result that you are looking for.

INGREDIENTS

Two 9-inch store bought Honey Maid Graham
    Cracker pie crusts

FILLING

3/4 cup sugar
1/2 cup cornstarch
1/4 teaspoon sea salt
4 cups whole milk
5 large egg yolks
2 teaspoons vanilla extract
2 large bananas, peeled and sliced
2 tablespoons lemon juice

TOPPING

2 cups whipping cream
2 tablespoons sugar
2 tablespoons rum

To make the filling combine the sugar, cornstarch and salt in a heavy saucepan and stir to mix. Add the milk, egg yolks and vanilla, whisk to combine and bring the mixture to a boil over a medium heat stirring constantly. After the mixture has come to a boil and thickened, continue to cook for 1 minute then remove the custard from the fire. Peel the bananas and cut into 1/2-inch slices then sprinkle on the lemon juice and combine. Place 1/3 of the warm custard mixture into the prepared pie shells, top with some of the banana slices and continue layering until all the bananas and custard are used up making sure it doesn't overflow the shell. Place the filled shells into the refrigerator for a good 4 hours to chill then just before serving, whip the heavy cream to soft peaks, add the sugar and rum, and decorate the top of the pie.

PLANET GYROS GO ROUND AND ROUND!

GYROS
RECIPES

There's an old Greek children's game, Gyros-Gyros-oli (similar to the Farmer in the Dell nursery rhyme), that describes the circular motion of the lamb spinning on the gyros spit. Gyros, or spitted spiced lamb, is actually a dish that made its way from the Middle East to Greece and then on to the States in such a big way that it has become one of America's and Chicago's favorite adopted foods. Modern day sliced-off-the-hot-vertical-spit gyros is a far cry from its lonely roots that date back easily to the time of Christ. The original dish, which comes from Turkey, was actually called, lahmacun, or dough stuffed with meat. The meat was typically lamb or beef that was heavily seasoned with sweet spices such as all-spice, coriander, cloves, cumin, pepper and garlic. The eating utensil that encased these meats came to be known as pita bread.

Middle Eastern flat bread--pita--came to America via Arab bakers who would bake the round, puffy, pocket circles to the delight of their ever- increasing American audience. Pita is usually described as having a light chewy texture reminiscent of a sweet wheat taste and best eaten fresh and slightly warmed straight from the oven. It's mind boggling to comprehend that pita bread has been around for thousands of years. It is common knowledge among food historians that Middle eastern bakers invented the process of turning wheat into flour and that Plato, in a few of his works, mentioned the pita bread. The first cookbook known to man was written in 330 B.C. by the Greek food philosopher, Archestratos, and it is also interesting to note that two other Greek food writers by the names of Dilphius and Athenaeus wrote extensive treatises on the art of Greek bread- making way back then.

Lahmacun was actually ground spiced meat that was encased in a small round of dough and baked in a communal oven called a fourno. Through the years, modern Turks renamed the dish doner kabob, basically changing it by taking the meat out of the dough and spit roasting it on a utensil called a kabob or metal skewer. History marched on, and it is noted through old Middle East cookbooks that utensils such as rotisseries or vertical spits called gyros (meaning something that spins around) became popular in these cultures, changing the way the meats were prepared. Pita was the daily bread of choice at the time and became a natural combination with the grilled meats. Greeks have enjoyed through the years two different styles of meat dishes--arni/katsikaki souvlas (spit roasted whole baby lamb or goat) and grilled kephtethes (are spicy beef and lamb patties that are molded around metal skewers and grilled). These delectable dishes are traditionally served on a pita with a topping of tomatoes, red onions, cucumbers, lemon juice and parsley, thus laying the culinary foundation for the gyros sandwich as we know it today.

Greek chefs experimented with these new-fangled contraptions that would spin the meat, and found that the simplest preparations were the best. Gyro, pronounced yeeh- roh, has been part of Greek street culture for hundreds of years. In Greece, open air stands or restaurants called souvlakia have served to droves of hungry tourists spit roasted or skewered marinated lamb, kid, or suckling pig, along with the traditional salads and the addictive cucumber and mint tzatziki. The smells and sensations of these open-air cooking stands totally engrosses your senses and is best described as getting a whiff of a grilled burger at a Fourth of July party. It's that good!

Modern-day gyros has been a work in progress in Chicago from the 50s and 60s when local Greek restaurants would painstakingly experiment in replicating their beloved open-air foodstuffs. Chefs would de-bone large chunks of seasoned lamb meat, skewer it, spit roast it over an open flame, then slice it to order as patrons filled the restaurant. The biggest problem they encountered was that whole spitted sides of lean lamb, usually about 4 to 5 feet long, cooked very rapidly, so not everyone got the same evenly roasted succulent cut of juicy meat. The other problem they encountered was that the cooking pit (usually of coals and hard wood) was so unmanageable and hot that it would literally burn the eyebrows off any respectable Greek who got too close (dripping grease most definitely causes flare-ups). A solution needed to be found. Marinating the meats was easy, but cooking it uniformly was the tricky part. Escalating lamb prices, ever watchful fire chiefs and the lack of pit space forced Greek chefs and owners to brainstorm. In addition, my research shows that at this time in history fast food was starting to take off, so Greek owners wanted to throw their hat into the ring and cash in on the sandwich craze. Through some ouzo-induced transformation, modern American gyros as we know it was born right here in the city.

In the early 70s, two local Greek businessmen, Chris Tomaras and Peter Parthenis, were working with Greek food service companies to develop an easier way to prepare and serve horizontal and vertical spit gyros. They found that ground lamb, beef and spices could easily be pressed into a large, tight mold, skewered through the middle then slowly rotated over a charcoal pit to cook. Think of it as a large tasty meatloaf that is molded around a skewer and cooked rotisserie style over the grill. Local Greek chefs liked the idea because the seasoned loaf would cook consistently. However, they disliked the fact that the horizontal spit it was cooked on would cause the sliced pieces to spill over the back and fall into the pit. (Kitchen rotisseries spin counter clockwise.) Chris Tomaras' company, Kronos Central, invented and patented the gyrokones, which is a large 20 pound cone of ground mixed meat and spices that is placed on a vertical spit that slowly spins around a flame broiler. When the meat is browned, juicy hot slices are cut off the cone and placed on pita bread to make an authentic Greek sandwich. Greek restaurant owners loved the cones and were more than happy to get rid of their old charcoal pits. Their enthusiasm persuaded both Peter and Chris to come up with a better contraption to cook these new-fangled cones. Peter owner of Grecian Delight Foods, just happened to be a recent graduate from the University of Illinois with a masters degree in engineering. Rumor has it that his garage became an engineer's design studio and within a year, he designed and improved a vertical broiler on which gyrokones could be cooked. His creation, the Autodoner, revolutionized the vertical spit business and is utilized worldwide. Kronos Foods also patented a vertical cooking machine, the Kronomatic gyros broiler. In my cooking career, I have been fortunate to have become acquainted with these two spirited entrepreneurs and find both men to be the leading proponents of modern Mediterranean style foods in this country. In addition to their warmth and generosity, their dedication to perfection has led their companies to dominate the market worldwide.

Now I don't expect you to go out and buy a 25 pound gyrokone or an autodoner, as they can easily serve a few hundred sandwiches. The recipe for gyros meat is a well-guarded secret and eating a sandwich out is something I highly recommend you experience first hand at any gyros restaurant around the city. Gyros joints are a culinary journey all in themselves, as most owners are proud to display their ever-spinning autodoner with the orangy flame that sears the meat beautifully. When you place your order, the cook uses a very thin carving knife to vertically slice the browned meat off the cone, from the top to the bottom, places the meat into a small skillet, then heats it on a griddle alongside lightly oiled fresh pita bread. The meat is then piled high on the warmed pita, topped with a tasty onion and tomato salad and a generous dollop of tzatziki sauce. Some joints like to enliven the gyros after slicing it by giving it a quick griddle to extra crisp the meat, but I find this sacrilegious! For you out-of-towners who don't live near a gyros joint, don't fear because both companies are currently marketing family packs of pre-portioned gyros meat, pita and tzatziki sauce that can be bought at your local grocery store or restaurant supply house.

Spiro's Classic Gyros

This is the original mouth watering, mind blowing, greasy Mediterranean spice infused, tzatziki slathered and onion breathed Greek sandwich that will most definitely take the edge off of anything that's ailing you!

1 pound pre-sliced gyros meat, Kronos Central
    or Grecian Delight
4 fresh white pita breads
1 medium red onion, thinly sliced
2 medium Roma tomatoes, quartered
2 tablespoons parsley, chopped
1 tablespoon olive oil
Dash of sea salt, black pepper and garlic powder

TZATZIKI SAUCE

1 large English hothouse cucumber, peeled and
    finely diced
1 teaspoon sea salt
2 cups plain yogurt
4 medium garlic cloves, minced
2 tablespoons fresh mint or dill, minced
1 tablespoon red wine vinegar
1/4 teaspoon sea salt
1/4 teaspoon black pepper
Dash of garlic powder, onion powder and Tabasco
1 tablespoon olive oil

At least 4 hours before preparing the gyros make the tzatziki sauce. Place the diced cucumbers and 1 teaspoon of sea salt in a bowl and mix. Pour the cucumbers into a fine mesh colander set over another bowl to let the excess water drain off. One hour later, combine the remaining tzatziki ingredients including the cucumbers in a mixing bowl and refrigerate for 3 hours. Pre-heat the oven to 400°. In a small mixing bowl place the onions, tomatoes, salt, pepper, garlic powder, parsley and oil, and toss to combine. Lightly brush a little olive oil onto one side of the pitas and place on a baking pan. Lay the sliced gyros slices on top of another baking pan and when the oven is hot, cook the meat for 4 to 5 minutes until little bubbles of grease appear on the top. Remove the pan from the oven and place the pita pan in the oven to heat until warm. To make the sandwich lay the warm pita on a plate, top with 6 or 7 slices of meat, ladle on a good dollop of tzatziki sauce and then lightly sprinkle on the tomato and onion salad.

Greek Salad with Feta

Everyone loves a classic Greek salad. The sharp creamy taste of the feta is a perfect complement to the fresh and springy greens, tomatoes and olives.

INGREDIENTS

12 large Romaine lettuce leafs, cleaned and dried
1 small English hothouse cucumber, sliced
1 medium red onion, thinly sliced
1 medium green pepper, cut into rings
4 medium sized Roma tomatoes, cut into wedges
1/3 pound feta cheese, cubed
20 Kalamata olives
12 canned anchovy fillets

SALAD DRESSING

1/2 cup olive oil
3 tablespoons red wine vinegar
1/2 teaspoon sea salt
1/4 teaspoon black pepper
1/2 teaspoon dried oregano

In a small mixing bowl combine all the dressing ingredients. Cut the Romaine leaves into bite-size pieces over a large mixing bowl. Add the rest of the ingredients except the dressing and gently toss. Re-stir the dressing and pour over the salad, mix with a tong to combine and serve.

Grecian Grilled Butterflied "Leg O Lamb"

SERVES A SMALL CROWD

Modern style American gyros has come a long way and there are those purists who insist on using only grilled baby lamb for their gyros. This is a simple and easy recipe, but just be sure to slice the meat very thinly and not over cook it.

INGREDIENTS

1 small leg of lamb about 3 to 4 pounds, de-boned and butterfly cut

MARINADE

3/4 cup olive oil
1/4 cup red wine vinegar
2 tablespoons Dijon mustard
8 large garlic cloves, minced
1 tablespoon dried oregano
1 tablespoon dried rosemary
2 teaspoons sea salt
1 teaspoon black pepper

Have your butcher butterfly a small leg of lamb being sure to remove all excess fat. Combine all the remaining ingredients in a small mixing bowl. Place the lamb into a large Ziploc bag, add the marinade and seal the bag. Place the bag into the refrigerator and every 2 to 3 hours aggressively jostle the bag so that the marinade infuses the meat. The next day remove the bag from the refrigerator and let the lamb sit on the counter for at least 2 hours to come to room temperature. Light a charcoal grill and when the coals are hot, grill the lamb for 40 to 45 minutes until the internal temperature reaches 130 to 135° for medium rare to medium. (Reserve the excess marinade to baste the lamb while it's cooking.) Let the meat rest 10 minutes on a serving platter before cutting into bite-size pieces.

Easter Time Barbecued Whole Baby Lamb a la "My Big Fat Greek Wedding"

SERVES A SMALL CROWD

For all of you Greek pyromaniacs who need to grill on the front lawn, this is the perfect recipe for you. Every few years I entertain a large group of chefs and barbecue a whole lamb which is the main course. There is nothing more beautiful than watching a few tipsy chefs lovingly baste and slowly turn such a delectable beast.

INGREDIENTS

One 12 to 14 pound baby lamb, gutted and
    ready for the grill
6 fresh lemons, halved

BASTE

4 cups olive oil
2 cups lemon juice
1 cup white wine
1/3 cup sea salt
2 tablespoons black pepper
1/2 cup dried oregano
1/2 cup garlic cloves, minced

20 pounds of charcoal

The day before cooking the lamb, go into your front yard and dig a pit that is 2 feet wide by 6 feet long by 6 inches deep. The next day line the pit with long pieces of aluminum foil. At this point you will need a Greek contraption called a souvla and two iron poles with forked ends. (The souvla is basically the spit that the lamb is threaded on and the poles are what holds the souvla in place.)

The day that you are ready to cook the lamb, pound the poles in the ground about 7 feet apart at each end over the length of the pit so that the souvla sits exactly 18 inches above the top of the pit. Using half the charcoal, makes two piles exactly 1 1/2 feet away from the poles at each end. Light the fire and let the charcoal go to gray. While the charcoals are heating, rub the lamb all over with the sliced lemon halves and give it a good sprinkling inside and out with some garlic salt and pepper. Pass the souvla through the animal's butt and then carefully through the stomach cavity and lastly, through its chin and out its mouth. Using metal wire, tie the front and back legs to the skewer and make sure that the back of the animal is straight on the souvla. Using the wire again, skewer and sew the stomach cavity closed and also tie up the shoulders and middle back making sure the lamb is secure to the rod. When the coals go gray, place the souvla onto the poles, then look at the lamb and determine where the fleshier parts are such as the legs and the shoulders. (The legs and shoulders are a lot meatier and take longer to cook so it is imperative that most of the heat from the fire is sitting under those two fleshy parts.) Carefully spread out the charcoal so that it is now hitting every part of the lamb. Now taking turns, rotate the spit slowly and every 15 minutes baste the lamb. As the fire burns down you will need to throw on each pile a few charcoal briquettes to keep it going. A lamb roasted like this takes about 3 to 4 hours. A clear indication that it is nearly cooked is when the flesh shrinks away from the bones. If certain parts of the lamb are cooking faster than the other, just remove that section carefully using a sharp carving knife and let the other parts keep cooking.

Backyard Greek Party

SERVES 6 TO 8

I didn't want to leave you hanging out in the front yard all day so here are few dishes to set on your table along with the lamb. All the recipes are easy and can be doubled and prepared a few days in advance.

Grilled Flat Bread

MAKES 12 PIECES

INGREDIENTS

5 cups all-purpose flour
1 3/4 cups whole wheat flour
1 package active dry yeast
2 1/2 teaspoons sea salt
1/2 cup parsley, minced
4 tablespoons olive oil
2 1/3 cups warm water 105 to 115 F

In the mixing bowl of a heavy-duty stand mixer, add the flour, salt, yeast, parsley and oil. Attach the flat beater, put the machine on to low speed and with the machine running, slowly add the water until it forms a shaggy mass around the paddle. Now replace the flat beater with the dough hook and knead at medium speed until the dough is smooth and elastic and forms a round ball, around 4 to 5 minutes. If the dough seems sticky and won't form a ball, add a little bit more flour until it does. If the dough seems too dry, add 1 to 2 tablespoons more of water until the dough comes together. Remove the ball to a lightly floured work surface, hand knead for a minute and then place into a oiled plastic container, cover and let rise until doubled in size for about 1 1/2 to 2 hours. Turn the risen dough out onto a lightly floured work surface and knead it briefly. Cut the dough into 12 equal pieces. Using the knuckles of your hand or a small rolling pin, roll each piece of dough into a rough 5 or 6-inch circle. Lightly brush the round with a little olive oil and then place oil side down on a piece of parchment paper. (You will need twelve cut pieces of parchment paper to separate the bread.) Repeat the process with the remaining dough pieces, then stack the rounds on top of each other separated by the parchment. Cover with a piece of plastic wrap and refrigerate for an hour. Pre-heat a charcoal grill and adjust the cooking grid 4-inches above the coals. Clean the grill grate with a wire brush and when the coals go to gray, lightly brush the grate with a little olive oil. To grill the pitas, grasp a corner of the parchment paper and flip one round of dough onto the grill and peel off the paper. Grill the bread for 2 to 3 minutes on each side turning once with a spatula until the bread is lightly flecked and brown on both sides. Repeat with the remaining dough then place into a decorative basket to keep warm.

Marinated Olives with Feta Cheese and Roasted Red Peppers

SERVES A SMALL CROWD

INGREDIENTS

2 pounds assorted brined Greek olives, black and green
1 medium red onion, halved and thinly sliced
1 medium head fennel bulb, halved and thinly sliced

MARINADE

1/2 cup olive oil
1/4 cup lemon juice
2 tablespoons balsamic vinegar
4 medium garlic cloves, minced
1 teaspoon sea salt
1/2 teaspoon black pepper
1/4 teaspoon dried oregano
1/4 teaspoon dried thyme

1 pound Greek feta cheese, cubed

1 Recipe Roasted Red Peppers

In a large mixing bowl combine the olives, onion, fennel and peppers. In another small bowl combine the marinade ingredients and then pour over the olive mixture and toss. Refrigerate the olive mixture for 2 days to marinate. Remove the olives from the refrigerator, toss again and then combine with the cubed feta to serve.

Roasted Red Peppers

SERVES 6 TO 8

INGREDIENTS

3 large red peppers
2 large garlic cloves, sliced
1/4 cup light olive oil
1/2 teaspoon dried oregano
Dash of garlic powder
1/4 teaspoon sea salt
1/8 teaspoon black pepper

Cut the peppers in half, core and remove all the pits and seeds. Cut each half into 8 long strips. Heat a large high-sided non-stick skillet, add the oil and garlic, and let the garlic steep in the hot oil for exactly 1 minute. Now add the peppers and sauté over medium heat for 3 to 5 minutes being sure to toss the peppers so that they are all covered with the hot oil. Reduce the heat to low, season with the salt and pepper only, and continue tossing and sauteing for another 10 minutes. When the peppers just take on a touch of brown on their skin and are softened, add the oregano and garlic powder and toss the skillet a few more times to redistribute the seasoning. Immediately pour the hot peppers into a Pyrex bowl and cover with a piece of plastic wrap to steam and infuse the flavors. When the peppers are cooled, toss gently, store in a glass container and refrigerate until needed.

Taramosalata (Fish Roe Dip)

MAKES 2 CUPS

INGREDIENTS

6 thick slices Italian bread
1/4 cup tarama
2 tablespoons red onion, minced
3 medium garlic cloves, minced
2 tablespoons lemon juice
Dash of red wine vinegar, sugar and Tabasco
1/2 cup light olive oil

Using a sharp knife remove the crusts from the bread and let the pieces dry out over night. The next day in the container of a food processor, place the tarama, onion, garlic, lemon juice, vinegar, sugar, Tabasco and oil and process until it is smooth and emulsified. Fill a bowl with cold water, drop the bread slices into it and then when the bread is soaked, squeeze out as much water as possible and drop them into the food processor tube. Now process the dip until it is light and fluffy and then scrape into a serving bowl and chill.

Melitzanosalata (Roasted Eggplant Dip)

MAKES 2 CUPS

INGREDIENTS

2 medium sized eggplants
1 large tomato, peeled and diced
2 tablespoons olive oil
2 tablespoons red wine vinegar
2 tablespoons lemon juice
2 large garlic cloves, minced
2 tablespoons red onion, minced
1/4 teaspoon sea salt
1/8 teaspoon black pepper
1/4 teaspoon dried marjoram or oregano

Pierce the eggplants all over with the tip of a sharp knife and then grill on a hot grill for about 30 minutes until the eggplants are charred all over and very soft. Remove to a platter and when cool enough to handle, skin, remove the seeds and chop the eggplant into very fine pieces. Place the eggplant and tomato into a medium sized mixing bowl. In another mixing bowl combine the remaining ingredients and then pour over the eggplant and thoroughly combine until well mixed. Chill for a couple hours before serving.

Spanakopita (Spinach and Cheese Pie)

INGREDIENTS

1 pound phyllo dough
2 cups clarified melted butter

FILLING

4 bags fresh spinach, cleaned and dried
2 tablespoons olive oil
4 large garlic cloves, minced
1/2 cup green onion, minced
1 small leek head, chopped
1 3/4 pound feta cheese
2 cups small curd cottage cheese
4 tablespoons parmesan cheese
2 tablespoons fresh dill, chopped
3 large whole eggs
1/4 teaspoon sea salt
1/4 teaspoon black pepper
Dash of Tabasco, nutmeg and cumin

To prepare the filling remove the stems from the spinach and coarsely chop the leaves. In a large skillet heat the olive oil and then add the garlic, green onion and leek and stir cook for exactly 1 minute. Add the spinach and cook until the leaves start to wilt and release their liquid. Place the cooked spinach into a small colander set over a mixing bowl and let the mixture cool for 10 minutes. Squeeze the spinach to release all the water. While the spinach is cooling, place the remaining ingredients for the filling into a large mixing bowl and using a heavy wooden spoon, combine until well mixed and slightly smooth. Add the cool spinach and combine again until smooth. Pre-heat the oven to 375°. Remove the phyllo from the package and lay the stack of phyllo sheets onto a clean counter with the longest side facing you. Using a ruler and a sharp knife, cut the phyllo into three sections each about 5 1/2-inches wide. Cover all of the cut piles with a slightly damp kitchen towel to keep from drying out. Working with two cut pieces stacked on top of each other lay the pastry on the work surface short ends facing you. Brush both strips lightly with the clarified butter down the center. Working quickly with two strips at a time, place 1 tablespoon of the spinach-cheese filling in the center of the strips 1-inch from the bottom. Fold the sides in over the filling, butter the folds and roll into a tight cylinder shape. Butter the finished roll and place onto a non-stick baking sheet seam side down. Finish making the rest of the pies and bake in the oven for 15 minutes. Re-brush with the butter and bake for another 10 to 15 minutes until the phyllo is golden brown. Place on a wire rack to cool.

Tiropitas (Cheese Pies)

MAKES ABOUT 40 PIECES

INGREDIENTS

1 pound phyllo dough
2 cups clarified melted butter

FILLING

1 3/4 pounds feta cheese
1 pound small curd cottage cheese
1/3 cup parmesan cheese
3 large whole eggs
1/4 teaspoon black pepper
Dash of Tabasco, nutmeg and cumin
1/3 cup parsley, minced

To prepare the filling place all the ingredients into a large mixing bowl and using a heavy wooden spoon, combine until well mixed and slightly smooth. Pre-heat the oven to 375°. Prepare, stuff, roll and bake as in the above recipe for spinach pies.

Cucumber Salad with Dill

SERVES A SMALL CROWD

INGREDIENTS

2 large seedless cucumbers
1 1/2 teaspoons sea salt

1 cup sour cream, full fat
2 teaspoons lemon juice
1/4 teaspoon celery salt
1/4 teaspoon black pepper
1 1/2 teaspoons sugar
2 dashes Tabasco
2 dashes garlic powder
2 tablespoons dill, chopped

Cut the cucumbers into 1/8 - inch pieces and place into a large mixing bowl. Sprinkle on all of the sea salt and then gently mix so all the salt is evenly distributed. Now pour the cucumbers into a colander set over a bowl to drain excess liquid and cover the colander with plastic wrap. Set aside for 1/2 hour. Combine the rest of the ingredients in a small mixing bowl, cover with plastic wrap and refrigerate for 1/2 hour. After a half an hour, gently squeeze out any excess water from the draining cucumbers and then place into a medium sized mixing bowl. Using a plastic spatula fold in the dressing, cover with plastic wrap and refrigerate for a few hours before serving.

Beet, Green Bean and Tomato Salad

SERVES A SMALL CROWD

4 medium sized beets, unpeeled
1/2 pound green beans, trimmed
4 large Roma tomatoes, quartered
1/4 cup raspberry vinegar
1/4 cup light olive oil
Large pinch of sugar
1/4 teaspoon sea salt
1/8 teaspoon black pepper

In a small mixing bowl combine the vinegar, olive oil, sugar, salt and pepper. Place the beets into a medium sized saucepot, cover by 2 inches with cold water, add 1/4 teaspoon of salt, bring to a boil and simmer for 20 to 30 minutes until a knife pierces the beets easily. When the beets are cooked, remove from the water, cool slightly and gently rub off their skins with a paper towel and then set aside. Bring 1 quart of lightly salted water to a boil and cook the green beans until they are crisp to the taste. Immediately remove with a kitchen skimmer to a bowl containing ice cubes and water to stop the cooking process. When the green beans are cool, drain thoroughly in a strainer and then dry with a paper towel. Using a sharp kitchen knife, slice the beets 1/4 -inch thick and then place into a large mixing bowl and add the green beans. Re-stir the dressing, add about half to the salad and toss to mix. Now add the tomatoes to the bowl and again toss to mix. Re-season if needed and then refrigerate for at least 1 hour.

Red Potato, Pickle and Egg Salad Vinaigrette

INGREDIENTS

2 pounds small red new potatoes,
    cleaned and halved

1/3 cup olive oil
1/4 cup apple cider vinegar
3/4 teaspoon sea salt
1/2 teaspoon black pepper
2 large garlic cloves, minced
2 medium stalks celery, finely chopped
4 green onions, white and some of the
    green part finely chopped
8 radishes, sliced
1 large dill pickle, finely chopped
4 tablespoons fresh dill, chopped
2 tablespoons parsley, chopped
2 hard boiled eggs, coarsely chopped

Steam the new potatoes in a vegetable steamer placed over an inch of hot water for 12 to 15 minutes until tender. Remove to a large mixing bowl and cool slightly. While the potatoes are steaming, combine the olive oil, cider vinegar, salt, pepper, and garlic cloves and mix well. In another large mixing bowl combine the remaining ingredients until well blended and then add the dressing and stir slightly with a wooded spoon until well mixed. Arrange the slightly cooled potatoes in one layer cut side up onto a serving platter and then gently spoon all the mixed dressing onto the potatoes. This dish is best served at room temperature.

Rice and Orzo Pilaf

INGREDIENTS

2 tablespoons olive oil
3 medium garlic cloves, minced
1 medium onion, minced
1 small red pepper, diced
1 cup tomatoes, diced
1 cup white rice
1/2 cup orzo
1/2 teaspoon sea salt
1/4 teaspoon black pepper
2 3/4 cups chicken stock
1/2 fresh lemon
2 tablespoons parsley, chopped

Pre-heat the oven to 375° In a medium sized earthenware casserole heat the olive oil and saute the garlic, onion and red pepper for 2 minutes. Add the rice and orzo and saute for another 2 minutes. Add the salt, pepper, diced tomatoes and stock, bring to the boil, stir, cover and cook in the oven for 20 to 25 minutes. When the pilaf is cooked remove from the oven, squeeze on the lemon juice, sprinkle on the parsley, stir to combine, re-cover and let it rest 10 minute before serving.

Baklava

INGREDIENTS

1 pound phyllo dough
1 cup clarified melted butter
3 cups walnut pieces, lightly toasted and
   finely chopped
2 cups sliced almonds, lightly toasted
   and finely chopped
1/3 cup fresh breadcrumbs
1/4 cup sugar
2 teaspoons ground cinnamon
2 teaspoons grated lemon peel

SYRUP

2 cups sugar
1 1/2 cups water
1 small cinnamon stick
3 whole cloves
3/4 cup honey
2 tablespoons lemon juice

Pre-heat the oven to 350°. In a mixing bowl combine the walnuts, almonds, breadcrumbs, sugar, cinnamon and lemon peel until well mixed. Butter a 9 by 13-inch glass baking dish and line with three sheets of phyllo brushing each lightly with some melted butter and letting the dough overlap the sides of the pan. Sprinkle about 1/2 cup of the nut mixture over the phyllo. Now repeat with the remaining sheets of phyllo dough alternating two sheets of buttered phyllo and the nut mixture. The very top should just be two buttered sheets of phyllo. Using a razorblade, carefully cut through the top layer of phyllo making lengthwise strips 1 1/2-inches wide and then cut diagonally making diamond shapes. Trim off any excess phyllo dough that is overlapping the sides of the pan. Bake in the hot oven for about 1 hour or until golden brown. Remove the pan from the oven and set on a wire rack to cool completely. While the baklava is cooling, make the syrup by combining all the ingredients in a saucepan, bring to a boil, stir and cook for 10 minutes. Remove from the fire and cool to lukewarm and then carefully pour the syrup over the cooled baklava. Cover lightly with aluminum foil and set aside at room temperature for several hours or overnight. Carefully cut the diamonds and serve.

EAT-A-PITA/GOBS OF KABOBS

PITA

RECIPES

I don't want to get into to some long culinary sermon, but the Middle Eastern community in Chicago is huge and so are the foodstuffs that this brotherhood has to offer. Typically speaking, the Middle East encompasses Syria, Jordan, Lebanon, Israel, Egypt, Turkey, Iraq, Iran and the gulf states around the Arabian border. The earliest settlers in the Chicago land area were the Assyrians and Syrians who were most typically known as small merchants specializing in embroidered lace, Persian rugs, ornate wood novelties and sweet foodstuffs that were lavishly presented at the 1893 World's Fair. Early city census reports indicated that small pockets of middle easterners were immigrating to Chicago and Detroit around the turn of the century. Political upheaval in the Middle East produced a massive influx of refugees who immigrated to Chicago in the late 1970s and settled into neighborhoods scattered around the city.

I've always had a peaked interest in Middle Eastern cuisine since I spent so many years working for some of the best Greek chefs the city had to offer. One of my earliest cooking jobs was at the infamous Lake Point Tower Club located on the eightieth floor of a surrealistically glass lined building that overlooks Navy Pier and beautiful Lake Michigan. The head chef, Nick Tselentis, a true Greek from Corfu, was a master of continental cuisine but also had encyclopedic knowledge and was fervently devoted to the culinary landscape of his home and the Middle Eastern countries that surrounded it. Nick's enthusiastic after work seek-and-destroy missions were always the highlight of my week as we would hop on the "EL" train and visit Greek and Middle Eastern markets that were buried treasures on the Chicago ethnic scene in the early 1980s. Quite a treat for a Polish kid from the Northwest side of Chicago! Nick's mission in life was to seek out freshly made pita bread and feta cheese, silky paper-thin phyllo dough, golden couscous, rose water, baby lamb, Greek olives, dates and fresh pomegranates. Mind you, on these jaunts I was actually an observer and package carrier rather than an active participant, as I didn't speak the language. However, the sensory overload of smells, sensations and wild hand gesturing along with the bitter- tasting Turkish coffee has left an indelible mark.

Continental cuisine at the time was a mainstay for most restaurants around the city, But Nick's infectious enthusiasm for turning out fanciful mezze literally turned around the way private clubs displayed their culinary expertise. The chef and I, who luckily worked the lunch crowd, would knock out such delectable and artistically presented dishes as baba ghanoush, garlic infused hummus, stuffed grape leaves, tabouleh, fattoosh, lemony lentil soup, shish kebab, rice pilaf, tsaztziki and pistachio baklava. Mind you, these were limited daily specials that would sell out very quickly, thus changing my culinary perception of stuffy French haute cuisine. Middle Eastern and Greek cooking revolves around such foodstuffs as currants, dates, figs, fancy nuts, a shit load of assorted olives, sesame, small grains and peas, grape leaves, flavored honeys and preserves, dried lemons and limes, orange blossom water, and flavored syrups. For a young cook early in the game, this was a heavy sensory overload that taught me the fine art of delectably and cautiously seasoning food with sweet spices. To give you an example of what I'm talking about, pick up a small jar of a spice called Baharat, which is a Middle Eastern blend of nutmeg, peppercorns, coriander, cumin, cloves and paprika, carefully unscrew the cap, and take a deep "Tony Manero" whiff of the spice to experience the aroma sensation for yourself.

Since I've already given you recipes devoted to the Greeks, I wanted to turn you on to some great easy recipes that revolve around Middle Eastern culture. My experience with this food is to present it as simply and easily as possible, using the freshest ingredients that you can find. Dips, fresh salads and kabobs are undoubtedly the most well recognized and beloved of this food type around the city. If you're lucky, you may find a street vendor to offer it up fresh in a nicely warmed pita and if not, the following recipes will help you make your own.

Chicago has a slew of Middle Eastern restaurants such as Pita Ria, Rezas, Pars Cove, Schwarma King and Noon O Kabob who turn out beautiful spicy and flavorful mezze, salads, sandwiches and kabobs to the delight of adventurous patrons. Visiting with the owner is a big part of the show so enjoy their hospitality, sit back and let them tantalize your taste buds with their delectable delights.

Middle Eastern Lemonade

SERVES 4

A tart and lemony concoction!

INGREDIENTS

3/4 cup fresh lemon juice
3/4 cup sugar
1 tablespoon orange flower water
4 tablespoons fresh mint
8 cups soda water

Ice cubes

Pour the lemon juice, sugar, orange flower water and mint into the bottom of a large glass pitcher. Using a plastic spoon, stir the mixture until the sugar dissolves and creates a slurry. Fill the pitcher 1/4 of the way with ice cubes, add the soda water, stir with a spoon until well chilled and serve.

Homemade Pita

INGREDIENTS

7 cups all-purpose flour
4 1/2 teaspoons active dry yeast
2 1/2 teaspoons sea salt
1 teaspoon sugar
1/3 cup olive oil
2 1/2 cups warm water 105 to 115F

In the mixing bowl of a heavy-duty stand mixer add the flour, salt, sugar, yeast and oil. Attach the flat beater, put the machine on to low speed and with the machine running, slowly add the water until it forms a shaggy mass round the paddle. Now replace the flat beater with the dough hook and knead at medium speed until the dough is smooth and elastic and forms a round ball, around 4 to 5 minutes. If the dough seems too sticky and won't form a ball, add a little bit more flour until it does. If the dough seem too dry, add 1 to 2 tablespoons more of water until the dough comes together. Remove the ball to a lightly floured work surface, hand knead for 1 minute and then place into an oiled plastic container and cover until risen and doubled in size about 1 1/2 to 2 hours. Turn the dough out onto a lightly floured work surface and knead it briefly. Cut the dough into 12 equal pieces. Using the knuckles of your hands or a small rolling pin, roll each piece of dough into a rough 6 to 8-inch circle and place the circles onto baking sheets leaving about 1-inch between them. Cover with a kitchen towel and let rest for 30 minutes. Pre-heat the oven to 500°. Bake the pitas on the middle rack of the oven for 8 to 10 minutes until bubbly and lightly browned. **When removing the pitas from the oven, stack on top of each other hot to create the flat textured pieces.** Cover with a towel to keep warm.

Cucumber Tzatziki Dip

MAKES ABOUT 3 CUPS

1 large English hothouse cucumber,
  peeled and finely diced
1 teaspoon sea salt
2 cups plain yogurt
4 medium garlic cloves, minced
2 tablespoons fresh mint or dill, minced
1 tablespoon red wine vinegar
1/4 teaspoon sea salt
1/4 teaspoon black pepper
Dash of garlic powder, onion powder
  and Tabasco
1 tablespoon olive oil

Place the diced cucumber and a teaspoon of sea salt in a bowl and mix. Now pour all the cucumbers into a fine mesh colander set over another bowl to let the excess water drain off. An hour later combine the remaining tzatziki ingredients including the cucumbers in a mixing bowl and refrigerate until needed.

Hummus Dip

SERVES 4

An addictively cool, lemony garlic infused spread of mashed chick peas, tahini and spices.

Two 14 ounce cans chick peas, well drained
1/4 cup tahini (sesame seed paste)
4 large garlic cloves, minced
2 tablespoons cold water
2 tablespoons olive oil
1/4 cup fresh lemon juice
1/2 teaspoon sea salt
1/4 teaspoon black pepper
1/4 teaspoon cumin
Dash of garlic powder, onion powder, Tabasco
  and sweet paprika

In the bowl of a food processor, place the chick peas, tahini, garlic cloves, water, lemon juice and olive oil. Secure the lid and pulse the mixture until semi smooth. Add the rest of the ingredients to the bowl and pulse again until the mixture is completely smooth. Pour into a glass bowl, cover and chill for 4 to 6 hours before using.

Baba Ghannouj

SERVES 4

A spicy dip that is similar to hummus, but uses roasted eggplant instead of chick peas.

INGREDIENTS

2 medium eggplants
1/3 cup tahini (sesame seed paste)
4 large garlic cloves, minced
1/3 cup parsley, chopped
1/2 teaspoon sea salt
1/4 teaspoon black pepper
1/4 teaspoon cumin
Dash of garlic powder, onion powder and Tabasco
1/3 cup fresh lemon juice
2 tablespoons olive oil

Preheat the oven to 450°. Slash the eggplants with a sharp knife and bake on a non stick cookie sheet for about 40 minutes until the insides are soft. Cool the eggplants, carefully remove the skin and discard. Place the eggplant pulp into the bowl of a food processor with the garlic, tahini, salt, pepper, cumin and spices and then cover and pulse until semi smooth. Add the lemon juice and olive oil and pulse again for another 30 seconds. Pour into a glass bowl, cover and chill for 4 to 6 hours before using.

Chilled Cucumber Mint Salad

SERVES 4

INGREDIENTS

2 large seedless cucumbers, peeled
1 1/2 teaspoons sea salt

1 cup sour cream, full fat
2 teaspoons lemon juice
1/4 teaspoon celery salt
1/4 teaspoon black pepper
1 1/2 teaspoons sugar
2 dashes Tabasco
2 dashes garlic powder
2 tablespoons mint, chopped

Cut the cucumbers into 1/8 - inch pieces and place into a large mixing bowl. Sprinkle on all of the sea salt then combine. Now pour the cucumbers into a colander set over a bowl to drain excess liquid, cover with plastic wrap then set aside for 1/2 hour. Combine the rest of the ingredients in a small mixing bowl, cover with plastic wrap and refrigerate for 1/2 hour. After 1/2 hour, gently squeeze out any excess water from the draining cucumbers then place into a medium sized mixing bowl. Using a plastic spatula, fold in the dressing, cover with plastic wrap and refrigerate for a few hours before serving.

Jerusalem Salad

A cool and refreshing salad of tomatoes and cucumbers drizzled with a lemony tahini dressing.

INGREDIENTS

4 to 5 vine ripened Roma tomatoes
2 medium seedless cucumbers
1 small red onion, peeled

TAHINI DRESSING

1 cup plain yogurt
1/4 cup tahiini (sesame seed paste)
2 tablespoons lemon juice
2 large garlic cloves, minced
2 tablespoons parsley, minced
1/4 teaspoon sea salt
1/8 teaspoon black pepper
2 tablespoons olive oil
Dash of Tabasco, garlic powder and onion powder

Using a sharp chef's knife, quarter the tomatoes, slice the cucumbers and red onion and combine in a large mixing bowl. In another mixing bowl, combine the remaining ingredients and whisk until smooth. Gently place the tomato-cucumber mixture onto a large serving platter and drizzle over the tahini dressing. Garnish with a sprinkling of fresh cracked black pepper.

Tabouleh Salad

Undoubtedly the best known and loved Arab dish in the States is tabouleh. A delectable salad made from cracked wheat, diced tomato, cucumber, parsley, green onions, olive oil, lemon juice and mint.

INGREDIENTS

1/2 cup fine grain quick cook bulgur wheat
1/4 cup lemon juice
1/3 cup olive oil
1 cup parsley, minced
2 scallions, minced
2 tablespoons fresh mint, minced
4 plum tomatoes, chopped
1 medium seedless cucumber, peeled and chopped
1/2 teaspoon sea salt
1/4 teaspoon black pepper
Dash of garlic powder, onion powder and cayenne
    pepper

Place the bulgur wheat into a fine mesh strainer and rinse under exceedingly hot water for 5 minutes and then drain and cool. In another medium sized mixing bowl, combine the remaining ingredients until well blended and then mix in the bulgur wheat, pour into a glass serving bowl, cover and refrigerate for 4 to 6 hours.

Kibbeh

Not so much a salad, but a savory appetizer! Kibbeh is a deep fried and flavorful croquette of cracked wheat, minced meat, pine nuts, onions and sweet spices.

INGREDIENTS

1 cup fine grain quick cook bulgur wheat
1 pound lean ground beef or lamb
2 tablespoons olive oil
1 small onion, minced
2 large garlic cloves, minced
1/4 cup pine nuts, slightly ground
1/2 teaspoon sea salt
1/4 teaspoon black pepper
Dash of cayenne and tabasco
1 whole large egg
1/4 cup tomato sauce
Pinch of all-spice, cinnamon, cloves, ginger and nutmeg

Corn or Peanut Oil for frying

Place the bulgur wheat into a fine mesh strainer and rinse under exceedingly hot water for 5 minutes and then drain and cool. In a large non-stick skillet, heat the olive oil and saute the onion, garlic and pine nuts for 2 to 3 minutes and then cool. Place all of the ingredients into a large mixing bowl and using yours hands, mash together as if you were making meatballs. Divide the mixture into 16 equal pieces and roll into a nice ball. Freeze the croquettes for 20 minutes on a baking sheet. Pour 2 inches of corn oil into a saucepan and heat to 375°. Deep fry the kibbeh a few at a time until golden brown for about 2 to 3 minutes on each side. Serve with cucumber mint salad.

Middle East Sandwiches

Most Middle East fast food joints around the city serve up a healthy portion of street food that usually centers around 6 varieties of local favorites that you can eat on the go. Mediterranean style chicken tenders and spiced burgers can be had at any of these places along with a dose of shish kabobs in assorted flavors; lamb, beef or chicken. I dig em all! The famed sandwich (schawarma) that is similar to the Greek gyros usually comes in a spicy lamb or chicken variety and will definitely get your juices flowing. Probably two of the most easily recognized and sought after Middle Eastern sandwiches are the falafil and kefta kabob. Both are typically served on a heated pita with cucumbers, tomatoes, lettuce and onions topped with a dollop of cool lemony tahini sauce. Falafil is actually a mixture of ground chick peas, vegetables and spices that are shaped into tasty patties and then deep fried until crisp. Kefta kabob is made of a fragrant meatloaf type mixture that is usually skewered and then grilled or broiled. Both are utterly delicious and worth a try.

Fabulous Falafil

SERVES 4

INGREDIENTS

2 cups cooked chick peas
2 tablespoons olive oil
2 medium garlic cloves, minced
1/3 cup celery, finely minced
1/3 cup scallions, finely minced
1/2 teaspoon sea salt
1/4 teaspoon black pepper
Dash of cayenne
1/4 teaspoon cumin
1/4 teaspoon turmeric
1 large whole egg
1/4 teaspoon baking powder
2 tablespoons tahini paste
1/4 cup fresh breadcrumbs
Dash of Tabasco, garlic powder and onion powder

Corn or peanut oil for frying

Heat the olive oil in a small skillet and sauté the garlic, celery and scallions for 2 to 3 minutes until soft and then cool. Place the chick peas into a large mixing bowl and using a potato masher, mash the peas thoroughly. Add the rest of the ingredients and mix with a kitchen spoon until well combined. Cover the bowl and refrigerate for 2 to 3 hours. Pour 2 inches of corn oil into a saucepan and heat until 375°. Using lightly floured hands, divide the mixture into 16 equal pieces, roll into a ball and deep fry for 2 to 3 minutes on each side until lightly golden brown. Serve on a warm pita with a topping of Jerusalem salad and its dressing.

Kefta Kabob

INGREDIENTS

1 pound 85% lean ground beef or lamb
2 tablespoons olive oil
3 medium garlic cloves, minced
1 small onion, minced
1/2 teaspoon sea salt
1/4 teaspoon black pepper
1/2 teaspoon dried oregano
1/8 teaspoon all-spice
2 tablespoons fresh mint, chopped
2 tablespoons parsley, chopped
1 large whole egg
1/4 cup whole milk
1/4 cup parmesan cheese
1/4 cup fresh breadcrumbs
Dash of Tabasco, garlic powder and onion
   powder

In a small skillet, heat the olive oil and sauté the garlic and onion for 2 to 3 minutes until soft. Remove from the fire and chill. In a large mixing bowl, combine the remaining ingredients plus the chilled garlic and onions and knead with your hands until it all comes together. Using lightly oiled hands, divide the meat mixture into 12 to 16 equal pieces and roll into a meatball shape. Place onto a baking sheet and chill in the freezer for 20 minutes. While the meat is resting, turn on your broiler to medium. Remove the pan from the freezer, lightly flatten down each ball into a patty and broil for about 6 to 7 minutes on each side until nicely golden brown. Serve on a warm pita with a topping of Jerusalem salad and its dressing.

Basic Kabob Recipe

This is an all-purpose marinade that takes well to chicken, pork or beef. A good 24 hour marinade will leave the meat tender and sweet. I also like to marinate the vegetables along with the meat so that the whole kabob has a wonderful taste.

INGREDIENTS

2 pounds cubed chicken breast, pork, or beef
1 large onion, med. cubed
1 large green pepper, med. cubed
1 large red pepper, med. cubed
16 small mushroom caps

MARINADE

1 1/2 cups canola oil
1/3 cup red wine vinegar
2 tablespoons lemon juice
1 tablespoon garlic, minced
1 1/2 teaspoons sea salt
1/2 teaspoon black pepper
1/8 teaspoon dried marjoram, thyme and oregano

Place all the marinade ingredients into a medium sized mixing bowl and whisk until smooth. Place the meat and vegetables into another mixing bowl and cover with the marinade. Cover with plastic wrap and refrigerate for 1 to 2 days being sure to toss to redistribute the marinade. The next day alternate the meat and vegetables decoratively onto metal skewers and grill for 4 to 5 minutes on each side until the meat is cooked. Serve with a cool mint tzatziki.

Chapli Kabob

This is a really old Indian dish that I learned from a good chef friend of mine. The heavily seasoned, spicy meatloaf-like mixture is formed into longish cigar shapes and then carefully skewered and grilled.

INGREDIENTS

2 tablespoons olive oil
3 medium garlic cloves, minced
I small onion, minced
2 pounds ground lamb
I large whole egg
1/2 cup breadcrumbs
1/4 cup toasted pine nuts, ground
I tablespoon tahini (sesame seed paste)
1/4 cup parsley, minced
I teaspoon sea salt
1/2 teaspoon black pepper
1/4 teaspoon ground coriander
1/8 teaspoon ground cumin
1/8 teaspoon ground fennel

Heat the olive oil in a small skillet and then saute the garlic and onion for 2 to 3 minutes without burning. Remove from the fire and chill. In a large mixing bowl combine the remaining ingredients including the chilled garlic and onions, and knead with your hands until it all comes together. Using lightly oiled hands, scoop out about 1/2 cup of meat, roll it into a meatball shape and then place onto a baking sheet. Finish with the rest of the meat, cover with plastic wrap and place in the freezer for 20 minutes. Light a grill while the meat is resting. Remove the pan from the freezer and again using lightly oiled hands, re-roll the balls into a long cigar or alligator shape. Carefully run a skewer lengthwise through the meat and grill for 4 to 5 minutes on each side until the meat is cooked. **I know this is a lot of meat but that's the way the recipe works. If you are nervous about grilling it, pre-heat the oven to 350°, make 1/4 cup size meatballs then cook in the hot oven for 25 minutes.)** Serve this kabob with a side salad of chilled couscous, cucumber, tomato and dill.

Oriental Kabob

This is my favorite kabob that is reminiscent of the Pacific rim. It is always a hit at the hibachi bars. Beef and chicken are the ideal choice but try substituting shrimp or scallops.

INGREDIENTS

2 pounds chicken breast, cubed
2 cups fresh pineapple, cubed
1 large onion, med. cubed
1 large red pepper, med. cubed

MARINADE

1 cup soy sauce
1/2 cup orange juice
1 tablespoon sesame oil
1/4 cup honey
2 tablespoons ginger, minced
1 tablespoon garlic, minced
2 scallions, minced
1/2 teaspoon black pepper
Dash of red pepper flakes

Place all the marinade ingredients into a large bowl and whisk until smooth. Add to the bowl the cubed chicken, red pepper and onion chunks, stir to combine, cover with plastic wrap and refrigerate for 3 to 4 hours to marinate. Light a grill, decoratively skewer the meats, vegetables and pineapple on 4 long skewers and then grill the kabobs for 4 to 5 minutes on each side. Serve this kabob with a side of fluffy oriental fried rice.

Tandori Kabob

This classic Indian dish of chicken marinated in a spicy and fragrant dressing is typically cooked in a large clay pit, but grilling also renders the meat succulent and sweet.

INGREDIENTS

2 pounds chicken breast, cubed

MARINADE

2 cups plain yogurt
1/4 cup lemon juice
1/4 cup canola oil
2 tablespoons ginger, minced
2 tablespoons garlic, minced
1 tablespoon ground cumin
2 teaspoons paprika
2 teaspoons ground coriander
1 teaspoon cinnamon
1 teaspoon sea salt
1/2 teaspoon cayenne pepper
Dash of cloves
2 drops red food coloring, optional

Place all the marinade ingredients into a mixing bowl and whisk to combine, add the chicken cubes, cover with plastic wrap and refrigerate overnight. The next day light the grill, skewer the chicken and grill for 4 to 5 minutes on each side. Serve this kabob with a fresh side salad of mango relish.

Ole Margarita Kabob

SERVES 4

A spicy Tex-Mex kabob infused with tequila, lime juice, peppers and cilantro. This dish will most definitely leave you with visions of Baja beaches and chilled Coronas.

INGREDIENTS

2 pounds chicken breast, cubed or
   shrimp

MARINADE

1/2 cup canola oil
1/2 cup gold tequila
1/2 cup lime juice
2 tablespoons sugar
1 teaspoon sea salt
1/2 teaspoon black pepper
1 large jalapeno, minced
4 large garlic cloves, minced
1/4 cup green onion, minced
1/2 cup cilantro, chopped

Combine all the marinade ingredients in a mixing bowl and whisk until smooth. Add the cubed chicken or shrimp, re-mix, cover with plastic wrap and refrigerate overnight. The next day light the grill preferably with mesquite, skewer the chicken or shrimp and grill for 4 to 5 minutes on each side. Serve this kabob with fresh salsa and hot sauce.

Jamaican Jerk Kabob

SERVES 4

Jamaican Jerk chicken is extremely addictive if cooked over a slow fire with the addition of spiced wood to lightly smoke the meat.

INGREDIENTS

2 pounds chicken breast, cubed
2 cups fresh pineapple, cubed

MARINADE

3/4 cup light soy sauce
1/2 cup red wine vinegar
1/4 cup canola oil
2 green onions, minced
1 habanero pepper, minced
1/4 cup brown sugar
2 teaspoons fresh thyme
1/4 teaspoon cloves
1/4 teaspoon nutmeg
1/4 teaspoon all-spice

Combine all the marinade ingredients in a mixing bowl and whisk until smooth. Add the cubed chicken, re-mix, cover with plastic wrap and refrigerate for 4 to 6 hours. Light the grill, skewer the chicken and pineapple and grill for 4 to 5 minutes on each side. Serve this kabob with bottled jerk sauce and cilantro infused white rice.

MAXWELL STREET MEXICAN AND BEYOND

MEXICAN

RECIPES

As most are well aware, I relocated my family to southern California a few years back to pursue the life of a food writer, avid farmer and recipe consultant. I've also become a devotee of the Hispanic culture that permeates this region. Exceedingly fresh San Diego style fish tacos, carnitas, tamales and beans are pretty typical fare here, and Baja, which is right over the border, boasts some of the best sport fishing that the West coast has to offer.

So, many years back I was approached by a chefs' collaborative to donate time and money to NAFTA, an organization that works with Mexico to supply fresh produce such as tomatoes, cucumbers, corn, carrots, peppers, etc. to neighboring U.S. states across the border. This is about a 2,000 mile stretch from the ocean to south Texas if you look at the area on the map. I'm an adventurous guy, so hell, why not hop into the Jeep, cruise the border and see what these small towns have to offer to us neighboring gringos? I could probably write an amusing book about my Western adventures which would include highlights of getting kicked by a mule, some wild Tequila-induced dancing parties, naked steer-wrestling and endless days panning for fools' gold in the Colorado River, but this book's about food, street food to be exact, and let me tell you that Mexican and Tex-Mex cooking are sweeping this country by storm. It is my opinion, and that of many food critics, that Chicago undoubtedly produces some of the quintessential Hispanic and Latino cooking north of the border. To take it a step further, if you are adventurous and really want to see some of the best street food in action, just turn your attention to the Maxwell Street market in the city.

To give you a little history, Hispanic culture has been steadily making its way onto Chicago's big shoulders since the early 1900s. In the beginning Latino immigrants were sparsely recruited to work on the railroads, and by 1910 The Mexican Revolution laid the groundwork for passing sweeping reform of immigration laws in the United States, thus limiting European entry. History books denote that escalating poverty, joblessness and the sinking peso sent the Mexican economy down the tubes, thus creating a mass exodus in the 1950s and the 60s towards the large cities such as New York, Chicago and Los Angeles. Slowly but steadily Hispanic culture trickled into the Chicago land market, settling in the Pilsen area that was first inhabited by the Irish and the Germans. Pilsen is often referred to as Chicago's port of entry for displaced immigrants seeking a better life. Much like Chicago's European immigrants, the Hispanic population improved their lives through hard work, determination and frugalness, moving on to more affluent suburbs. I've always had an affinity for Hispanic culture because it mimics my Polish heritage for hard working family-oriented people who just want to have a better life.

My earliest experiences with this culture were through my father who was a Polish and Hispanic immigration lawyer. Our jaunts through the city to visit neighboring ward captains and my dad's clients always led to some interesting hole-in-the-wall restaurants, street vendors or mercados where my love for Mexican food was fueled. One of the interesting facets of my father's character was that he was typically a 9 to 5 suit and tie kind of guy but he also possessed a gentler side that was drawn toward communities or people of poverty and need. My dad and some of his closest friends earned a reputation around the city for practicing a type of law that is known as tavern familia, basically meaning if you own a small business and you need immigration help, we'll bring the office to you. I always thought it was odd that these guys would settle a case for a shot and a beer, a pair of shoes, a couple of live chickens or just a plate of homemade food. Many adolescent questions were raised about these people and where they came from and my father's answer was," just as Warsaw is the heart of Poland, Chicago's Hispanic culture is a melting pot for the people of the interior regions of Mexico."

I take a very reverent view when it comes to authentic Mexican cooking. I was never impressed with the Americanized Latin versions that are doled out at chainlike places around the city. Standardized dishes such as the super- neon, sweet Margarita, cheese loaded nachos, and combination plates are so far separated from actual regional Mexican cooking that they blend into a category that foodies call Tex-Mex (a combination of American Indian and Spanish cuisine). Chicago's first taste of south-of-the-border food came in the form of the San Antonio Chili Company stand that was set up at the Chicago World's Fair of

1893. A few years later historians note that homemade tamales were being vended from street carts around the city to an increasing adventurous audience. Regional Mexican cuisine, like many other cuisines, is based on maybe a dozen or so great local dishes that simmer and cook away for hours in clay pots, adobe grills, or old wood stoves, preferably outdoors. Mexico's climactic conditions are favorable for growing exotic herbs, fruits, vegetables and grains and for raising wild game, cattle and pork.

Chicago's Hispanic community is huge with over a half million people scattered throughout the city and suburbs (some say the largest population outside of Mexico City), and then factor in that most immigrated from the interior of Mexico from such spots as Oaxaca, Puebla, Michoacan, Veracruz, Jalisco, Guanajuato, Yucatan and Guerrero. From a chef's perspective, this is an enormous, warm patchwork quilt of tastes, sensations, spices and emotions that brings this culture together as a fine work of art. As to who would produce the best authentic Mexican cuisine out of the bunch is anyone's guess because it's all good. There are literally hundreds of small Hispanic markets and restaurants that line the streets of Chicago that come and go as the passing wind. The key to success and what separates them from the rest, is a family's style of spicing the mole or tweaking the recipes that are representative of their home town. Some of the best Mexican street food can be had at Maxwell Street market, an open air forum that accentuates Chicago's diverse ethnic heritage.

The most beloved regional type of Mexican cooking from the city centers around a street food called antojitos or little whims. Antojitos, made from fresh corn masa, then garnished with a savory topping, are what I like to refer to as Mexican appetizers or canapes that can be eaten at a street party while standing up and enjoying a few cold cervesas. Maxwell Street market has been a Chicago mainstay since 1912 when newly transplanted immigrants hocked everything from socks and magazines to old tools, antiques and foodstuffs to adoring crowds who jammed the street every Sunday morning. One of the highlights of this open-air flea market is that there are about two dozen Hispanic street vendors who entice your culinary senses with beautiful full-flavored, hand-made antojitos that can only be found in Chicago. Most vendors are housed in small makeshift 15 x 15 multicolored booths equipped with miniature grills or flattop griddles on which the food can quickly be re-heated or prepared.

These vendors offer up such "mamasita" delicacies as seafood cocktails made of shrimp, octopus, avocado, onion and cilantro bathed in a ketchupy hot sauce with a garnish of lime. There is also smoked grilled fresh corn-on-the-cob that is brushed with chili lime butter and fresh queso, and a dazzling array of freshly prepared tacos that consist of grilled carne asada, chorizo, egg and potato, de los chicharones (pork skin), de los ojos (boiled cow's head with eyeballs), lengua (tongue), barbacoa (BBQ beef), cesos (brains) or cachete (cow's cheek). Most of the vendors add a special taste sensation to the tacos by heating the homemade corn tortillas in chorizo grease and providing the patron with a plethora of fresh red and green salsas. For the more adventurous, they also offer antojitos in the form of pupusa, which are hand rolled little boats of masa that are stuffed with cheese, pork and beans, grilled, then garnished with a pickled cabbage and carrot salad along with a smoked chili sauce.

Another favorite is called the Mexican flag huaraches, which is a flat, oval, hand-shaped masa tortilla that is quickly fried, slathered with black beans, garnished with Chihuahua cheese, green and red salsa, then topped with a healthy portion of grilled carne asada, onion and cilantro. Other hand-formed and grilled antojitos include, horachitos (masa mixed with black beans and grilled), empanadas filled with sweet potatoes, chalupas, which are canoe-like boats filled with shredded chicken topped with a green salsa and garnished with onion, cilantro and queso fresco, or sopas meaning little round rafts that are filled with refried beans, chorizo, potatoes, red and green salsa, lettuce, tomatoes, onions and cheese. All utterly delicious!!! As you can see, the selection is endless depending on what time of the year you happen to be there. If you are visiting and your heartburn starts to kick in, don't fear because the market does offer aquas frescas, horchata, licuados or jugos, all being some kind of fresh fruit hand-squeezed liquid libation, and there's a Walgreen's Drug Store right up the road where you can get a quick Alka Seltzer fix. I want to inform you that there are very few markets outside of Mexico where you can enjoy such a variety of earthy fare and it's really cool to just stroll around and take in everything else this experience has to offer.

By no means is Maxwell Street market the only game in town, but it comes pretty close to offering a huge variety of street foods of Chicago's Hispanic culture. If by chance you can't make it down there, I've put together a good collection of authentic recipes for you to prepare at home.

BIRRIA DE CHIVO

Man, if I had a dollar for every time I've been asked about this local favorite, I'd for sure own a small pickle farm up North by now! It has been my experience working in kitchens for the last 25 years that many of the most prolific cooks come from the interior of Mexico and tend to be the driving work force behind many of the 4 star restaurants in the city. These cooks work hard, play harder and really enjoy simple dishes that they learned from their grandmas and moms, fare that rivals any braises that come out of France.

In a nutshell, braise is a cooking term that means to brown meat in hot oil, cover tightly and cook slowly in the oven with a small amount of liquid until the meat can be pulled apart with a fork in about 3 to 4 hours. Birria de chivo (goat stew) or birria de borrego (mutton stew) are typically prepared using a two-step process. The first step is to braise the highly aromatic, seasoned meat until it is rendered tender and juicy. The second part is to reconstitute and re-season the braising juices to make a soul-satisfying soup or stew. A whole cow's head, lamb shanks or veal brisket are sometimes substituted.

Hispanic cooks actually fancy Birria around the Christmas holidays where it's traditionally cooked in a charcoal-sealed earthen dug pit in the backyard that is covered with banana leaves for 12 to 15 hours. (Think of it as a Hawaiian pig roast at a luau.) After 12 to 15 hours, the meat is gently peeled off the head and bones and the soup is made from the remains. That's a lot of work! Half of the cooked meat is re-seasoned to use for tacos while the other half goes back into the soup. I've been making this soup for years and every cook has their own variation on the theme depending on where they come from, whether it is Texas, Jalisco or Michocan. However all cooks agree that the seasoning should contain three different pepper types. Ancho adds a rich mahogany flavor, cascabel adds a medium heat index and guajillo chiles add an earthy hotness and depth to the dish. The adobo, or seasoning spice, also contains sweet spices such as cumin, ginger, cloves and cinnamon to mask the gaminess of the chivo; it's a delicate balance but it works. I've given a lot of thought to the proper preparation of this stew and have decided to take the easy route where you can cook it all in one small covered turkey roaster. **Please note that the roaster has to be at least a 5 to 6 quart size to achieve the proper braise.**

Birria Estilo Jalisco

SERVES 6 TO 8

INGREDIENTS

1/4 cup canola oil
3 to 4 pound bone-in goat meat, lamb shank,
      pork shoulder or beef chuck

AROMATIC SOUP STOCK

2 tablespoons canola oil
4 large garlic cloves, minced
1 medium onion, diced
2 dried cascabel chiles
1/2 teaspoon dried oregano
2 cups diced tomatoes with juice
1 tablespoon corn starch
8 cups chicken stock
1/2 cup cilantro, chopped

ADOBO

5 medium garlic cloves, sliced
1 medium onion, chopped
4 dried ancho chiles
3 dried cascabel chiles
4 dried guajillo chiles
1/4 teaspoon each dried cumin, cinnamon,
      oregano and thyme
2 small bay leaves
2 whole cloves
1 teaspoon sea salt
1/2 teaspoon black pepper
1 fresh lime, juiced
4 tablespoons cider vinegar
2 cups chicken stock

Pre-heat the oven to 350°. In a large non-stick skillet, heat the oil and brown the meat on all sides then remove to a serving platter. In the same skillet saute the adobo garlic, onion and chiles for 5 to 6 minutes without burning. Add the remaining adobo ingredients, bring to a simmer and cook for 20 minutes then remove from the heat and cool. While the adobo is cooling, prepare the aromatic soup stock by heating the oil in a sauce pan and saute the garlic, onion and chile for 3 to 4 minutes. Add the remaining stock ingredients, bring to a boil then slowly simmer for 1 hour.

Scrape all the reduced adobo ingredients into a bowl of a cuisinart, then puree into a fine paste. Push the paste through a fine mesh strainer and season the meat with exactly half of the adobo paste (slather it on with a spatula). Arrange the meat in the bottom of a turkey roaster, ladle on 3 or 4 cups of the seasoned stock, cover and cook for 2 to 3 hours until the meat is fork tender. After that time, remove the meat to a serving platter, strain the remaining cooking liquid into a soup pot, de-grease then add the remaining stock and simmer for 30 minutes more. Chop the cooled meat into bite size pieces and place into a hot non stick skillet with no oil. When the pan and meat start to sizzle, spoon on 2 to 3 tablespoons of the remaining adobo paste and toss until hot. Garnish the soup with some of the meat or use as a filling for tacos.

"CARNE EN SU JUGO"

When I released my first cookbook, I thought it would be a good idea to have my own website to interact with people and trade recipes. Bad idea! I was deluged with requests for such items as Scandinavian head cheese, pickled pigs feet and other oddities that drove me to the brink of shutting the website down. For kicks, when I bought a new computer my wife went through every old e-mail and kept a ledger as to what people requested. I was surprised to see dozens of entries for two local dishes, birria and carne en su jugo, two Hispanic delicacies. Birria de chivo (goat) or borrego (mutton) is actually a savory goat stew that's cooked in an earthen dug pit in the backyard around the Christmas holiday. The meat from the goat's head and carcass are finely chopped and the remaining bones and juices are transformed into a soup-like stew garnished with onions, cilantro, salsa and limes. Some people like to just use the heads while some favor the use of the entire carcass.

Carne en su jugo, meaning meat cooked in its own juice, is an old-world Hispanic dish favored by our local Mexican community that originates from Jalisco and Guadalajara. There seems to be a lot of confusion when it comes to the making of this savory soup, so I contacted a rancher/chef I know who lives down Jalisco way to get the scoop. In its simplest form, CESJ is a subtly-flavored beef broth enriched with red or green chilies and chili beans and typically garnished with a nice salad consisting of radish, avocado, diced onion, cilantro, lime and chili de arbol. The coup de gras to this savory soup is the addition of a grilled skirt steak and rashers of crisp bacon. The meat, cooked medium rare. is thinly sliced, then placed on top of the garnished broth which is then blended into the soup. The confusing part in making the dish is that there are opposing factions who think that their way is the best. Let me digress a little here! In no uncertain terms, the main component of the soup is the stock or broth. Traditionally, ranchers liked to use a fresh whole cow's head (eyeballs, tongue, hairy face and all) to create the stock. There's no question that the preferred meat choice is the whole cow's head because it produces a rich and gelatinous broth. Unfortunately, you better have a really big stock pot and a lot of time on your hands because the average head weighs about 30 pounds and takes around 10 hours to cook. Thrifty Mexican chefs I know actually prefer using the head because it yields a lot of savory meat from the jowls, tongue, brain, snout and ears that can be used in all kinds of taco fillings.

Restaurants around the city produce three different kinds of jugo: one is clear, one is red and one is green. The red, or chili based soup is a favorite from the Jalisco region of Mexico. The broth is traditionally seasoned with a dried chili called guajillo, meaning big pod, or chili morita, meaning little mulberry. Chefs from Guadalajara prefer a green-based jugo that is enriched with a slurry of tomatillos, cilantro, green onions and jalapenos. Both versions are utterly delicious and utilize the same cooking technique by producing a flavorful stock that is then garnished with salad and grilled steak. I actually prefer the Jalisco style since I've worked with so many great cooks from that region. I've been making this soup for years and I can greatly appreciate all the small mom-and-pop taquerias around town that stick to the "old-fashioned way" by using the cow's head to flavor the stock. I know a lot of cooks who own jugo restaurants around the city and every one is completely different; most definitely, all their recipes are handed down from generation to generation. I would be remiss if I didn't let you know that there are two theories relative to the proper garnishment for jugo. Some chefs feel that the meat used to cook or season the broth should not be used as a garnish for the soup, while others feel that the seared steak elevates the soup to aristocratic heights. You be the judge!

Jalisco Carne en su Jugo

INGREDIENTS

3 to 4 pounds oxtails, beef chuck or rump roast
1 cup all-purpose flour

1 medium smoked hock
1/2 small calves foot
6 tablespoons achiote oil
8 large garlic cloves, sliced
1 large onion, chopped
2 medium carrots, chopped
2 large celery stalks, chopped
2 bay leaves
2 whole cloves
10 whole black peppercorns
1 tablespoon dried oregano
6 dried chili guajillo pods or 1 to 2 tablespoons
    chipotle chili powder
2 cups diced tomatoes with juice
3 1/2 quarts cold water
3 tablespoons granulated beef base

Two 14 ounce cans red chili beans, well rinsed

STEAK GARNISH

2 slices hickory smoked bacon, diced
3 medium garlic cloves, minced
1 small onion, diced
Pinch of Lawry's seasoned salt
4 six ounce skirt steaks

SALAD GARNIS

1 cup sliced radishes
1 cup sliced avocado
1 cup cilantro, chopped
1/2 cup onion, diced
1/2 cup sliced jalapenos
Red pepper flakes
Lime wedges

Using a sharp knife clean the meats of any excess fat then lightly dust with the flour. Rinse the hock and calves foot then dry. In a large stock pot heat the oil and brown the meat on both sides for 3 to 4 minutes then remove to a serving platter. In the remaining oil saute the garlic, onion, carrots and celery for 3 to 4 minutes. Add the remaining ingredients except the beans, but including the browned meats, hock and calves foot, bring to a slow boil and then reduce the heat and simmer for 3 hours being sure to remove any impurities and foam that float to the top. After that time, strain the broth into a clean pot through a fine mesh strainer and add the beans to the strained stock and simmer slowly for 30 minutes more. Reserve the cooking meat to use as a garnish or proceed with the optional steak garnish. In a large non-stick skillet, saute the bacon until it starts to render its fat and turns lightly brown. Add to the pan the garlic, onion, season salt and stir cook for 3 to 4 minutes until lightly browned. Push the bacon-onion mixture to the side, add the steaks and saute for 2 to 3 minutes on each side then remove from the fire. Slice the steaks into thin strips and then lay on to the bottom of 4 soup bowls. Sprinkle on top of that the bacon-onion mixture then also a handful of the salad garnish. Carefully ladle on top of that the warm bean broth and serve.

Alright, it's a fictitious name that I thought would look cool in the book so don't go trying to find her, just get your butt down to the market! The following recipes are a compilation I've collected from a handful of obliging street vendors so feel free to master them and set up a cart on the corner of your own block.

Horchata

MAKES A QUART

Horchata is a cool and pleasing drink made from rice, almonds, cinnamon and sugar that is marinated overnight then strained and sweetened.

INGREDIENTS

1 cup raw rice
1/2 cup slivered almonds
2 small Mexican cinnamon sticks
1 quart warm water
1/2 cup sugar
1/2 teaspoon vanilla or almond extract

Place the rice into a fine mesh strainer and rinse under cold water for 1 minute. In a large mixing bowl combine the rice, almonds, cinnamon and warm water, cover and let it soak together overnight in the refrigerator to infuse. The next day using a ladle, remove 2 cups of the liquid from the bowl and set a side. Carefully pour the remaining ingredients in the bowl into an electric blender and puree until it is as smooth as possible. Pour the blended mixture back into the large bowl, combine with the remaining 2 cups of liquid plus the sugar and vanilla, and whisk until well blended. Strain all the ingredients through a fine mesh strainer and then pour into a glass pitcher, refrigerate overnight and serve chilled over ice.

Tamarindo

MAKES A QUART

Tamarindo is served as an agua fresca at most Mexican markets or street fairs. Tamarind pulp can be bought at any Hispanic market and possesses a sweet and sour lemony flavor that is very refreshing.

INGREDIENTS

One 4 ounce block tamarind pulp
1 1/2 quarts boiling water
3/4 cup sugar

Place the block of tamarind in a large bowl and cover with the hot water. Soak for 30 minutes to soften the tamarind and then using a potato masher, mash the pulp thoroughly to separate the seeds and fibers. Cover with plastic wrap and refrigerate overnight. The next day strain through a fine mesh strainer into a pitcher, stir in the sugar and serve chilled over ice.

Limonada

A cool and satisfying Mexican style lemonade.

INGREDIENTS

2 fresh Mexican limes, sliced
1 1/2 cups fresh Mexican lime juice
1 1/2 cups sugar
1 quart sparkling water

Ice

Place the sugar and fresh lime juice into the bottom of a glass pitcher and using a long kitchen spoon stir to combine. Throw a few of the lime slices into the bottom of the pitcher, add 2 handfuls of ice, a couple more lime slices, 2 more handfuls of ice and then pour in the sparkling water and any remaining lime slices. Swirl the liquid in the pitcher until all is well combined and serve.

Lupe's Camarone Cocktail

The Mexican version of shrimp cocktail!

INGREDIENTS

1 pound medium sized shrimp,
   pre-cooked and chilled

COCKTAIL SAUCE

1 cup ketchup
1/2 cup spicy V-8 juice
2 large garlic cloves, minced
2 Serrano chilies, seeded and minced
1/3 cup celery, minced
2 tablespoons cilantro, minced
3/4 teaspoon sea salt
1/4 teaspoon black pepper
2 tablespoons lime or lemon juice
1 teaspoon Worcestershire sauce
1/2 teaspoon Tabasco
Dash of celery salt and garlic powder

Clean, peel and de-vein the shrimp and then cover and refrigerate for a few hours. Combine the cocktail sauce ingredients in another bowl and mix until smooth. Cover and refrigerate for at least 4 hours. When you are ready to serve the shrimp, place a lettuce leaf into the bottom of four cocktail glasses. Now divide the shrimps up evenly among the glasses, ladle on a dollop of the sauce and garnish the side of the glass with a few avocado spears, red onion rings, a cilantro sprig, lime wedges, a pickled jalapeno and a couple of saltine crackers.

Marta's Grilled Roasted Corn Etole

The quintessential Maxwell Street market street food! Some vendors in the city like to dip the steamed corn into melted margarine, roll it in parmesan cheese, slather it with mayo and sprinkle it with red pepper!

INGREDIENTS

8 ears fresh corn, silks removed but
  husks left on
1 stick unsalted butter, softened
Juice of 2 limes
1 tablespoon chili powder
2 large garlic cloves, minced
2 tablespoons cilantro, chopped
1/2 teaspoon sea salt
1/4 teaspoon black pepper
Dash of paprika and cayenne pepper

1 cup crumbled queso fresco (optional)

Heat your charcoal grill to medium high making sure that the rack is 4 to 5 inches above the coals. Place the corn into a large bucket filled with water for 10 minutes to soak. While the corn is soaking, combine the remaining ingredients except the queso and set aside until needed. Place the corn directly onto the grill, close the lid and cook for 15 minutes turning occasionally until the corn is steamed through, hot and crispy. Using kitchen mitts remove the corn from the fire, unwrap the husks and immediately spread on the butter mixture. Place on a serving platter and sprinkle on the fresh queso.

Cheech's Wake-Up Flying Saucer

SERVES 4

After a heavy night of Tequila drinking this dish will most certainly wake you up!

INGREDIENTS

4 fresh corn tortillas
I cup canola oil

2 cups Refried Beans Recipe
2 cups Monterrey Jack cheese, shredded
I cup Guacamole Recipe
I cup sour cream
I cup Fresh Salsa
I cup Pickled Jalapenos, sliced
1/2 cup cilantro, chopped
Table Green and Red Sauce

Pre-heat the oven to 400°. Heat the oil in a medium sized skillet and fry the corn tortillas on each side for about I minute. Carefully spread about 1/2 cup of beans on each tortilla, sprinkle on the cheese and bake in the hot oven for 6 to 7 minutes until the cheese is melted. Remove from the oven and garnish the center of each flying saucer with a dollop of guacamole, sour cream, fresh salsa, a sprinkling of jalapenos and cilantro, and a splash of red and green sauce.

Juan's Breakfast Taco with Chorizo, Potato and Egg

SERVES 4

The Mexican version of a Zone Diet breakfast if served with a side of tomatoes.

8 fresh corn tortillas, warmed
12 ounces fresh bulk chorizo
4 medium sized red potatoes, peeled
   and 1/2-inch cubed
2 tablespoons unsalted butter
2 tablespoons canola oil
6 whole large eggs, beaten

1 recipe Table Red Sauce
Fresh cilantro leaves

Cook the potato cubes in a pot of lightly salted water for 10 minutes until al dente and then drain and cool. In a medium sized non-stick skillet, place 2 tablespoons unsalted butter and 2 tablespoons of olive oil and when hot, saute the potatoes for 10 minutes until lightly golden brown. While the potatoes are cooking, saute the chorizo in another skillet until fully cooked about 6 to 8 minutes. Drain through a strainer to remove all excess grease. Add the chorizo to the skillet with the potatoes and then carefully fold in the beaten eggs and cook for 2 to 3 minutes until well combined. Divide the mixture among the 8 tortilla shells and serve with a topping of red chili sauce and chopped cilantro leaves.

Luisa's Flautas with Red Chicken, Guacamole, Salsa and Sour Cream

SERVES 4

Savory stuffed flautas are a very popular snack in northern Mexico. In the States, kids enjoy them as taquitos which are prepared with shredded chicken meat in a spicy red sauce that is rolled into a tight flute, deep fried and garnished with a creamy guacamole and salsa.

INGREDIENTS

16 fresh large corn tortilla shells
1 quart canola oil for frying
1 recipe Guacamole
1 recipe Fresh Salsa
Sour cream

One 4 pound fresh chicken, quartered and
   excess fat removed
1/4 cup all-purpose flour
1/4 cup canola oil

SPICY TOMATO SAUCE

2 tablespoons canola oil
2 large garlic cloves, minced
1 medium onion, sliced
1 medium red or green pepper, sliced
3/4 teaspoon dried thyme
1 bay leaf
3 tablespoons tomato paste
1 1/2 cups tomato sauce
1 1/2 cups beef or chicken stock
1/4 cup dry white wine
1/4 teaspoon sea salt
1/8 teaspoon black pepper
Dash of Tabasco, cayenne and Worcestershire
   sauce
1 to 2 large dried red pepper pods

Pre-heat the oven to 375°. To prepare the spicy sauce heat the oil in a medium sized pot over medium heat, add the garlic, onion and peppers and cook stir until softened about 3 minutes. Add the bay leaf and thyme and cook for another minute to release their oils. Add the rest of the tomato sauce ingredients to the pot, bring to a boil and then reduce the heat and simmer slowly for about 10 minutes. While the sauce is simmering place a large non-stick skillet over medium heat and add the 1/4 cup of canola oil. When the oil is hot, quickly dredge the chicken pieces into the flour and then saute in the hot oil for 3 to 5 minutes on each side until golden brown. Remove to a medium sized earthenware casserole. Ladle all of the spicy tomato sauce over the chicken, cover tightly and bake for 1 1/2 hours until cooked. Remove the casserole from the oven and when cool, chill completely overnight. The next day carefully remove the chicken pieces from the red sauce, remove the meat from the bone and lightly shred. Place the pieces into a medium sized bowl, ladle over some of the spicy tomato sauce and combine. Heat 2 inches of canola oil in a large cast-iron skillet until it reaches 350°. Using a kitchen tong, dip the tortillas into the heated oil for just a few seconds to soften then remove to a paper towel to drain. Place about 3 tablespoons of the chicken filling onto the center of each tortilla in a strip down the middle, roll as tightly as possible and secure through the center with a toothpick. (Like rolling a tight cigar) When all the flautas are rolled, cook three to four at a time in the hot oil for 1 to 2 minutes until crispy and golden brown. Drain on paper towels and serve with a good dollop of guacamole, salsa and sour cream.

Mexican Flag Huarache

This favorite antojito consists of a flat oval shaped masa tortilla that is quickly fried, slathered with beans, Chihuahua cheese, green and red chile sauce and a dose of spicy beef.

INGREDIENTS

2 cups prepared masa dough, see page 339
1 recipe Spicy Refried Beans, warmed
1 cup Chihuahua cheese
Table Red and Green sauce
1 recipe Spicy Beef

Garnish of shredded lettuce,
    guacamole, salsa and pickled jalapenos

SPICY BEEF

2 1/2 pound boneless beef chuck roast
2 tablespoons canola oil
8 large garlic cloves, crushed
1 medium onion, diced
1 medium jalapeno, sliced
1 large tomato, diced
1 tablespoon tomato paste
1/2 teaspoon sea salt
1/4 teaspoon black pepper
1/8 teaspoon chili flakes
1 teaspoon cumin
1 teaspoon oregano
2 teaspoons chili powder
3 cups beef stock

To prepare the spicy beef heat the oil in the bottom of a medium sized pressure cooker and brown the meat on both sides then remove from the pot. Add the garlic, onion and jalapeno to the hot oil and saute for 2 to 3 minutes. Add the rest of the ingredients to the pot including the meat, secure the lid, bring to a gentle hiss and cook for 20 to 25 minutes. When the meat is cooked, remove from the pot with some of its juices and shred with forks until needed. Work the masa until very soft and smooth and then divide into eight equal parts. Roll each into a ball and then flatten into a 6-inch oval canoe shape about 1/4-inch thick. Heat 1/4 canola oil in the bottom of a large non-stick skillet and working in batches of four, fry the huarache for about 2 minutes on each side until slightly speckled brown and then place onto a serving platter. Working quickly, spread the warm beans over the top of the canoes, ladle some red sauce on the far left, green sauce on the far right and place in the center a healthy portion of the spicy beef. Top with the queso and garnish.

336 Street Food CHICAGO

Heime's Excellent Steak Tortas with
Grilled Chilies, Peppers and Onions

This is an updated Mexican grilled steak sandwich that I think you'll enjoy. I got the recipe from a Tex-Mex chef that I know down San Diego way and he typically prepares this dish on a flattop griddle.

INGREDIENTS

2 pounds sliced skirt steak

STEAK MARINADE

2 tablespoons canola oil
1/2 cup orange juice
1/4 cup lime juice
3 large garlic cloves, minced
1/4 cup cilantro, chopped
2 small jalapenos, chopped
2 teaspoons ground cumin
1 1/2 teaspoons chili powder
1 1/2 teaspoons garlic salt
1/2 teaspoon Mexican oregano

VEGETABLE GARNISH

2 tablespoons canola oil
2 small jalapenos, quartered and deseeded
1 large onion, peeled, halved and sliced thin
1 green pepper, halved and sliced thin
1 red pepper, halved and sliced thin
1/2 teaspoon Lawry's Garlic Salt

4 Mexican Bolillos or French rolls, split and
   lightly toasted

The night before making combine the marinade and marinate the steaks overnight. The next day pre-heat a large flat cast iron griddle and when hot, pour on the canola oil and quickly sauté the onions and peppers for 4 to 5 minutes until slightly browned. Season with the garlic spice and push to the far side of the griddle. Remove the steaks from the marinade and griddle fry in the pepper grease for 2 to 3 minutes on each side. To serve the tortas, place a piece of steak into the roll, top with the griddled vegetables and accompany with a side of beans, rice, salsa and jalapenos.

Rosa's Red Chile Pork Tamales

MAKES ABOUT 16 TO 20 PIECES

Everyone loves homemade tamales and I urge you to give this recipe a try. Working with the dough can be a little tricky so have one of your Hispanic friends show you the ropes.

INGREDIENTS

2 1/2 pounds recipe prepared Masa Dough, see page 339
25 extra large dried corn husks

PORK FILLING

2 1/2 pounds boneless pork shoulder, cubed
2 tablespoons canola oil
6 medium garlic cloves, minced
1 medium onion, minced
1 large jalapeno, minced
1/2 teaspoon sea salt
1/4 teaspoon black pepper
1/8 teaspoon chili flakes
1 teaspoon cumin
2 teaspoons oregano
One 14 ounce can Italian plum tomatoes, chopped
One 14 ounce can mild or hot green chilies, drained and chopped
1 cup chicken stock

The night before making the tamales you must make the filling. Heat the oil in the bottom of a medium sized pressure cooker and when hot, brown the cubes on all sides and then remove to a serving platter. Add the garlic, onions and jalapeno to the pot and saute for 2 to 3 minutes without browning. Place all the remaining ingredients into the pot including the pork, cover tightly with the lid, bring to a gentle hiss and cook for 20 to 25 minutes. **After 25 minutes, check inside the pot to make sure there isn't too much liquid. If there is, continue cooking until the liquid has evaporated.** Refrigerate the pork filling overnight. To make the tamales, soak the corn husks in water until they are soft for about 30 minutes and then dry. Place the masa into the bowl of an electric mixer, add 1/4 cup chicken stock and mix on medium high speed until the masa is light and fluffy. Lay the husks out onto a clean/dry work surface and using a kitchen spoon, spread about 1/4 cup of the masa over the middle of the husk, leaving 1/2 -inch borders along the sides and a 4-inch border at the top. Spoon about 1/4 cup of the pork filling down the center of the masa, lift the sides of the corn husks up to the center to meet each other and gently press to seal the masa together making a tube shape that encases the filling. Fold the top edge of the husk over the roll. The tamale should be about 4-inches long and 1 1/4-inches wide. Repeat with the remaining masa and filling, cover and refrigerate for 3 to 4 hours. To cook, place the tamales folded end down and standing upright in the steamer insert of a large stock pot. Steam over boiling water for 30 minutes until the masa is firm and serve warm with hot chili sauce.

Basic Masa Dough

MAKES 2 1/2 POUNDS

INGREDIENTS

2/3 cup lard
1 1/2 teaspoons sea salt
1 1/2 teaspoons baking powder
2 1/2 pounds prepared masa (6 cups)
1 cup chicken broth, warmed

In the bowl of a heavy-duty mixer combine the lard, salt and baking powder with the paddle attachment on high speed until light and fluffy. Lower the speed to medium, add the prepared masa along with 1/2 cup of chicken stock and beat until well mixed about 3 to 5 minutes, adding the rest of the stock along the way to incorporate in. To test the dough, drop 1/2 teaspoon of masa into a cup of cold water and if it floats, it's ready. If not, keep beating the mixture until it passes the water test.

Homemade Pickled Jalapenos

MAKES A QUART

INGREDIENTS

3/4 pound fresh jalapenos
1 medium onion, peeled and sliced thin
1 medium carrot, peeled and sliced
6 large garlic cloves, peeled and sliced
3/4 cup water
1 1/2 cups white vinegar, 5%
1 tablespoon canola oil
1 tablespoon sea salt
1 1/2 teaspoons sugar
2 small bay leaves
1/4 teaspoon dried oregano
1/4 teaspoon dried thyme
1 teaspoon dried marjoram
1 teaspoon cumin seeds, lightly crushed
A few black peppercorns

Thoroughly wash and slit the tip of each pepper. Place the garlic, dried herbs and peppercorns into the bottom of a pickling jar and then layer the jar with the jalapenos, onions and carrots. In a saucepan bring the water, vinegar, oil, salt and sugar to a boil and then pour over the jalapenos until they're fully covered, Seal the jar tightly and when cool to the touch, refrigerate for 1 week before using. Be sure to shake the jar every once in a while to mix.

Fresh Salsa

MAKES 2 TO 3 CUPS

4 medium sized ripe hothouse
    tomatoes
1 small onion, minced
2 tablespoons jalapenos or serranos,
    minced
2 tablespoons cilantro, chopped
2 teaspoons lime juice
1/2 teaspoon sea salt
1 tablespoon canola oil

Core and dice the tomatoes and then place into a medium sized mixing bowl. Add the rest of the ingredients and carefully using a kitchen spoon fold the salsa together. Cover and chill for 2 to 3 hours before using.

Guacamole

MAKES 2 TO 3 CUPS

INGREDIENTS

3 medium ripe haas avocados
1 tablespoon lime juice
2 large garlic cloves, minced
3/4 cup Fresh Salsa
1/2 teaspoon sea salt
1/4 teaspoon black pepper
Pinch of chili powder
2 tablespoons cilantro, chopped

Using a sharp chef knife peel, core and dice the avocados and place into a medium sized glass mixing bowl. Sprinkle on the lime juice, mix to combine and then add the rest of the ingredients. Gently fold together using a kitchen spoon, cover and chill for a few hours before using.

340   Street Food CHICAGO

Table Red Sauce

INGREDIENTS

1 pound fresh ripe tomatoes
2 or 3 serranos, chopped
3 large garlic cloves, minced
1/2 small onion, minced
1/2 cup cilantro, chopped
1/4 teaspoon sea salt
1/4 teaspoon sugar
1/2 cup chicken stock
1 tablespoon canola oil

In a food processor combine all the ingredients except the oil and process to a puree. Heat the oil in a non-stick saucepan and cook the puree over low heat until slightly thickened about 15 minutes. Chill for a few hours before serving.

Table Green Sauce

MAKES 2 TO 3 CUPS

INGREDIENTS

1 pound fresh ripe tomatillos
2 or 3 fresh jalapenos or serranos,
   chopped
3 large garlic cloves, minced
1/2 small onion, minced
1/2 cup cilantro, chopped
1/4 teaspoon sea salt
1/2 cup chicken stock
1 tablespoon canola oil

In a food processor combine all the ingredients except the oil and process to a puree. Heat the oil in a non-stick saucepan and cook the puree over low heat until slightly thickened about 15 minutes. Chill for a few hours before serving.

Mexican Rice

INGREDIENTS

1/4 cup canola oil
2 garlic cloves, minced
1 small onion, diced
1/4 cup green pepper, diced
1 small carrot, diced
2 cups long grain rice
1/2 teaspoon sea salt
1/4 teaspoon black pepper
1 tablespoon chili powder
1 teaspoon cumin
1/2 cup diced tomatoes
3 cups chicken stock
1/2 cup fresh peas
1/2 cup fresh corn kernels
Dash of Tabasco

Heat the oil in a medium sized non-stick saucepan and when hot, add the garlic, onions and peppers and sauté for 1 minute. Now add the rice to the pan and sauté for 5 minutes until lightly golden brown. Add the remaining ingredients, bring to a simmer, cover the pot, reduce the heat and cook slowly for 15 to 20 minutes until the rice is fully cooked. Gently fluff before serving.

Spicy Refried Beans

INGREDIENTS

2 tablespoons bacon grease
3 medium garlic cloves, minced
1 small onion, minced
1/2 teaspoon sea salt
1/4 teaspoon black pepper
1/4 teaspoon dried oregano
1/4 teaspoon cumin
1 teaspoon chili powder
1 to 2 tablespoons pickled jalapeno juice
Two 15 ounce can whole cooked pinto or black
    beans, drained
1 cup chicken stock
Dash of onion powder, garlic powder and
    Tabasco

Heat the bacon grease in a medium sized non-stick saucepan and when hot, add the onion and garlic and sauté for 2 to 3 minutes. Add the remaining ingredients, bring to a slow simmer and cook for 20 to 25 minutes over low heat. Using a wooden kitchen spoon, mash the beans to give it a more rustic texture.

Excellent Frijoles

INGREDIENTS

1 tablespoon canola oil
1/4 cup bacon, minced
3 large garlic cloves, minced
1/2 small onion, minced
1 small jalapeno, minced
1 cup diced tomatoes
Two 15 ounce cans pinto beans, drained
1 teaspoon Creole spice
2 cups chicken stock
Dash of Tabasco, onion powder and garlic powder
1/3 cup cilantro, chopped

Heat the oil in a non-stick soup pan and add the bacon, garlic, onion and jalapeno and saute for 3 to 4 minutes. Add the rest of the ingredients, bring to a slow boil and then reduce the heat and simmer for 20 to 25 minutes until the beans take on good taste.

THE ASIAN CONNECTION

ASIAN

RECIPES

For some strange reason my life has been full of brief encounters of greatness with movie stars, politicians, rock stars, and world-class chefs who have enriched and enlightened my world with memorable stories that center around food. By now most people know of my friendship with Julia Child or my late night bull sessions with Wolfgang Puck. When my last cookbook, The New Polish Cuisine came out, I was invited by a few book designers from Harcourt Brace to go on a junket with them to Hong Kong to see my book actually go to press. Now mind you, although I consider myself to have an educated palate, my experiences with Chinese cooking are strictly Americanized versions of chop suey, egg rolls, won ton and pot stickers. The fear of being trapped in Hong Kong for a week, eating fish eye soup and slimy eel sushi, caused my stomach to have pre-dinner palpitations and convinced me to stock up on the Pepcid!

The flight to Hong Kong on Northwest was really long, yet my journey was comfortable and entertaining, as the plane was full of shoeless businessmen wearing kimono robes who gleefully told stories about the people and the food of China while enjoying a scotch or two. My luck was such that a few seats up from me was a fellow chef by the name of Kevin Chuk, who was an instructor in Hong Kong at the Chinese Cuisine Training Institute, one of the biggest culinary schools in that country. Chefs are like sticky fly paper in that we attract each other, and the next thing you know, we were accompanied by another great chef, Martin Yan, the Don Juan of Asian cooking shows in this country. Both Martin and Kevin were returning from a chefs' convention in San Francisco and were going home to teach some seminars at the institute, to which I was gratefully invited.

Hong Kong is a mystical magical place that is actually a bustling port city renowned for its food culture and dining, boasting about 6,000 restaurants and almost an equal amount of street stalls that seem to cook 24 hours a day!! After a day of resting up, I was surprised to get a knock on my hotel room door from Kevin's assistant who was kind enough to arrange a 2-day culinary sightseeing tour in this vast and fast-paced city. There's no question that the food of China is truly wonderful, but it also encompasses a rich history that I would like to share with you.

Chinese cuisine is divided into eight or nine different regions, or wards as we say in Chicago, each possessing its own individual local specialty or taste. China's culinary traditions date back some 12,000 years with actual written recipes being developed some 3,000 years ago. It's said, that like the French, Chinese cuisine is based on technique with a national collection of 80,000 recipes. It's also my observation that the Chinese take the cooking profession very seriously and often show disdain for the Americanization of their culinary dishes. The country in itself is huge with over a billion people living in some 400 million square miles, with most of the population jammed into the big cities, dwelling in small apartments one on top of another. One of the wildest bits of information I received about this great country is that only 10 to 15% of the land is suitable for farming and growing crops. It was explained to me later that all the dishes of this land are wok-cooked very quickly, due to the fact that there is limited wood and natural fuels, yet such an enormous population. (It's also interesting to note that the country is shaped like a slightly tilted overflowing wok!)

A long bus ride up to the Szechuan province opened up my eyes to some truly beautiful land and farms that were over flowing with the growth of long beans, garlic chives, mini bok choy, winter melon, Chinese eggplant, water chestnuts, ginger, turnips, Napa cabbage, soybean sprouts, broccoli and snow peas; the list and variety is endless. Since I only had five days, my sightseeing had to be cut short, but I can tell you as a chef I was amazed by this country's expansive culinary world. It's funny spending a week in a foreign land and not eating at one fine dining restaurant, but instead enjoying the street foods at makeshift stalls that seemed to be crammed at all hours. Kobuki, my guide, was actually an apprentice chef at the Hong Kong Institute. Her father worked for the Chinese government and Kobuki was being groomed for a chef position to cook at one of the local embassies. I found her not only to be a fascinating individual whose knowledge of Hong Kong street food was unlimited, but I also thought she possessed a hippie- like spiritual earthiness in her approach to interpreting Chinese cuisine. Since Hong Kong is such a bustling city, quick-service street food is the food of choice, but not your ordinary burger and fries kind of deal. (Another interesting note is that the Chinese consume more bagged chips and nuts than any other country in the world!)

Street vendors in China are given a lot of leeway in setting up makeshift restaurant stalls, which are illegal and considered dangerous in the States. The novelty and unfamiliarity of the scene entices you in. Kobuki quickly steered me through tangled and jammed blocks of shops hawking kitchen utensils, electronics, stuffed animals and mind-boggling arrays of fresh vegetables, meats and fish. My day trip to Szechuan territory had most definitely left me in a spicy frame of mind so I was glad to settle down at a joint that was literally built around an old Good Humor truck with the guts ripped out of it to accommodate the cook. It was a funky makeshift restaurant, with rickety tables, no more than 20 seats and a profusion of table condiments that included cured cabbage salad, homemade peppers, dipping sauces and good 40 ounce beers--my kind of joint!

It's kind of scary when you don't know the language and eyes are upon you, but my dining companion assured me that no fish heads would grace the table. A quick sip of beer, pop the Pepcid, and out comes the cook's wife with a huge tray full of decorative soup bowls loaded with assorted fresh ingredients that you are allowed to choose from to mix and match depending on what you want to eat. **She is looking at me and holding it under my nose!** (Jean Banchet of Le Francais fame used to do this routine for years before the meal.) A quick glance reveals no fish heads or innards and luckily, Kobuki now steps in with some wild hand gesturing, head bowing and language that reassures me I am working with a professional. With chopsticks in hand, we enjoy the kimche-like turnip salad that supplies just enough heat to wake up the senses and offset the cold Chinese beer. Jet lag from the day is slowly kicking in, but conversation with other patrons and an ever watchful eye of the cook who has now fired up his propane-induced wok to a fiery red ember glow, keeps me awake in the chilly and misty Hong Kong air. It's not until you're in this situation that you realize the power of a well-tuned fire-eating wok that sears your food so fast and clean that no wonder it's called one of the original sought after street foods of the world.

Our meal majestically begins with chilled lotus root, cucumber and radish salad, followed by salt and pepper octopus, ginger duck soup with spring pea wonton, spicy ma pa tofu, fragrant eggplant and mushrooms, stir fried pot herbs, spicy chicken with orange cashews, black bean chili clams on fried noodles, hot and sour pork with cabbage, Szechuan special lobster. Cookies and mango ice cream top it all off. It's difficult to describe the experience; you just had to have been there, but all the dishes were exceptionally prepared, beautifully presented and most definitely Chinese street and quick.

I was really torn as to whether to include this chapter in this book, since most of Chicago's Chinese and Asian communities are known for sit down restaurants or carry out, not exactly street food per se, but it deserves merit. The Asian community in Chicago is very large and local chowhounds most definitely have a voracious appetite for foods from the spicier regions such as Szechuan, Canton and Hunan. The last 10 years have witnessed a profusion of Asian restaurants, markets and new age Chinese dumpling houses that are scattered throughout the city and at malls around the suburbs. You can walk into any Asian market in the city and buy frozen egg rolls, spring rolls, pot stickers, dumplings, fresh noodles, soups, sauces and condiments; the variety is endless, as is the demand in Chicago for this type of cuisine. I am often asked by fellow chefs where to find the best Asian food in town and my response is always the same, "Head to Chinatown." I choose this destination not only for its diverse culture and strong ethnic heritage, but also for restaurant owners who take their profession very seriously in giving you the most authentic Asian food in Chicago. As of late, I've had really good food at three restaurants that I think you will also enjoy, all located in the Chinatown Mall: Lao Sze chuan, Spring World and Little Three Happiness.

Just a side note: It has recently come to my attention that there is some controversy among local chowhounds that some of these joints might possibly have two sets of menus, one for American patrons and a different one for Asian patrons. With all due respect, I have analyzed this situation very carefully and have come to the conclusion that if you are not an adventurous carnivore accustomed to eating chicken feet, duck tongues or an occasional testicle or two, you aren't missing out on anything!

The following popular recipes are a good representation of what can be had at most Asian restaurants around the city. Be careful and keep a large glass of ice water near as some of the dishes can be really spicy.

Chilled Lotus Root, Cucumber and Radish Salad

SERVES 4

A refreshing salad to cool down the palate before the heat arrives!

INGREDIENTS
1 pound fresh lotus root, peeled and sliced thin
1 seedless cucumber, sliced thin
1 bunch red radishes, cleaned and sliced thin

DRESSING
4 tablespoons sugar
1/3 cup rice wine vinegar
2 tablespoons cilantro, chopped
1 tablespoon lime juice
1 tablespoon ginger, minced

Bring a small pot of water to the boil, add the lotus root and cook for 2 to 3 minutes until al dente crisp. Drain and cool. Place the radish, cucumber and lotus root in a medium sized mixing bowl. Combine the ingredients for the dressing in another small bowl. Pour all of the dressing over the salad, mix to combine and serve.

Chinese Chicken and Rice Soup

SERVES 4

The Chinese equivalent to mom's chicken soup. The secret to this dish is in the broth so make your stock carefully.

STOCK
5 cups chicken stock
1 tablespoon soy sauce
1 teaspoon sesame oil
1/4 teaspoon sea salt
1/8 teaspoon black pepper
2 quarter slices fresh ginger
3 medium garlic cloves, sliced
2 scallions, chopped

2 tablespoons peanut oil
1 cup long grain rice, pre-cooked and chilled

GARNISH
2 tablespoons Chinese chives, minced
2 tablespoons scallions, minced

Place all the ingredients for the chicken stock into a saucepot, bring to a slow simmer and cook for 20 minutes to infuse. While the stock is simmering, heat the peanut oil in a medium sized non-stick skillet and when hot, add the rice making a large pancake. Fry the pancake for 2 to 3 minutes until lightly browned on the bottom, then carefully flip over patting down on the cake and cook for another 3 to 4 minutes until crisp. Strain the hot stock, pour into Chinese soup bowls, sprinkle on the chives and scallions, then carefully cut the rice cake into small wedges and place a piece into each soup bowl.

Crispy Pork Dumplings with Dipping Sauce

SERVES 4

Wontons or dumplings are easily one of the oldest dishes in Chinese culture dating back to 206 B.C. Varieties and shapes are endless and can be had at any oriental restaurant around the city.

INGREDIENTS

2 or 3 packs frozen thin wonton skins

DIPPING SAUCE

2 tablespoons soy sauce
1 tablespoon seasoned vinegar
1 tablespoon sweet chili sauce
1 tablespoon green onion, minced
1 teaspoon cilantro, minced
1/2 teaspoon garlic, minced
1/4 teaspoon ginger, minced
1 teaspoon hot chili oil

FILLING

1 1/4 pounds fatty pork butt, ground
1 whole large egg
1 small shitake mushroom, minced
1/2 cup water chestnuts, minced
2 tablespoons scallions, minced
1 tablespoon ginger, minced
2 teaspoons garlic, minced
2 teaspoons sesame oil
2 tablespoons soy sauce
1 tablespoon rice wine
1 teaspoon sugar
1/2 teaspoon sea salt
1/4 teaspoon black pepper

Place all the filling ingredients into a large mixing bowl and thoroughly combine. Lay the wonton wrappers on top of a lightly floured work surface and place a heaping teaspoon of the filling into the center of each shell. Pick up a filled shell and lay it in the palm of your hand, then flip the skin in half diagonally pressing the 2 sides together. Repeat with the remaining shells, place onto a parchment lined sheet pan and refrigerate for 1 hour. Combine all the dipping sauce ingredients and set aside. Bring a large pot of lightly salted water to a boil then reduce to a simmer. Cook the dumplings a few at a time for about 3 minutes until they float to the top. Immediately remove to a serving platter. Heat 2 tablespoons of oil in a large non-stick skillet and when hot, gently fry the dumplings for 2 to 3 minutes on each side until lightly browned. Serve with the dipping sauce.

Spicy Salt and Pepper Shrimps

SERVES 4

An addictively simple recipe that will most definitely wake up your taste buds! Some joints around town substitute small fresh water smelts when in season for the shrimps which also makes for good eatin'!

INGREDIENTS

2 pounds medium sized fresh shrimps,
   left in shell
4 tablespoons peanut oil
1 teaspoon sea salt
1/2 teaspoon sugar
1/4 teaspoon chili powder
1 tablespoon garlic, minced
1 tablespoon Anaheim chili, minced

Heat the oil in a large wok over high heat and when white hot, pan-fry the shrimps for 3 to 5 minutes until they turn a bright orange color. Sprinkle on the salt, sugar and chili powder and toss the wok until the shrimps are coated on all sides with the spice. Cook for another 2 minutes until the spice caramelizes onto the shrimp. Add the remaining garlic and chili, cook for another minute and serve immediately.

Szechuan Eggplant, Green Beans and Mushrooms

SERVES 4

Eggplant is undoubtedly one of the most treasured vegetables to the Chinese. This recipe is musky, dark and rich and can be eaten hot or cold.

INGREDIENTS

1/2 pound small Chinese eggplant
1/2 pound thin Chinese green beans
1/2 pound assorted mushrooms such as;
    shitake, oyster, golden needle or enoki
2 tablespoons peanut oil

SZECHUAN SAUCE

2 tablespoons peanut oil
1 tablespoon garlic cloves, minced
2 teaspoons ginger, minced
2 scallions, minced
4 ounces ground pork
2 tablespoons soy sauce
1 teaspoon red wine vinegar
1/2 teaspoon sugar
1 tablespoon chili paste
1 teaspoon sesame oil
1/2 cup chicken stock

Using a sharp chef's knife cut the eggplant in half then cut the halves into thin crescent moon sized slices. Trim the green bean ends and cut into 3-inch pieces. Also cut the mushrooms into bite size pieces. Heat 2 to 3 tablespoons of peanut oil in a large wok over high heat and when white hot, add the eggplant and green beans and stir-fry for 3 to 4 minutes until lightly wilted. Now add the mushrooms and cook for another 2 to 3 minutes then pour into a strainer to remove any excess oil and juices. Place the wok back over the heat and when hot, add the oil and stir-fry the garlic, ginger and scallions for 1 minute. Now add the pork and stir-fry until it takes on a nice brown color. Add the remaining sauce ingredients, let it come to a boil, stir to combine, reduce slightly and then add the vegetables back to the wok. Cook for 1 minute more then serve.

Kung Pao Chicken

This dish is hot-hot-hot!!!

INGREDIENTS

1 pound chicken breast, cubed 1/2 -inch
1 tablespoon cornstarch
2 tablespoons peanut oil

AROMATICS

2 tablespoons peanut oil
1 tablespoon garlic, minced
2 teaspoons ginger, minced
1 cup red and green bell pepper, cubed
6 to 8 small dried red chili pods
1/4 cup raw peanuts

PAO SAUCE

2 tablespoons soy sauce
2 tablespoons rice wine
1 tablespoon Chinese vinegar
1 teaspoon sugar
1 teaspoon cornstarch
1 tablespoon chili bean sauce
1 tablespoon hoisin
1 teaspoon sesame oil
1/2 cup chicken stock

Place the cubed chicken into a medium sized mixing bowl, sprinkle on the cornstarch and thoroughly combine until all of the pieces are coated. Place all the ingredients for the Pao sauce into a small bowl and combine. Heat a large wok over high heat, add 2 tablespoons of peanut oil and when white hot, stir-fry the chicken for 3 to 4 minutes until lightly browned then remove to a serving platter. Add the remaining oil to the wok and stir fry all of the aromatics for 2 to 3 minutes. Return the chicken to the pan, stir-fry a minute more and then add the sauce. Bring to a quick boil, stir and simmer for 1 to 2 minutes until all the pieces of chicken are coated and then scoop out onto a decorative platter to serve.

Black Bean Garlic Clams

This is an old Cantonese dish everyone seems to like. Be sure to track down exceedingly fresh clams from your local fish market before attempting this recipe.

INGREDIENTS

2 dozen littleneck clams, cleaned
2 cups water

SAUCE

1 tablespoon peanut oil
2 tablespoons salted black beans, rinsed
1 large red jalapeno, chopped
2 teaspoons garlic, minced
1 teaspoon ginger, minced
2 tablespoons scallions, minced

3/4 cup chicken stock
2 tablespoons soy sauce
2 tablespoons rice wine
1 teaspoon cornstarch
1 teaspoon sesame oil

Pour the water into a large saucepot and bring to a boil. Add the clams, cover and cook until they open, about 5 minutes. Drain the liquid from the clams and set aside. Heat the oil in a large wok over high heat and when white hot, stir-fry the black beans, jalapeno, garlic, ginger and scallions for 2 minutes. Add the remaining sauce ingredients to the wok, bring to a quick boil and let reduce for 1 to 2 minutes. Now add the clams to the hot sauce, cook for 1 minute more and scoop the sauce and clams onto a serving platter.

Ma Pa Tofu

This popular dish was invented by the wife of a well known Chinese chef by the name of Chen Ling Fu. The chef's wife had such a pock marked face the dish became known as Tou-fu of the pock marked wife.

INGREDIENTS

12 ounces fresh bean curd, cubed

2 tablespoons canola oil
2 large garlic cloves, minced
1 green onion, chopped
4 dried red chiles
2 tablespoons black bean garlic sauce
8 ounces ground pork
3/4 cup sliced bamboo shoots

FRAGRANT SAUCE

3/4 cup chicken stock
2 tablespoons soy sauce
1 teaspoon sesame oil
1 teaspoon chili garlic paste
1 1/2 teaspoon corn starch
Pinch of sugar

Bring a small pot of water to a simmer and blanch the bean curd for 2 minutes then remove to a serving platter. Combine all the fragrant sauce ingredients then set aside. Heat the oil in a wok and stir fry the garlic, green onion and red chilies for 2 to 3 minutes. Add the ground pork and stir fry until lightly browned. Add to the pan the bean curd, black bean garlic sauce and bamboo shoots and toss for 2 minutes more. Now add the sauce liquid, stir to combine, bring to a boil then simmer for 2 minutes until the sauce is reduced and slightly thickened.

Crispy Duck "Mu shu" in Lettuce Leaves

SERVES 4

This is a newer version of an old classic that I know you'll love!

INGREDIENTS

1 small pack bean thread noodles
2 cups peanut oil
1 medium head iceberg lettuce, leaves
  separated

2 cups leftover Peking duck, chopped
1 tablespoon garlic, minced
2 teaspoons ginger, minced
2 cups napa cabbage, sliced
1 cup carrots, cut julienne
1/4 cup green onion, chopped
1/2 water chestnuts, sliced
1/2 cup bamboo shoots

SAUCE

1/4 cup chicken stock
3 tablespoons soy sauce
2 tablespoons rice wine
2 tablespoon oyster sauce
1/4 teaspoon black pepper
1 teaspoon sugar
1/2 teaspoon cornstarch

1 cup hoisin for lettuce

Place the 2 cups of peanut oil into a medium sized wok over high heat. Using your hands, separate the bean thread noodles and carefully deep fry them in the hot oil. (They will puff up instantly so you might have to do the whole bag in separate batches.) Drain on paper towels until needed. Combine all the sauce ingredients in a small bowl. Remove all but 1 tablespoon of hot oil from the wok, then stir-fry the duck pieces for 2 to 3 minutes until lightly crisped and remove to a serving platter until needed. Add all the vegetables to the wok and stir-fry for 3 to 4 minutes until wilted. Add the sauce to the wok, toss with the vegetables, bring to a quick boil then add the duck pieces. Cook for 1 minute more then pour out onto a serving platter. To serve, spoon about 1 tablespoon of hoisin onto a lettuce leaf, sprinkle on some of the fried bean thread noodles then spoon on a good portion of mushu. Fold the lettuce over and eat like a taco.

Gold Mango Ice Cream

A cool and satisfying end to any spicy meal.

INGREDIENTS

1 pound fresh mango pulp
2 tablespoons lemon juice
3 large egg yolks
1/3 cup sugar
1 cup whole milk
1 cup whipping cream

Peel the mango and cut away the flesh from the stone. Measure out one pound of mango pulp and puree with the lemon juice in a food processor until smooth. In a medium sized mixing bowl, whip the yolks and sugar until light. Bring the milk to a boil in a heavy duty saucepan, add the egg mixture and cook stirring constantly until it boils then remove from the heat. Stir in the whipping cream and the mango puree, transfer to a container and cool to room temperature. When cool, freeze in an ice cream maker until ready to serve.

THAI-ED UP, KOREAN-ED & VIETNAMESE-ED!

THAI

RECIPES

I recently gave a cooking demonstration at a local restaurant in the city and was surprised as to how many guests showed up. In a late night conversation about my new project, Street Food Chicago, I was introduced to members of two local food groups called Chowhound and LTH Forum. In a nutshell, these highly devoted restaurant epicureans have led the forefront of internet chat about Chicago's culinary scene, far surpassing the topics covered by any local media. Although they are small in number, I was highly impressed by their exuberance and appetite to push the culinary envelope just a little bit further and to showcase some local restaurants and ethnic groups that don't get much attention. In the midst of our conversation, pens were drawn and my sparkling new, white chef's apron became a chalkboard of ideas for additions to this book.

I've traveled a lot over the last couple of years hocking my first book and spending major down time in overbooked airports. When you travel late as I like to do, you usually run into two different types of people, businessmen and military who are off to some exotic port. When you're laid up in Ohio for six hours, undoubtedly the conversation will center around Chicago's food. I've seen business guys bite their hands with envy over the talk of a deep dish stuffed pie, and I've even witnessed a guy chow down about 12 fully loaded Chicago red hots because he didn't think they'd last in his carry-on cooler when his flight was delayed. Oh, the magnetism of Chicago food, but pizza and hot dogs aren't the Windy City's only culinary attraction. Chicago boasts around 90 different ethnic groups whose foodstuffs all add to the mix, but only a few stand out enough to change the city's food landscape and perception of the way Chicagoans eat.

The Asian community has been around these parts since the early 1870s with the building of the Transcontinental Railroad System. However, the cultures of the Thai, Vietnamese and Korean people didn't filter into our city until the 1950s and 60s brought about by the onset of war and poverty in their homelands. Lenient immigration laws and the desire to Americanize led these industrious people to set up shop in some of the most distressed and poverty ridden parts of the city. There's no doubt that the Chinese introduced Chicago to oriental food around the 1920s when egg rolls, wonton soup and broccoli and beef were known as exotic delicacies usually served in not so luxurious venues. South Chinatown on the near west side is home to some 10,000 Asians and the neighborhood boasts some 40 restaurants, all squeezed into an eight block area. This part of town has become a culinary destination for the millions who travel through the city.

Local food historians note that it wasn't until the early 60s that the eyes of the world turned their attention to southeast Asia, specifically Thailand, Vietnam and Korea. GI vets coming home from the wars reminisced about exotic and fragrant spices, pristine seafood, larger-than-life shrimps and lobsters and the over abundance of root vegetables and rare fruits. Small mom-and-pop Asian markets and restaurants started to appear on the horizon without any critical acclaim. If you grew up in the city at that time, most people's first taste of Pan-Asian cooking came in the form of two well known restaurants, Trader Vic's in the Palmer House and Kon Tiki Ports located a little bit shy of O'Hare. Fanciful frilled concoctions such as the Zombie and Tortuga accompanied dishes like crab Rangoon, batter fried shrimp, sweet and sour chicken and barbecued pork spareribs, adorned with a side of chow mein and fried rice. My childhood remembrances tend to lean towards the more outlandish Asian decorations and koi ponds than on the validity of the food.

Years passed, trade relations improved and, fortunately for us, these ethnic groups have toughed it out and stuck around. Korean cuisine and culture, relatively new to the Chicago area, has transfixed the way we eat and is slowly but surely making its way into the mainstream dining experience. Korean food, which is actually a combination of Chinese and Japanese rolled together, adheres to the strict principles of being earthly, robust and spicy with a distinct flair of delicacy for good measure. Korea is a rough, mountainous region next to China, and it is said that its earliest influences came from the Mongolians who taught them the arts of hot pots and barbecue pit cooking. Wars changed the face of their land and in a harmonious act to find their true ying and yang, Koreans adapted a more Japanese-influenced culinary style. Korean cooking is colorful in the respect that it brings together five basic flavors: salty, sweet, sour, hot and bitter (soy, honey, vinegar, chilies and ginger). It is my opinion that in the states, most Korean restaurants are more heavier meat and sauce induced than their respective home-style counterparts, which include more seafood and vegetables. Also the dishes here are on the tamer side as far as the heat and spice factor in an effort to entice the American palate.

Korean restaurants are typically divided into four different groups: barbecue joints, sushi bars, dumplings houses and noodle counters. However, here in the city you can usually find everything you want under one roof. To really enjoy Korean food is to eat communal style. Most restaurants specialize in serving you family style with a wide array of panchan that centers around one main dish, either hot pot or Mongolian grill. Panchan is basically a dozen or so small dishes of pickled and marinated vegetables served as an accompaniment to accentuate the flavors of the main course. An assortment can include small bowls filled with stuffed cabbage pickle, pickled radish leaf, dried anchovy dipping sauce, spiced bean curd, fragrant chili with sesame, egg and seaweed dip or sprouts with watercress. Finger-sized appetizers abound with a selection of scallion pancakes with kimchi, steamed vegetable dumplings or fried vegetable fritters with dipping sauce. Even though most dinners come with a side of sticky rice and some type of soup, savvy diners save their appetite for a serving of bi bim bap (a hot pot filled with rice, beef, spinach, bean sprouts, shitake mushrooms, dikon, watercress, carrots, fried egg, hosin and chili sauce) or the infamous Korean barbecue that patrons can grill at their table. Two of the most popular are galbi (beef short ribs) and bulgulgi (sliced beef,) both marinated in a spicy sauce and most often cooked by you at your table, hibachi style. Meat isn't the only popular dish; shrimp, octopus and squids are also marinated and grilled and a wide array of noodle dishes can be had. I've always favored the spicy hot pots of tofu, chicken, seafood and meats as well as sizzling rice pots that contain kimchi, vegetables and eggs. Most restaurants offer a wide assortment of beers and wines, but the most popular drink is a martini-like concoction called soju tinis, a vodka-like Korean liquor that is enlivened with a dash of fresh fruit puree or vegetable juice, to the delight of its customers.

Thai and Vietnamese cuisine, often referred to as Asian fusion, has been brewing on the back burner in the city for the last 25 years. My first experience with Thai cuisine was in the late 70s at a restaurant called The Bangkok, which specialized in classic Thai. Beautifully prepared dishes such as chicken satay, mee krob som tum, tom yam, green curries and pad Thai enticed my senses with a taste of the orient, a far cry from my classical French training roots. Thailand, which is a virtual peninsula of streams and waterways, has always been a fertile growing ground for pristine chilies, sprouts, cabbage, bamboo shoots, mustard greens, broccoli, garlic, ginger, lemon grass, cucumbers and straw mushrooms. These quick harvested vegetables are beautifully combined to create a distinctive cuisine that is based on balance and possesses the four taste attributes of hot, sour, salty and sweet. Not to be outdone, Thai chefs also heavily utilize the use of herbs and spices such as red chilies, cumin, coriander, peppercorns, cloves, cinnamon, mace, nutmeg, cardamon, lemon grass, ginger and galanga.

Thailand has a rich culinary tradition that dates back to the 13th century. This uniquely visual cuisine is a combination of Chinese and Indian that is synthesized together to create a mind-blowing rhapsody of aroma, flavor and vision. Food writers that I know have a specific way of approaching Thai food and the dining experience associated with it. They describe a fiery and calming cuisine that enlightens your senses with spices and herbs perfectly blended together to enhance the overall taste sensation. Local chowhounds claim there are a good 30 Thai restaurants around the city that specialize in street food, family style and royal Thai. Three that I have enjoyed through the years are Spoon Thai, Young Thai and Tac Quick. I don't want to get into who has the best food because they're all good. Thai and Vietnamese food was originally hawked by Asian street food vendors who would knock out beautiful and quickly prepared snacks and more substantial fare that could be eaten on the go. I tend to like places that add little twists and nuances to their family recipes just as long as they don't use too much fish sauce. Luckily for anyone who is interested, Chicago is home to several outstanding mom-and-pop operations that serve great food in a family style setting. This small list of recipes is pretty typical of the fare that can be found, but insiders or those in the know always ask for the secret Thai menu!

Spicy Hot Cabbage Kimche

MAKES 1 QUART

The equivalent to the American pickle! Kimche is utterly delicious served as a side salad or accompaniment to any grilled dish.

INGREDIENTS

2 pound head Napa cabbage, chopped
1/3 cup pickling salt
1 quart cold water

SEASONING

1 small white radish, peeled and shredded
2 scallions, minced
1 small white part of leek, sliced
1 tablespoon garlic, minced
1 1/2 teaspoons fresh ginger, minced
1 teaspoon sugar
1 teaspoon lemon juice
1 tablespoon pickling salt
1 to 2 tablespoons coarse ground Korean chili powder
4 tablespoons cold water

Place the cabbage into a large mixing bowl, sprinkle on the salt, mix thoroughly and then pour on the cold water. Cover the cabbage with a small plate to insure that it's submerged in the salt water. (The cabbage needs to soak for 4 hours.) While the cabbage is in the brine, combine the seasoning ingredients in a mixing bowl. After 4 hours pour the cabbage into a strainer, rinse with cold water and using yours hands, squeeze gently to remove any excess liquid and then combine with the seasoning mix. Place the cabbage salad into a glass storage jar, cover and refrigerate 3 to 4 days before using.

"Bulgalbi" Grilled Barbeque Beef Short Ribs

SERVES 4

Korean BBQ restaurants around the city offer up this easy dish that is usually cooked on a small grill at your table. Extremely addictive!

INGREDIENTS

3 to 4 pounds beef short ribs

MARINADE

3/4 cup soy sauce
1/3 cup rice wine or sake
5 tablespoons sugar
2 tablespoons sesame oil
1 tablespoon hot chili paste
1/4 teaspoon black pepper
1 1/2 tablespoons garlic, minced
1 tablespoon fresh ginger, minced
1/3 cup green onion, chopped

Cut the ribs in to 2 inch lengths then place into a heavy duty one gallon reseal-able plastic bag. Combine the marinade ingredients in a mixing bowl, pour over the ribs, re-seal and refrigerate for up to 4 hours. Heat a grill or broiler and grill the ribs for 3 to 4 minutes on each side or until browned and cooked through. Do not over cook.

Quick "Bi Bim Bap"

This Korean rice and vegetable hot pot is usually artfully decorated, but what's the point since you mix it all together anyway. Thinly sliced sirloin of beef can be substituted for the chicken!

INGREDIENTS

3/4 pound raw chicken breast, thinly sliced
1 small shitake mushroom, thinly sliced

MARINADE

1/3 cup soy sauce
1/4 cup rice wine
2 teaspoons sugar
1 tablespoon garlic, minced
3 tablespoon green onion, minced
1 tablespoon toasted sesame seeds
2 teaspoons sesame oil
Pinch of salt and pepper
1 tablespoon chili bean paste

VEGETABLE GARNISH

1/2 cup fiddlehead fern sprouts
1/2 cup bean sprouts
1/2 cup zucchini, julienne
1/2 cup red bell pepper, julienne

3 cups fresh cooked short grain rice

Preheat the oven to 450°. Place in the oven a 10-inch Lodge cast iron skillet to keep hot. Combine all the marinade ingredients and marinate the chicken and mushrooms for half an hour. While the chicken is marinating, bring a pot of lightly salted water to the boil and blanch the vegetable garnish for 1 minute Drain and dry. Using a kitchen tong, remove the chicken and mushrooms from the marinade and place into the hot skillet in the oven to cook for 2 to 3 minutes. Re-open the oven, add 3/4 cup of the marinade and let that cook for another 2 to 3 minutes. Now stir the meat, pour on the vegetable garnish, pat on top of that the rice, re-close the oven and let that cook for another 8 to 10 minutes until the top of the rice is slightly crispy. After that time place the skillet in the center of the table on a trivet, stir with chopsticks and eat.

Green Papaya Salad with Chili, Lime & Blue Crab

SERVES 4

Som Tam Thai is a mouthwatering salad that really perks up the senses.

INGREDIENTS

1 medium green papaya, (not ripe)
   peeled and shredded
1 cup thin green beans, sliced
1 cup green cabbage, chopped
8 cherry tomatoes, quartered
4 medium garlic cloves, minced
4 small Thai chilies, minced
1/3 cup fresh lime juice
4 tablespoons Nam Pla fish sauce
1 tablespoon honey
1/4 teaspoon sea salt
1/3 cup roasted peanuts, chopped
1/4 cup cilantro, chopped

1 cup fresh blue crabmeat, chilled

Place the papaya, green beans, cabbage and tomatoes in a large mixing bowl and thoroughly combine. Place the garlic, chilies and salt into a mortar and pestle and then mash together for 2 minutes. Add the honey, lime juice and fish sauce to the mash and stir to combine. Sprinkle the peanuts, cilantro and crabmeat over the vegetables, pour on the dressing, carefully mix with a tong and serve.

Classic Pad Thai

This sweet, sour and salty noodle dish can be had at any stall throughout Thailand. The variations are endless so feel free to experiment on your own.

INGREDIENTS

8 ounces flat rice stick noodles

2 tablespoons canola oil
1 tablespoon garlic, minced
1/2 small red onion, diced
1/4 cup scallions, chopped
2 cups fresh bean sprouts
1/4 cup unsalted peanuts, chopped
1/4 teaspoon sea salt
1/8 teaspoon red chili flakes
3/4 pound pork loin, fresh ground
2 large whole eggs, beaten

SAUCE

1/3 cup chicken stock
3 tablespoons fish sauce
2 tablespoons rice vinegar
1 teaspoon sugar
1 to 2 tablespoons tamarind puree

1/4 cup cilantro, chopped

Pre-cook the noodles, rinse and set aside. Heat the oil in a large wok and stir fry the garlic, onion, scallions and pork for 2 minutes. Add the remaining ingredients except the sauce and continue to stir fry for another 2 minutes. Stir together the sauce ingredients, add to the wok, cook for 2 minutes more, pour onto a platter and garnish with the cilantro.

Fiery Pepper Beef in Lettuce Cups

This is actually an appetizer, but my wife likes to order it as her entree. The leftover cups make a delightful and heart healthy cold lunch for the next day.

INGREDIENTS

1 pound beef flank steak, thinly sliced and chopped

MARINADE

5 medium garlic cloves, minced
5 medium Serrano chilies, chopped
1/2 cup cilantro, chopped
3/4 cup fresh lemon juice
3 tablespoons fish sauce
4 tablespoons light brown sugar
1/2 teaspoon sea salt
1/4 teaspoon black pepper

GARNISH

1 small stalk lemongrass, chopped
1 small red onion, chopped
1 small hothouse cucumber, chopped
3 Roma tomatoes, chopped
1/2 cup fresh mint, chopped
8 small lettuce cups, cleaned & dried

DIPPING SAUCE

1/2 cup fish sauce
1/4 Thai chilies, minced
2 tablespoons garlic, minced
2 tablespoons fresh lime juice

Combine all the marinade ingredients in a mixing bowl until dissolved, add the meat and marinate for one hour. In another bowl combine the vegetable garnish excluding the lettuce cups and refrigerate until needed. Lastly combine the dipping sauce in a small bowl and set aside. After a few hours place the lettuce cups onto a large serving platter and into each cup, add 2 to 3 tablespoons of the vegetable salad. Strain the meat from the marinade and stir cook in a lightly oiled hot wok for 2 to 3 minutes. Place some of the meat mixture into each lettuce cup and spoon over a little dipping sauce to serve.

"Cha Gio" Crispy Spring Rolls

MAKES ABOUT 30 PIECES

Crispy little delectable buffet treats that are typically wrapped with a lettuce leaf to eat and hold in the dressing.

INGREDIENTS

1 ounce dried cellophane noodles
1 ounce dried cloud ear mushrooms

2 tablespoons canola oil
2 large garlic cloves, minced
1/4 cup red onion, minced
1/4 cup scallions, minced
1 cup finely grated carrot
2 tablespoons fish sauce
1 to 2 teaspoons sugar
1/4 teaspoon sea salt
1/8 teaspoon black pepper
1/2 pound fresh ground chicken breast
1/2 fresh ground pork loin
1 large whole egg

30 to 40 pieces rice paper

DIPPING SAUCE

1 tablespoon garlic, minced
1 teaspoon chili paste
1 Thai chili, minced
1/4 cup Vietnamese fish sauce
1/3 cup cool water
2 tablespoons fresh lime juice
1/4 cup sugar

Soak the cellophane noodles and mushrooms in warm water for 20 minutes and then drain, dry and chop. Combine the ingredients for the dipping sauce in a small bowl and stir to mix. In a small skillet heat the oil and sauté the garlic, onion, scallions and carrots for 2 to 3 minutes until slightly softened and then cool. In a large mixing bowl combine the chopped noodles, mushrooms, sautéed vegetables and the rest of the ingredients except the dipping sauce. Thoroughly combine with a wooden spoon. Now working on a clean surface pour about 2 inches of warm water into a rectangular baking dish, add a few rice papers and soak for 3 to 4 minutes until pliable. Drain on a kitchen towel and blot dry. Place a good heaping spoonful of filling onto the center of each rice paper and roll up tightly, egg roll style sealing the end with a little warm water if needed. Repeat with the remaining papers and filling and then deep fat fry in canola oil at 350° for 3 to 4 minutes until crispy brown. Serve with the dipping sauce.

Sweet and Sour Chicken Cabbage Salad

SERVES 4

This dish is the Vietnamese version of our American style Chinese chicken salad. Very cool, refreshing and great on a buffet table.

INGREDIENTS

2 cups pre-cooked shredded chicken, chilled
3 cups Napa cabbage, shredded
1 cup carrots, shredded
1 small red onion, sliced
1/2 cup mint, chopped
1/4 cup cilantro, chopped
4 tablespoons roasted peanuts, crushed

DRESSING

1 tablespoon garlic, minced
1 tablespoon Thai chili peppers, minced
4 tablespoons canola oil
4 tablespoons Vietnamese fish sauce
4 tablespoons fresh lime juice
2 tablespoons rice vinegar
2 tablespoons sugar
1/4 teaspoon sea salt
1/8 teaspoon black pepper

Combine all the dressing ingredients in a jar, cover and marinate for one hour. In a large mixing bowl combine the remaining ingredients, pour on some of the dressing, toss to mix, pour onto a platter and sprinkle with colorful shrimp chips to serve.

Pho Bo "Hanoi Beef Noodle Soup"

All LTHers love their Pho Bo so I thought I would include a recipe in the book. The secret is to really degrease the stock before adding the vegetable garnish.

INGREDIENTS

2 pounds oxtails, well trimmed of fat
2 pounds beef chuck
1/4 cup canola oil

SOUP GARNISH

1 cup bean sprouts
8 ounces rice noodles, pre-cooked
1 small red onion, halved and sliced
2 tablespoons green onions, chopped
2 tablespoons assorted san leaf herbs, chopped
1/4 cup cilantro, chopped

STOCK

12 cups cold water
1/4 cup Vietnamese fish sauce
3 tablespoons beef base
1 small chunk ginger root, quartered
5 large garlic cloves, sliced
1 medium onion, sliced
1 small leek, sliced
1 medium carrot, sliced
1 medium celery, sliced
1 small cinnamon stick
5 whole cloves
5 star anise
1 teaspoon sea salt
1/2 teaspoon whole black peppercorns
2 large Serrano chilies, chopped

In a large non-stick skillet heat the oil and brown the oxtails and beef chuck for 3 to 4 minutes on each side. When the meat cools place into a large soup pot, cover with the water, fish sauce and beef base, bring to a boil and simmer slowly for 45 minutes being sure to remove any impurities that float to the top. Now add the remaining stock ingredients to the pot and again simmer slowly for another 2 hours until the soup takes on a good taste. Using a tong remove the meat to a serving platter to cool and then strain the soup through a fine mesh strainer into a medium sized soup pot. Re-season the soup if it needs it. Pick the meat off the bones, slice the chuck and then return to the finished broth. Divide the garnish evenly among four deep soup bowls, ladle on the hot meat broth and then serve with a side of chili sauce, bird peppers, lime and soy.

INDIAN

RECIPES

I'm going to make this chapter short and sweet! Ask any classically trained French chef what cuisine or food they like to eat or would convert to if they had the chance, and you guessed it, Indian food is their answer; "Why?" you ask. Because of its mind-blowing profusion of chilies, herbs, legumes and exotic spices that totally engulf any erogenous part or orifice of a chef's soul! India and its foods are described by food writers as being rich, sensuous, enchanting and alluring, to say the least. Five thousand years plus of civilization have transformed this great nation into a mysterious melting pot of culture that just seems to draw you in.

In my younger years I landed a cool job as a cook at a French restaurant called Jovan's, located on Huron. Situated next door was an emerging Indian restaurant named India Star. Our kitchen back doors were no more than 20 feet apart, and during our evening breaks we cooks would share a quick beer, a smoke and exchange dishes of fancy foods from our respective establishments. Over a two-year period of making soups, stocks and sauces, I had to endure the sweet and intoxicating odors that emanated from their kitchen into ours. I struck up a friendship with a young Indian cook by the name of Raj Patel. Raj was an interesting character. He was visiting our country on a working visa, perfecting his craft so that he could land a job as a personal chef for a bigwig in the New Dehli justice department. My impression of Raj was of a mild mannered, slight of frame and highly spiritual person who had a God-given talent for cooking technique and the subtle use of exotic spices. Since we both shared Sunday as our day off, we would occasionally venture up to Devon Ave., the Indian-Pakistani neighborhood of Chicago, to visit Raj's family as well as some shop and restaurant owners that he knew. It was on those visits where I learned a little Indian history.

The Indian and Pakistani community is fairly new to Chicago. Most started settling here during the 60s. There was a time in the city when the Indian community was known as non-settlers due to the fact that they came here to study in our great universities only to return back home upon completion of their education. Unfortunately during the late 70s and 80s, affirmative action put a stranglehold on their university studies and work force, but fortunately for us their business spirit took over, they assimilated and they now own Devon Avenue. I learned many cool and interesting facts from Raj on our culinary excursions. The first was that Indian chefs borrow a lot of technique from the French cooking style such as slicing, sauteing and braising. Second, most people's notions of Indian cooking revolve around heavy meat-laden curry dishes, which is not true as half the nation is vegetarian. Just like French and Italian bakers, Indian cooks take very seriously their homemade flat breads, called naans, traditionally cooked in a tandori oven and used as an eating utensil instead of a fork or a spoon. Another observation is that an Indian meal is all about balance and harmony. Each part of the meal should complement the other, whether it be color, flavor, texture or aroma. The Indian people carry that philosophy over to their everyday lives in native dress, music, videos and inner serenity.

Indian cuisine is divided into four types. The northern style is mostly non-vegetarian and draws influences from their Arab, Persian and Mughal neighbors. This region has a propensity for heavy sauces and the wide usage of chicken, mutton and lamb. The southern area is known for its lighter vegetarian fare. Curries and rice dishes abound and the Kerala coast boasts some of India's best seafood dishes. Steamed foods are usually fragrant with coconut, malabar pepper, turmeric and coriander. The eastern region is typically known for its simple country-style fare of highly seasoned curries as well as masalas of vegetables, legumes and seafood. This area also produces some of India's best traditional desserts and sweets. Last but not least, the west Indian region is known as the lightest and is more Mediterranean style in taste and texture. Famed dishes from this area are typically lamb or chicken curry with vegetables, pork vindaloo and goan- style seafood of shrimp, crab, lobster, oyster and pomfret.

My friendship with Raj lasted for years, and rather than returning to India to pursue his career, he became a culinary consultant for some of the oldest Indian restaurants in Chicago, New York and Los Angeles. I've enjoyed many a fine dish of Indian food and find that the simplest preparations are always the best. Quality gourmet stores around the city now carry pre-packaged curry and masala mixes so Indian meals come together in a snap. **Chef Raj's wisdom: "Indian cuisine is always based on the freshest ingredients available whether it is the spices, vegetables or meats." If in doubt, throw it out!**

Naan

Naan is traditionally cooked in a hot tandoor oven, but can be easily baked on a pizza stone that fits in your conventional oven.

INGREDIENTS

4 cups all-purpose flour
1 teaspoon active dry yeast
1 1/2 teaspoons sea salt
1 teaspoon sugar
1/2 teaspoon baking powder
2 tablespoons nigella seeds
1/2 cup plain yogurt
1/4 cup whole milk, slightly warmed
1/4 cup water, slightly warmed
1 large whole egg
1/4 cup canola oil

In a large mixing bowl combine the flour, yeast, salt, sugar, baking powder and nigella seeds. In another bowl whisk together the yogurt, milk, water, egg and oil. Make a well in the center of the flour, slowly pour in the liquid mixture and using your hands, mix the ingredients until they all come together in a shaggy ball. Let the dough rest for 15 minutes covered with a kitchen cloth. Knead the dough until it comes together in a slightly smooth mass then divide it into 8 to 10 pieces. Cover with plastic wrap and a kitchen towel and let rest for 2 hours. Pre-heat the oven to 550° with the pizza stone placed on the middle rack. (It's imperative that the oven and pizza stone are really hot.) To form the naan, on a lightly floured work surface, press down with the palm of your hand onto each one of the balls shaping them into a circle of about 4 to 5-inches in diameter while pressing out any air pockets. Now carefully pick up each piece, stretch it into a tear-drop shape then cook 2 to 3 at a time on the hot pizza stone for 2 to 3 minutes until they puff up and are lightly browned. Repeat with the remaining dough.

Bombay Salad

This light and refreshing salad is famous throughout India and can be bought at any street corner stall.

INGREDIENTS

3/4 pound fresh paneer cheese
1/2 cup red onion, diced
1 1/2 cups Roma tomatoes, diced
2 1/2 cups English cucumber, diced
2 small Serrano chilies, minced

DRESSING

6 tablespoons canola oil
4 tablespoons fresh lemon juice
1/2 teaspoon sea salt
1/4 teaspoon black pepper
Dash of cayenne and cumin
3 tablespoons cilantro, chopped
3 tablespoons mint, chopped

Using a sharp chef's knife thinly slice the paneer and lay out onto a serving platter. Combine all the vegetables in a mixing bowl and in another bowl, combine all the dressing ingredients. Toss the dressing with the vegetables and arrange over the cheese to serve.

Vegetable Fritters

Vegetable fritters are a nice, light and easy appetizer to make for a summer party or picnic.

INGREDIENTS

2 pounds assorted baby vegetables such as, cauliflower, eggplant, onion rings or sweet potatoes
2 tablespoons canola oil
1 teaspoon sea salt

BATTER

1 3/4 cups chickpea flour
1 1/4 cups cold water
1 teaspoon sea salt
1/4 teaspoon cayenne pepper
1/2 teaspoon ground coriander
1/2 teaspoon ground cumin
1/4 teaspoon turmeric
1/2 teaspoon baking soda

Using a sharp chef's knife slice all the vegetables into thin strips, season with the salt and oil and let rest. In a mixing bowl combine all the batter ingredients until completely smooth and let rest covered for 30 minutes before using. Heat a heavy duty iron skillet with about 2-inches of canola oil to 350°. Carefully dip the vegetables into the batter then deep fry for 3 to 4 minutes until lightly golden brown and crispy. Drain on paper towels before serving.

Spicy Indian Tikkas Kabob

SERVES 4

Chicago's Indian community up off of Devon Avenue is easily the most fragrant area around. Tikka Kabobs come together in a snap and are great on the grill.

INGREDIENTS

2 pounds raw chicken breast

MARINADE

1 cup plain yogurt
2 tablespoons lemon juice
2 tablespoons canola oil
1 tablespoon chili paste
1 tablespoon garlic, minced
2 teaspoons ginger root, minced
1 teaspoon sea salt
1 1/2 teaspoons garam masala
Dash of red food coloring

Wood Skewers

In a medium sized mixing bowl combine all the marinade ingredients until smooth. Using a sharp chef's knife cut the chicken breast into bite size cubes. Place in the marinade and refrigerate for 3 to 4 hours. Heat a charcoal grill, skewer the breast meat and grill for 6 to 8 minutes being sure to turn the skewers as they cook. Serve the tikka kabobs on freshly made naan with a sprinkling of diced onion, chopped cilantro, mint, green chilies and lemon juice.

372   Street Food **CHICAGO**

Fragrant Pullaoo Rice

Rice dishes abound throughout all of India and this is a simple and delightful one to make.

INGREDIENTS

4 tablespoons unsalted butter
1 small bay leaf
6 whole green cardamom pods
One 2-inch cinnamon stick
2 whole cloves
1/4 teaspoon ground turmeric
1/3 cup white raisins
1/4 cup raw cashews
1 1/2 teaspoons fresh ginger, minced
1 teaspoon sugar
1/4 teaspoon sea salt
1 cup basmati rice
1/2 cup fresh green peas
1 3/4 cups chicken stock

Heat the butter in a small non-stick pot and when hot, saute the bay leaf, cardamom, cinnamon and cloves for 2 minutes. Add the remaining ingredients except the peas and stock and saute for another 3 to 4 minutes. Now add the stock, bring to a boil, then gently simmer for 20 minute. After 20 minutes stir the peas into the rice, cover tightly and let steam for 10 minutes more off the fire before serving.

Tandoori Prawns

Quick, easy to prepare and utterly delicious on the grill.

INGREDIENTS

2 pounds jumbo shrimp, peeled and de-veined
1 tablespoon lemon juice

MARINADE

1 cup plain yogurt
1 tablespoon garlic, minced
1 tablespoon ginger, minced
1/4 teaspoon sea salt
1/8 teaspoon black pepper
1 teaspoon paprika
1 teaspoon ground cumin
1 teaspoon ground coriander
1 teaspoon ground turmeric
1 teaspoon garam masala

Combine all the ingredients for the marinade in a mixing bowl. Season the shrimps with the lemon juice then add to the marinade. Cover and refrigerate for 3 to 4 hours. Heat a grill to medium high and using a kitchen tong, remove the shrimps and place on the grill. Grill for 2 to 3 minutes on each side until firm and cooked. Serve with a side of fragrant rice.

Pistachio Ice Cream

MAKES ABOUT 1 QUART

The Indian culture loves their sweet treats and ice creams especially those that soothe the palate after a spicy meal.

INGREDIENTS

3 1/4 cups half and half
3 tablespoons sliced almonds, finely ground
3/4 cup shelled pistachios, finely ground
2/3 cup sugar
6 large egg yolks

In a saucepan over medium heat bring the half and half, almonds, pistachios and half of the sugar to a simmer stirring occasionally to make sure the mixture doesn't burn. Remove from the fire and let the mixture infuse for 30 minutes. Meanwhile in a large mixing bowl beat the egg yolks and remaining sugar together until pale yellow. Once the milk and nuts have finished infusing, pour the mixture through a fine mesh strainer into a clean saucepan and bring to a simmer. Now carefully pour a little of the hot milk into the egg yolk mixture whisking constantly as the liquid is added, then pour the egg-milk mixture back into the saucepan. Over medium low heat cook the mixture by constantly stirring with a wooden spoon until it thickly coats the back of the spoon. When the mixture is thickened, immediately place the saucepan into a bowl of ice cubes. Stir to cool it down as quickly as possible. When cool strain through a fine mesh strainer into a clean bowl. Refrigerate for 4 hours then freeze according to directions on your ice cream maker.

THE OTHER ETHNIC SIDE

ETHNIC

RECIPES

If you read up until this point, you could undoubtedly feel my pain in the choosing of the recipes for the book. "It's all good!" Chicago with its melting pot metropolis conjures up visions of the past, present and future and its perception of street food changes daily. Cloistered around the city are areas known for specific ethnic specialties such as, German, Ukrainian, African and Indian in the form of small grocery stores that tantalize your taste buds with daily lunch buffet specials. Typically three items such as curried goat, plantain chips and spiced cabbage or a falafel sandwich with pita, hummus and jasmine rice will run you about 5 bucks. I find these places to be the best deal in town!

Over the last few years I've noticed a distinctive trend conquering Chicago's "fast food market" known as the slow foods movement. In a nutshell slow foodies abstain from the chains and embrace a more natural old world and healthier style of cooking. Artesian bakeries, organic farmer's markets and slow braised dishes are in. I'm happy to say that a lot of local mom and pop joints have jumped on "the natural bandwagon" and are featuring a handful of their national dishes at bottom basement prices to grateful foodies. Not to be forgotten, here's several ethnic recipes I've enjoyed over the years.

Nigerian Egusi Stew

Good egusi soup or stew recipes are difficult to come by so I worked this one out with a fellow chef who worked for "Vee Vee's African Restaurant". It has the hardiness of a good gumbo without the roux. As a side note, a small smoked hock or calves foot can be added to the pot. Red palm oil and egusi seed are essential to the outcome of the dish.

INGREDIENTS

1/3 cup red palm oil
3 pounds assorted meats, goat, mutton, tripe or
   bush meat
2 tablespoons Creole spice

4 large garlic cloves, minced
1 medium onion diced
2 medium celery stalks, diced
1 medium red pepper, diced
2 cups okra, sliced
1 cup diced tomatoes
2 tablespoons tomato paste
1 cup toasted egusi seed, ground
2 tablespoons minced dried smoked crayfish
1 teaspoon dried oregano
1 teaspoon dried basil
1 bay leaf
2 small red chili pods
1/2 teaspoon sea salt
1/4 teaspoon black pepper
8 cups chicken stock
Dash of Tabasco and Maggi

3 cups assorted greens such as collard or kale,
   cleaned and chopped

Season the meat with the Creole spice then brown in the palm oil for 3 to 4 minutes and remove to a serving platter. In the remaining palm oil, saute the garlic, onion, celery, red pepper and okra for 3 to 4 minutes. Add the remaining ingredients to the pot including the meats and except the greens, bring to a boil then simmer slowly for 1 hour and a half. After that time add the greens and let the stew cook for another hour.

Argentinean Chimichurri

Often called the Argentine version of pesto, chimichurri is a cool and refreshing marinade and side sauce that compliments grilled pork skewers, chicken breast or flank steak.

INGREDIENTS

2 pounds pork tenderloin, chicken breast or
   flank steak

MARINADE

1/2 cup olive oil
2/3 cup sherry vinegar
1 bunch Italian parsley
1/2 bunch cilantro or mint
6 medium garlic cloves, minced
1/2 small onion, diced
1/2 cup diced red pepper
1/2 cup diced tomato
2 teaspoons dried oregano
2 teaspoons paprika
1 fresh bay leaf, crushed
1 teaspoon sea salt
1/2 teaspoon black pepper
Pinch of red pepper flakes

Cube the pork or chicken breast and skewer. Leave the flank steak whole. Finely chop the parsley, cilantro or mint, place into a mixing bowl, add the remaining ingredients and let set for 1 hour to infuse. Place the skewers or flank steak into a resealable bag, pour on half of the sauce, seal and refrigerate for 4 hours. Grill the meat on a hot fire for 3 to 4 minutes on each side, then serve with the remaining chimichurri sauce.

Fish and Chips

British restaurants and pubs seem to be popping up all over Chicago land, and I couldn't think of a simpler dish to have with a nice cold ale than this one.

INGREDIENTS

2 pounds sea bass or cod fillets

BEER BATTER

1/2 cup beer
1/2 cup cold water
1/2 teaspoon sea salt
1/4 teaspoon black pepper
1/4 teaspoon baking powder
3/4 cup all-purpose flour
1/4 cup corn starch
Dash of Tabasco and Creole spice

1 cup all-purpose flour for breading

1 quart canola oil
3 pounds Idaho potatoes

Combine the beer batter ingredients in a mixing bowl and whisk until smooth. Heat the canola oil in a deep fat fryer until 325°. Clean and scrub the potatoes and cut into 1/4-inch thick fries. Place the potatoes into a pot of ice water and let rest for 10 minutes, thoroughly drain and dry in a colander. Working in batches, pre-blanch the chips for 3 to 4 minutes in the hot oil until they turn white and opaque in color then remove to a paper towel lined baking pan. Increase the heat to 375°, dredge the fish fillets in the reserved flour then carefully dip into the beer batter. Quickly add a couple of handfuls of the French fries back to the fryer, also lay in the hot oil 1 or 2 of the fish fillets and fry for 3 to 4 minutes until golden brown. Remove to a serving platter, season with some Creole spice, lemon wedges and malt vinegar.

"Ya Man" Curried Goat

Every righteous brother I know enjoys this Jamaican specialty that pops up on lunch counters around the city. One to two cups of canned coconut milk can be added to the finished stew to enrich the broth.

INGREDIENTS

3 pounds pristine fresh cubed goat meat

4 tablespoons canola oil
3 large garlic cloves, minced
2 medium onions, sliced
1 large carrot, sliced
1 large celery stalk, sliced
1 scotch bonnet pepper seeded and sliced
1 teaspoon dried thyme
1 large bay leaf
2 tablespoons quality curry powder
4 tablespoons all-purpose flour
2 tablespoons red wine vinegar
1/2 cup dry white wine
7 cups beef stock
1 cup diced tomatoes
1/4 teaspoon sea salt
1/8 teaspoon black pepper
Dash of garlic powder, Tabasco and
Worcestershire sauce

2 large potatoes, peeled and diced

Heat the oil in a large pot and brown the cubed goat meat then remove to a platter. In the remaining oil saute the garlic, onions, carrots, celery and pepper for 3 to 4 minutes. Add the thyme, bay leaf, curry powder, flour, salt and pepper and cook for 1 minute more. Now add the red wine vinegar and white wine, let it reduce until dry then add the remaining ingredients except the potatoes. Bring to a boil then slowly simmer for 2 hours. After 2 hours, add the potatoes and cook for another 20 minutes.

Monday Red Beans & Rice

This New Orleans Monday night special can be had at any Creole restaurant around the city. Some cooks like to mash the stew while others favor the beans left whole. You decide!

INGREDIENTS

I pound dried light red kidney beans, rinsed
2 tablespoons canola oil
I pound Andouille or kielbasa sausage, sliced
I cup diced ham steak
3 medium garlic cloves, minced
1/2 cup onion, minced
1/2 cup celery, minced
1/2 cup green pepper, minced
1/2 cup green onion, minced
I small jalapeno, minced
Pinch of red pepper flakes
I tablespoon Creole spice
I bay leaf
9 cups chicken stock
Dash of Tabasco and Worcestershire sauce

I to 2 teaspoons gumbo file powder

Place the kidney beans into a large pot of water, bring to a boil then immediately remove from the fire, drain and let cool. Heat the oil in another medium sized non-stick soup pot and saute the sausage and diced ham for 3 to 4 minutes until lightly brown then remove. In the remaining oil, saute the garlic, onion, celery, green onion and pepper for 3 to 4 minutes. Add the seasoning, beans, meats and remaining ingredients except the file powder. Bring to a slow simmer, cook partially covered for 2 hours then uncovered for 1 hour. While the beans are cooking, cook some fresh rice by placing 3 cups water, 1 cup converted white rice and 1 tablespoon butter in a small saucepan. To serve, off the fire stir the file powder into the bean stew, place some rice in a serving bowl and ladle on the beans and sausage.

Cuban Empanadas

Every culture known to man has some kind of savory stuffed dough whether it be beef, turkey, vegetable or seafood. Latin markets around the city churn out these delectable street foods but they're just as easy to make at home.

DOUGH

2 cups all-purpose flour
1/2 teaspoon sea salt
1 teaspoon baking powder
1 teaspoon sugar
6 tablespoons butter flavored shortening
1 whole large egg and 1 yolk
1/2 cup ice water

CHICKEN FILLING

2 tablespoons canola oil
2 large garlic cloves, minced
1/2 small onion, minced
1 small jalapeno, minced
3 cups cooked chicken breast, diced
2 tablespoons white wine
1 cup chicken stock
1/2 teaspoon sea salt
1/4 teaspoon white pepper
1/4 cup cilantro, chopped
Shot of lime juice

1 quart canola oil for frying

Mix the flour, salt, baking powder and sugar in a medium sized mixing bowl. Cut the butter into the mixture using a pastry blender. Make a well in the center of the flour mixture and place the eggs and water in the well. Using a wooden spoon, stir the mixture until well blended. Wrap in plastic and refrigerate for 1 hour. While the dough is chilling, make the filling by heating the oil in a skillet and saute the garlic, onion and jalapeno for 2 to 3 minutes. Add the remaining ingredients and cook until the liquid dissipates and the mixture has good taste. Stir the cilantro into the mix. After 1 hour on a lightly floured work surface, roll out the dough until 1/8-inch thick. Using a 2 1/2-inch round pastry cutter cut the dough into neat circles. Place about a tablespoon of filling in the center of each circle, fold over and crimp the edges with a fork. Heat the oil in a deep fat fryer to 365° and fry the empanadas for 3 to 4 minutes until golden brown.

Cheese Crepes with Jam

Whether your Lithuanian, Ukrainian or Russian, you just got to love a plate full of these Eastern European pancakes!

INGREDIENTS

1 1/4 cups all-purpose flour
1/3 cup sugar
2 teaspoons baking powder
1/2 teaspoon baking soda
1/4 teaspoon sea salt
1 cup whole milk
1 cup farmer's cheese
2 tablespoons unsalted butter, melted
3 whole large eggs, separated
1 tablespoon lemon juice

Assorted jams or compotes such as,
apricot, raspberry or blueber

In a mixing bowl stir together the flour, sugar, baking powder, baking soda and salt. In another bowl whisk together the milk, cheese, melted butter, egg yolks and lemon juice. Add the cheese mixture to the flour and whisk until well combined. In another clean mixing bowl whisk the whites until they form stiff peaks then gently fold into the pancake batter. Heat a griddle, lightly butter and spoon on silver dollar sized pancakes being sure to leave enough room in between. When the pancakes are brown/ spread with the jam, sprinkle with powdered sugar and serve.

Homemade Sheboygan Brats

YIELDS 5 POUNDS

Ya Hey Der to all my German friends up Nort! I get a lot of requests for sausage recipes and thought this would be a nice one to share.

INGREDIENTS

3 1/2 pounds trimmed pork butt
1 1/2 pounds veal shoulder
2 1/2 teaspoons sea salt
1 1/2 teaspoons ground white pepper
1 1/2 teaspoons ground mace
1/2 teaspoon ground ginger
Large pinch of nutmeg

1 cup whole milk
2 large whole eggs
1/4 cup fine breadcrumbs

12 feet 32 to 35 mm hog casing

Cube the meat and place in the freezer for exactly 1 hour. Remove and grind through a 3/8-inch plate of a meat grinder. Season the ground meat with the dry spices and mix with your hands. In a separate bowl combine the milk, eggs and breadcrumbs, mix until well blended and using your hands work into the meat. Refrigerate the meat mixture for at least 6 to 8 hours, stuff into the casing and tie off into 5-inch lengths. Refrigerate or freeze until needed. Will freeze up to 2 months.

Laotian Spiced Long Beans & Scallops

SERVES 4

Laotian-Thai fusion dishes are cropping up at many establishments around the city. This one is most definitely sweet as well as hot!

INGREDIENTS

1/2 pound small bay scallops
1/2 pound thin green beans, cooked al dente
1/2 cup flour

2 tablespoons canola oil
3 medium garlic cloves, minced
1/2 teaspoon turmeric
1/4 teaspoon sea salt
1 tablespoon brown sugar
1 tablespoon fish sauce
2 tablespoons soy sauce
1 tablespoon red chili paste
1/2 cup light chicken stock

Heat the oil in a wok, lightly flour the scallops then saute in the hot oil for 2 to 3 minutes tossing the wok so they brown on all sides. Cut the pre-cooked green beans into 2-inch long pieces and add along with the garlic to the skillet. Cook for another 2 to 3 minutes until slightly brown. Add the remaining ingredients to the wok except the chicken stock, stir and toss to coat, then add the chicken stock. Cook until the sauce thickens slightly then serve over a bed of pre-cooked brown rice.

Updated Colcannon

Having grown up in a Polish-Irish neighborhood, I can attest to this quintessential street soul food we call taters and mash. Steamed new potatoes are essential to the flavor of the dish.

CABBAGE MASH

1 slice hickory smoked bacon, diced
2 tablespoon olive oil
3 medium garlic cloves, minced
1 small onion, diced
1 medium head green cabbage, cored and diced
1/2 teaspoon sea salt
1/4 teaspoon black pepper
4 tablespoons chicken stock
2 dashes Tabasco

TATERS

2 pounds whole new potatoes, scrubbed
4 tablespoons unsalted butter
1 cup whole milk, hot
Dash of garlic powder, onion powder and nutmeg

In a large non-stick skillet heat the oil and sauté the bacon until slightly brown, add the garlic and onion, sauté for 2 to 3 minutes then add the cabbage and sauté again for another 3 to 4 minutes. Add the rest of the seasoning, lower the heat, cover and cook for 20 minutes then remove from the fire. Steam the new potatoes for 30 minutes, peel warm and mash with the butter, hot milk and seasoning. While the potatoes are still warm, add the cabbage mixture, stir with a wooden spoon and serve.

Zucchini Latkes

Jewish delis around the city produce wonderful and addictive foodstuffs. I started noticing a trend of multi colored latkes and I thought this would be a good one to include.

SEASONED OIL

2 slices hickory smoked bacon, minced
3 large garlic cloves, chopped
6 black peppercorns, crushed
1 cup canola oil

LATKES

2 large baking potatoes, scrubbed and peeled
1 medium zucchini
1 large whole egg
1/2 teaspoon sea salt
1/4 teaspoon black pepper
1/8 teaspoon baking powder
Dash of Tabasco
1 tablespoon parsley
1/4 cup matzo meal

Preheat the oven to 400°. In a small skillet saute the bacon until it starts to render it's fat and turn lightly brown, then add the garlic, peppercorns and oil, cook for 5 minutes and remove from the fire. Using a hand grater, grate the potatoes through the large hole into a large bowl. Using your hands pick up the potatoes and squeeze out as much moisture as possible then return to the bowl. Grate on top of that the zucchini and mix. In another bowl whisk together the remaining ingredients except the seasoned oil then fold into the potato mixture. Heat a griddle, brush on some of the seasoned oil, then spoon on small batches of latke mix. Cook on both sides until brown, place on a non-stick sheet pan and let bake 20 minutes until crisp and browned.

Fragrant Yaki Soba

The Japanese love their noodles morning, noon and night and this is most definitely a great street food to be had.

INGREDIENTS

3/4 pound soba noodles, pre-cooked

2 tablespoons peanut oil
1 cup carrots, julienne
2 cup Napa cabbage, shredded
1 cup fresh bean sprouts
1/4 cup green onion, minced

SAUCE

1/3 cup soy sauce
2 tablespoons teriyaki sauce
1 tablespoon honey
1 tablespoon ground coriander
1/4 teaspoon ground turmeric
1 teaspoon garlic, minced
1 teaspoon ginger, minced

Combine the ingredients for the sauce in a small bowl then set aside. Heat the peanut oil in a large wok and stir fry the vegetables for 3 to 4 minutes. Separate the noodles, add to the wok and stir fry for 2 minutes more. Now add the sauce to the back of the pan, stir fry and toss the noodles and vegetables until well coated.

Peruvian Paella

Paella wears many hats, but this South American dish is hotter than most with the addition of almonds, green aji pepper and cilantro. No need to add saffron.

INGREDIENTS

1/3 cup olive oil
1 pound chicken breast, cubed
1 1/2 pounds small raw shrimp, peeled and cleaned
1/2 cup dried chorizo, diced
1/4 cup slivered almonds

1 medium jalapeno or aji pepper, diced
5 medium garlic cloves, minced
1 medium onion, diced
1/2 cup red pepper, diced
2 cups short grain rice
1 cup diced tomatoes
3 1/2 cups chicken stock
1/4 cup dry white wine
1/2 cup fresh peas
1/2 cup fresh corn kernels
1/2 teaspoon sea salt
1/4 teaspoon black pepper
16 fresh clams
1/2 cup cilantro, minced

Heat 4 tablespoons of the oil in a 14-inch paella pan and when hot, brown the chicken, shrimps, chorizo and almonds for 3 to 4 minutes then remove to a serving platter. Add the remaining oil to the pan and saute the pepper, garlic, onion, red pepper and rice for another 3 to 4 minutes. Add the meats and almonds back to the pan along with the diced tomatoes, 2 cups of chicken stock and white wine. Stir with a wooden spoon, reduce the heat to a bubbling simmer and cook for 10 minutes. Sprinkle over the peas, corn, salt and pepper. Give the paella a good stir, push the clean clams onto the top of the rice, add the remaining chicken stock, cover with a piece of foil and simmer another 10 minutes until clams crack open and the rice Is cooked. Before serving, sprinkle on the cilantro.

Huevos Fritos Con Chorizo Y Patatas

Chicago's been blessed with a few great Spanish restaurants and markets and sometimes the easiest dishes are the best.

INGREDIENTS

4 round Cubano rolls, toasted

1/2 pound bulk chorizo sausage
2 tablespoons unsalted butter
3 medium garlic cloves, minced
1 small onion, diced
1 small red pepper, diced
1 1/2 cups cubed potatoes, pre-boiled
  and diced
4 whole large eggs
1/4 teaspoon sea salt
1/8 teaspoon black pepper
Pinch of fresh thyme leaves

Heat a 10-inch non-stick skillet until hot, then cook the chorizo sausage for 3 to 4 minutes until slightly browned and cooked through, then pour into a fine mesh strainer to remove the grease. In the same skillet add the butter and sauté the garlic, onion red pepper and potatoes for 5 to 6 minutes. In a separate bowl whisk together the eggs, salt, pepper and thyme leaves. Return the chorizo sausage to the skillet, cook for a minute more then add the egg mixture being sure to push it around with a wooden spoon. Turn the heat to low, cover the skillet until the eggs set then carefully using a flipping motion, flip the torta and cook for 2 more minutes covered. Let it cool slightly, cut into wedges and serve on the toasted rolls.

Portuguese Codfish Cakes

My dear chef friend, Eduardo Feliz, turned me on to this recipe years ago and it's been a hit with my Italian in-laws ever since. Chicago has a handful of Portuguese restaurants that specialize in "petiscos" meaning little tastes.

INGREDIENTS

1 pound boneless salt cod
2 pounds russet potatoes
2 tablespoons unsalted butter
2 tablespoons olive oil
4 large garlic cloves, minced
1 medium onion, minced
1 medium scallion, minced
1/3 cup parsley, minced
2 large whole eggs plus 1 yolk
1/4 teaspoon white pepper
Dash of Tabasco, Worcestershire, lemon juice
and garlic salt

Rinse the salt cod under warm water for 5 minutes, place into a bowl, cover and refrigerate for 24 hours. Rinse again under warm water the next day, place into a pot covered with water, simmer for 5 minutes, cool and drain. While the cod is draining, cook the potatoes in boiling water for 30 minutes, drain, skin and pass through a ricer into a large bowl. Heat the butter and oil in a skillet and saute the garlic, onion and scallions for 3 to 4 minutes and then chill. Using your hands, break apart the salt cod over the potatoes. Season with the remaining ingredients and form into small cakes. Cover the cakes and refrigerate for 4 hours. After 4 hours heat a medium size cast-iron skillet with 2 inches of canola oil to 350°. Gently fry the cod cakes on each side for 2 to 3 minutes and then serve with a side of tartar sauce and lemon wedges.

DESSERT RECIPES

If I had to choose one dessert that defined the city, it would most definitely have to be cheesecake!

Chicago Style Turtle Cheesecake

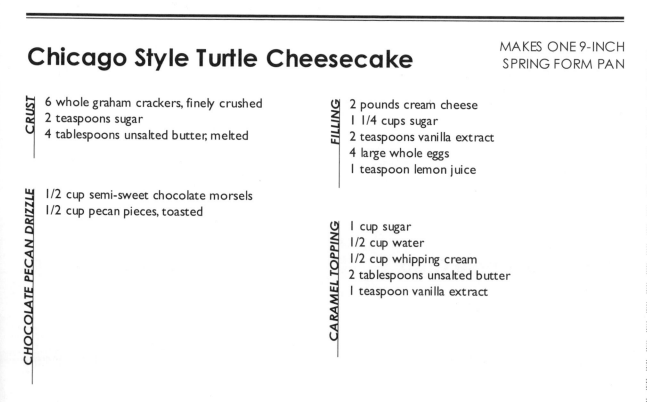

CRUST
6 whole graham crackers, finely crushed
2 teaspoons sugar
4 tablespoons unsalted butter, melted

CHOCOLATE PECAN DRIZZLE
1/2 cup semi-sweet chocolate morsels
1/2 cup pecan pieces, toasted

FILLING
2 pounds cream cheese
1 1/4 cups sugar
2 teaspoons vanilla extract
4 large whole eggs
1 teaspoon lemon juice

CARAMEL TOPPING
1 cup sugar
1/2 cup water
1/2 cup whipping cream
2 tablespoons unsalted butter
1 teaspoon vanilla extract

Pre-heat the oven to 350°. Prepare a 9-inch spring form cake pan by brushing the interior with softened butter and place a circle of buttered parchment paper onto the bottom of the pan. In a bowl combine the crushed graham crackers, sugar and butter and then pat onto the bottom of the parchment lined pan. Bake the crust in the hot oven for 5 minutes and remove.

Put the cream cheese into the work bowl of an electric mixer and using the paddle attachment, beat on low speed until smooth. With the machine running, add the sugar, lemon juice and vanilla in a slow stream. Turn off the machine, scrape the sides down with a plastic spatula and then slowly add the eggs one at a time until fully incorporated. Pour all the batter over the prepared crust and bake in the hot oven on the middle rack for exactly 40 minutes. After 40 minutes, turn the heat off and open the door slightly ajar to remove any excess heat from the oven. Now close the door and let the baked cheesecake sit in the warm oven for another hour and a half to set. After that time remove the cake to a cooling rack for one hour and then wrap the entire pan in plastic wrap and refrigerate overnight.

The next day remove the cheesecake from the refrigerator and make the caramel topping. In a small saucepan combine the sugar and water and bring to a boil over medium heat. Increase the heat to high and cook the mixture for 6 to 7 minutes until it turns light amber. Remove the pan from the fire, stir in the heavy cream and then return the pan to medium heat and stir until smooth. Remove from the fire again, stir in the butter and vanilla extract, pour into a bowl and refrigerate for 45 minutes. After 45 minutes, drizzle the caramel over the entire cheesecake. To make the chocolate topping, place the morsels into the top of a double boiler and stir to melt. Let cool for 10 minutes and then drizzle over the caramel cheesecake and sprinkle on the pecans. Refrigerate the cake for an hour before serving.

Almond Coffee Cake   SEE PAGE 26 FOR RECIPE

Lemon Babka   SEE PAGE 27 FOR RECIPE

Chocolate Glazed Pachki   SEE PAGE 28 FOR RECIPE

Mom's Hot Apple Crisp   SEE PAGE 180 FOR RECIPE

Homemade Italian Ice   SEE PAGE 229 FOR RECIPE

Really Smooth Italian Ice   SEE PAGE 229 FOR RECIPE

Uncle Tony's Jumbo Cannoli   SEE PAGE 230 FOR RECIPE

Cousin Chic's Frozen Eclairs   SEE PAGE 231 FOR RECIPE

THE PANTRY

MISC.

RECIPES

Chicken Stock

INGREDIENTS

4-5 pounds raw chicken bones or one large
   stewing chicken of equal weight
3 quarts cold water
2 large garlic cloves
1 medium onion, chopped
2 medium carrots, chopped
1 medium celery stalk, chopped
1 leek, white and some of the green part, chopped
1 bay leaf
6 sprigs parsley
6 sprigs thyme
1 teaspoon sea salt
8 black peppercorns

Rinse the chicken bones under cold water for 5 minutes to remove impurities, and then put them in a large stockpot. Add the water and set the pot over high heat. Bring to a boil and then skim off any froth that comes to the top.

Reduce the heat so that the liquid is barely simmering.

Add the rest of the ingredients and simmer for 2 hours. Skim off any froth that has risen to the top with a kitchen spoon.

Strain through a fine mesh conical sieve into a bowl and cool it as quickly as possible.

Veal or Beef Stock

INGREDIENTS

8 pounds veal or beef bones
One half calf's foot, split lengthwise,
    chopped, and blanched
2 large garlic cloves
1 medium onion, chopped
2 medium carrots, chopped
1 medium celery stalk, chopped
1/2 cup mushrooms, sliced
2 bay leaves
3 sprigs tarragon
6 sprigs parsley
6 sprigs thyme
4 tablespoons tomato paste
1/2 cup dry white wine
1 teaspoon sea salt
8 black peppercorns
6 quarts cold water

Preheat the oven to 425°F.

Rinse the bones under cold running water for 5 minutes to remove any impurities.

In a large roasting pan, place the bones in the pan. Roast about 35-45 minutes until browned. Add the tomato paste and vegetables and toss to coat and return to the oven and roast until the vegetables and bones are well browned, about 20 minutes more. Keep tossing and checking.

Remove from the oven and transfer the bones and vegetables to a large stockpot.

Pour off the fat from the roasting pan and deglaze with the white wine scraping up all of the sediment. Set the pan over high heat and reduce the wine by half, then pour the wine into the stockpot.

Pour the water over the bones and the vegetables, then add the bay leaves, tarragon, parsley, thyme, sea salt, and black peppercorns and bring just to a boil over high heat.

As soon as the liquid boils, reduce the heat so that the liquid is barely simmering. Skim off any froth that has risen to the top with a kitchen spoon.

Simmer the stock for 3 1/2 to 4 hours skimming as necessary. Strain through a fine mesh conical sieve into a bowl and cool it as quickly as possible.

Spicy Tomato Sauce

INGREDIENTS

2 tablespoons olive oil
2 large garlic cloves, minced
1 medium onion, sliced
1 medium red or green pepper, sliced
3/4 teaspoon dried thyme
1 bay leaf
3 tablespoons tomato paste
1 1/2 cups tomato sauce
1 1/2 cups beef or chicken stock
1/4 cup dry white wine
Dash of cayenne pepper
Dash tabasco
Dash of Worcestershire sauce
1/4 teaspoon sea salt
Freshly ground black pepper

Heat the oil in a medium pot over medium heat, add the garlic, onion, and peppers and cook, stirring until softened, about 3 minutes. Do not let the vegetables brown.

Now add the bay leaf and thyme and cook for exactly 1 minute to release their oils.

Add the rest of the ingredients to the pot and bring it to a boil, and then reduce the heat and simmer slowly for about 10 minutes.

Walnut Filling

INGREDIENTS

1/3 cup fresh almond paste
1 tablespoon unsalted butter
1/4 cup light or dark brown sugar
1/4 cup sugar
1 tablespoon all-purpose flour
3/4 teaspoon ground cinnamon
1 teaspoon vanilla extract
3/4 cup lightly crushed walnut pieces

Combine all the ingredients in a medium sized mixing bowl, and working quickly, cut the butter into the mixture with a pastry blender until the mixture is evenly distributed. Do not over mix.

Clear Glaze

INGREDIENTS

1/2 cup sugar
1/4 cup water
1 tablespoon light corn syrup

Place the ingredients in a small saucepan over medium heat and bring to the boil. Remove from the heat and cool.

Butter Cream Icing

INGREDIENTS

5 tablespoons shortening
3 tablespoons sugar
3/4 cup powdered sugar
1 egg white
1/8 teaspoon vanilla extract

Combine all the ingredients in a medium sized mixing bowl, then set over a warm bain Marie. Whisk until completely smooth, and then remove from the heat.

Chocolate Glaze

INGREDIENTS

1 1/4 cups powdered sugar
3 tablespoons unsweetened cocoa powder
1 1/2 teaspoons light corn syrup
1 tablespoon shortening, melted
2 tablespoons water
1 teaspoon vanilla extract

Combine all the ingredients in a medium sized mixing bowl, then set over a warm bain Marie. Stir with a wooden spoon until completely smooth and warm.

INDEX

INDEX

INDEX